SLOW

Cornwall
& The Isles of Scilly

Local, characterful guides to Britain's special places

Kirsty Fergusson

EDITION 4

Bradt Guides Ltd, UK
The Globe Pequot Press Inc, USA

Fourth edition published September 2023
First published 2012
Bradt Guides Ltd
31a High Street, Chesham, Buckinghamshire, HP5 1BW, England
www.bradtguides.com

Print edition published in the USA by The Globe Pequot Press Inc,
PO Box 480, Guilford, Connecticut 06437-0480

Text copyright © 2023 Kirsty Fergusson
Maps copyright © 2023 Bradt Guides Ltd; includes map data © OpenStreetMap contributors
Photographs copyright © 2023 Individual photographers (see below)
Project Manager: Anna Moores
Cover research: Pepi Bluck, Perfect Picture

ISBN: 9781804690987

British Library Cataloguing in Publication Data
A catalogue record for this book is available from the British Library

Photographs
© individual photographers credited beside images & also those from image libraries
credited as follows: Alamy Stock Photo (A); AWL Images (AWL); Dreamstime.com (DT);
Shutterstock.com (S); SuperStock (SS)

Front cover Godrevy Lighthouse, St Ives Bay (Guy Edwardes/AWL)
Back cover Looe (ian wookcock/S)
Title page Polperro (SS)

Maps David McCutcheon FBCart.S

Typeset by Ian Spick, Bradt Guides
Production managed by Zenith Media; printed in the UK
Digital conversion by www.dataworks.co.in

AUTHOR

Kirsty Fergusson is an award-winning travel writer who grew up in the West Country and spent several years living in the far west of the Cornish peninsula. With a background in horticulture and garden writing, a degree in Art History and a PhD in French philosophy, she brings a unique perspective to even the most well-trodden destinations, writing as much for local residents as for curious travellers.

Her taste for immersive, solo travel began with a student Interrail pass – the story appears in Bradt's travel-writing anthology, *Roam Alone* – while the opportunity for travel writing was kindled during a botanising expedition through the wilds of Mongolia on horseback, where she found herself describing the world around her for a blind companion. It turned out to be the unconscious start of a journey into the Slow ideal of immersive, unhurried and sustainable travel – a journey always enlivened with her trademark sense of humour and penchant for plant-led curiosity. She currently lives in southwest France and has branched out into leading and organising garden tours, in England, France and further afield. She can be contacted on SlowCornwall.

AUTHOR'S STORY

Before I came to live in the far west of Cornwall in the spring of 2009, I remember poring over my OS maps and being enthralled by the dramatic contours of the coastline, the empty moors dotted with archaeological symbols, the deep meandering estuaries and the strange poetry of the place names. The cluster of islands that lay where the sun set on the horizon fired my imagination too, as I stood on the cliffs near my new home, close to Land's End.

I was fortunate that year, and in the years that followed, to have time to explore my adopted county out of season, on foot and by bicycle (and occasionally in a canoe): it was an eye-widening, if slightly random immersion, that revealed an exhilarating diversity in local identity. Living on a cider farm, I learned how to make craft cider, and the weekly delivery run helped me discover many of the special pubs and eateries found within these pages. I learned to sail a dinghy, abandoning evening club races to follow dolphins around the shores of Mount's Bay, and talked to farmers and market gardeners at village shows and rallies. And twice I had the huge privilege of being a judge in the Food and Farming pavilion at the Royal Cornwall Show in Wadebridge. An additional impetus to my Cornish travels came from my meandering career in gardening and garden journalism. Cornwall lacks for nothing in horticultural variety and richness, and there are few trails I have followed that have not had to include a small wiggle to take in a lush collection of those hardy exotics which thrive in sheltered coombes up and down the peninsula. Without realising it, I had embarked on a Slow exploration of Cornwall. So when Bradt, who had published a piece I'd written years earlier about looking for peonies in Mongolia, announced they were looking for new authors, I jumped at the possibility of more Slow exploring, relishing the opportunity to spend time in the places with which I was less familiar.

For this fourth edition, I am delighted to be returning to the Isles of Scilly as well as to my favourite parts of rural, urban and coastal Cornwall, re-immersing myself in familiar locations among old friends, and having the opportunity to explore some less familiar places and forge new connections.

It was in a Redruth café that I found myself in conversation with Clive Baker, who teaches Cornish. Clive taught me the meaning of the Cornish word, *hirath*. It means the sense of deep belonging to a place that can lead to extremes of emotion through either attachment or separation. (Try expressing that in one English word!) But Cornwall and Scilly can have that effect on you; and where there is a sense of *hirath*, I believe you find individuals and communities living well, savouring and contributing to the special quality of their surroundings and a willingness to share it with others. Scillonians and Cornish alike are alert to the growing demand for a sustainable approach to tourism, having seen more than their fair share of unsustainable industries come and go. Time after time in conversation, 'Slow', I discovered, proved valuable shorthand for so much that Cornwall, Scilly and their admirers aspire to in the 21st century.

PREFACE TO THE FOURTH EDITION

As so many have said, crossing the Tamar is more like visiting another country than another county: the climate, the geography, the language, the slightly mysterious character of Cornwall that is seductively distinct and infinitely rewarding, not least for the horticulturally inclined. So it is that the first day of spring in Cornwall is prescribed not by the equinoctial calendar (as the rest of the country would have it), but by flowers.

In 2023 that day fell upon Monday 27 February, and as luck would have it, I was there when the precise moment arrived. The precise moment? Well yes, it was early in the morning and I was with Gary Long, Trewithen's long-standing head gardener, squinting up into the purple canopy of a huge magnolia, counting the open blooms. It was the last of six 'champion' *Magnolia campbellii* trees – each one located in a different garden between St Austell and Penzance and planted between 1860 and 1976 – to be officially recorded as having fifty or more blooms apiece; the fuzzy black winter jackets had split to reveal the purplest of petals. Three hundred blooms on six separate trees and spring is declared in Cornwall! The date has ranged between February 10 and March 3 since the idea was hatched in 2013 by hotelier Toby Ashcroft, concerned that visitors to Cornwall were arriving too late for the great magnolia spectacle. April or May might well be the preferred month for garden visiting to begin in earnest in the rest of the country, but not so in Cornwall, where many of the greatest gardens welcome visitors from early March or even mid-February, which is when Caerhays opens its gates.

Most of the research for this new edition was done in February, under (mostly) blue skies, though there was one memorable night when the sky over the north coast danced with green and purple light. Moorland and coast-path walks were scented with gorse and narcissi and despite the cold nights, sheltered gardens brimmed with camellias and spring bulbs. On Tresco, even the agapanthus (which even in the south of England are not expected to bloom until mid-summer) were in flower! Beaches were empty and even the A30 was easy to navigate. And finding a seat in one of the new wave of excellent cafés and restaurants, dedicated to the promotion of Cornish food, was a doddle. Local residents had time to talk, unhurried by the stresses of an increasingly intense tourist season. No doubt about it – February is a grand month to visit Cornwall and Scilly to savour a Slow spring, ahead of the rest of the country.

ACKNOWLEDGEMENTS

I am hugely grateful to all those who stopped what they were doing in order to chat and answer my questions and show me round their gardens, houses, museums, churches, bed and breakfasts and campsites, or point me in the right direction. The present edition is built on the kindness and helpfulness of all those who assisted with previous editions, so I have no hesitation in including their names here, too.

These people include, in no particular order, Jake Jackson, Cherry Warne, Jane Nancarrow, Nigel Bowman, Paul Corin, Gil and Neil Faiers, Claire and David Thomas, Mike and Sandra Hockley, Robin Haddy, Helen Rawe, Ian Sandbrook, Katie Thomson, Tim and Luke Marshall, Adam Bates, Dave Morgan, John Harris, John Hogarth, Ann Giles, the late Ed Prynn, Annie Sturrock, Christopher Hart, Claire Lewis, Jon Ross, Henrietta Boex, Annabelle Read, Lisa di Tomasso, Alex Phillips, James Treseder, Ben Quinn, Simon Stallard, Dean Evans, Kingsley Rickard, Viv Hendra, Harry Gott, Jonathan Jones, John Price, Malcolm Beaton, Henry Garfitt, Ruth Huxley, Jennie Trevithick, Kate and Sam Hicks, Phil and Sheryl Moon, Carolyn and Tom Screech, Laura Richards, Jim Wallwork, David Keast, Steve and Sheila Perry, Reg and Sue Sheppard, Neil and Ruth Burden, Julie Tamblyn, Jo Craig, Lynda Small, Barry Mays, Sir Richard Carew Pole, Joy Cheeseman, Jamie Parsons, Mark Camp, Lois Humphrey, John and Dee Watt, Mark Harris, Michael and Kim Spencer, Sioux Dunster, James and Mary St Aubyn, Joe Hemming, Hugh Chapman, Gaz O'Neil, Emily Whitworth Wicks, Chris Gregory, Will Wagstaff, Oriel Hicks, Barney McLaughlin, Amy Hiron, Gary Long, Louise Danks and her dad Chris, Charles Inkin, Sam and Kitty Galsworthy, Adi Harvey, Danni Dixon and many others – volunteer coastguards, churchwardens, the ladies in the John Betjeman Centre, dog-walkers, farmers, National Trust car-park attendants (especially Annie at Cape Cornwall) and volunteers – who all helped along the way.

I'd also like to make a special mention of CoaST (Cornwall Sustainable Tourism) – a fantastic social enterprise working hard to ensure that tourism in Cornwall benefits local communities, economies and environments. Thanks to you all, especially Manda, who helped enormously in the initial stages of my research and put me in touch with so many good people across the county.

I am extremely grateful to Charlotte Winterbourne and Tegen Shipp from Wildcard and Anna Mahoney and Victoria Bond from the Islands' Partnership for organising my flight to Tresco with Penzance Helicopters; what an experience!

For this fourth edition, I'd like to say a special thank you once again to Glyn and Martin Winchester as well as Nick, Alice and dog Finny, for such a homely welcome in Falmouth and unstinting efforts to promote the book – Cornwall is lucky to have you! And a big thank you also to Chella and her children in Upton Cross for hospitality and valuable inside information.

I remain indebted also to Tim Locke, whose book, *Slow Sussex and the South Downs National Park*, was the model and inspiration for the first edition.

It's a particular pleasure to mention all those at Bradt who have been involved and supportive from the start – Adrian Phillips, Donald Greig, Janet Mears, Hilary Bradt and Rachel Fielding. For this edition, I'd like to thank Claire Strange and Anna Moores for their patience and encouragement. And huge, heartfelt thanks to Samantha Cook, who had the unenviable task of editing the first draft of this new edition. It would be only half the book it is today without your eye for detail and accuracy – I am truly indebted to you

SUGGESTED PLACES TO BASE YOURSELF

These bases make ideal starting points for exploring localities the Slow way.

BODMIN page 119

A tangle of tracks and footpaths past rushing rivers and wooded valleys, open moorland with brooding Neolithic stones, remote villages and vintage pubs on the doorstep of this historic town.

THE CAMEL ESTUARY page 70

Between a rugged coastline ruled by slate and surf, Methodist chapels and hedonist beaches, John Betjeman country rubs up against a seafoodie paradise at Padstow.

TRURO page 256

A cathedral city perfect for pottering, with lots going on; explore cycle trails over the mining heartland of Cornwall and take part in the renaissance of Camborne and Redruth.

PENZANCE page 335

The essence of Cornwall is in its toe-tip: artists' colonies and archaeology, brooding moors and crumbling tin-mines, surf, fishing fleets – and a supremely romantic bay.

ATLANTIC OCEAN

THE ISLES OF SCILLY page 385

Unwind and live the Slow dream on your chosen island amid pristine white beaches, aquamarine seas and sub-tropical plant life.

N
0   10 miles
0   15km

St Agnes Head

Cornwall

St Agnes

CHAPTER 9
page 330

Navax Point REDRUTH
CAMBORNE

ST IVES

CHAPTER 6
page 216

Hayle

Penwith A30 Hayle

Hayle

St Just

Sennen PENZANCE HELSTON *Helford*

Land's End *Mount's Bay* Trelowarren

CHAPTER 10
page 384

St Martin's

Tresco

Isles of Scilly

St Mary's

Mullion

CHAPTER 8
page 294

The Lizard
Lizard Point

TRELOWARREN page 328

From this historic estate, discover the wooded creeks and tiny fishing villages, iconic gardens and lonely moors in the wild far south of Cornwall.

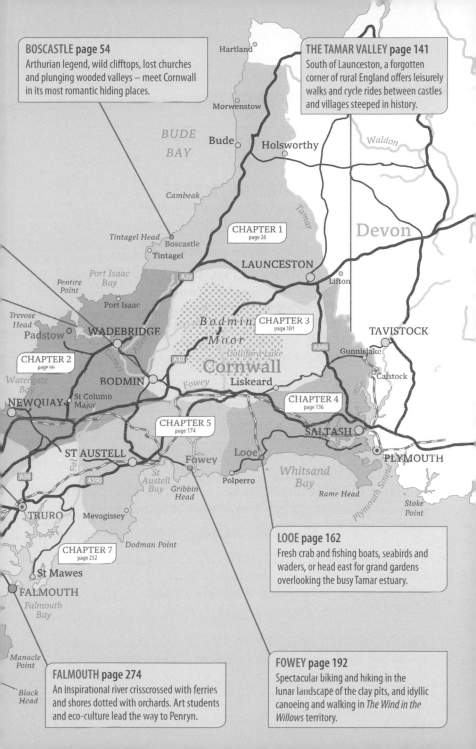

BOSCASTLE page 54
Arthurian legend, wild clifftops, lost churches and plunging wooded valleys – meet Cornwall in its most romantic hiding places.

THE TAMAR VALLEY page 141
South of Launceston, a forgotten corner of rural England offers leisurely walks and cycle rides between castles and villages steeped in history.

Hartland

BUDE BAY
Bude
Holsworthy

Morwenstow

Waldon

Cambeak

CHAPTER 1
page 26

LAUNCESTON

Tamar

Devon

Tintagel Head   Boscastle
Tintagel

A39

Lifton

Port Isaac Bay
Pentire Point
Port Isaac

Bodmin Moor

CHAPTER 3
page 104

TAVISTOCK

Trevose Head
Padstow

WADEBRIDGE

A30   *Colliford Lake*
Cornwall

A388   Gunnislake

Calstock

CHAPTER 2
page 66

Camel   *Allen*

A30

BODMIN   *Fowey*   Liskeard

St Columb Major

CHAPTER 4
page 136

Watergate Bay
NEWQUAY

CHAPTER 5
page 174

SALTASH

ST AUSTELL   Fowey   Looe   PLYMOUTH

A39   *Fal*

A390   *St Austell Bay*
Gribbin Head

Polperro

Whitsand Bay

Rame Head

Plymouth Sound

Stoke Point

TRURO   Mevagissey

Dodman Point

CHAPTER 7
page 252

LOOE page 162
Fresh crab and fishing boats, seabirds and waders, or head east for grand gardens overlooking the busy Tamar estuary.

St Mawes

FALMOUTH
Falmouth Bay

Manacle Point

Black Head

FALMOUTH page 274
An inspirational river crisscrossed with ferries and shores dotted with orchards. Art students and eco-culture lead the way to Penryn.

FOWEY page 192
Spectacular biking and hiking in the lunar landscape of the clay pits, and idyllic canoeing and walking in *The Wind in the Willows* territory.

CONTENTS

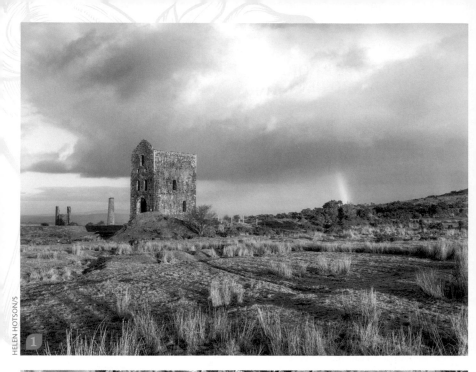

GOING SLOW IN

CORNWALL & THE ISLES OF SCILLY

Five million people come to Cornwall each year as visitors, and a further 50,000 travel on to the Isles of Scilly, and more ink has been spilt by writers attempting to capture the county and the archipelago than over any other part of Britain. It's not hard to see why: Cornish and Scillonian beaches are astonishingly beautiful, washed by tumbling surf that has travelled the Atlantic, while photogenic fishing villages, squeezed into rocky coves, have long served to define Cornwall at its most picturesque.

But Cornwall is more complex and infinitely more diverse than that. There are the post-industrial, granite-built towns of Redruth and Camborne as well as the whitewash-and-thatch villages of the Roseland peninsula; among the mountains of white china clay spoil there are moments of startling natural and manmade beauty, while the wild moors of Bodmin and Penwith are strewn with the skeletal husks of the tin-mining industry and evidence of prehistoric communities lingers in stone. Meanwhile, Scilly is in the process of transforming itself – with no loss of beauty or character – into a cultural and sporting destination like no other part of the country can offer.

Then there's the remarkable heritage of unspoilt country churches, holy wells and pilgrim routes, lying quietly beside busy roads and brash resorts; and colonies of artists, shifting with the times around Lamorna, St Ives, Redruth, the Tamar Valley, Falmouth and Penryn.

The almost-island geography of Cornwall means you are rarely more than a few miles from the sea. The variety is seemingly infinite: the

◀ **1** Bodmin Moor, strewn with the remnants of Cornwall's mining history, page 105.
2 Golitha Falls: come to this picturesque spot when it's quiet to look for otters and dippers, page 126.

rugged north coast with its jutting cliffs of slate and granite, towering sand dunes and windy beaches, where Arthur fought and St Piran landed; or the gentler south coast, with its lush subtropical gardens running down to sheltered coves, busy estuaries, rambling rivers and storm-lashed harbours where old fishing communities still survive.

No wonder, then, that dozens of guidebooks exist to help holidaymakers get the most out of their precious week or fortnight, listing Cornwall's 'unmissable' sights, its 'Top Ten Beaches', swankiest celebrity-run restaurants or coolest surf bars and festivals. The Slow concept isn't like that. Slow travel is about taking the time to get to know a place and what contributes to its uniqueness, rather than encouraging an anxious, superficial lightning tour, aimed at ticking as many cultural, gastronomic or geographical boxes as possible. But it's not about travelling at a snail's pace either. The reward of Slow travel is the understanding that immersion in one place often leads to insights into what makes up the bigger picture.

A TASTE OF CORNWALL & THE ISLES OF SCILLY

It's not so long ago that Cornwall's culinary identity rested squarely on its traditional pasties and cream teas, while crab sandwiches and early asparagus were push-the-boat-out treats. And it would probably be fair to say that until recently (with one or two noble exceptions) Scillonian cuisine was best described as … conventional.

How things have changed! Both Cornwall and Scilly have completely reinvented themselves as high-class foodie destinations and I'm struck by the pace at which this change is occurring. It started, we all remember, with **Rick Stein** in Padstow, who was followed by a large scoop of celebrity chefs nailing their colours to the Cornish mast and doing much to promote not only the superb local seafood but also award-winning Cornish cheeses, meats and charcuterie. Nevertheless, for me, it was the celebrated chef **Sanjay Kumar** who deserved most applause for spreading the word about Slow Food through Cornwall. He summed up the Slow concept perfectly in remembering his mother's words at the dinner table: 'Chew, don't gulp!'

I think it's fair to say that Cornwall's reputation as a top foodie destination has changed direction over the past few years. You no longer

THE SLOW MINDSET

Hilary Bradt, Founder, Bradt Travel Guides

> **We shall not cease from exploration**
> **And the end of all our exploring**
> **Will be to arrive where we started**
> **And know the place for the first time.**
> T S Eliot, 'Little Gidding', *Four Quartets*

This series evolved, slowly, from a Bradt editorial meeting when we started to explore ideas for guides to our favourite part of the world – Great Britain. We wanted to get away from the usual 'top sights' formula and encourage our authors to bring out the nuances and local differences that make up a sense of place – such things as food, building styles, nature, geology, or local people and what makes them tick. Our aim was to create a series that celebrates the present, focusing on sustainable tourism, rather than taking a nostalgic wallow in the past.

So without our realising it at the time, we had defined 'Slow Travel', or at least our concept of it. For the beauty of the Slow movement is that there is no fixed definition; we adapt the philosophy to fit our individual needs and aspirations. Thus Carl Honoré, author of *In Praise of Slow*, writes: 'The Slow Movement is a cultural revolution against the notion that faster is always better. It's not about doing everything at a snail's pace, it's about seeking to do everything at the right speed. Savouring the hours and minutes rather than just counting them. Doing everything as well as possible, instead of as fast as possible. It's about quality over quantity in everything from work to food to parenting.' And travel.

So take time to explore. Don't rush it, get to know an area – and the people who live there – and you'll be as delighted as the authors by what you find.

have to go to the big-name restaurants in Padstow, Newquay or Rock to fall in love with Cornish food, for even larger crowds seem to be drawn to places like Simon Stallard's **Hidden Hut** (page 289) – a coast-path café near Portscatho, where outdoor evening cook-ups sell out online in seconds. A host of other informal venues that celebrate seasonal, local produce cooked simply but with passionate regard for the quality of the ingredients – and often served at shared convivial tables – have sprung up. **Argoe** in Newlyn (page 350), Ben Quinn's **Canteen**, now at Mount Pleasant Eco Park (page 420), **The Crab Shack** on Bryher (page 415) or **On the Quay** in St Mary's (page 398) are just a handful of places to be found among many listed in these pages where travellers and locals alike feel as though they are among friends, drawn together by a love of good food, cooked by good people.

Nor do you have to eat out to get a taste of the way things are heading. I admire the way that village and community shops have pitched in to support local producers and I've derived huge pleasure, while researching this edition, from making a point of buying all my weekly groceries – from salt and ketchup to flour and teabags – from Cornish suppliers or producers in village shops and from farmers' markets and the **Great Cornish Food Store** in Truro (page 263). A rising number of artisan bakeries – **Vicky's**, **Baker Tom's** (page 239), **Stones** (pages 242 and 278), **Da Bara's** (page 292) – have acquired devoted followings too, and the peculiarly Cornish saffron bun is selling in record quantities from Sennen to Bude. Ice cream has also become an artisan affair, and coupled with the Kea plum – that most desirable and local of fruits – is something you'll not find anywhere else in the country. Cornish-grown and -blended tea? Look no further than Tregothnan. Gorse-flavoured chocolate, tasting naturally of coconut? That's made in Cornwall, too.

Cornish ciders, ales, craft gins and wines have made a powerful impact on the drinking scene in recent years. There are almost 50 Cornish and Scillonian breweries and micro-breweries at the time of writing, while ciders made with Cornish apples can hold their own among the best that Devon and Somerset can offer and the latest generation of sparkling wines from **Camel Valley** and **Polgoon** continue to scoop awards by the bucketful. And as for gin … you might be forgiven for thinking that distilling botanical gin has become Cornwall's main industry, for every village shop now seems to present a mind-boggling array of gins, each with its own distinct identity. But perhaps I'm not alone in thinking that **Westward Farm** on St Agnes in the Isles of Scilly produces some of the finest botanical flavoured gins ever tasted. No doubt about it: Cornwall and Scilly have become hugely rewarding destinations for foodies of every persuasion.

With such an abundance of local produce and culinary talent, it's no surprise to discover that Cornwall and Scilly host more festivals dedicated to food and drink than any other region of Britain. Some celebrate a local speciality, such as the **Falmouth Oyster Festival** or the **Newlyn Fish Festival**, others bring all kinds of specialist growers and producers together, like the **Food and Farming pavilion** at the

Royal Cornwall Show in Wadebridge (page 80), or the **Taste of Scilly Festival** held every September (page 392) – a wonderful excuse for an island-hopping, gastronomic adventure. Porthleven, St Ives, Mevagissey and Rock are also riding the wave of success, hosting food-and-drink festivals that attract greater numbers each year.

Away from the hustle of the foodie-fests, I've also discovered the joys of foraging in Cornwall. **Rachel Lambert** (⌂ wildwalks-southwest. co.uk), a neighbour of mine when I lived near Penzance, introduced me to the thrill of returning to the kitchen with a bag filled with fresh green alexanders, wild sorrel, crunchy pennywort, pungent three-cornered leeks and young nettle tips. I must give special mention also to **Liz Woods**, whose blog, *Feasts and Festivals*, opened my eyes to the rich traditions of celebratory Cornish cooking, from stargazy pie to hot spiced cider; the blog became a book, *Cornish Feasts and Festivals* (Alison Hodge, 2013), and the recipes are now an established part of my own culinary adventures. Another individual making tireless and inspirational efforts to promote quality Cornish produce is **Ruth Huxley**. Her books, *The Great Cornish Food Book* (Cornwall Food and Drink Ltd, 2014) and its companion volume, *The Great Cornish Fish Book* (Cornwall Food and Drink Ltd, 2015), present a very contemporary picture of the richness and diversity of the Cornish culinary scene and are highly recommended. Ruth has also been instrumental in the opening of a terrific shop called, appropriately, the Great Cornish Food Store (page 263), beside Truro's Waitrose.

So, what has become of the humble pasty and cream tea? The good news is that they are as popular as ever, but the bar has been significantly raised. The long-established supremacy of **Ann's Pasties** (page 320) is now challenged by the likes of Nicola Willis at **The Dog and Smuggler** in Falmouth (page 278) or **Gear Farm** close to Gweek (page 329). And a Cornish cream tea – jam first, cream on top unless you want to be thrown out of the county and into Devon, where they practise the heresy of putting cream on first – is still a fine objective for a clifftop or moorland walk.

Wherever possible, I have given details of local producers, good shops, farmers' markets and festivals at appropriate points in each chapter, but the following websites provide useful directories for the whole county. You can find more information about the food and drink to be enjoyed on Scilly on page 391.

⊘ cornwallfoodanddrink.co.uk
⊘ foodfromcornwall.co.uk (lists all farmers' markets)
⊘ greatcornishfood.co.uk
⊘ visitcornwall.com/love-Cornwall-food-and-drink
⊘ visitislesofscilly.com/tasteofscilly

A SLOW APPROACH

In this book, one of a series of Slow Travel guides to parts of Britain by local authors, I've taken a Slow look at both the well-known and the less familiar parts of Cornwall and Scilly, taking time to chat with local residents and allowing curiosity to get the better of me at every turn. Inevitably, every question answered raised two more; every branching footpath and backroad was an invitation to double back on the chosen route and start again.

I could easily have continued my journey for years and written a book ten times as long. Instead, I must apologise to those special places which did not make it into this book, and to those which did, but deserved more space. But if this line of approach encourages readers – seasoned residents and visitors as well as newcomers – to embark on their own Slow Cornish or Scillonian adventures, then to my mind, this book will be serving its purpose.

It was exciting to meet people tuning into their region in this way. A farming family in the Tamar Valley I spoke to were intrigued by the prospect of going on holiday within their county to unknown Porthcurno; children in their last year at St Buryan primary school were beside themselves with excitement at the prospect of the traditional end-of-year camping trip to the Isles of Scilly, just 30 miles (or a world) away from home. The idea of having an adventure waiting for you on your doorstep, so to speak, is immensely appealing. And a couple who live in Gorran Haven were inspirational: they had spent their Slow honeymoon staying at The Gurnard's Head near Zennor and exploring the north coast of West Penwith on the open-topped, double-decker bus that runs along the clifftops between St Ives and Land's End.

---

1 Camel Valley Vineyard, page 123. 2 Walking the South West Coast Path in north Cornwall. 3 Cycling a disused railway bridge on the Camel Trail. 4 Local produce at Truro's farmers' market, page 262. ▶

PLASTIC-FREE COASTLINES

Surfers against Sewage (⊘ sas.org.uk) is a charity dedicated to the protection of oceans, beaches and wildlife. What started out in 1990 as a gathering of surfers and other beach users utterly fed up with and disgusted by the state of their beloved Cornish coast became a huge grass-roots movement that continues to contribute enormously to the cleaning of beaches and monitoring of sewage spills, not just in Cornwall, but all over Britain. Now, under the slogan of 'plastic is the new sewage', the St Agnes-based charity is leading the charge against single-use plastics and has been instrumental in the creation of hundreds of plastic-free communities in Britain and Europe. Their headquarters are at Wheal Kitty (page 224). All Slow travellers will, I know, be rallying to the cause.

Taking the Slow approach and stopping to appreciate what the landscape and the local populations have to say has not always made for comfortable listening. Paddling a canoe up a wooded creek of the Fal, looking for orchards of the Kea plum, I came across a (human) community facing extinction as pressure to cash in on the lucrative holiday-rental possibilities of their homes reared its head. In various parts of the peninsula I discovered head gardeners striving to maintain standards on vastly reduced budgets and museums – including the Royal Cornwall Museum in Truro – fighting for their future.

The impact of second homes on small communities needs no retelling, but nevertheless I was shocked to hear a local voice asking where the next generation of lifeboatmen and women would come from if 85% of the village houses were second homes. On Scilly, where many businesses and community buildings have visibly benefitted from EU funding, I heard more than one anxious conversation about the impact of Brexit.

But independent resilience in the face of adversity and the ability to adapt have long been the signature of both coastal and inland Cornwall and the Isles of Scilly, too. There is much to celebrate in the present determination to support and promote local, sustainable, low-carbon businesses – including tourism – which continue to gain momentum and shake up our attitudes to how and where we travel, eat, sleep and spend our days. Ben Quinn, founder of Canteen which now opens its welcoming doors at Mount Pleasant Eco Park (page 420), summed it up like this: 'There has to be a triple bottom line – there's the economic one, of course, but we must give equal status to the social and environmental impacts of what we do. It's not all about profit.'

Cornwall may be Britain's most popular holiday destination and provide a second home to thousands, but familiarity can all too often make us blind to what gives a place its unique identity, and deaf to the quieter voices that inform and give new definition to that special sense of place. Tuning into the Slow concept not only illuminates that uniqueness, it also creates an awareness of Cornwall's future direction and the positive part that we, as visitors or residents, can play in helping shape that future.

FURTHER READING

Among the many classic works on Cornwall and Cornish life, and in addition to the food books mentioned on page 17, the following were especially helpful while researching this guide and will be enjoyed by those wanting more specialist information: *The Cornwall Gardens Guide* by Douglas Ellory Pett, *Secret Beaches: Southwest* by Rob Smith, *Gourmet Cornwall* by Carol Trewin and *101 Cornish Lives* by Maurice Smelt. Philip Marsden's *Rising Ground* is inspirational and will touch all readers who come to Cornwall and the Isles of Scilly in search of 'the spirit of place'.

HOW THIS BOOK IS ARRANGED

There are ten chapters, starting from the Devon border and travelling west to end at the Isles of Scilly. Each chapter follows the same format. No charge has been made for the inclusion of any business in this guide.

MAPS

Each of the ten chapters begins with a map, with places numbered as they appear in the text. The ♀ symbol on these maps indicates that there is a walk in that area. There are also sketch maps for these featured walks. That should be enough to get you started; the pink-covered OS Landranger maps 190 and 200 to 204 cover the county in excellent clarity, at 1:50,000.

For walkers, the more detailed and more numerous orange-covered OS Explorer maps at 1:25,000 show more features, such as field boundaries – these are especially handy if you're walking through farmland or trying to locate a Bronze Age burial chamber on the moors (though if you're just following the coast path the Landranger sheets are generally adequate).

ACCOMMODATION, EATING & DRINKING

At the end of this book I've listed some accommodation – a mixture of bed and breakfasts, campsites, self-catering cottages and one or two very special hotels – places that struck me for their location or friendliness or character, or a mixture of the three. For further details and additional listings, go to ⊘ bradtguides.com/cornwallsleeps.

The hotels, bed and breakfasts, hostels and self-catering options are indicated by the symbols ♠ or ⌂ under the heading for the area in which they are located. Campsites are indicated by ▲.

Under places mentioned in the text I've also added a personal selection of cafés, pubs and a few restaurants, plus anything else involving food and drink that has struck me as being useful. These listings are far from exhaustive; they're simply good (some notably good) pit stops I happen to know about.

PRACTICAL INFORMATION

As far as possible, I've included telephone numbers and websites, and opening times if they're unusual in any way (and these are marked with the icon ☺). It's always wise to check opening times before setting out, although in my own experience, discovering a 'Closed' sign has nearly always resulted in another – unexpected – door opening. In a few cases I have included grid references for places that take a bit of searching for. The main **tourist information centres** (TICs) are listed in each chapter; the official all-Cornwall website is ⊘ visitcornwall.com and the Isles of Scilly website is ⊘ visitislesofscilly.com. Both are excellent one-stop references for places to eat and sleep as well as festivals, activities and local attractions.

I have also outlined, at the start of each chapter, some of the most feasible options for exploring Cornwall using **public transport**; as you'll soon discover, the bus network has had a radical shake-up and now you can hop on any bus and go anywhere in Cornwall for just £5/day or £20/week. Well-priced family tickets make leaving the car at home a real option now. Hurrah. All details are to be found at ⊘ firstbus.co.uk/cornwall. The air and sea routes to Scilly are also described at the start of Chapter 10.

WALKS & CYCLE RIDES

Cornwall is famous for its long- and short-distance walks, and there are many references within these pages to the Cornwall section of the **South West Coast Path** (which follows the entire coastline and is waymarked with an acorn motif; see ⊘ southwestcoastpath.com for further details) as well as coast-to-coast routes such as **The Saints' Way** and **St Michael's Way** and some lesser-known routes, such as the **Copper Trail** and **Tinners' Way**. All these are well documented and easy to find online or in print; the circular walks I have suggested will often make partial use of these longer routes, but will only make sense on the ground if you are equipped with the appropriate OS Explorer map for the area.

I must mention also a fantastic app, iWalk Cornwall, developed by Cornish brothers John and Dave Alden. It works for both Android and Apple and currently reveals more than 300 carefully thought-out circular walks all over the county. Allowing the app to identify where you are also shows what routes are closest to your current position. If you don't have a smartphone, the routes can be downloaded from the website; there's a small charge to pay for downloading each route. I thoroughly recommend it and make reference to the app throughout this guide on several of my own suggested routes.

I mention a few good cycle rides, following **Sustrans NCN Route 3** (the Cornish Way), the **Clay Trails** and routes of my own devising. Cornwall is fantastically hilly, which I thought was a curse, until I found myself feeling slightly let down by the flatness of the extremely popular **Camel Trail**. No uphill struggles, but no downhill, freewheeling exhilaration either. If staying in Penzance, St Austell or Truro, you'll notice the appearance of new green, electric bikes, activated with the Beryl Bikes app. It's early days at the time of writing, but if these prove to be a popular means of getting about we can expect to see them in more towns all over Cornwall.

The Isles of Scilly, meanwhile, are too small to attract serious walkers, but strollers and Slow explorers will be captivated by the tangle of paths and narrow lanes that thread about each island. Bikes are used for short A-to-B journeys as tarmac roads are in very limited supply here.

PLACES DESCRIBED WITHIN THE MAIN TEXT

The first place in each chapter, numbered **1**, is marked on the relevant chapter map with a '1', so you can see its location. The second place is marked with a **2**, and so on. The sites, and thus the numbers, are arranged in a roughly geographical order. Food and drink (and occasionally other) listings are included at the end of some entries.

FEEDBACK REQUEST

At Bradt Guides we're aware that guidebooks start to go out of date on the day they're published – and that you, our readers, are out there in the field doing research of your own. You'll find out before we do when a fine new family-run hotel opens or a favourite restaurant changes hands and goes downhill. So why not tell us about your experiences? Contact us on ✆ 01753 893444 or ✉ info@bradtguides.com. We will forward emails to the author who may post updates on the Bradt website at ⬧ bradtguides.com/updates. Alternatively, you can add a review of the book to Amazon, or share your adventures with us on Facebook, Twitter or Instagram (@BradtGuides).

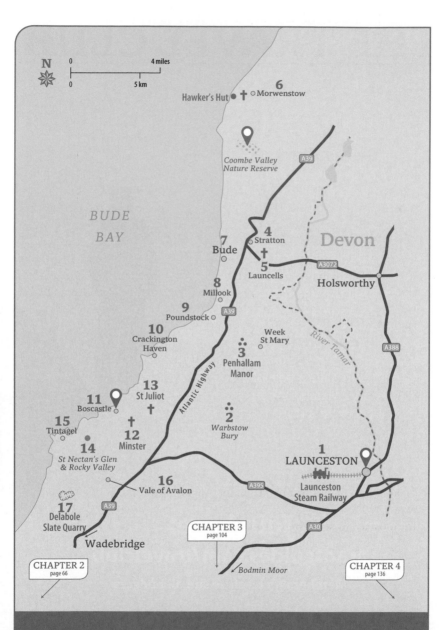

N

0   4 miles
0   5 km

Hawker's Hut **6** ○ Morwenstow

Coombe Valley Nature Reserve

BUDE BAY

7 **Bude**

4 Stratton

Devon

5 Launcells

A3072

Holsworthy

8 Millook

9 Poundstock

A39

Week St Mary

River Tamar

A388

10 Crackington Haven

3 Penhallam Manor

13 St Juliot

11 Boscastle

2 Warbstow Bury

15 Tintagel

12 Minster

14 St Nectan's Glen & Rocky Valley

1 LAUNCESTON
Launceston Steam Railway

16 Vale of Avalon

A395

A39

17 Delabole Slate Quarry

Wadebridge

A30

CHAPTER 3
page 104

Bodmin Moor

CHAPTER 2
page 66

CHAPTER 4
page 136

LAUNCESTON & THE NORTHEAST

1

LAUNCESTON & THE NORTHEAST

Geographically, Cornwall does not lend itself to neat chapter divisions, but **Launceston**, perched with strategic precision just on the Cornish side of the Tamar, and right beside the main arterial road through the county, is a good place to start exploring the wild northeast coast and its gentler, rural hinterland.

If you exclude the tourist honeypots of Bude, Boscastle and Tintagel, northeast Cornwall is one of the least well-known parts of the county, but the rewards for Slow explorers are rich and worth savouring. It's truly a land of contrast: here are some of the most unspoilt rural farmscapes in the West Country, grazed by chubby Ruby Red cattle and dotted about with orchards, woods and fields bounded by streams and narrow lanes, while the coast, for miles south of the Devon border, is terrifyingly ragged and perilous. Vicious reefs of razor-backed rocks jut into the sea and black beaches emerge at low tide beneath formidable cliffs. The coast path rears and plunges with exhilarating – or daunting – gusto, testing walkers to the extreme; yet I love the fact that a mile or two inland, among the dipping hills, visitors on wheels can meander and potter along sheltered lanes designed for donkey carts, stopping in villages with names that hail from the Anglo-Saxon side of the Tamar – Stratton, Marhamchurch, Week St Mary – or ramble between some of the most leafily sequestered churches in the county, many having carved oak pew ends of exceptional quality.

Travelling westwards, gaps in the cliffs open up and a tiny harbour or beach squeezes in among a scramble of cottages. Experienced boardmasters ride the wild surf, their vans and V-Dubs camped along the clifftops. Around **Bude**, where the waves at last roll safely on to wide, sandy beaches, the natural drama of the coast seems to draw breath before embarking on another roller coaster ride, rich in appeal to geologists, through **Crackington Haven** and **Boscastle**, rising to a wildly romantic climax at **Tintagel**. For me, however, the romantic coastline of Arthurian legend is eclipsed, just a mile short of Tintagel, at the head of the Trevillet Valley. Here, in **St Nectan's Glen**, a 60-foot waterfall descends through a halo of granite and foliage to a sequence of shallow rock pools and falls of staggering beauty and spiritual significance to latter-day Arthurians, pilgrims and healers alike. No-one should miss this very special place.

Relics of Cornwall's gritty industrial past are never far from view wherever you find yourself on the peninsula, but just inland from Tintagel, Britain's oldest and largest slate quarry at **Delabole** remains in robust health and offers a rival identity to a region stamped everywhere with the image and legend of Arthur.

GETTING AROUND

The last **train** from Paddington to Bude ran in 1966 and Launceston station, which connected passengers (including Mrs Simpson and her king) with Waterloo and Padstow, closed in the same year. Today, the nearest you can get by train to this part of Cornwall is Gunnislake, 15 miles south of Launceston, at the end of the branch line from Plymouth. The two-carriage train shuttles up and down the Tamar Valley, providing picturesque views and an invaluable resource for residents and visitors on both sides of the river. A Tamar Valley Line Ranger ticket gives you unlimited access to the trains for a day.

Driving around this part of Cornwall is mostly enjoyable, though you must be prepared for long spells of reversing down narrow country lanes, where large farm machinery and limited passing places make for interesting encounters.

BUSES

Following the pandemic, there was a major reorganisation of Cornwall's bus services and the result is a very modestly priced and truly joined-up service which really should – and let's hope it does – take a lot of the pressure off Cornwall's road network. Everything you need to know is on ⊘ firstbus.co.uk/cornwall, where there's a link to ⊘ traveline.com, which helps you plan your route. Day and week tickets covering the whole of Cornwall are available for individuals and families for less than the cost of an ice cream each.

CYCLING

Many of the cyclists you meet in this challenging part of the county will be Dutch or German and following the *Hart van Engeland* route – an illustrated cycle guide that takes them from the Hook of Holland, via Harwich, London, Stonehenge, Bristol and Bude, to Land's End. Others will be following the European VéloWest from North Devon, via Bude, Bodmin Moor, the Camel Trail (page 87), Goss Moor, the Eden Project, Lanhydrock and then back over Bodmin Moor to Launceston. The **Atlantic Trail website**, *&* bude-area.co.uk/atlantictrail, has lots of shorter – though no less demanding – variants on these routes.

Keen cyclists based in Launceston might like to know that convivial rides of 40–60 miles start every Sunday morning from **Launceston Cycles**, Pennygillam Industrial Estate, Launceston PL15 7FU. Beginners' evening rides start here in the summer months, too (◼️Launceston Velo); and novice riders will enjoy the routes starting from **Bude Bike Hire**, which also has the added benefit of having a great café next door (see below). The online Sustrans shop (*&* shop.sustrans.org.uk/books-and-guides) sells laminated maps with the routes and other helpful information; even with a map, in the knitwork of tiny lanes around Bude, the clearly signed waymarkers at every junction are invaluable.

 ## CYCLE HIRE

Bude Bike Hire The Weir, Whalesborough EX23 0JD *&* 01288 362234 *&* budebikehire. co.uk. This friendly shop has moved out of Bude and is now to be found a couple of miles south, beside The Weir café (page 50) on the canal towpath. Bikes can be hired by the day or week for adults and children, and a handful of easy routes around Bude that take in the quieter roads and canal towpath are suggested. They also offer bike repair, maintenance and sales as well as collection and delivery within a 15-mile radius. And there's the very nice café next door.

WALKING

Walkers will find it difficult to resist the drama of the **coast path** in this extremely wild and rugged part of Cornwall, and buses trundle up and down the steep coast roads, making it possible to plan a linear route and get back to the day's point of departure. Perhaps, however, the best way for day-walkers – or those looking for more of a stroll than a hike – to get the most out of the coast path is to choose a circular route which takes in a section of path and loops back inland through the

i TOURIST INFORMATION

Note that the TICs in Boscastle and Tintagel have closed.

Bude Crescent Car Park, EX23 8LE ✆ 01288 354240 🖱 visitbude.info
Launceston White Hart Arcade, PL15 8EP ✆ 01566 772321 🖱 visitlaunceston.co.uk

deep, narrow and often wooded valleys that characterise the immediate hinterland. I've suggested **two longish circular walks** in this chapter that follow this formula, starting at Sandymouth Beach (page 48) and Boscastle (page 52), as well as some **shorter strolls** from Morwenstow to Hawker's Hut (page 42) and Poundstock church to Millook (page 51). The footpath that follows the Trevillet as it rushes down Rocky Valley makes a lovely approach to the coast near Tintagel and reveals a labyrinthine surprise to the curious (page 59).

For terrific views inland of most of the region described in this chapter, climb the Iron Age hillfort at Warbstow Bury (page 38) or take a literary stroll through and around Launceston in the footsteps of the poet Charles Causley (page 35).

1 LAUNCESTON

What a thoroughly likeable town this is. From its Norman fortress at the top of the hill to the little steam railway at the bottom, from its handsome Georgian terraces and ancient granite churches to its narrow streets and inviting shops, this is a place made for Slow exploration. But for me what clicks about Launceston is its unselfconsciousness and lack of pretension: it enjoys its history and local culture without clobbering you with them. I talked to the novelist Jane Nancarrow, who grew up here, about how impressed I was with 'Lanson' (as it is pronounced by those who live here). 'Oh!' she said, politely surprised, 'Us locals think so too, but we're never overwhelmed with visitors here. I think most people zoom past on the A30 and don't think to stop.' John Betjeman was pretty taken with Launceston too; Castle Street, he decided, has 'the most perfect collection of 18th-century town houses in Cornwall'.

The quiet prosperity shows in the shops that line the narrow streets off the Town Square, but glance up above shop doorways and you will see relics of previous trades and crafts, such as a gilded boot, a pair of cherubs and an Art Deco café sign. There was a genuine affability among the shopkeepers that you would be hard pressed to find on a similarly hot July day in a seaside town further down the peninsula. But Adi Harvey, who formerly ran the much-missed No. 8 café and now runs the superb Westgate Street Deli (page 36), admits that behind that affability is a lot of anxiety, much of which could be relieved by easier, cheaper parking in the town centre and reduced business rates. It was a sentiment I heard echoed up and down the peninsula.

LAUNCESTON CASTLE

Castle Lodge, PL15 7DR ✆ 01566 772365 ☉ closed in winter; English Heritage

The castle dominates the skyline as you approach the town, an archetypal one-pot sandcastle of a fortress, sitting solidly atop its grassy slopes. As you look from high ground to the west, its lonely grandeur is thrown into relief by the gentle, rolling landscape; Turner painted it in 1811 and again in 1851, captivated by its dramatic silhouette, against ferocious skies and flaming sunsets.

A gang of tiny knights in homemade cloaks and chain mail waved their swords

"The castle dominates the skyline as you approach the town, an archetypal one-pot sandcastle of a fortress."

and giggled as I panted up the steps to the summit of the castle keep. In fact, Launceston Castle has never seen much in the way of military action and its ruins are testament to neglect rather than battle-scars. When William the Conqueror handed much of Cornwall over to his half-brother, Robert, the Norman chose this natural hill above the hamlet of Dunheved to assert his presence with a wooden motte and bailey fort. It overlooked a thriving Saxon town, Lan-Stephan, with its markets and church dedicated to St Stephen half a mile away, across the River Kensey. Over the next two centuries, as Dunheved and its castle grew in wealth and importance and the balance of power and commerce shifted away from Lan-Stephan, the name shifted too, giving way to the more euphonic 'Lanson'. The older town became known as St Stephens, Launceston's somewhat diminished and forgotten parent.

Stone replaced wood and under Henry III's younger brother, Richard, Earl of Cornwall, the castle acquired its granite walls and a touch of medieval splendour. When Richard died in 1271, his son Edmund fancied a change of scene and moved his seat of power to Restormel, further west. The castle at Launceston remained, functioning as a prison (George Fox, founder of the Quakers, endured a particularly foul incarceration here in 1656) and courtroom for the assizes, but without the lavish upkeep it had previously enjoyed, fell into slow decay. By the time of the Civil War it offered no real protection and the Battle of Launceston was fought outside its undefended walls. I left my giggling knights to their imagined battles.

THE HISTORIC CENTRE

Once through the medieval **Southgate arch**, all roads seem to lead to **St Mary Magdalene** in the town centre. Even if you don't go inside (it's mostly a late Victorian restoration) there is plenty to be impressed with on the outside. Every square inch of this grand church is covered in carvings, so fluid and detailed in their execution that they look as though they have been hewn from butter rather than granite. On the entrance porch, look out for St George on the point of impaling a very nasty dragon and St Martin offering half his cloak to Christ disguised as a beggar. The arms on the shields are those of Henry Trecarrel who, it appears, had already commissioned the carved stones for his new manor house at Higher Larrick (page 133), but changed his mind following the awful death of his young son in 1511 and poured his wealth into the building of a new church instead.

On the east gable, the figure of St Mary appears, lying down and surrounded by musicians and choristers. Fashion-conscious visitors should note that ever since the church's completion in 1524, local legend has had it that a pebble thrown which lands – and stays – upon her back will bring good luck, specifically in the form of new clothes. If you think the massive square tower at the other end of the church, which is simply ornamented by a clock and the odd gargoyle, looks a little off-centre and mismatched, you would be right: built on the instructions of the Black Prince, the tower pre-dates the rest of the church by almost 150 years.

The construction of this church coincided with the declining fortunes of the splendid 12th-century Augustinian priory at the foot of the hill, dissolved on the instructions of Henry VIII in 1539. Precious little

---

1 Market stalls in the town centre. **2** The castle, dominating Launceston's skyline. **3** Jake Jackson, former curator of Lawrence House Museum. **4** Carvings decorate every inch of the exterior of St Mary Magdalene. ▶

STUDIOGEORGE/S

TIM KNIGHT/S

KIRSTY FERGUSSON

remains to be seen today, but the Norman font is to be found in St Thomas's Church, just across the road, while up the hill, in Town Square, the arched entrance to the White Hart Hotel was reputedly plundered from the ruins in the 16th century. The old **Prior's Bridge**, built by the monks to carry them dry-footed across the River Kensey, makes a picturesque detour en route to the steam railway station, which occupies much of the priory's former footprint.

The handsome, Georgian brick-built houses on **Castle Street** which impressed Betjeman so much, were largely built on the wealth generated by the quarterly assizes. (How Launceston's lawyers and landladies must have mourned when, in 1838, the county court was removed to Bodmin.) But the most striking of all the houses was funded by the chance purchase of a winning lottery ticket. In 1760, the Constable of the Castle, one Coryndon Carpenter, bought a lottery ticket and gave it to his girlfriend. The prize was an incredible £10,000. Needless to say, he promptly married her and built the grandest house on the street, which is now the **Eagle House Hotel** (⊘ **theeaglehousehotel.com**). Do pop in – it's been given a terrific makeover and now boasts a giant gin distillery within its elegant interior.

LAWRENCE HOUSE MUSEUM
9 Castle St, PL15 8BA ⊘ 01566 773277 ⊘ lawrencehousemuseum.org.uk ⊙ check website for opening times

Major renovations began on this delightful museum in 2022, since when various parts of the collection have been displayed on a rotating basis in a pop-up museum in the town centre (opposite the Co-op in Broad St). I wondered as I entered the pop-up if I might bump into Jake Jackson, the former curator, whom I had first encountered in 2011. He'd been carrying a painted 13th-century floor tile from the old priory in his hand. 'This is probably my favourite period of Launceston's history,' he smiled, 'when the castle and the priory were at the height of their magnificence and the whole town prospering.' Launceston's long history, from the Bronze Age onwards, is brought to life in this fine Georgian house, with intriguing detours into the particular passions of its inhabitants. The pharmacist and former mayor of Launceston, William Wise, for example, collected and pressed over a thousand wild plants growing around his home town. His herbarium runs to six volumes and a new page is chosen for display each week, appropriate to the season. Down in the basement, next to

A SCHOOLMASTER POET

Many people will have read – and probably remember – a poem by Charles Causley during their schooldays. 'Timothy Winters', for example, which begins:

> Timothy Winters comes to school
> With eyes as wide as a football pool,
> Ears like bombs and teeth like splinters:
> A blitz of a boy is Timothy Winters.

Simple, clear formal and read by adults and children alike, Causley's poetry was quite out of tune with British poetry in the second half of the 20th century. He drew endlessly for inspiration on Cornwall and Launceston, where he lived by the river, close to the Prior's Bridge, for all but the war years, and the Charles Causley Festival (⊘ causleytrust. org) is held here in June. The Causley Society has produced a map of Launceston showing buildings and places that the author wrote about, which is as good a way as any to discover the town; you can pick one up in the Visitor Information Centre (page 30). Although a fondly remembered teacher at the local secondary school for many years, Causley was far from sentimental about children: 'you walk among them at your peril'.

Causley died in 2003, aged 86, not long after receiving a prestigious literary award. 'My goodness,' he is reported to have said, 'What an encouragement.'

the Victorian kitchen, I caught up with Mr Jackson again and asked him if he'd known the poet Charles Causley, a much-loved native of the town. 'Actually that's his desk we're standing beside,' he replied, 'and yes, we were schoolmasters together in Launceston.' I shall look forward to hearing the new curator's tales of Launceston when I next visit.

LAUNCESTON STEAM RAILWAY

St Thomas Rd, PL15 8DA ⊘ 01566 775665 ⊘ launcestonsr.co.uk

Cornwall is not short of enterprising, energetic (and often eccentric) collectors who have dedicated their lives to the object of their passion. For Nigel Bowman it's all about steam locomotives and motor vehicles from the heyday of British engineering. From the moment in 1965 when he decided to give up a teacher training course in order to restore *Lilian*, a steam locomotive he had found languishing in a Welsh slate quarry, Nigel's passion and determination produced remarkable results. From the station booking office and tea room, housed in a building first erected at the 1919 Ideal Home Exhibition, the 2½ miles of track run on the old bed of the North Cornwall Railway, following one of the prettiest stretches of the River Kensey to Newmills, where most people get off for a picnic or go for a walk before catching a later train back to Launceston for a peep at the railway museum and workshops.

ST STEPHENS

The original heart of Launceston, before the castle was built, the district of St Stephens is now little more than a cluster of (mostly newish) houses on the road north to the coast. But before the Norman Conquest, it was a town of some importance – there was a mint here, producing coins stamped with the monarch's head and the church tower served as its vault. Practical but profane, and in 1140 the tower was at the centre of a dispute which resulted in its destruction. The whole church was rebuilt in the 13th century, but a further 200 years passed before it received another tower. On the south door, look out for the ring knocker, which was hammered by those seeking 40 days' sanctuary from earthly justice for that brief (1540–1603) period of eccentric generosity to criminals who were able to reach one of the eight English sanctuaries.

Just after crossing the Kensey, you'll see an **octagonal stone building**, built on the instructions of the Duke of Northumberland in 1829 to house the old market cross and act as a place from which election results could be proclaimed. Not that the duke was without political prejudice: a die-hard Tory peer, who never doubted that his man, Sir Henry Hardinge, would win the vote. Even today, after a general election, the winning candidate for Cornwall North is driven from the Round House, as it is known, up the hill to Launceston in a Land Rover for the post-electoral celebrations.

¶¶ FOOD & DRINK

Launceston is well served by local suppliers, but the town tends to be overlooked by outsiders, perhaps seduced by Tavistock's plethora of food shops and famous weekly farmers' market, just 11 miles away. But locals know they have a good thing on their doorsteps, and high-quality local produce is easy to come by.

Delis, farm shops & markets

Slow foodies will make a beeline for the **Westgate Street Deli** (✆ 01566 772089 ✆ westgatestreetdeli.co.uk). Local businessman Adi Harvey, who used to run the very popular No.8 café – which has, alas, closed – has created a triumphant sequel in this fabulous deli that also serves take-away breakfasts and lunches. Meat comes from the celebrated butcher Philip Warren (whose former shop the deli now occupies), and bread from the Cornish Sourdough Bakery (⊘ cornishsourdoughbakery.co.uk). Adi's daughter now runs a very attractive refill store, Let's Get Naked, next door in the arcade. Fish comes fresh from Brixham in **Hamilton's** van in Town Square on Fridays. A mixed market, incorporating the former **farmers' market**, is held in the Town Square on the second Saturday of the month (Mar–Dec) and on Fridays local crafts and produce are sold in the church hall, next to St Mary Magdalene.

Pubs

Launceston's pubs can be a bit daunting for non-locals but the **Bell Inn** (⊘ 01566 779970 ⊘ bellinnlaunceston.co.uk), the oldest pub in town, in Tower Street beside the church, is full of charm and has been sensitively updated after the owners stripped the walls to discover 20th century frescoes depicting scenes of medieval village life. The food menu is simple (homemade pork pies, pasties and scotch eggs), but everything is very nicely done and complements the real ales and ciders on tap.

Outside Launceston, the **Eliot Arms** (⊘ 01566 772051 ⊘ theeliotarms.co.uk) at Tregadillet, just a mile or so west, or the **Springer Spaniel** (page 142), six miles south at Treburley, are both child-friendly and have mouth-watering menus based on seasonal and locally sourced produce as well as Cornish ales. Well worth the ten-minute drive or taxi ride.

Restaurants

New to the scene, very close to Springer Spaniel pub, is a lovely farm shop and café, **Tre, Pol & Pen** (page 142).

Food@cowslip Newhouse Farm, St Stephens PL15 8JX ⊘ 01566 772654 & 01566 772839 ⊘ cowslipworkshops.co.uk. A couple of miles out of town and deservedly popular with locals, Newlands Farm has been farmed by the Colwills for a century and the family are passionately organic in their approach. Home-cooked food from the farm is served in a converted barn or the colourful garden outside, and there are exhibitions of paintings or textile art to visit all through the year. Jo Colwill runs textile art workshops here, which have an international following.

A WRIGGLING ROUTE TO MORWENSTOW

North of Launceston, the roads soon narrow between high hedges, concealing a rolling, agricultural landscape. The River Ottery is

THOMASINE BONAVENTURA

The extraordinary life of a shepherd's daughter began in Week St Mary where Thomasine Bonaventura was born in or around 1450. She was just a girl, minding her father's flock, when she was spotted by a travelling merchant from London. There was clearly something about Thomasine that impressed John Bunsby, who later returned to her parents' house and invited her to return with him to be his wife's maid. Her acceptance turned out to be one of those life-changing decisions. After several years in London, the wife died and Thomasine became the next Mrs Bunsby. John died soon after and Thomasine inherited his wealth. She remarried, again to an affluent merchant, and when he too died her grief was matched only by the size of her bank account. Her third marriage, to Sir John Percyvall, later Lord Mayor of London, saw Thomasine moving in the highest circles and a favourite at the court of Henry VII. But

in 1504, wealthy and childless Thomasine was widowed again. She sounds like an ambitious, social-climbing adventuress, but nothing could be further from the truth. Right from the start of her unexpected affluence, she set about distributing her wealth in her native parish, helping her parents and the poor, building roads and a much-needed bridge, purchasing woodland to enable a degree of self-sufficiency among local indigents and providing St Stephen's Church at Launceston with a new tower. With no taste for London life after the loss of her third husband, she spent her remaining years back in Week St Mary, overseeing the building of a chantry and a free grammar school. The chantry is long gone, but the school was restored by the Landmark Trust; over the stone-arched doorway, Thomasine's legacy is remembered with a simple carved T.

glimpsed, rushing towards the Tamar, beneath ancient granite bridges, and old Cornish estates lie hidden among trees and parkland in the valleys. Turn west off the B3254, which runs straight and fast to Bude and Kilkhampton (the most northerly town in Cornwall) and you're in a maze of looping lanes, isolated farms and tiny hamlets, where shops and pubs are few and far between. Village churches and holy wells are rarely disappointing in these parts and the few mentioned in this chapter by no means tell the whole story.

2 WARBSTOW BURY

♥ SX203906

Travelling westwards, if you feel hemmed in by the narrow lanes, this huge and ancient hillfort is a good place for a pause or picnic. No great climb is involved: a small car park is just a few yards from the summit and the views are stupendous. Look back to Launceston Castle or north for a panoramic view of the coast as far as the glittering satellite dishes of GCHQ Bude on the headland close to Morwenstow. The barrow in the middle is known as the Giant's Grave or King Arthur's Grave, though less romantic souls have decided it is simply a medieval rabbit warren. Kept neatly cropped by sheep, it is best not to bring dogs during lambing in spring.

3 PENHALLAM MANOR
Use the small car park at ♀ SX224979, a mile west of Week St Mary; English Heritage

The half-mile walk through peaceful, airy woodland to the excavated remains of Penhallam Manor is a treat at any time of year, and you are likely – even in high summer – to have the ruins in the leafy clearing to yourself. Discovered when the site was being prepared for tree planting in the 1960s, emergency excavations were carried out and the knee-high remains of a four-square and moated, medieval manor house were exposed. Inhabited from about 1170 until it was abandoned in 1428 and left to decay for over 500 years, there can be few more atmospheric places for the imagination to take root and flourish. The footpath continues on, skirting **Ashbury Hill**, to **Week St Mary**, but unless you retrace your steps, you will have to take the road out of the village as there are no footpaths to get back to the car park.

4 STRATTON
All the road signs point to Bude as you travel north up this last finger of Cornwall, but if the temptation to unpack the surfboard can be resisted, Stratton justifies a generous hour or two, much of which might well be spent in the **Tree Inn** on Fore Street (✆ 01288 352038 ⊘ treeinn.co.uk) soaking up the history (and Cornish ales). It's always good to find a pub which is still the hub of village life, although the post office and village shop have moved a few doors along from its ancient courtyard. Formerly

"Stratton justifies a generous hour or two, much of which might well be spent in the Tree Inn."

Stratton Manor, the building that the pub now occupies was also at the hub of Civil War history. The Royalist army, under Sir Ralph Hopton and Sir Bevil Grenville, whose house at Stowe Barton lay just outside Kilkhampton, plotted their tactics here as the Parliamentarians closed in and took up position on an Iron Age earthwork close by (now occupied

THE CORNISH GIANT

Anthony Payne was born in Stratton Manor (now the Tree Inn; page 39) and served Sir Bevil Grenville as a bodyguard. A giant of a man, standing at seven feet and four inches and with an impressive girth to match, he was not, however, all brawn. Quick-witted, funny and highly intelligent he proved an incredible asset to the Royalist army and survived the battles of Stamford Hill and Lansdowne Hill and went on to serve Sir Bevil's son, Richard, during the Siege of Plymouth. Payne accompanied the body of Sir Bevil, who died at Lansdowne Hill, back to the Grenville family church at Kilkhampton, a few miles up the road from Stratton where his memorial stone can be seen. The giant soldier returned definitively to Stratton when he retired, and when he died, his coffin had to be lowered through a section of ceiling before it could be transported to St Andrew's which, fortunately for all, is just a few steps up the hill.

by the Bude golf course). But the Royalists won the day at the Battle of Stamford Hill, named after the defeated Earl of Stamford.

St Andrew's Church is a fine, 12th-century building, enthusiastically renovated inside during the late 19th century. The Victorian restorers can be forgiven though: they didn't touch the rather battered tomb of the 13th-century knight, who lies cross-legged on the sill of a window, in the north aisle, or the stunning Tudor ceilings, which are typically Cornish 'wagon-style', and they handed the design of the east window showing the four evangelists, to none other than Edward Burne-Jones and William Morris. In the porch, an old wooden door taken from Stratton's little lock-up is studded with nails that spell CLINK, a term which originated in the West Country for a jail with just one or two cells.

5 LAUNCELLS

Launcells is not so much a village as a scattering of tiny hamlets, a mile southeast of Stratton. Tucked away in a leafy coombe beside a trickling holy well lies its parish church, St Swithin's, described by Betjeman as 'the least spoilt church in Cornwall'. Inside the 15th-century building are the original floor tiles, made in the Barnstaple potteries and decorated with a raised design of pelicans, lions, griffins and flowers. The finely carved Tudor bench-ends are exceptional, and a further treasure was

◄ 1 The church of St Morwenna and John the Baptist, Morwenstow. 2 The ruins of Penhallam Manor. 3 View towards Morwenstow Beach. 4 Hawker's Hut, Morwenstow.

discovered in 1929, when underneath layers of limewash, fragments of a large painting depicting the sacrifice of Isaac was revealed on the wall of the south aisle. Outside, in the churchyard, is the grave of the Bude inventor Sir Goldsworthy Gurney (page 45).

6 MORWENSTOW

🏠 **Coombe** (page 417)

Just two miles from the border with Devon at Marsland Mouth, and only a few hundred yards from some of the highest and most treacherous cliffs on the north Cornish coast, Morwenstow lacks nothing in romantic appeal of the most wuthering kind. As you approach from the road (as opposed to the coast path), the excellent **Bush Inn** (page 43) and working blacksmith's forge face each other across a wide and windy sort of village green.

As you move on towards the cliffs, the object of many a visitor's journey to this far-flung spot is the lonely **church of St Morwenna and John the Baptist**, its graveyard filled with the sad stories of shipwrecked souls, while a straggling congregation of 'smugglers, wreckers and dissenters' once found their way into the pews. In the sheltered dip below the church stands a handsome house, built in 1837 as the **vicarage** by the eccentric vicar of Morwenstow, Robert Hawker, at his own expense. It's now run as an upmarket bed and breakfast, but a footpath passes close by and you can get a good look at the quirky chimneys, which were designed to reflect other church towers of significance to Hawker.

It's a short step from here to join the coast path, for sublime clifftop views across the sea to Lundy Island and far south along the ragged coast to Bude, far-off Tintagel and the misty beyond. A 30-minute walk (well mapped on a board at the field gate between the tea room and the lychgate to the church) takes you south along the coast path, where a sign indicates a narrow flight of steps, leading down the cliff to a small wooden cabin, hardly bigger than a sentry box. **Hawker's Hut**, built from planks salvaged from shipwrecks, was a favourite haunt of the vicar, from which he could scan the sea, compose highly charged verse and smoke his opium pipe. A little further on, turn inland at a kissing gate for a

"It's a short step from here to join the coast path, for sublime clifftop views across the sea to Lundy Island and far south."

THE VICAR OF MORWENSTOW

Enough has been written about Robert Stephen Hawker to fill several volumes, and though a Devonian by birth (he was born in Plymouth in 1803) he is one of Cornwall's best-loved eccentrics, not least because he penned the words to 'The Song of the Western Men'. (These rousing verses on the subject of Bishop Trelawney's incarceration in 1687 by James II have become the 'Cornish National Anthem', sung lustily at rugby matches and any other suitable occasion.)

Stories abound of the parson who went about in a sailor's jersey, who was not afraid to climb down the dizzying cliffs to haul up the shredded bodies of the shipwrecked and plied his congregation with gin to give them the courage to lend him a hand, who dressed as a mermaid and sang on a rock at night, who got Tennyson all fired up about King Arthur and who, towards the end of his eventful life, married a 19-year-old Polish governess and converted to Roman Catholicism.

But there was more substance to Hawker than these extreme examples might suggest. When he and his first wife arrived at Morwenstow in 1835, the church had been without a vicar for a century; the vicarage was in ruins and the church decayed. Hawker flung himself into a programme of rebuilding, adding a school and bridge to the parish, as well as the new rectory. He farmed intelligently and with the formidable energy and commitment that characterised everything he set his heart upon, and for good measure, added the Harvest Festival to the church calendar.

Hawker would no doubt have raised a cynical eyebrow to his enduring reputation and popularity; 'Posthumous fame is of little value,' he wrote. 'It is like a favourable wind after a shipwreck.'

signed route to the tea rooms, or for a longer walk (with steep paths), carry on and descend the coast path before turning left to follow the Tidna Valley for almost a mile back up to the village.

FOOD & DRINK

Bush Inn Morwenstow EX23 9SR ℰ 01288 331242 ℰ thebushinnmorwenstow.com. The Bush has stood here since the 13th century, when it was a hostel for pilgrims crossing the peninsula between the north Devon ports and Fowey to the south. In the main bar you can still see the Celtic fish symbol cut from serpentine stone, and a monastic cross is carved into the flagstone floor by the door leading into the garden, while in the middle bar, a tiny window known as a 'Leper's Squint' allowed scraps of food to be passed to beggars. Daphne du Maurier is known to have visited and it's reasonable to think that this building was the model for her novel *Jamaica Inn*, rather than the eponymous tourist-trap in the middle of Bodmin Moor. History apart, these days the Bush has acquired a well-earned reputation for its food, and the owners are great supporters of local producers. Line-caught sea bass comes straight from the sea below and game from the surrounding woods and fields can occasionally be found on the menu.

Little Pig Farm Shop and Café Kilkhampton EX23 9PZ ✐ 01288 321739
⌂ littlepigfarmshop.co.uk. A superb farm shop offering beef and lamb from the farm as well as seasonal fruit and veg, bread from the wonderful Electric Bakery in Bude (page 50) and home-cooked pasties and cakes. The café, serving breakfasts, lunches and teas, is a new addition and a terrific pit stop. A footpath leads directly from the car park to Bude, a 40-minute walk away.

Rectory Farm Tea Room Morwenstow EX23 9SR ✐ 01288 331251 ⌂ rectory-tearooms. co.uk ⊙ Easter–Oct. Built in part from beams salvaged from shipwrecks and oozing cottagey charm, this is a great pit stop for walkers looking for a substantial and delicious cream tea. The farm next door supplies organic meat and eggs to the kitchen and all the veg is sourced locally too; homemade soups, pasties and tarts make it a popular lunchtime destination.

ALONG THE COAST FROM MORWENSTOW TO TINTAGEL

Brace yourself if doing this on foot; the coast path is vertiginous in places and the threading clifftop roads take guts and a steady hand for those on two wheels (or four) as well. All traffic seems to be heading for Bude, and south of Bude, Boscastle and Tintagel are the big draw. However, away from the honeypots, the countryside and beaches are remarkably empty and a happy hunting-ground for naturalists and geologists alike. There are some grand circular walks to be done, taking in small sections of the coast path, wooded, stream-fed valleys and a lot of local history too.

7 BUDE

⌂ **The Beach at Bude** (page 417)

Bude hit the big time when the railway arrived in 1898 and Edwardian families and grandees alike hastened to its wide sandy beaches and the romance of its unspoilt hinterland. However, the arrival of the trains was bad news for Bude's harbour and canal, which had transported sand and coal inland for over a century. The closure of the railway in 1966 heralded lean times for Bude, and it's taken a long time – despite the town's vigorous attempts to reinvent itself as a surfing, family-oriented rival to Newquay with a well-established international jazz festival at the end of August and September food festival – for the town to escape the feeling that a loss of substance has occurred somewhere down the line. But on my last visit to Bude, I came away thinking the town was really on the up, with some exceptionally good places to eat, drink and sleep. Much had also been made of its resources for cyclists and walkers, as well as its beach and watersports. Local footpaths and cycle trails had been clearly waymarked, the TIC was full of colourful maps and suggested routes, the attractive beach huts for hire had been given a fresh coat of paint and the canal was providing a lot of fun for novice paddlers in kayaks and canoes.

Bude is a town of two halves, with the bulk of its hotels, shops and restaurants gathered around the hugely popular, sandy **Summerleaze Beach**, with its colourful, practical beach huts and wonderful natural swimming pool in the rocks. (Surfers tend to gravitate towards **Crooklets Beach**, a little to the north.) Across the River Neet, the canal, wharves and peculiar castle-like building are a rich hunting-ground for Slow explorers as well as walkers looking for a good place to stretch their legs.

SIR GOLDSWORTHY GURNEY

Gurney was of the same generation of incredibly bright and inventive Cornishmen – Humphrey Davy and Richard Trevithick were his friends – who transformed both industry and daily life with their inventions. Born in Padstow in 1793, Gurney was qualified and running a medical practice in Wadebridge before he was 20. In his youth, and throughout his career as a London surgeon, Gurney was intensely focused on solving scientific problems such as getting steam-driven wagons on the roads. In this he succeeded and his cheap but highly profitable 'buses' were soon running between Cheltenham and Gloucester. He was put out of business by horse-drawn transport companies who, foreseeing their ruin if he was allowed to continue, fixed road tolls so that mechanised transport was severely penalised. Gurney also devised a new bright light, the 'Bude Light', by injecting oxygen into a flame and bouncing the light through crystals and mirrors. At a stroke, London's streets and theatres, and even the House of Commons – which had hitherto been lit by smoky candles – were transformed. Limelight, it was called.

But Gurney never found himself in the limelight and despite a host of other inventions which improved mine safety and launched telegraphy, he remained obscure. His castle, the first building in Britain to be built on sand, stabilised by a concrete raft, and the millennium sculpture at its gates, are how Bude remembers him today.

IAN WOOLLOCK/S

SS

TRAVELLIGHT/S

KIRSTY FERGUSSON

THE MUSEUM OF WITCHCRAFT AND MAGIC

The **Bude Canal** was an ambitious project, begun during the 18th-century 'canal boom', and conceived to link Bude harbour with Plymouth via the River Tamar. By 1820, it was possible to ferry goods to within spitting distance of Launceston, 35 miles away, but given the hilly terrain, barges were only used for the first two miles. Thereafter, as the land rises to a height of 350 feet in six miles, the three-branched canal was constructed on a much smaller scale and without locks. Ingeniously, goods were transferred from the barges into boats with wheels (tub boats), winched up on ramps with rails by horses. Lime-rich sea sand was ferried up the canal for use as fertiliser on farms and the tub boats and barges came back filled with grain or slate where they were transferred to ships in the harbour. Cheaper fertilisers and railways eventually made the canal redundant and it ceased to operate commercially in 1891. There is water still in the first two miles to Helebridge, but beyond that nearly all trace of the canal's three branches has disappeared.

Beside the car park stands the decidedly Victorian Bude Castle, overlooking Summerleaze Beach. Now the **Bude Castle Heritage Centre** (℘ 01288 353576 ⊘ thecastlebude.co.uk), it was once the home of Bude's most inventive son, Sir Goldsworth Gurney (page 45), for whom it was built in 1830. Admission is free and inside are exhibits relating to Gurney's life and numerous inventions, a research library dedicated in the main to the history of Stratton and Bude, an interactive shipwreck map as well as a shop and café.

Outside, in front of the gateway to the castle, is a tall and pointy sculpture, striped with bands of colour, representative of sand and sea and sky. This is the **Bude Light 2000**, designed to celebrate Bude, Gurney and the millennium by Carole Vincent and Anthony Fanshawe. In order to be impressed you really need to see it at night, when its fibre-optic lights turn it into a brilliant beacon, and not with a parking cone on its nine-foot peak (Bude youth, eh?).

"You really need to see the Bude Light 2000 at night, when its fibre-optic lights turn it into a brilliant beacon."

◄1 Crooklets Beach, Bude. 2 Crackington Haven is popular with surfers and geologists alike. 3 Boscastle. 4 Geological formation known as 'chevron folds', at Millook. 5 Exhibits in Boscastle's Museum of Witchcraft and Magic.

A wander up Coombe Valley

❋ OS Explorer map 126 or OS Landranger map 190; start: Sandymouth Beach car park
♀ SS202100; four miles; moderate.

This walk, which can be extended, starts between Bude and Morwenstow. It takes in the woods that now bury the site of the Grenville family seat at Stowe Barton, the prettiest of whitewashed hamlets clustered around a working watermill, **Coombe Valley Nature Reserve**, an isolated beach and freshwater pool – and finishes with a blast along the cliffs, if arriving by car. The bus from Bude stops at Kilkhampton (where there are shops and a pub), a good and hilly mile along a pretty footpath to Stowe Barton.

1 Park in the **Sandymouth Beach** car park and follow the coast path north along the clifftops until you reach the waymarker with a flower symbol indicating the path inland that follows the ridge of a steep valley across fields to the lane, where you turn left.

2 You reach the National Trust site of **Stowe Barton**. Just before the farm, cross the lane and take the footpath across a field, skirting a bungalow, and walk down the gentle slope towards the woods.

The remains of one of the Grenvilles' great manor houses lie here among woodland. The Tudor manor was home to generations of distinguished Grenvilles, including Sir Richard (of Spanish-trouncing fame) and his grandson, hero of the Civil War, Sir Bevil. Bevil's son, Sir John, whose Royalist exploits made him a wealthy man under Charles II, demolished the old house and replaced it in 1679 by what was described as 'by far the noblest house in the west of England'. Daniel Defoe passed by and gasped at the quality of the woodcarving in the chapel, which he described as worthy of Grinling Gibbons.

John's daughter, however, had other ideas. Less than 70 years after its completion, on her instructions, the house was taken apart and sold off as she relocated the family seat to Stowe in Buckinghamshire.

3 Follow the footpath signs to Coombe down through the wooded valley nature reserve.

4 The whitewashed cottages and working watermill at **Coombe** have been pleasingly restored by the Landmark Trust which lets the cottages for holidays. Electricity is generated by the watermill. The Hawkers rented a cottage here while waiting for the new rectory at Morwenstow to be completed.

From Coombe, walk on the road beside the stream down to **Duckpool**, where the stream gathers in a natural hollow.

5 As you arrive at the beach, note the lack of swimmers. Duckpool is notoriously unsafe, but attracts a few brave and experienced surfers, regardless of the grasping currents and tides.

Turn left to find the coast path back to Sandymouth, a good mile away to the south. The views are superb – but it's a daunting climb up from the beach for weary legs.

If you'd rather start the walk on the clifftop, there is parking at Duckpool. If your legs are up to it, you can extend the walk to Northcott Mouth, where there is also parking. A footpath takes you across fields to join the lane down to Sandymouth. This extra loop adds a couple of miles.

Dog walkers will be pleased to know that their four-legged companions are allowed on the beach at Sandymouth all year round. The Sandymouth café is open from Easter weekend to the end of October and weekends at other times of the year.

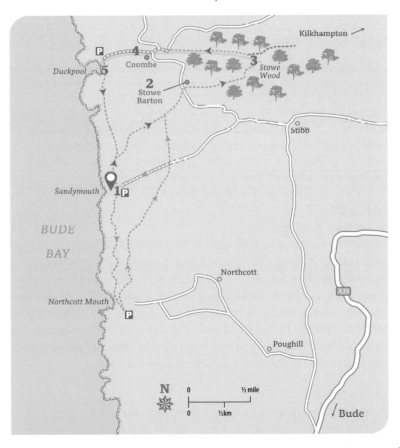

¶¶ FOOD & DRINK

Bude has numerous places to eat and drink, catering largely for ravenous surfers and bucket-and-spading families, but on my most recent visit it was evident that some exciting new ventures were putting the town on the map in a very positive way.

Electric Bakery The Depot, King's Hill EX23 8PQ ♪ 01288 356604 𝕕 electricbakery.co. A new bakery/café (outdoor seating only) that has acquired a devoted following in a very short time. Finnish rye bread, einkorn flour loaves, Italian ciabatta and French almond croissants sell out in a flash, but everything can be reserved online. Saturday lunches are a Slow Food treat, featuring the likes of tempura broccoli or confit chicken.

Rosie's Kitchen Crooklets Beach EX23 8NE ♪ 01288 354238 𝕕 rosieskitchen.co.uk. A friendly café right on the beach that warms up in the evening with wood-fired pizzas and a licensed bar.

Temple 10 Granville Terrace EX23 8JZ 𝕕 templecornwall.com. Availability of local ingredients – from lobster to cauliflower – dictates the daily-changing menu here. Lunches daily; two-course evening meals at weekends, reservations by email only. There's no booking for the informal terrace and tapas bar upstairs – first come, first served.

The Weir Whalesborough Farm, Helebridge EX23 0JD ♪ 01288 361207 𝕕 weir-restaurant-bude.co.uk. A café and wildlife centre, perfectly placed at the halfway point of the Bude Canal walk. Open all day and great for families, walkers and cyclists. Descriptions of short (and shortish) circular walks from the tea room are available for 50p; they are best used in conjunction with an OS map.

8 MILLOOK

🏠 The Beach House (page 417)

Follow the coast road south, passing Widemouth Bay, and the narrow road rears and plunges like a wild horse, leaving you slightly breathless by a tiny clutch of houses in a deep cleft of the cliffs, with just enough room for a couple of cars to park at the roadside. The stream that tumbles down from the surrounding hills gathers in a sheltered pool above the pebbly beach: stand beside it and turn right to gaze at the zigzag rock formations ('chevron folds') in the cliffs, where sandstone and shale have buckled to form extraordinary patterns.

¶¶ FOOD & DRINK

The Break The Beach House, Marine Drive, Widemouth Bay EX23 0AW ♪ 01288 361256 𝕕 beachhousewidemouth.co.uk. Overlooking – and with direct access on to – Widemouth Beach, this is a lovely spot for a drink or a bite at any time of day. Sundowners accompanied by a spot of live music are very popular with locals of all ages. See also the accommodation chapter (page 417).

9 POUNDSTOCK

Poundstock spills over the A39 eastwards, but the core of the village lies in the wooded valley to the west. I was nosing around the 14th-century church of St Winwaloe when the church warden suggested I might want to look at the **Gildhouse** (⊘ poundstockgildhouse.co.uk ⊘ normally only Wed). This lovely building was probably constructed to house the masons working on the church and then acquired a new use as a village hall – a function it still serves today, having also done service as a poorhouse and village school. Close to the church, a footpath runs over the fields to the coast, dropping down into the tiny cove at Millook. A short, but steep circular walk can be made of it (the churchrwarden's favourite) by returning through oak woods owned by the Woodland Trust, then picking up the lane at Trevoulter Farm which takes you back to Poundstock. There's a good-sized car park at the top of the hill, behind the church.

¶¶ FOOD & DRINK

Cornish Coasts Farm Shop & Café Middle Penlean EX23 0EE ⊘ 01288 361380 ⊘ cornishcoasts.co.uk. Licensed café serving breakfasts and lunches that make the best of the farm's produce. It's right on the A39, about five miles south of Bude, making it a great pit stop for tired travellers.

10 CRACKINGTON HAVEN

🏠 **Pencuke Farm** St Gennys (page 417)

Paradise for surfers and geologists, with easy parking, a pub and two very good cafés, Crackington Haven's geography makes it unusually good for spectators. Climb just a short way up the coast path to the village tennis court and you have a close-up view of the action below in the sea, especially on an incoming tide. From the thoughtfully positioned bench there's a good view of the exposed cliff face on the far side of the beach where you may observe the 'Crackington Formation': compressed folds of sandstone and grey shale. 'Crak' is the onomatopoeic Cornish word for sandstone; you can almost hear the rock fracturing in your mouth. The Haven shop-cum-café (page 53) in the car park sells a leaflet giving details of a walking trail for the geologically curious. To the south,

A walk around Boscastle

❋ OS Explorer map 111 or OS Landranger map 190; start: Boscastle main car park
📍 SX100914; seven miles; demanding.

A challenging walk taking in both Minster and St Juliot, a spectacular stretch of coast path with seals and dizzying cliffs, a waterfall, a terrific farm shop and café as well as Boscastle's ancient harbour. Have a look at the iWalk Cornwall app for a shorter, circular route if this seems too daunting.

1 From the main car park in Boscastle follow the signed footpath through oak woods uphill along the valley beside the Valency.

2 After almost a mile, you will see a wooden footbridge crossing the river, offering a detour to Minster church (see 3). Soon after passing the footbridge the path forks. Take the left-hand route with the steps.

3 If you wish to detour to **Minster church**, follow the signed footpath over the wooden footbridge and return by the same route. Alternatively, at dry times of the year when the river is running low, a pretty yet steep, looping route is available. Soon after leaving the Boscastle car park you will see granite sleepers, laid as stepping stones over the river. Upon crossing them, the path ascends through woodland to the church. Pick up the path to the footbridge (2 on the map) in the lowest corner of the churchyard.

4 Reach **Newmills**, a pretty hamlet with a ruined mill. Continue on the footpath, keeping the river on the right until the path is crossed by another path. At this point, you can make a shortish detour to **St Juliot Church**, or turn left up a farm track. At the next junction, turn left and follow the footpath across fields to the road (B3263). Cross the road with caution and find the footpath on the far side by the entrance to Trebyla Farm.

5 Make your way past the campsite and over fields towards the hamlet of **Beeny**.

6 Turn right at the tarmac road and left at the next junction. You will soon see the footpath to the coast path on your right.

beyond the headland of Cambeak, High Cliff is just that – Cornwall's highest cliff at 732 feet; there's easy access from the road that avoids the substantial ascent from Crackington Haven itself.

🍴 FOOD & DRINK

The Cabin EX23 0JG ☎ 01840 230238 🖥 cabincafecrackington.co.uk. Perched just above the car park, this café is justly proud of its locally sourced, home-cooked produce, and the

7 On reaching the coast path, turn left and walk south to Boscastle harbour. Just after the Boscastle Farm Shop entrance, turn around and look back to see the spectacular waterfall which drops sheer into Pentargon Cove.

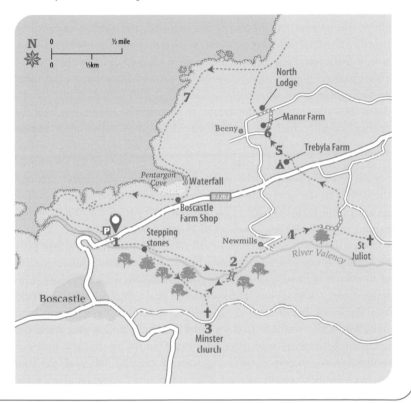

beef in the pasties comes directly from **Dizzard Farm** (which has a good farm shop), three miles north on the coast-hugging road to Bude. Look out for their summer evening BBQs.
Coombe Barton Inn EX23 0JG ✆ 01840 230345 🖰 coombebarton.co.uk. Cornish ales and grand views over the beach.
The Haven Beach Café and Shop EX23 0JG ✆ 01840 230774. On the other side of the car park from The Cabin, and run by a local family who know how to catch a fish or two – fish which often find their way on to the menu. Local crab is on offer too, and if it's quiet

and you're not in a hurry, friendly chat about what's going on in the village and the rest of Cornwall.

11 BOSCASTLE

Until 16 August 2004, Boscastle was just a picturesque harbour, its cottages, tea rooms and pubs jostling for space in a narrow valley watered by a small river, the Valency, and its tiny tributaries in the wooded hills above. Then the rain came and by the following morning, everyone had heard of the Boscastle flood. Miraculously, no people were killed – but two unfortunate dogs in locked cars were washed away in the torrent. Two hundred people, sheltering in the ground-floor bar of the hotel by the bridge, were warned by a local motorist who had just driven down the valley and seen the danger to get out fast; 20 minutes later the ceiling beneath which they had gathered caved in. Fallen trees, higher up the valley, were thought to be responsible for causing the swollen river to burst; then cars, swept along from the village car park, jammed against the bridges and the water rose. Firemen searching through the debris in the aftermath of the flood thought they had discovered a corpse, but it turned out to be a waxwork of Joan the Witch, a star exhibit in the **Boscastle Museum of Witchcraft and Magic**.

Today, the flood and the witchcraft museum are what give Boscastle its strongest identity and its own brand of curiosity value. A native of Boscastle (whose grandmother fought a battle with the MoD, who wanted her to dig up her tennis court to grow potatoes during World War II) shook her head and sighed, 'So much has been rebuilt, and so authentically restored that it's hard to believe unless you knew the village in its antediluvian days'. The Pixie House by the new harbour footbridge, for example, with a gloriously sagging 300-year-old roof has been entirely rebuilt, while totally respecting its spectacular degree of irregularity. The museum, too, was resurrected and continues to attract both the curious and the convinced.

The entrance to the S-shaped harbour is practically invisible from the sea, and given extra concealment by Meachard Rock. Both sides of the harbour offer a good leg stretch: the footpath on the south side leads to a white, castellated watchtower for coastguards, once the site of an

1 Minster – Boscastle's mother church. 2 The waterfall at St Nectan's Glen. 3 Delabole Slate Quarry. 4 Labyrinth carving, Rocky Valley. ▶

Iron Age hillfort, from which you look over the Forrabury Stitches, a medieval 'stitchmeal' field system; to the north of the harbour, the narrow, rocky track climbs to Penally Point. If there is a heavy swell, about an hour before or after low tide, you'll be rewarded with an impressive display of water jetting horizontally into the harbour mouth from a blowhole, known locally as the Devil's Bellows.

Boscastle Museum of Witchcraft & Magic

PL35 0HD ✆ 01840 250111 ⊛ museumofwitchcraftandmagic.co.uk

The museum has experienced many changes since it first opened in 1960, when lurid tableaux depicting sacrifice and ritual added a frisson of excitement to the slightly dusty library and curious exhibits, divided into sections such as Herbs & Healing, Protection, and Cursing and Divination. Simon Costin, who became director in 2013, introduced the magic – both into the museum's title and its exhibits. With a

WICCA MEN

Cecil Williamson was a colourful character: film director, MI6 spy and practitioner of magic. His large collection of magical objects grew when author Gerald Gardner joined him at his house, named 'The Witches Mill' on the Isle of Man. Gardner was in the process of founding the neo-pagan religion, Wicca, but both men were strong characters and eventually fell out and Williamson moved, along with his collection and wife Gwen, to the mainland in 1954.

After several ventures on the mainland, each meeting with some hostility, Williamson finally settled in a two-storey building in the harbour at Boscastle, which in 1960 opened as The Witches House – today's Museum of Witchcraft and Magic – and where it has remained ever since.

The next director of the museum was Graham King. During a walk in the English countryside in 1996, he encountered and was made welcome by a group of early road protestors, the Dongas Tribe, gathering to celebrate the ancient Tan Hill Fair. It was this encounter that set in motion King's decision to leave behind his previous life as a specialist camera manufacturer and led to his purchase of the museum from Cecil Williamson.

King made the 200-mile journey on foot to Boscastle, where at midnight on 31 October that same year the purchase was finalised. King and his team went on to develop The Museum of Witchcraft into one of Cornwall's most popular museums, which passed into the hands of current director, artist and art director, Simon Costin, in a splendidly theatrical ritual with appropriate lighting and costumes at midnight on 31 October 2013.

background in art direction, his long professional interest in evoking a sense of the magical on stage has served the museum well – his sense of style and subtle use of lighting has transformed the ever-growing collection. 'I want the objects to tell their own story … by trying to explain too much, you can destroy the magic, so I hope to bring some poetry and nuance to the collection and to use lighting and shadow to conceal as much as they reveal.' One of the most popular exhibits, brought to the museum by Costin's predecessors, is a scrying mirror (used rather like a gypsy's crystal ball) … I'm not sure I would dare look at it!

¶¶ FOOD & DRINK

Boscastle Farm Shop Pentire Point, Widemouth PL35 0HH ✆ 01840 250827
⌖ boscastlefarmshop.co.uk. Award-winning farm shop and café, surrounded by National Trust farmland. In summer it hosts barbecues and hog roasts with music. A 50-yard path leads straight on to the coast path above Pentargon Cove.

12 MINSTER

Though Boscastle has changed, its mother church, known simply as Minster, hidden in the wooded hills a mile from the harbour, is seemingly timeless and far from the madding crowds below. A lovely walk from the main car park in Boscastle follows the River Valency up into the woods and brings you to the churchyard which in spring is full of daffodils and wild garlic followed by a lush pageant of wildflowers, ferns and grasses – no surprise to learn it is an SSSI (Site of Special Scientific Interest). The church originates from 1150, but was restored and extended in 1507. Look closely and you will see an enigmatic carving of a pair of scissors dating from this period on the western face of the tower wall. A major restoration was carried out, again in Victorian times, and yet more work was done following the 2004 flood, when water rose to a height of six feet inside the church.

13 ST JULIOT

⌂ **The Old Rectory** (page 417)

Many of Cornwall's medieval churches were in a dismal state of repair by the 19th century and subject to necessary, if occasionally over-enthusiastic, Victorian renovation. Thomas Hardy in his younger days worked as an architect and in that capacity came to Boscastle in 1870 to draw up a plan for restoring the church of St Juliot, Victorian style. He stayed in the vicarage and later married the vicar's sister-in-law, Emma Gifford.

**I found her out there
On a slope few see,
That falls westwardly
To the salt-edged air,
Where the ocean breaks
On the purple strand,
And the hurricane shakes
The solid land.**

Hardy wrote this in 1914, two years after Emma's death, when he came back to Cornwall to revisit the place of their courtship. She had encouraged him to write and his third novel (though the first published under his own name), *A Pair of Blue Eyes*, is all about their early days together. But Hardy, as is well known, was not especially nice to his wife over the 38 years of their marriage and remorse leaks out in his poems.

14 ST NECTAN'S GLEN & ROCKY VALLEY

⊘ st-nectansglen.co.uk

On the road from Boscastle to Tintagel a roadside car park, signed 'St Nectan's Glen', is the starting point for an idyllic mile-long walk through ferny oak woods, alongside a shallow, splashing river of outstanding loveliness. The path culminates abruptly in a steep flight of rocky steps, leading to the spot where St Nectan wisely retreated during the bloody battles of the 6th century. Of the hermitage, only his cell remains, burrowed into the bedrock below the Victorian cottage that incorporates the old chapel walls and is now a shop and ticket office. But the main reason for coming here is the **waterfall**, which cascades 60 feet, emerging through a halo of rock to fall into the kieve, a deep hollow, where baptisms of every stripe are regularly performed. Around the pool and the shallow springs and beaches, the trees and rocks are festooned with ribbons, coins and other offerings to the undoubtedly happy spirits of this magical place.

A lot has changed here since the change of ownership in 2014, and if you knew the place in the days when it was visited by only a handful of spiritually curious adventurers who were met by Barry, the previous owner, sitting at the entrance gate in his plastic chair, you may well feel nostalgic. Now, there are all sorts of timber buildings – housing a very nice café, a room for groups to hire, toilets, accommodation and (on the bank holiday weekend when I last visited) hordes of noisy families building (or shying pebbles at) little cairns in the shallow water. The wooden walkway and steps down to the waterfall have been greatly extended so you can see other parts of this astonishingly beautiful valley, including another waterfall, although finding a quiet spot from which to drink in the beauty may not be so easy.

"The trees and rocks are festooned with ribbons, coins and other offerings to the spirits of this magical place."

The valley of the Trevillet has more surprises to offer on its journey to the sea. On the other side of the B3263, heading towards Tintagel, the footpath marked **Rocky Valley** descends through ruined woollen mill buildings and emerges, twisting above the river, to deliver a breathtaking view of the sea and the rugged, rocky cliffs that frame it. But before hurrying across the wooden bridge below the ruined mill, turn right and there on the rock face are two finely chiselled but entirely enigmatic seven-fold labyrinths, carved for reasons unknown perhaps 1,500 – or just 200 – years ago.

A local woman, out walking her dog, remarked, 'You know, Tintagel is almost a red herring once you know this valley'. I know what she meant: the spirit of the Trevillet from the waterfall to the sea surely inhabits all the myths and legends that have, over the centuries, come to settle a mile away upon Tintagel.

15 TINTAGEL

🏠 **Mill House Inn** Trebarwith (page 417)

Drive through Tintagel on a hot summer's day, when the car parks are bursting, the pavements crowded and the gift shops brimming with Arthurian knick-knackery and you might well be tempted to give it a miss, which would be a shame, because if you ditch the car and get out on to the coast path things change dramatically. Standing at a lonely distance from the village, high on the cliff above the sea, **St Materiana's Church** has more than something of the lighthouse about it. Inside the Norman building, a 12th-century granite font carved with crude faces at each of its rounded corners and serpents in between, stands on an oddly decorative plinth of small upright slates. Much of the woodwork in the church is unusual too: the reredos looks as though it was made out of old carved bench-ends, depicting the Passion and local coats of arms. In the south transept, a Roman milestone, discovered in the lychgate wall during repair works in 1889, now points the way to heaven; the inscription suggests it was made in the time of Emperor Licinius, who died in AD324.

Tintagel Castle

Castle Rd, PL34 0HE *✆* 01840 779084; English Heritage

From the clifftop path, the once-fortified island reveals itself in all its natural grandeur. But let's be clear: the castle ruins are very ruined and the rocky island fortress is definitely more rock than fortress. It has been well established that a 5th- or 6th-century monastery and trading post stood here, and relics of Mediterranean oil and wine jars have been found. The **Arthurian connection** is largely due to Geoffrey of Monmouth's 12th-century manuscript, which makes Tintagel the place of Arthur's conception, and a century later Prince Richard – the Earl of Cornwall responsible for building Launceston Castle's stone walls – used the myth to reinforce his own magisterial status in Cornwall.

The ruins seen today are the remnants of the castle Prince Richard built, which occupied both the island and the closest part of the mainland, where the most significant remains of the castle are to be found. But Arthur's name remains more potent at Tintagel than Richard's and the idea of an Arthurian stronghold more exciting than a rocky island; so when a piece of inscribed slate was discovered during excavations on the island in 1998, pro-Arthurian excitement knew no bounds. In Latin, it read: 'Artognou, father of a descendant of Coll, has had [this] made'. Cynics may shrug, but in the end, the place, in all its wild and windswept glory, is bigger than the academic disputes that surround it. (I reserve my cyncism for the village, which having been known to all and sundry as Trevena for the best part of a millennium, adopted the name of its castle as a marketing ploy in the mid-19th century, when Pre-Raphaelite interest in the Arthurian legend was at its peak and tourism was booming.)

TINTAGEL: **1** The new bridge linking the mainland and island at Tintagel. **2** Rubin Eynon's spectral statue *Gallos* was inspired by the legend of King Arthur. **3** The 14th-century post office. ▶

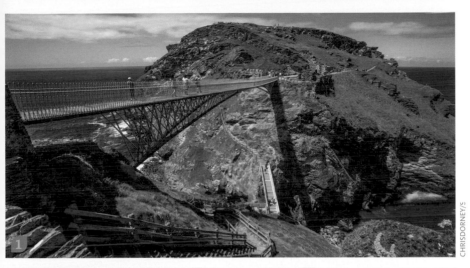

A good morning or afternoon is needed to do justice to the whole site, with its beaches, caves, vantage points and hundreds of steps. Not so long ago, the slog uphill back to the village was even more daunting than it is today, and the site's inaccessibility to less-able visitors led to the – inevitably controversial – decision to build a bridge across the chasm that separates the cliff from the great lump of rock that is Tintagel Castle. The new bridge – of spectacular modern design, constructed in steel and oak – won the inaugural Building Beauty Award in 2022. Lead judge, Stephen Bayley, summed up the judges' decision: 'the designers … have generated something graceful, perfectly poised, restrained: nothing here is unnecessary, but what is necessary has been finessed to the point of beauty.' The charge to cross the bridge to the great lump of rock is an eye-watering £17 for an adult.

King Arthur's Great Halls
Fore St, PL34 0DA ℐ 01840 770526 ◈ kingarthursgreathalls.co.uk ⊖ closed Mon

Abandon all scepticism before entering: the grey, slightly uninviting façade and entrance conceal a splendid secret, revealed within the huge ex-Masonic hall added on to the back of the house. (A very fine coastal garden was destroyed in the process, but you can't make an omelette, etc.) The secret is this: 72 quite simply sublime **stained-glass windows** created in 1930 by Veronica Whall, a gifted pupil of William Morris. There are flowers, jewel-like, along the aisles, while in the hall a great triptych centres upon Merlin at the darker end and Arthur at the sunlit one. The granite structures and sculpted architectural decoration are genuinely enthralling too. More than fifty Cornish quarries sent their finest granite here, the stones ranging from black or pinky grey to ochre and sparkling white, to be sculpted into wall-mounted shields, a canopied throne and Round Table. (Old quarrymen come just to remember the now defunct quarries in the solid craftsmanship.) The hall is no longer in use as a Masonic lodge, but once a year a terrific banquet is held for members of the Fellowship of the Knights of the Round Table of King Arthur.

As if all that were not enough, a large **antechamber**, hung with ten paintings by the Edwardian artist William Hatherall, prepares the visitor for the experience in the great hall. The paintings show scenes from Mallory's 16th-century telling of the Arthur legend, and the disembodied voice of Robert Powell, as Merlin, is suitably enchanting.

The man with the extraordinary vision and the means to realise all this was Frederick Thomas Glasscock, one half of Monk & Glass Custard, upon which the British Empire was nourished. Early in the 20th century the company was sold to Bird's and Glasscock retired to Tintagel to pursue his extravagant dream. It was completed to his exacting satisfaction in 1933, and the following year he embarked on a lecture tour of the States to promote interest in all things Arthurian. Sadly, he died on the journey back to Tintagel.

The Old Post Office

Fore St, PL34 0DB ℘ 01840 770024 ☺ closed winter; National Trust

Among the modern shops and houses on Tintagel's main street, this quaint anomaly, with its higgledy-piggledy roofs, slumping walls and stumpy chimneys, looks like it has been dropped into the present out of a fairy tale. Built in the 14th century for a well-to-do farming family, it served briefly as a post office in Victorian times and is now owned by the National Trust. The pretty cottage garden to the rear offers picnic space – if you can find a free spot.

¶¶ FOOD & DRINK

Tintagel is fairly bursting with cafés, pubs and tea rooms, but it's not all Excaliburgers and Magic Merlin Milkshakes. Ales from **Tintagel Brewery**, brewed at Condolden Farm in the hills behind the village, are a real treat. Look out for Castle Gold, Harbour Special and Cornwall's Pride at the **Cornishman Inn** and the **Tintagel Arms Hotel**. Located at the castle end of Fore Street and Atlantic Road, **Pengenna Pasties** (⌂ pengennapasties.co.uk) is an upmarket bakery doing a roaring trade in pasties (you can watch them being made from a street window).

Charlie's Café Fore St, PL34 0DA ℘ 01840 779500 ⌂ charlies.cafe. Housed in a 14th-century cottage, almost opposite the Old Post Office, this café is a good option for breakfasts, lunches and tea. Lovely crab salads and sandwiches, and a shop selling local produce at the back.

16 VALE OF AVALON

℘ 01840 213947 ⌂ thevaleofavalon.co.uk

Just north of the hamlet that goes by the gory name of Slaughterbridge, close to the supposed site of Arthur's last battle, the **Vale of Avalon** (formerly known as the Arthurian Centre) might sound like a theme park, but it's probably of equal interest to archaeologists and Arthurian scholars as to imaginative children. Behind the café and children's play area, a half-mile walk through fields takes you past the partially excavated site of an **Iron Age village** and around a wooded clearing, which has been identified as Camlann, where Arthur and the evil Mordred fought their last battle in AD542. From here, the path drops down to a little river and the cobbled terrace, uncovered in 2005, that was once part of a 17th-century garden created by Lady Falmouth, who lived at Worthyvale Manor, just out of sight behind the trees. The restoration

"A wooded clearing has been identified as Camlann, where Arthur and the evil Mordred fought their last battle in AD542."

of the garden is a slow yet ongoing project, which advances as and when funds allow. From a wooden platform you look down the steep and muddy riverbank to where the greatest treasure lies, lapped by the rippling water: the **Arthur Stone**. This great stone must have lain here undisturbed for nearly a thousand years until Lady Falmouth identified it as useful material for a footbridge and the historian Borlase gently pointed out its significance. Two hundred years later, Tennyson fought through the brambles to gaze at it in wonder. Now scholars and Arthurians wrangle over the meaning of the two inscriptions, one in Latin, one in Ogham (a rare Celtic script which identifies the stone as 6th century). This seems to indicate that the stone was carved around the time of the battle, but only wishful thinking can make the almost illegible letters spell out Arthur's name.

¶¶ FOOD & DRINK

Hilltop Farm Shop and Tea Room PL32 9TT ✆ 01840 211518 ⌖ hilltopfarmshop.co.uk ⊘ closed Sun. Less than a mile from the Vale of Avalon, just off the B3314 shortly before the junction with the A39, this wonderful place is going from strength to strength. Packed with everything you could ever wish for from a Cornish deli-cum-greengrocer, and the home-cooked lunches, cakes and scones are top drawer. Seriously recommended.

17 DELABOLE SLATE QUARRY
Pengelly, Delabole PL33 9AZ ⌖ delaboleslate.co.uk

It was a bank holiday and this working quarry was therefore closed the first time I arrived in Delabole. But the viewing platform from which the vast hole in the ground (in fact, the biggest manmade hole in the country) can be seen is next to the car park at the start of a footpath which follows the mile and a half circumference of the giant crater. From here peregrine falcons nesting in the cliffs can be seen soaring on thermals, eyeing the ducklings and baby gulls foolish enough to venture out into the still, blue pool that fills the bottom of the quarry. On the brow of the hill where the quarrymen have erected a jokey 'slate-henge' complete with altar ('They're still looking for a sacrificial virgin', remarked a passing dog-walker from the village) the views to Bodmin and the west are outstanding. George Hamilton, who rescued the mine from dereliction in 1999 and whose four sons all work with him in a workforce of about 30, is a community-hearted man determined to do his best for the village where he grew up. The summer afternoon tours are no longer running, but the public footpath around the quarry is well worth the detour.

¶¶ FOOD & DRINK

The Bettle and Chisel 114 High St, Delabole PL33 9AQ ✆ 01840 211402. Aptly named after slate-splitting tools, this inn serves St Austell ales and good, locally sourced, home-cooked pub grub beneath old photos of the quarry and its workforce. A field is generously provided for campers (no showers, just pub toilets) behind the building.

Sea View Farm Shop Higher Tynes PL30 3LR ✆ 07966 201945 ⚲ seaviewfarmshop.co.uk. Just 4 minutes' drive south of Delabole, this terrific farm shop and café – right in the middle of a working farm – draws both locals and visitors for breakfasts, lunches and teas, music nights and lovely views.

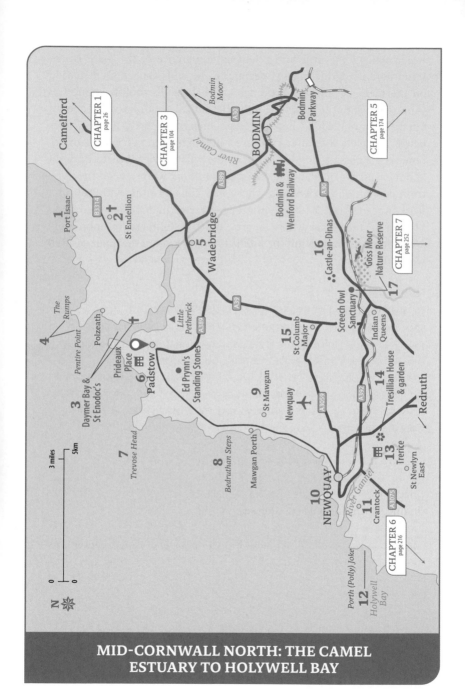

MID-CORNWALL NORTH: THE CAMEL
ESTUARY TO HOLYWELL BAY

2

MID-CORNWALL NORTH: THE CAMEL ESTUARY TO HOLYWELL BAY

The year-round appeal of breaking surf and sandy beaches makes this stretch of the Cornish coast one of the most visited parts of Cornwall, and while Newquay and Rock may not be everybody's idea of paradise (at least, everybody not of Bermuda shorts-wearing age), **Padstow** fulfils an alternative vision of Cornish bliss with its pretty houses, working harbour and abundance of upmarket eating establishments where fresh fish and seafood are given celebrity status.

Researching this chapter, I seem to have spent rather more time among the quieter backwaters of the region, looking for angels in the architecture or otters in the **Camel**, often finding myself ambling in Betjeman's footsteps: pottering about **Wadebridge** and revisiting his words in quiet churchyards or on windy headlands. I discovered too, that music is particularly strong in these parts. The now-famous voices of a group of local men can be heard singing Cornish songs of the sea on the beach at Port Isaac on summer evenings, and the Easter and summer concerts in the lovely church at St Endellion have also found audiences from far beyond the Tamar.

"Often just a mile or two away from the big tourist attractions, there are unsung valleys and villages to explore."

Inland, a landscape of river valleys, woods and fields is crossed by the hugely popular **Camel Trail**, while the **Saints' Way**, used by traders and pilgrims for more than 1,000 years, offers a superb walking route through hidden Cornwall from Padstow to Fowey on the south coast. Off the beaten track, but often just a mile or two away from the big tourist attractions, there are unsung valleys and villages to explore, dotted with prehistoric stones, Iron Age hillforts and secluded churches.

GETTING AROUND

The A39, dubbed **Atlantic Highway**, is the main route across north Cornwall; it's single-carriageway for much of the way and can be very slow. Inevitably the spur roads off to Newquay and Padstow get very congested in the high season and the traffic is nose to tail around Wadebridge during the three days of the Royal Cornwall Show in early June and the first weekend in April when the 'Chelsea of the West', as the Cornwall Garden Society's Spring Flower Show is known, is in progress.

TRAINS

Bodmin Parkway station is your best bet for the Camel estuary towns and villages; **Newquay** fares rather better with its own branch line from Par on the main London–Penzance line, and its station is right in the town centre.

BUSES

Wadebridge and Newquay are the **hubs**. Buses run from Newquay to Crantock and Holywell, making it easy to walk the three-mile stretch of coast path between them, taking in lovely Porth Joke Beach on the way. Frequent, **direct buses** run from Newquay to Padstow and Wadebridge, where you change for services to Rock, St Endellion and Port Isaac. Check ⊘ firstbus.co.uk/cornwall for up-to-date details of winter and summer services.

FERRIES

The *Black Tor* shuttles **between Padstow and Rock** all through the year during daylight hours, though points of embarkation vary with the tides (⊘ padstow-harbour.co.uk/ferry) and a water taxi provides an evening service from Easter until the end of October. Both services carry foot passengers and bikes. A summer-only ferry **crosses the Gannel** from the Fern Pit landing in Newquay to Crantock Beach (page 92) when the tide is too high to use the footbridge.

WALKING

Coast-path walking is rather spoilt by development around Polzeath and Newquay, but there are some glorious **circular routes** where you

TOURIST INFORMATION

Newquay Marcus Hill, TR7 1BD 𝒮 01637 838516 𝒶 visitnewquay.org
Padstow North Quay, PL28 8BL 𝒮 01841 533449 𝒶 padstowlive.com

can feel you've left the world of mass-tourism behind. North and west of Padstow, for example, **well-marked footpaths** loop from Trevone to Stepper Point (page 85) or around the windswept headland at Trevose. Further south, an understandably popular stroll takes in the beach at Bedruthan Steps (page 89), with its monumental stacks of rock, one of the great sights of the north Cornish coast. This is best viewed from the heights of the coast path, well served by frequent buses that ply between Newquay and Padstow.

Inland, you may find the Wadebridge to Padstow section of the **Camel Trail** (page 87) rather too popular with cyclists for enjoyable walking; turn instead to the **Saints' Way** (page 87), which begins in Padstow and follows an ancient overland route to the south coast, through unexpectedly lush green valleys, far from the madding crowds.

CYCLING

Sustrans NCN Route 3 (the Cornish Way) splits at Bodmin, offering cyclists the choice of a south- or northbound coastal route, before joining up at Truro. The northern route makes use of the busy, level **Camel Trail** (page 87). Beyond Padstow the route is quieter but hilly, wiggling past St Columb Major, Newquay and Trerice.

CYCLE HIRE

There's no shortage of places to hire bikes along the Camel Trail, but it's wise to book ahead (online booking is now generally available) in the summer months – an indication of how popular the trail has become. Evening rides in the summer are now offered by most hire companies, when the trail is not so busy. Padstow and Wadebridge have a number of options; all offer bikes with tag-alongs or trailers for children and/or small dogs.

Bikesmart Eddystone Rd, Wadebridge PL27 7AL 𝒮 01208 814545 𝒶 bikesmartcornwall. co.uk. Free car parking for customers.
Bridge Bike Hire/Go By Cycle Camel Trail, Wadebridge PL27 7AL 𝒮 01208 813050 𝒶 bridgebikehire.co.uk. One-way trips can be organised with drop-off in Padstow. Part-refund on long-stay car parking charges.

Camel Trail Cycle Hire Eddystone Rd, Wadebridge PL27 7AL ℞ 01208 814104 ℞ cameltrailcyclehire.co.uk. Free car parking for customers and indoor bike parking available. Cheaper rates after 15.00 in the summer.

Padstow Cycle Hire South Quay, Padstow ℞ 01841 533533 ℞ padstowcyclehire.com. Indoor bike parking for small charge (very useful if you've just cycled up from Wadebridge); one-way trips possible with drop-off in Wadebridge.

Trail Bike Hire Unit 6, South Quay, Padstow PL28 8BL ℞ 01841 532594 ℞ trailbikehire. co.uk. These guys are competitively priced and offer evening hire from late Jul to late Aug at reduced rates.

AROUND THE CAMEL ESTUARY

'Heyl' is Cornish for estuary, of which there are just two on the north coast of Cornwall. There's the Hayle estuary (page 230), further to the west and this, the Cam-heyl or 'crooked estuary', the last before the Taw and the Torridge meet between Bideford and Barnstaple, way up the coast in Devon. The Camel is superbly rich in wildlife and is one of the few estuaries in the West Country where salmon are flourishing, a mark of a healthy river. Birdwatching from the western shores, where access is made easy by the Camel Trail, is especially rewarding in winter, when flocks of migrants join the natives dipping their beaks in the rich estuarine mud.

To the east and west of the wide estuary mouth, strings of fine, sandy beaches look out towards rocky islets, where seals and seabirds keep a distant eye on the surfing and seafood-loving human crowds who flock here in numbers equal to the winged visitors.

1 PORT ISAAC

x **Cornish Tipi Holidays** Tregeare (page 418)

There's not much elbow room in the steep, narrow streets of this immoderately photogenic fishing village (one of the lanes is called Squeeze Belly Alley, which gives a good indication of the limitations on space), so it's not surprising that cars are banned in the summer months. Two big car parks on the cliff above the harbour take the strain and the walk down to 'the Platt' (as the beachy harbour is known locally) is full of charm and offers a great vantage point over the action below.

Because of the good view and terrific acoustics of the harbour, this spot gets packed on summer evenings when the **Fisherman's Friends** assemble on the Platt for an informal concert of shanties and Cornish folk songs. They used to sing every Friday, but other commitments and the vagaries of the weather mean that concerts are often impromptu and announced at the last minute on social media. The singers, who all grew up in and around Port Isaac, sang together in the Methodist chapel as lads, and kept on meeting to sing even after work claimed them as fishermen, coastguards, potters, lifeboatmen, builders, artists, hoteliers and shopkeepers. There's no leader among them – each man takes his turn to start a song and the sound of their voices builds a full, rich orchestra of harmonies. These rugged types have

"This spot gets packed on summer evenings when the Fisherman's Friends assemble on the Platt for an informal concert of shanties and Cornish folk songs."

acquired a modestly unexpected fame over the past few years: there's even been a film loosely based on their story. But I love the tale of how they were asked to sing in the foyer of the Royal Albert Hall for the BBC Folk Awards and found an unexpected fan: 'David Attenborough came and listened to us and he refused to go into the Hall until we'd finished our set: "No, I'm staying here," he said.' In 2013, the shocking news was announced that one of the ten singers and the tour manager had been killed in a freak accident while setting up the stage for a performance in Guildford. There was no more singing for a long time after that terrible day.

For years, the village was the backdrop to the popular TV series, *Doc Martin*. Themed tours of the village are still popular with fans of the series from all over the world. To book, visit ⊘ portisaactours.com.

Port Isaac doesn't sound very Cornish, but it's a corruption of Issick, meaning wheat, which was exported from here in large quantities from medieval times onwards. Slate was exported too, and Welsh coal landed here. Pilchard fishing was big business in the 18th and 19th centuries and the old pilchard cellars have found a wide variety of uses: one of them is now the lifeboat station. Fish is still landed here, and crab and lobster are cooked on the slipway and sold in the fish market where, if you come in the morning, you'll see the local chefs in their aprons putting in their orders for the day.

Less than a mile to the east, **Port Gaverne**, a long, finger-shaped cove, has one of the safest beaches on the north Cornish coast: pebbly at high tide, but revealing firm sand and rock pools as the tide retreats.

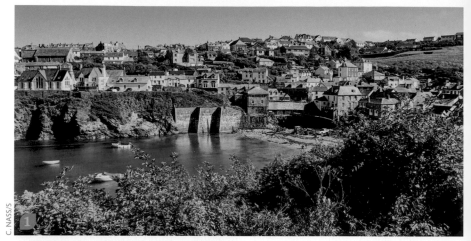

A fine three-mile **walk** west along the coast path takes you round Kellan Head from where there are magnificent views across Port Quin Bay to the Rumps before dropping down into **Port Quin**, a shingle harbour with a scattering of houses, tucked away at the sheltered end of a Cornish fjord. This once busily populated fishing village was able, like its bigger neighbour, Port Isaac, to add substantially to its income by exporting local slate. The railways stole the trade from the quays and the pilchard industry dried up; almost overnight it became a ghost village. Now there's just a small cluster of holiday cottages, including a castellated Victorian folly, Doyden Castle, perched on the south side of the water, all immaculately restored by the National Trust. You can make this a circular walk, returning to Port Isaac by a well-signposted, straightforward inland route across the fields to Roscarrock Manor, one of the oldest farms in Cornwall. There are Roscarrock family tombs in St Endellion (page 73). After Roscarrock there's a plunging coombe to negotiate, and then Port Isaac appears ahead.

ⓉⓉ FOOD & DRINK

Port Isaac is stuffed with characterful cafés, pubs and restaurants, with cream teas, pasties and locally caught fish on their menus.

The Mote 9 Fore St, PL29 3RB ✆ 01208 880226 ⬦ the-mote.co.uk. This restaurant and bar, in a cosy little former smuggler's cottage, is particularly good at championing home-grown (or home-fished) food.

2 ST ENDELLION

There's something very special about this village community and the church that stands at its centre, well known these days for its world-class music festivals in spring and summer. There's an Arthurian connection, too: St Endelienta, to whom the church is dedicated, was reputedly the god-daughter of King Arthur (Tintagel, of course, is just a few miles up the coast). And, as any good godparent would do, Arthur slew the villain that killed Endelienta's favourite cow. The girl revealed her saintliness by bringing the beast back to life and when she died, it carried her to the place where the first church was built to remember her. There's

◀ **1** Port Isaac. **2** Fulmars can be seen from Pentire Headland. **3** Revellers at the Rock Oyster Festival. **4** St Enodoc's Church and Daymer Bay.

MUSIC AT ST ENDELLION

What began in 1958, when some college friends got together to renovate the old rectory and put on a few concerts in the church, has grown to become what is now one of the most prestigious musical events in Cornwall. Actually, there are two main events: the Easter and summer music festivals, made special by the mixture of amateur and top-flight professionals, rising and established musicians who keep coming back, finding the creative energies and glorious atmosphere of St Endellion completely irresistible. So irresistible that the **summer festival** now fields a full symphony orchestra and 75-strong chorus for the annual centrepiece opera. The virtuous circle that generates this kind of passion and energy is in no small part due to the late Richard Hickox, who ran the festival for 40 years; members of his family are still very much involved.

The **Easter festival** is never without a major choral and orchestral oratorio, but the intimacy of the church lends itself equally well to evening concerts of chamber music, song recitals and even jazz. Tickets to these events sell out with predictable rapidity, but there are open rehearsals in the mornings and just before the opening of the festival, where local musicians from across Cornwall 'come and sing' with members of the festival chorus under the direction of one of the festival conductors. After just three hours' rehearsal, there's an informal performance.

The two festivals are now supported by a year-round arts programme, organised by Endelienta (⊘ endelienta.org.uk). This also includes the excellent **North Cornwall Book Festival**, held in late September. Under the leadership of Cornish novelist Patrick Gale, big names turn up each year.

mention of the church again at the end of the 13th century, when the same bishop who ordered the building of Glasney College in Penryn (page 271) awarded it collegiate status. Endelienta's shrine, carved in the 15th century by a local sculptor known simply as 'the Master of St Endellion', has been used as an altar since the 1920s, when a very sensitive restoration was started. The darker roof beams date from this period, but the lighter wood, smothered in carved decoration, is early 15th century; the older bench-ends can also be dated to this period.

It must be the lack of stained glass in the windows that makes the building seem so light and airy; it's hard to imagine what it would have been like when a high wooden rood screen separated the nave from the sanctuary. This (like so many) was removed during the Reformation, but there's still a reminder of where it once stood. The narrow stone staircase set into the north wall spirals up to an eight-foot drop, but when the screen was in place, it provided the means by which candles could be placed along its top or draped with a veil during Lent. In the bell tower an amusingly illustrated 18th-century 'poster' gives rhyming advice to bell-ringers on how they should behave. The tower isn't often open, but there's an identical poster beside the bell-ropes in the equally attractive church in **St Kew**; the little, leafy village a couple of miles to the south makes a rewarding detour for secular reasons too: the pub does excellent food.

FOOD & DRINK

Cornish Arms Pendoggett PL30 3HH ☏ 01208 880335 🖰 cornisharmsinn.co.uk. Often the location for happy, post-concert gatherings, 'The Doggett', as it is known affectionately, is a free house serving decent pub food (daily, after 17.30 only) and 'PSB' – Pendoggett Special Brew, brewed specially for the pub by Sharp's. Some areas are suitable for dogs.

St Kew Farm Shop & Café St Kew Highway, PL30 3EF ☏ 01208 841325 🖰 stkewfarmshop.co.uk. An excellent farm shop selling pork from Gloucester Old Spots, local lamb and homegrown fruit and vegetables. The café is open for breakfast and lunch, with gourmet pizzas on Fri eves.

St Kew Inn St Kew PL30 3HB ☏ 01208 841259 🖰 stkewinn.co.uk. A St Austell Brewery pub in a very pretty village; log fires, lovely garden and extremely good food.

Trevathan Farm Shop and Restaurant Almost opposite the church in St Endellion PL29 3TT ☏ 01208 880164 🖰 trevathanfarm.com. The café and large shop selling farm food as well as gifts is much appreciated by musicians and audiences during concert season.

3 DAYMER BAY & ST ENODOC'S CHURCH

The poet Sir John Betjeman (1906–84) spent his childhood holidays at Trebetherick and later came to live here by **Daymer Bay**, remembering sunny clifftop picnics and stormy beach walks in his verse. The west-facing beach has lost none of its charm for holidaying families; though the sea is saturated with surfers and windsurfers, there are still the simple pleasures of rock-pooling and crabbing at low tide on Trebetherick Point. Brea Hill looms above the beach, creating a 'wind shadow' that keeps the windsurfers on their mettle; footpaths wind around the

"Though the sea is saturated with surfers and windsurfers, there are still the simple pleasures of rock-pooling and crabbing."

hill and across the fairways of a golf course to **St Enodoc's Church,** where the Poet Laureate found his final resting place. The tiny, but lovely granite church, with its delightfully asymmetrical 13th-century

CORNISH ANGELS

Once you start looking for them, churches and churchyards of mid- and north Cornwall are a-flap with angels: all smiles and wings, decorating the corners of gravestones or at the base of roof arches, on fonts and bench carvings, windows and brackets. Henrietta Boex, from Falmouth, has made a study of them: 'It's not so much a local preoccupation with angels,' she says, 'as local availability of fine-quality slate, which permits fine-line chiselling and doesn't weather like softer stones, which is why they're so noticeable around here. When you start noticing them, you realise that both naive and skilled artists across the centuries had great fun drawing faces and hairdos, trumpets and wings, using their chisels almost like pencils.' Start looking in the churchyard at St Kew...

stone tower (I imagine a father-and-son team of masons building it at slightly different speeds) nearly suffered the same fate as St Piran's Oratory and Church on Penhale Sands (page 221), disappearing beneath the windblown sand on several occasions over the centuries. It's not hard to imagine: the church nestles so deeply among the dunes that you look down upon its slate roofs from the highest point of the churchyard. A nice (but possibly tall) story relates how, at one point, the vicar and his congregation had to enter the church by a trapdoor in the roof. By the middle of the 19th century 'the sands had blown higher than the eastern gable, the wet came in freely, the high pews were mouldy-green and worm-eaten and bats flew about, living in the belfry'. This was written by the son of the vicar who launched a major effort to remove the sand in the 1860s and oversaw the restoration of the church. A new bell was hung in the tower, claimed from the wreck of an Italian ship that had foundered on the infamous Doom Bar sand spit.

Doom Bar

Padstow's harbour is one of the safest on the north coast, but it's not always easy to approach thanks to the bank of silt and sand that blocks the estuary at low tide and is dangerously invisible at other times. Hundreds of ships have foundered upon it since it started to make its shifting presence felt over 500 years ago. Sharp's Brewery, in Rock, a 30-minute walk south along the coast path, has given its name to its best-selling flagship ale; you'll see Doom Bar in pubs all across Cornwall and beyond the Tamar, too.

Tresoddit

During the 1980s, *Guardian* cartoonist Posy Simmonds cast her wry gaze over the changing fortunes of neighbouring Rock and Polzeath, both of which have been identified as the model for her fictional Cornish fishing village, Tresoddit.

'The little hamlet holds its breath and gazes out to sea and waits for the safe return of its wayfaring ones,' began one classic strip, suggesting an absent fishing fleet. The streets of Tresoddit are silent, while locals 'eke out a doleful existence'. But then there's a glimpse of a sail: 'They're back up at Crab Pots,' a local reports. 'Car's in the lane … got their dinghy on the trailer.' In the final frame we see a crowd of London families meeting up at the Jolly Fisherman pub, complaining about traffic jams at Okehampton (the location of the last Waitrose on the A30 route into Cornwall) over gin and tonics. 'The fleet blows into its haven for a sojourn, which must be all too brief. But, for a short while, the streets are full of merry mariners … and all the tills ring.'

OYSTERS & OYSTERCATCHERS

On the tidal shores of Porthilly, with its pretty church standing almost on the beach a little south of Rock, Tim Marshall's family farm is thriving. Tim has been farming Pacific oysters for more than two decades. These oysters grow much faster than the native oyster raised in the Helford and Fal rivers – it takes just two years for little 'spats' the size of a fingernail to grow into palm-sized beasts and there's a ready market for them in the upmarket hotels and restaurants that have sprung up around the estuary.

Tim rears his oysters in netting sacks, laid out on racks along the shoreline, so they get washed and fed by each returning tide. Now joined by his son, Luke, the pair have added mussels, clams and samphire to the menu.

It's fortunate that oystercatchers pose no real threat to his business. Using their long bills to stab through shell, they feed on small shore crabs or cockles and mussels in the estuary mud and you'll occasionally see flocks in winter on grassy fields, looking for worms. 'They'll eat oysters too', says Tim with a grimace, 'but we've all got to eat'.

Held over a June weekend in the grounds of Dinham House, near St Minver, the **Rock Oyster Festival** (⌂ rockoysterfestival. co.uk) started in 2010 as an arts, food and music festival and continues to draw a friendly, family-orientated crowd. Billed by its originator, Charlie Anderson, as a 'locals' festival' that you'd be 'happy to take your granny to', the festival remains true to Charlie's vision with top names in both the kitchen and on the stage.

This clichéd image of Rock/Tresoddit is a little weatherworn these days, partly overtaken by unsavoury images of well-heeled youth partying on the beach, but more importantly by Rock's emerging identity as a serious sea-foodie destination to rival Padstow, a ferry ride away across the estuary.

¶¶ FOOD & DRINK

Little Avalon Café Bar Valley Campsite, Polzeath PL27 6SS ✆ 07970 298254 ⌂ littleavalonpolzeath.com. A campsite café, run by Kato with a warm, friendly vibe. Special attention is given to promoting local produce.

Restharrow Farm Shop Trebetherick PL27 6SQ ✆ 01208 862340. A family-run, low-key shop selling seasonal vegetables at reasonable prices, handy for campers staying on the farm.

4 PENTIRE POINT & THE RUMPS

🏠 **Moyles Farm** St Minver (page 418)

A square-headed chunk of land, circumscribed by a sublime section of the coast path, juts out into the sea above Polzeath. It's carpeted with wildflowers – thrift, sea campion, kidney vetch, gorse and, a Cornish rarity, harebells which appear in spring. Unbelievably, it was destined for commercial development in the 1930s, but saved by local opposition who raised funds and donated the land to the National Trust. At its westernmost reach is **Pentire Point**, described by Betjeman, looking up from Trebetherick, as having the form of a sleeping lion; it's a grand perch for gazing out over Padstow Bay.

The northeastern knobble of rock is **The Rumps**, surmounted by an Iron Age cliff-fort, one of three known to have existed on the headland. Binoculars come in really handy here: the lump of rock a few hundred yards out to sea, known as the Mouls, is home to masses of nesting seabirds, including fulmars and a handful of puffins. There used to be many more puffins (tour-boat operators in Padstow still refer to it optimistically as Puffin Island), but predation by great black-backed gulls has caused a severe decline in numbers.

"It's carpeted with wildflowers – thrift, sea campion, kidney vetch, gorse and harebells which appear in spring."

Between the two points, a memorial stone beside the cliff path records that the poet Laurence Binyon wrote 'For the Fallen' here in 1914, and quotes the fourth verse, heard each year at Remembrance Day services: 'They shall grow not old, as we that are left grow old …'

5 WADEBRIDGE

⌂ **Roskear** Tregunna (page 418)

Until the late 15th century, two villages faced each other across an unpredictable ford on the River Camel. On the west bank, there was Wade in the parish of St Breock; on the east bank Egloshayle, with its waterside church dedicated to St Petroc. The vicar of St Petroc, the Reverend John Lovibond, was also a sheep farmer, and clearly a wealthy one for he paid for a tower to be added to his church and in 1460 decided it was high time his flocks (both woolly and two-legged) were able to cross the Camel to the market in Wade without fear of drowning. The story goes that the piers supporting the 17 arches of the bridge were sunk on foundations made of woolsacks, which is why it's known as the **Bridge on Wool**, but this is likely to be an enthusiastically literal interpretation of the means by which the bridge was funded. Now only 13 arches are visible and it has twice been widened, but it's still an impressive sight and by far the longest medieval bridge in Cornwall. There's a healthy otter population on the Camel, and some have even been seen from the bridge, playing on the muddy shore late in the evening by the light of street lamps; kingfishers too, can sometimes be seen scooting underneath the arches.

Wadebridge is a busy place, servicing scattered communities over a wide rural area and it's full of the 'normal' kind of shops that have no place in swanky Rock and Padstow. But it's no Cinderella – Wadebridge, it would seem, is on the up. In the old town, Molesworth Street is wide and paved and home to a good assortment of independent shops, including the much-loved **Wadebridge Bookshop** (✆ 01208 812489 ⌂ wadebridgebookshop.co.uk), which holds regular talks by local authors, and book signings. Just off this street, the **Wadebridge & District Museum** (⌂ wadebridgemuseum.co.uk) found more secure premises after the last building slipped into the river (slowly enough for most of the collection to be rescued) a few years ago. The town's colourful history is brought alive here by the helpful volunteers, who will happily chat about the exhibits.

The town is also an important access point for cyclists and walkers embarking on the hugely popular **Camel Trail**, which follows the track of the old railway that once linked Padstow to Bodmin. In 1840, six years after the line opened, 1,100 people crowded on to three specially laid-on trains at Wadebridge for a day trip to Bodmin. The object of the excursion was to see the public execution at Bodmin Jail of the Lightfoot brothers who had been convicted of murder. Such was the entertainment then; Wadebridge's Regal Cinema, which opened its doors in 1931 (and is still going strong) clearly didn't arrive a minute too soon.

When the line closed in 1967, the Victorian station languished until rescue came in the form of a fund-raising volunteer group. It reopened in 1991 as the **John Betjeman Centre** (✆ 01208 812392 ☉ Mon–Fri), with additional new buildings to house the activities of the local U3A and over-55s groups. The Poet Laureate would have approved: he loved Victorian railway architecture and the cosy sociability of the community café seems a fitting tribute to the poet of 'trains and buttered toast'. The entrance houses a small collection of Betjeman memorabilia in a low-key sort of way – you're free to go in and inspect his desk, typewriter, spectacles and notes and gaze upon his sculpted bust. The charity Concern Wadebridge keeps the place open on weekdays only.

Wadebridge's rural hinterland

Immediately south and west of Wadebridge, a web of narrow lanes and footpaths takes you into hilly farming country, dotted with woodland and trickling tributaries of the Camel. There are some idyllic spots by the river, giving opportunities for spotting kingfishers and otters. Thanks to

FARMING, FOOD & FLOWERS

For three days in June each year, Cornish farmers and producers rally to the Wadebridge Showground for their county show, the **Royal Cornwall Show** (⊘ royalcornwallshow.org), in droves. It is a proper, traditional agricultural show, one of the best in the UK, and now it's become something of a showcase for Cornish Slow Food. In the Food and Farming pavilion you'll find many of the local producers listed in this guide and have the opportunity to sample the goods, chat to the people involved and leave with a bulging carrier bag.

Keen gardeners should also note that the Cornwall Garden Society's annual **Spring Flower Show** (⊘ cornwallgardensociety.org. uk/spring-flower-show), held over the first weekend of April, is held at the Wadebridge Showground. Dubbed the 'Chelsea of the West', this hugely popular event showcases the finest camellias, magnolias and spring-flowering bulbs for which Cornwall is so famous.

the **Camel Trail**, it's an easy stroll of just under a mile to Pendarvey footbridge; from here to Polbrock Bridge a mile upstream, the river, the surrounding woods and wetland meadows are all rich in wildflowers and outstandingly beautiful. The conservation walks branching off the main trail are well marked, bicycle-free and take in peaceful views of woodland and water.

Southwest of Wadebridge, narrow lanes zigzag past **St Breock**, with its pretty church tucked away on wooded slopes, and tiny **Polmorla**, where a handful of houses cluster around an ancient bridge at the bottom of a steep and leafy valley. The contrast with St Breock Downs, a mile or two to the south, could not be more startling: the exposed hilltops are crowned with wind turbines and an extraordinary collection of Neolithic standing stones, best appreciated on foot from the Saints' Way.

6 PADSTOW

It is a mean-looking place, of woe-begone aspect ... We imagine no one deliberately visits Padstow for its own sake, but those fond of a fine coast will find it a convenient resting-place for the night.
C S Ward, *Thorough Guide to North Devon and North Cornwall*, 1888

This remote little fishing port ... [which] endures that incessant and often intolerable wind ... faces on to a vast expanse of sand-flats which become at low tide a desert-like wilderness broken only by the inconspicuous trickle of the River Camel.
Roland Roddis, *Cornish Harbours*, 1951

Well, you can't accuse the old guidebooks of over-selling Padstow. Roddis worries that the decline of Padstow's fishing industry will result in the town delivering its soul to tourism, like the harbours he has seen at Volendam and Marken in Holland, where 'worst of all, they sell jellied eels by the dozen' to visitors. The man who saved Padstow from a fate of jellied eels is Rick Stein, whose many establishments now dominate the little town, to the extent that it goes by the sobriquet these days of 'Padstein'. Happily, the fishing fleet is healthy again, the fish market on South Quay lively, and the seafood restaurants along the quay packed throughout the summer. Even on a chilly grey day in February, when I last visited, there was a lot of activity in the harbour and lunchtime queues for Stein's fish and chip shop. Battered oysters were on the menu; it's good to see the celebrity chef has retained his sense of humour. Nevertheless, I can't say I was tempted to see if they had survived their battering.

Despite the crowds, the character of old Padstow still reveals itself in its narrow streets and haphazard terraces of old houses and cottages, which even Roddis was forced to admit 'typify all that is best in nautical architecture'. Sir Walter Raleigh, who held the exalted position of Warden of the Stannaries between 1585 and 1603, had a house and adjoining courtroom on Riverside (both private residences now) and older still is the Abbey House, on the far side of the quay, next to the Shipwright's Arms. The small **Padstow Museum** (⊘ padstowmuseum. co.uk ⊙ closed winter), in the Market Place, contains a cherished collection of documents, photographs and artefacts relating to Padstow's long history as a seaport. The finds from an archaeological dig that uncovered a Bronze Age cemetery at Harlyn Bay in 1900 are on display along

"Despite the crowds, the character of old Padstow still reveals itself in its narrow streets and haphazard terraces."

with a slightly creepy post-war 'Obby Oss' mask, used in the pagan festivities which continue – symbolically – to drive out winter from Padstow on May Day each year. And there's a riveting eyewitness account of the staggering bravery and dreadful loss of life when the harbour lifeboats attempted to rescue a stricken trawler on 11 April 1900.

A wander up Church Street, away from the busy harbour, brings you to **St Petroc's Church**, built in the early part of the 15th century on very ancient foundations – the thick base of the tower is a relic of the *second* church, built around 1100. The first, Celtic chapel dates from the 6th century and stood until AD981, when both the church and the monastery Petroc had founded were destroyed in a Viking raid. St Petroc's bones, which were originally buried here, have had a colourful history (page 121); his equally colourful life is recalled in the (modern) stained-glass window over the main altar, where he is shown with his famously rescued deer, as well as in the beautifully carved emblems of his saintliness in the canopies over the adjoining windows. But my prize for the best carving goes to a seat by the altar, fashioned from old bench-ends: it shows a fox in a pulpit, preaching to a flock of enthusiastic geese. (At least, five of them look interested; the other two have been distracted by something behind them.)

◄ **1** Bridge on Wool, Wadebridge. **2** Padstow harbour. **3** The interior of Prideaux Place. **4** Baby lobsters at the National Lobster Hatchery. **5** Cyclists on the Camel Trail.

A walk from Prideaux Place to Trevone

✾ OS Explorer map 106 or OS Landranger map 200; start: Prideaux Place ♥ SW915755; five miles (can extend to 8½ miles by taking in Stepper Point); moderate.

- -

This route takes in a terrific stretch of coast, fields of wheat and barley and a glorious beach, popular with families. An excellent picnic can be picked up en route at Padstow Farm Shop, and there are cream-tea pit stops at Trevone and at Prideaux Place. There are great opportunities for swimming too, particularly at low tide.

I left my car by arrangement in the car park at the Padstow Farm Shop, but there is a beach car park at Trevone and limited parking on the lane from Prideaux Place to the farm shop. If you are visiting the house and garden there is free parking at the end of the drive. The walk can be extended by following the coast path around Stepper Point.

1 **Prideaux Place** has two entrances. Start at the garden entrance on the B3276. With the gates behind you turn right and right again, following the lane uphill and keeping the garden wall on your right. After 700 yards look for the stile and footpath in the hedge on your left. This leads across fields to Trethillick Farm and the **Padstow Farm Shop** and its café (page 88).

2 Turn left out of the main drive-in entrance to the shop and take the farm track immediately ahead. After 150 yards, take the footpath on the left across fields and a footbridge crossing a stream, then more fields into **Trevone**. Cross the road and head for the Well Parc Hotel. With the entrance to the hotel on your right, follow the lane as far as the last house on the left. Take the track on your right which, with a dogleg, borders two fields running down to the cliffs.

3 The track joins with the coast path. Below, a magnificent natural swimming pool appears at low tide, surrounded by great slabs of rock. Turn right and follow the coast path to **Trevone Bay**, a lovely safe and sandy beach, with parking and all the usual opportunities for refreshment.

4 Climb the coast path and pass a giant collapsed cave (unfenced), the three-mile point in the walk. Soon after, a farm track appears on the right.

For the short route back, omitting Stepper Point: Turn right on to this track, turn left at the fork and continue to the hamlet of Crugmeer. Turn right on to the lane in Crugmeer and almost immediately left to pick up the footpath (indicated on your left) that runs through field after field of arable crops to join a farm lane, where you turn right for Prideaux Place.

Prideaux Place

PL28 8RP ✆ 01841 532411 ⊘ prideauxplace.co.uk ☉ summer only, Mon–Fri; check website for dates & times as they may vary

For the long route, taking in Stepper Point: Carry on along the coast path which goes around Stepper Point and continues, high above the dune-flanked River Camel, passing **St George's Cove**, where steps lead down to a small, but sheltered sandy beach, often busy with families escaping the crowds of Padstow. (If accompanied by a dog, note that between March and October the beach is out of bounds.)

5 At the war memorial, take the signposted footpath that leads inland to Prideaux Place – or continue on the coast path for just 765 yards to reach Padstow harbour for cafés and loo.

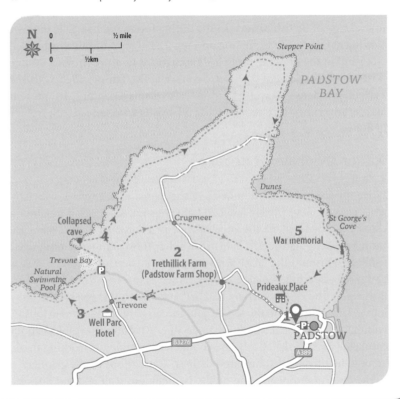

A short walk up the hill from the church brings you to Prideaux Place, home to the Prideaux-Brunes, who have lived here since it was built on the site of St Petroc's Monastery between 1588 and 1592. The Elizabethan house was extended and given a Gothic makeover in 1810, to bring it up to date with prevailing fashion, and the garden, which was the subject of a major overhaul, is a palimpsest of various dates and styles, from the restored 1730 formal 'Augustan garden' to the hornbeam *allée* and acer glade, planted in 2013.

In *Unwrecked England*, Candida Lycett Green describes Prideaux Place as 'about unwrecked as you can get' and she's right – inside the house, as the current owners, Peter and Elisabeth Prideaux-Brune, will tell you, 'there are 44 bedrooms, of which just six are habitable'. Some of them are just as the American army left them at the end of World War II and throughout the house you find yourself wandering through a microcosm of British history. In the dining room, for example, there's a carving of Elizabeth I trampling on a pig (the pig apparently symbolised vice) and in the drawing room a 'diplomatic' miniature shows a double portrait of Charles I and Oliver Cromwell. The family sided with the Parliamentarians, but won a pardon – also displayed – for 'past, present and future crimes' by later marrying off a sister to Charles II's Secretary of State.

National Lobster Hatchery

South Quay, PL28 8BL ✆ 01841 533877 ⊗ nationallobsterhatchery.co.uk

I love the straightforward honesty of the name, which tells you exactly what goes on here. Newly hatched baby lobsters don't stand much of a chance in open waters: the survival rate is less than 1%. (Lobsters are cannibalistic, which doesn't help much either.) So a number of designated fishermen around the coast send the hatchery berried lobsters, that is to say, egg-bearing, female lobsters rather than depositing them back in the sea. The eggs are safely hatched and after a few weeks, the baby lobsters are returned to the sea. Result: we can gorge ourselves on lobster without worrying that stocks are in decline. 'And how do you feel about eating lobster?' I asked Carly, the young marine biologist working there, among the tiny, semi-transparent babies. 'Can't afford it,' she grinned.

The one room open to the public is small, but well laid out and the first windows into the tanks behind the walls reveal examples of some whopping lobsters and lobster-lookalikes, such as crawfish, displayed in a child-friendly way. Facts and figures come next, aided by a short film. Then there are the babies, tray upon tray of finger-length crustaceans, each in their own cot-like unit, looking vulnerable and rather appealing.

Just a step away are some of Cornwall's most famous seafood restaurants, which you can now visit with your conscience appeased. That's the theory, anyway.

The Camel Trail & the Saints' Way

Padstow is the start – or finish – of two major walking routes. The **Camel Trail**, used perhaps by more cyclists than walkers, is a 17-mile level track that follows the route of an old railway, from the South Quay at Padstow along the estuary to Wadebridge (five miles), and on to Dunmere Halt (six miles) through deep, leafy cuttings beside a very picturesque stretch of the Camel. There's a family-friendly pub by the parking space at Dunmere, and from here you can take the mile-long route into Bodmin, or swing north, following the young river upstream to Wenfordbridge (six miles), just a short hop from the very pretty moorland village of Blisland (page 116). It's estimated that almost 500,000 walkers, cyclists, wheelchair users and horseriders use the trail each year, and at peak times in the summer months it can feel a bit like a healthy, green version of the A30.

The **Saints' Way** starts at the door of St Petroc's in Padstow and follows an ancient overland route taken by Celtic saints and medieval pilgrims travelling between Ireland or Wales and Brittany (where the route continues on to Santiago de Compostela), avoiding the dangers of sailing around Land's End. The 30-mile trail crosses some of Cornwall's most varied rural landscapes, dividing just south of the A30 to offer two equally enjoyable routes into Fowey.

You can use the first couple of miles of trail to make a decent circular walk up one side of Little Petherick Creek and down the other, following the creekside footpath to Tregonce, where a permissive footpath connects with the Camel Trail and crosses the iron bridge back to Padstow.

ᵀᵀ FOOD & DRINK

The whole town of Padstow seems dedicated to producing and selling high-quality food and drink that might be labelled 'Upmarket Slow'; it's a great place to push the boat out and indulge in some seriously good local cuisine.

With a preponderance of St Austell Brewery pubs around the quay, there's no problem securing a pint of Tribute, but if you're after a glug of Doom Bar from Sharp's, the local brewery, look out for the flowery frontage of the **Golden Lion** in Lanadwell Street (✆ 01841 532797 ♂ goldenlionpadstow.com).

There are also two special places a little way out of town that you wouldn't want to miss.

Padstow Farm Shop and **Roundhouse Deli** Trethillick PL28 8HJ (✆ 01841 533060 🖥 padstowfarmshop.co.uk). Half a mile on from Prideaux Place, on the lane to Stepper Point, this excellent place is unmissable. Fruit and veg from the old kitchen gardens as well as home-reared pork, beef and lamb, Cornish cheeses and smoked meats are always available. The farm also grows durum wheat, so a selection of homemade pasta is occasionally on sale too. The shop is big by any farm-shop standards, supplying several Padstow restaurants and offering an online shopping and delivery service. At the very tempting deli, salads, sandwiches, soups and casseroles make the most of the farm produce; bread comes daily from the Da Bara bakery. It is well worth the small detour out of Padstow and perfect for those heading out on the walk described on page 84 to pick up a pasty or slice of frittata.

Trevisker's Kitchen Trevisker Garden Centre, Padstow Rd, PL28 8LD ✆ 01841 541361 🖥 treviskers.com. Great breakfasts and lunches, with evenings and Sunday lunches bringing locals flocking to the table for terrific seasonal menus. The garden centre is a cut above the norm, too.

FROM TREVOSE HEAD TO HOLYWELL BAY

This sublime stretch of west-facing coast is famous for its superb sandy bays – Constantine, Watergate, Lusty Glaze and Fistral – beaches which are legendary among the surfing community. The cliffs behind them are also pretty special: battered by winds from the west and sculpted by the sea, a dramatic chaos of deep gorges, collapsed sea caves and colossal, isolated chunks of rock all make for spectacular coast path walks.

7 TREVOSE HEAD

The Doom Bar makes access to Padstow harbour difficult at the best of times, so the lifeboat has been stationed at Mother Ivey's Bay on the eastern side of Trevose peninsula since 1967 and crews must dash the five miles from Padstow by road. It's housed in an impressive piece of contemporary architecture, curved to accommodate the thrust of wind and waves and perched on piers at the far end of a glorious, shallow arc of golden sand that is rarely overcrowded. Trevose Head is owned by the National Trust and serviced by a National Trust car park. The toll on the lane out to the lighthouse and huge collapsed cave has been suppressed, as have the many 'Keep out' signs. The Trust's aim is to enhance and join up the wildlife habitats on the peninsula, and to extend the number of footpaths, making the area as accessible as possible.

8 BEDRUTHAN STEPS

Bedruthan Hotel (page 417), **The Scarlet** (page 418)

These monumental, flat-topped slabs of slate marching across the sand like a giant's stepping-stones (Bedruthan is the name of a mythical Cornish giant) are so large that in some cases they have individual names. One slab was ironically dubbed Samaritan Island in 1846, when a ship carrying a cargo of silks was wrecked on the unforgiving rock and locals rushed to save the precious cargo, ignoring the crew. Another is called Queen Bess Rock, as the profile of Elizabeth I could be discerned in its contours. It takes some imagination to see her these days.

At low tide, it's possible to walk around the northernmost rock (swimming is not an option in these dangerous waters) to Diggory's Island Sands — a perfect horseshoe of golden beach, edged with rockpools and caves. There's a steep, narrow path back up to the top of the cliffs from the beach, but the first part is a bit of a scramble.

The National Trust has several car parks along the clifftop road between Mawgan Porth and Porthcothan; at Carnewas Point there's a small visitor centre and friendly café.

FOOD & DRINK

Carnewas Tea Rooms PL27 7UW ℰ 01637 860701 ⌂ carnewas-tea-rooms.co.uk ☉ Feb half-term—end Nov & Dec w/ends (good weather only). Well placed for walkers, the café has been run by the same local family since 1984. Lunches, teas and ice creams and wonderful views from the clifftop gardens.

9 ST MAWGAN

Behind Mawgan Porth, the deep, wooded Vale of Lanherne is a world away from the frantic activity and windy exposure of the beach. St Mawgan is a Miss Marple kind of village, with church fetes, village cricket, a historic pub, pretty gardens open for charity and homemade jams and chutneys on sale at the garden gate. The restored 13th-century church is full of treasures: carved bench-ends, a 15th-century rood screen and a superb collection of brasses, mostly memorials to the Arundells of Lanherne. In the peaceful churchyard, a timber memorial,

PLANET GRANITE

The late Ed Prynn was a great British eccentric – you need only wander past the bungalow and garden where he lived, just outside St Merryn (PL28 8JZ, close to Rick Stein's pub, The Cornish Arms), to grasp the full extent of the retired quarryman's foibles. The self-appointed Chief Druid of Cornwall created a granite stone circle (each stone representing an important woman in his life), a giant dolmen ('the Angels' Runway'), an underground fogou (for ritualised re-birthing ceremonies) and other copies or interpretations of Cornish standing stones, and invited the curious – as well as the convinced – to share in the sacred energies of his extraordinary domain. He even claimed to have lifted a curse from the England football team before the World Cup in 2010. For all his eccentricity, though, Prynn was a man of persuasive charm: in 1987, he convinced Sir Rex Hunt, Governor of the Falkland Islands, to send him, free of charge, two massive stones excavated during the building of the islands' new airport: 'one to remember those who didn't return from the conflict and one to remember those who did'.

Prynn was generous to those who simply stopped to stare in wonder at his extraordinary garden. Its future, however, is by no means certain, as at the time of writing it was on the market.

shaped like the stern of a rowing boat, remembers the ten sailors who froze to death in their boat and were washed ashore in 1846.

The beautiful **Japanese Garden** and bonsai nursery (✆ 01637 860116 ⚲ japanesegarden.co.uk ☉ closed winter) might seem anomalous in such a quintessentially English village idyll, but it turns out to be less about acres of Zen gravel and more about woodland walks, beautifully planted with acers and azaleas, clipped 'cloud trees' and streams trickling into tranquil pools, crossed by small bridges.

10 NEWQUAY

🏠 **Lewinnick Lodge** (page 418)

Newquay is not an obvious destination for Slow travellers, and a sense of place cannot always be guaranteed in its hinterland of backstreets, teeming with – and catering for – an international crowd of party-loving surf-seekers and post-exam teenagers.

Problems associated with tourism – albeit high-class tourism – are not new to Newquay. The grand Headland Hotel caused riots when it

◄ **1** Bedruthan Steps. **2** The Japanese Garden, St Mawgan. **3** Fistral Beach, Newquay.

was built in 1900 on common land used for grazing and drying nets. The victory of tourism over local industry did not bring great happiness to the architect and entrepreneur Silvanus Trevail (page 205), but the hotel still stands, a lonely vision of upper-crust grandeur above the teeming surf of Fistral Beach.

It's a longish walk from one side of Newquay to the other, following the coast path along the clifftop seafront, but for much of the way there are gull's-eye views over the beaches and world-class surf activity to admire. If you can time your walk so the tide is in by the time you arrive at Pentire Point (allow a good hour from the cliffs above Lusty Glaze Beach) there's a delightful opportunity to cross the Gannel by ferry to Crantock Beach and return to Newquay by bus from Crantock village. A short detour might take you down to the historic **harbour**, engineered by the great Joseph Treffry (page 194), and once linked by a tunnel and tramway to the railway station. (The tunnel is still used by the pilot gig rowing team for storing their boats and the tramlines remain exposed on the approach to the station in Cliff Road.) High above the harbour, the route passes the Huer's Hut, a stubby whitewashed tower looking more like a Greek island windmill than a Cornish lookout post, from which the news was bawled that shoals of pilchards had arrived.

Fistral Beach

Beyond the Headland Hotel, a narrow peninsula separates Fistral Beach from Newquay's suburban fringes. The coast path cuts across the neck of the peninsula, but a footpath will take you all the way round the rocky promontory if you have the time or inclination – this is where you may well spot seals flopping on the rocky eastern shore. Looking more like a chapel on the beach than a former lifeboat station is the studio of local artist, Nicholas Williams. On the furthest point the octagonal tower was formerly used by coastguards and the deeply unpopular 'Preventative Men', whose job it was to observe and intercept smugglers.

Pentire Point East & the Gannel

The wide, grassy expanse of **Pentire Point East**, overlooking the mouth of **the Gannel** and the white sands of Crantock Beach, seems to conclude the east-to-west walking route, but there is a lovely treat ahead: halfway along a lane of suburban bungalows the Fern Pit Café (page 94) is the clifftop base of the Northey family, who have been ferrying passengers across the Gannel for over a century (⊘ fernpit.co.uk). Gill King (a Northey daughter) presides over the kitchen and – if you can find a quiet moment for a chat – will reminisce about family and local history, gig racing (she rowed in the winning gig at the Scilly championships some years back) or catching lobsters (her partner, Mark Smith, has been the boatman here since 1992). From the café garden you look down through a canopy of exotic plants to the hundred twisting steps that lead to the Fern Pit landing; I'll never forget that first glimpse of the jade-green water and Mark's boat ferrying a dog and its family across to dune-flanked Crantock Beach. While you wait for the boat there's a large tank of lobsters and crabs to peer into (beneath a sign that tells you your lobster will be cooked by the time you return) and panels telling the story of the Northey family business. At low tide, the bridge is exposed, but from mid-September to April, when the Fern Pit is closed (check ⊘ fernpit.co.uk for opening times), you'll have to head further upstream to find the next bridge at Penpol (which also disappears underwater at high tide). Failing that, the next crossing is the bridleway at Laurie Bridge and you'd have to be unlucky and hit a high spring tide to find it closed. A tide timetable takes the uncertainty out of the crossing.

Newquay Orchard
Yeoman Way, Tretherras TR7 2SL ⊘ 01637 877182 ⊘ newquayorchard.co.uk

This new community venture is a heartening sign that Newquay's identity is moving in a more sustainable direction. Local resident Luke Berkeley came up with the idea a few years ago and it's his energy and desire to create something transformative and sustainable for the benefit of the whole community that has seen the project develop with spectacular success. Newquay Orchard is just a 15-minute walk south from the town centre; open to everyone, all year round, the seven-acre site is rapidly maturing into cider-apple and dessert-fruit orchards, forest and market gardens and a community growing space. At present, the gardens are managed by a team of 120 volunteers, rewarded with free weekly veg boxes and lunch. At the heart of it all is an excellent café (page 94), established by Ben Quinn, a chef and restaurateur who is critically aware of the social and environmental impact of his business, launched as Canteen in 2016 in St Agnes and now growing into new locations. Good food and conversation at shared tables seem to be a natural consequence of this approach. Hats off to Luke Berkeley, Ben Quinn

NEWQUAY SPACEPORT

⌗ spaceportcornwall.com

It's not often that a small, regional airport hits the headlines, but the news that Newquay's little airport would be the first UK Spaceport, with the capacity for 'horizontal' satellite launches, has been causing a stir since the idea was first mooted in 2014. A horizontal launch is deemed to be less environmentally damaging than vertical ones, with fewer carbon emissions at lower levels, but nevertheless there's been considerable local anxiety about the impact of launches on the environment. In response, Cornwall Council says the aim is to ensure that any carbon emissions from the Spaceport are more than offset, in line with the council's plan to help Cornwall strive towards becoming carbon neutral by 2030. Furthermore, the argument goes, satellite-based technology can help to collect data and explore the impacts of climate change from space.

The first launch, where nine satellites were due to be sent into orbit, took place early in 2023 and ended in failure; but by the time you read this, successful launches will no doubt be a commonplace occurrence. Spaceport launches are monitored and supported by the satellite-tracking technology at Goonhilly Earth Station on the Lizard (page 327) – to the excitement of many, if not all, Cornwall now looks set to become a centre for space technology.

and his successors at the Heart & Soul café, and all the inspiring team who work here: it's the best thing to have happened to Newquay for a long time.

¶¶ FOOD & DRINK

Fern Pit Café Riverside Crescent, Pentire TR7 1PJ ✆ 01637 873181 ⌗ fernpit.co.uk ☺ closed in winter. A good old-fashioned café, run by the Northey family since 1910. Strong tea, crab sandwiches and slabs of cake – and breathtaking views to Crantock.

Heart & Soul Newquay Orchard, Yeoman Way, TR7 2SL (opposite the sports centre) ✆ 01637 877182 ⌗ newquayorchard.co.uk. Friends and strangers sit at shared tables for breakfasts and two-option lunch menus with veg and salads grown just a few steps away. Inexpensive and delicious.

Pavilion Bakery and Café 37 Fore St, TR7 1HD ⌗ pavilionbakery.com. This place opens early to the delight of dog-walkers and surfers looking for coffee and sourdough specials. Wholesome lunches on a Sri Lankan theme complete the menu.

Sprout The Old Printhouse, Crescent Lane, TR7 1FZ ✆ 01637 875845 ⌗ sprouthealth.co.uk ☺ closed Sun. This health-food shop and courtyard café offers delicious, wholesome salads, signature hummus and dishes made with local produce. Vegan heaven!

Trevilley Farm Shop Lane, TR8 4PX ✆ 01637 872310 ⌂ trevilleyfarm.com ⊙ all year, Mon–Sat. On the outskirts of Newquay, just off the road to Trerice (page 98), is a large farm shop plus kitchen making bread, pasties, soups and cakes, perfect for picking up picnic supplies. The shop provides a local-produce box-delivery scheme – handy if you are staying in self-catering accommodation.

11 CRANTOCK

Crantock is full of charm, though easily overlooked in the headlong rush to the beach. Thatched cottages, a village shop and two pubs cluster about a curious circular walled enclosure that was once used for corralling stray cattle until their owners could be found, known as the Round Garden. It's like an enclosed village green, with a few benches and fruit trees, much appreciated by walkers looking for somewhere quiet and sheltered to eat their pasties. (The village shop sells pasties from the St Agnes Bakery and hot drinks, too.).

Crantock Beach is a beauty, backed by steep dunes and separated from Newquay by the Gannel, whose wide, westward sweep makes it difficult to tell where river ends and sea begins. The west end of the beach, furthest from the car park, is safer for swimming (the mouth of the Gannel is treacherous and signs warn against swimming here) and where the dunes give way to cliffs and rocky inlets there's good exploring to be done at low tide. The first deep cleft in the rock is **Piper's Hole**; look up with care, because the cliff face is a sanctuary for fulmars and jackdaws. Just inside the cave on the right, a slab of rock has been carved with a figure of a woman, a horse and a sentimental verse, unmistakably Victorian in tone.

A few yards on from Piper's Hole, steep steps take you up to the coast path and the short walk to the granite headland, **Pentire Point**, where there's a collapsed cave, eclipsed in spring by the wildflowers.

Porth (Polly) Joke

I don't suppose adding my voice to the growing numbers of visitors who have 'discovered' this lovely, unspoilt beach will do it any good at all. In English, it would be Jackdaw Cove, for 'Joke' is a corruption of the 'jack' in jackdaw, and 'chough' (once pronounced 'choke') is similarly derived. There are plenty of jackdaws around, and since 2012 choughs have returned to their old haunts and are thriving, which is very pleasing to hear.

What's particularly nice is the way that cattle and sheep are able to wander down from the ancient pastures above, known as 'the Kelseys', to the beach, either looking for shelter or to drink from the trickling stream. It's National Trust land and policy to graze like this, and as they politely say on their notices, 'if the cattle concern you, there are other beaches at Crantock and Holywell'.

¶¶ FOOD & DRINK

Treago Farm Shop TR8 5QS ✆ 01637 030277 ⏁ treagofarm.co.uk ☺ May–Sep. Managed by a friendly young team, this is a very useful find for walkers as well as those camping at the farm. Hot and cold food and drinks as well as farm produce are all on sale, and fresh bread, cooked breakfasts and Sunday roasts are all popular options.

12 HOLYWELL BAY

When I said I was going to look for the holy well in the cave, the lady at the National Trust car park let me borrow a torch, passed on some rudimentary directions and pointed out that the tide had turned, so not to dawdle. It's not easy to find, but well worth the effort of looking. The cave lies roughly half a mile up the beach, once you've crossed the stream that lies between the car park and the dunes. The dunes give way to cliffs and it's beyond the first small indentation in the

"There, by torchlight, is an amazing sight: a colourful grotto of stepped pools."

rock face and before the deeper crook that marks the end of the beach that you must start looking. It's not easy to find, and impossible if the tide is too far in. But if you see a cluster of rocks, smothered in mussels, you're just about there. Look for a diagonal slit in the cliff and make for the left-hand side. Then you must climb carefully up the slimy 'steps' on your left and peer into the gloom ahead. And there, by torchlight, is an amazing sight: a colourful grotto of stepped pools, streaked with red and blue mineral deposits, curving away into the darkest recesses of the roof.

The other holy well (for Holywell is twice blessed with miraculous water) is less of an adventure to reach. The spring, enclosed by a Gothic arched structure, is in the Holywell Bay Fun Park, behind a newish wall. The owner of the fun park permits access provided cars are left at the park's own car park.

◀ **1** Thatched cottages in Crantock. **2** Porth Joke Beach.

AWAY FROM THE COAST

Inland from Newquay the landscape presents itself as a bumpy panorama of windswept hills; wind farms and isolated turbines dominate the exposed horizons. But down the deep lanes, narrow leafy valleys conceal a scattering of hamlets, farms and the long-defunct remains of industrial trams and railways. Nevertheless, in the summer months, you'll still see wisps of steam puffing above the trees below St Newlyn East, where three miniature trains still follow the route through Lappa Valley, a line engineered by Joseph Treffry in 1849 to serve the mine at East Wheal Rose.

13 TRERICE

Kestle Mill TR8 4PG ✆ 01637 875404 ⊙ closed Jan & Feb, Sat & Sun only Nov & Dec; National Trust

Buried in a green fold of the landscape just three miles south of Newquay, Trerice was clearly not built for commanding views. Shelter from the wind and clear spring water were much more important; when the wind is blowing hard on the north coast – and it's rarely otherwise – you only have to follow the deep lanes to Kestle Mill in order to appreciate the wisdom of building a house here. John Arundell built this devastatingly charming manor in 1570, on the site of a much older ancestral home. One wing has been lost, but what remains is comfortingly domestic, especially when seen from the rear courtyard, and the buildings are wrapped around by intimate gardens and an orchard, in which Elizabethan games of slapcock and skittles have been set out for visitors to play.

The emphasis is very much on hands-on engagement at Trerice, and the National Trust volunteers are keen to help everyone feel they have made some kind of personal contact with the house. It makes for a lively visit – while I was wandering through the great hall, lit by an astonishing window composed of 576 panes of glass, children and adults were trying on clothing, weaponry and armour; there were brasses to be rubbed and – on the day I visited – hats to be made.

Enjoyment is perhaps more important than authenticity at Trerice: it was a surprise to learn that the vast oak table in the great hall was

1 Castle-an-Dinas Iron Age hillfort near St Columb Major. 2 The Screech Owl Sanctuary. 3 Trerice house and gardens. ▶

the only piece of furniture the Trust had acquired with the house in 1953; everything else had come from other Trust properties. Even the great hall was a 19th-century reconstruction of what might have been. The gardens, however, have been the subject of a determined effort to supplant the prevailing 20th-century vision of what a garden should look like, and a new Elizabethan knot garden has been created in the orchard. Its design reflects the patterning of the plaster ceiling in the great chamber on the first floor; you can stand in the window there and look from the ceiling down to the intricately woven *parterre* of clipped yew hedging, infilled with a subtle mix of French lavender and insect-friendly summer-flowering bulbs and herbs.

14 TRESILLIAN HOUSE & GARDEN

TR8 4PS ☎ 07771 782202 ⌕ tresillianhouse.co.uk ⏰ tours are always available for guests; otherwise check ⌕ visitnewquay.org for open days

Newquay was once ringed by private estates, and a mile along the valley east of Trerice is Tresillian House. The entire house is available as self-catering accommodation for large parties, while the gardens are only open on special occasions. But if they are open, a visit is an absolute must for gardeners.

The organic walled garden, orchards, lake and lawns are models of Edwardian horticultural discipline. The man responsible is John Harris, who learned his craft the old-fashioned way, as an apprentice on a local estate, and has been at Tresillian since 1985. It has not always looked so impressive, though. The pale granite manor seen today was built in the first part of the 19th century, on the site of a much older house, the family seat of the Gully Bennets. The 23 acres of garden were landscaped in the prevailing style of lawns and lake, parkland trees and flowering shrubs, laurel hedging and – this being Cornwall – a profusion of camellias. The orchards and walled garden were set a little distance away from the house. Leonard Bennet, who inherited the estate in 1928, undertook the first renovation of the garden, but a further period of decline followed when the property was sold after World War II. Restoring the gardens, woodland and orchards has been a monumental undertaking, which suffered heartbreaking setbacks in 1987 and 1990, when storms ripped through the mature woodland garden. Undaunted, John Harris spent eight years clearing out the fallen debris and uprooted stumps and has planted 15,000 trees, including an orchard of apples which effectively form a library of old Cornish varieties, dating from 1800 or earlier. The cider apples go to Cornish cider-makers and are returned, appropriately, in liquid form.

15 ST COLUMB MAJOR

Built between the 12th and 15th centuries (and partially rebuilt in the 17th century after some local lads blew it up with gunpowder), the parish church in St Columb Major seems strikingly large for such a modestly sized town. Modest but certainly ambitious in Victorian times: when Cornwall was campaigning to have its diocese restored in the 19th century (page 259), William Butterfield, a champion of the Gothic revival, was invited by the town council to draw up plans that would transform the church into a cathedral. (A medieval moated manor house had already been rebuilt as a bishop's palace in preparation.) The town's self-confidence was misplaced – it was Truro that eventually won the bid to be Cornwall's cathedral city.

Each year (once on Shrove Tuesday and again 11 days later) the windows get boarded up in the town centre when the whole of St Columb Major turns out to watch a small silver ball being hurled, kicked and wrestled from one end of the parish to the other for the annual hurling matches. Hurling is a game which adheres to its own highly idiosyncratic rules and has been played here since medieval times. Divided into teams of 'townsmen' and 'countrymen' (the hurler's address determines the team he plays for) the scrabbling, jostling pack can spend hours getting the ball to a predetermined place on the parish boundary. Health and safety take a seemingly low profile. In the library, a helpful librarian drew my attention to a paragraph in an obscure pamphlet: 'throughout the centuries hurling at St Columb has been played without any interference from "outsiders". There is no organising committee, which is probably why the traditions and games have lasted to the present day. Unlike at St Ives, where the tradition is still also upheld, at St Columb the mayor and town council are not involved and the constabulary merely hold a watching brief and advise impatient motorists that "hurling" is in progress.' You watch at your peril.

16 CASTLE-AN-DINAS

📍 SW946622

Confusingly, there are two hills of the same name in Cornwall · the other Castle-an-Dinas is the site of a quarry near Ludgvan in Penwith.

This one, a couple of miles east of St Columb Major, is one of the largest hillforts in Cornwall and easily accessible from the road to Roche. There's a straightforward track from the car park to the summit – which at 700 feet gives fine views in all directions. To the south, beyond the flat, marshy expanse of Goss Moor Nature Reserve, the church tower of St Dennis rises from the centre of another Iron Age hillfort against a backdrop of the clay mountains. It seems reasonable to think that Dennis is a variation of Dinas (meaning hillfort), conveniently adapted to the name of a saint (albeit a Greek one) when the church was first established on the site.

"There's a lot of history to mull over while circumnavigating the wide circumference of the ramparts."

There's a lot of history to mull over while circumnavigating the wide circumference of the ramparts. Excavations of the interior in the 1960s identified two Bronze Age burial barrows dating from 2000BC and the possibility that an even earlier Neolithic causeway ran through the site. The construction of the ramparts came much later – around 1000BC – and there is evidence that people were still living here, thanks to a spring which rises damply against the innermost rampart, long after the withdrawal of the Romans. Romantics like to claim it as the site of King Arthur's hunting lodge. During the Civil War, a losing Royalist army camped here for two nights while Hopton wrangled with other generals over their decision to surrender to the Parliamentarians.

Some pretty nasty stuff took place on the summit in the 18th century, when a St Columb man, convicted of murdering two teenage girls, was imprisoned in a small cage (apparently attached to the stone slab now incised with a surveyor's benchmark) and left to starve to death. This, as well as other stories of murder and suicide, encourages regular posses of ghost hunters.

Geologically, the hill is unusually rich in wolframite, or tungsten ore. Steam-age tin miners despaired of wolfram because the ore was too hard and too heavy to work; it was only later that it was recognised as an ideal metal for modern weaponry and lightbulb filaments. The relics of Cornwall's only mining operation dedicated exclusively to wolfram, which lasted from 1916 to 1957, can still be seen: parts of the southern ramparts were cut away to allow the passage of an aerial ropeway connected to the buildings at the foot of the hill, by the car park.

17 SCREECH OWL SANCTUARY & GOSS MOOR NATURE RESERVE

Owl sanctuary: Trewin Farm, St Columb Major TR9 6HP ✆ 01726 860182
⊘ screechowlsanctuary.co.uk. Goss Moor: ⊘ visitcornwall.com

Like most people, I imagine, I thought the **Screech Owl Sanctuary** was a sanctuary for screech owls, but the truth is even more delightful. In actual fact, the sanctuary, based on the edge of Goss Moor, was set up by Carolyn Screech who had been rescuing owls since the age of eight and in 1990 established a rescue and rehabilitation centre that developed into the Screech Owl Sanctuary & Animal Park. The Screech family retired in 2019, when the reins were handed over to the Hopkins family, but the sanctuary continues to be a haven for sick and injured owls and the team work tirelessly in conservation, education and rehabilitation – providing the best possible support for all those in their care.

There's an impressive resident population of native and foreign owls, all on display in their carefully designed enclosures – from enormous Siberian eagle owls to tiny Indian scops owls like Iggy, who will sit comfortably in the palm of your hand – glaring, peeping and swivelling their necks through what looks like 359 degrees as only owls can do. One rescued tawny owl, admitted to the hospital as a baby in April 2005, is called Bob. As the care he required was quite intensive, Bob became more used to humans than owls and could not be released back into the wild. Today he is part of the sanctuary's flying team.

As well as the owls there is a variety of other animals that you can learn about at the regular educational feed and talk sessions, from raccoons and lemurs to emus, meerkats, goats and alpacas. And to further support the sanctuary's conservation work and make your visit extra special, personal encounters can be booked with the owls, foxes, lemurs, meerkats or wallabies.

For those who enjoy nature untamed or indeed, uncaged, the entrance to **Goss Moor Nature Reserve** – a wilderness of marsh and heath, traversed by the old A30 – is right on the doorstep, with parking just over the bridge that spans the new A30. Bikes are the easiest way to discover the five-mile level route that circles the moor. But it's the narrow footpaths that lead to the reserve's hidden secrets: a marsh fritillary trail, sequestered ponds fringed with willow and alder, the rusting remnants of the china-clay industry and otter hideouts along the trickling source of the Fal.

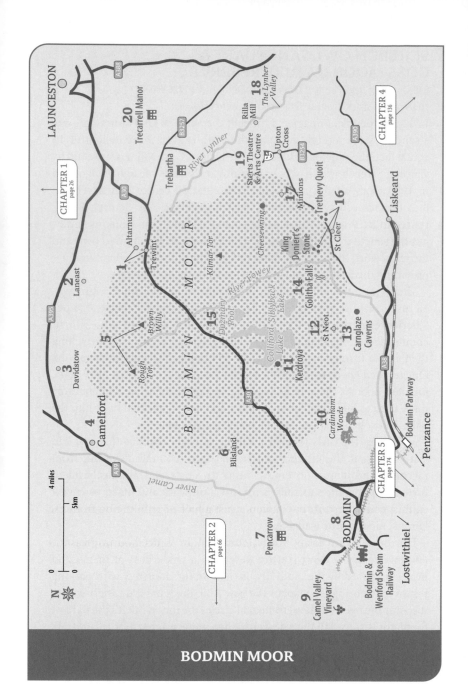

BODMIN MOOR

3
BODMIN MOOR

'Cornwall is like a frame without a picture,' say those who believe that Cornwall's coast is everything. It has to be one of the silliest platitudes ever uttered.

If your only perception of Bodmin Moor is a rather bleak stretch of granite moorland - often obscured by fog – sliced in half from east to west by the A30, then think again. This is where Cornwall hides some of its best treasures, generously revealed to those choosing to take the Slow approach. What I particularly enjoyed when researching this chapter were the exciting contrasts of landscape, culture and people within such a small area. On the east side of the Moor, I descended through dense woodland to find the rushing **River Lynher** at Rilla Mill, while just 20-odd miles away, west of Bodmin, I found myself on the sunny slopes of the **Camel Valley vineyards**, a glass of award-winning Cornish Brut in my hand. Yet just a few minutes before, or so it seemed, I had been stumbling over the rainswept summit of Rough Tor, looking down over the haunting emptiness of **Davidstow Moor**. There had been a lusty performance of *Twelfth Night* in a tented, outdoor theatre at Upton Cross, and rambling beside the **River Fowey**, where it rushed and tumbled through beech woods just a half-hour bike ride from the uncanny stillness of Dozmary Pool. There was dazzling stained glass in **St Neot**, and desolate **holy wells** in muddy fields; and not least, in Blisland, I found one of the best pubs encountered on my travels.

In places, you can't help but be reminded of Dartmoor, whose higher peaks loom on the eastern horizon. Goatish sheep, shaggy cattle and wild ponies graze among gorse and relics of the copper- and tin-mining industries; Neolithic standing stones litter the landscape. Bodmin is Dartmoor's condensed, less gentrified cousin. An air of self-sufficient remoteness clings like mist in Bodmin's hidden valleys and to the barren slopes of its highest peaks, **Brown Willy** and **Rough Tor**.

Village and farm shops are not a lifestyle option on Bodmin: they are vital lifelines for the rural community, and their precarious existence owes much to the support of visitors.

GETTING AROUND

Bodmin Moor is ringed by five towns – Bodmin, Camelford, Launceston, Callington and Liskeard – which are all linked by main roads; the Moor itself is bisected by the fast and furious A30. Once off these main arteries, however, be prepared for narrow lanes and even narrower medieval bridges or fords, steep gradients and, on the high Moor, animals dozing on the road.

TRAINS

The main line from London to Penzance stops at **Bodmin Parkway**, a couple of miles outside the town. The branch line which connected the station to the town centre now operates as a steam railway, which is fun, but not always practical, particularly during the winter months when it is closed. A train-timed bus service (55) runs between town and mainline station.

BUSES

While it is relatively easy to get between the five towns that encircle the Moor, it is not possible to cross the Moor from north to south by bus; ⊘ firstbus.co.uk/cornwall shows you what's possible and what's not on its very useful maps.

The impressive **visitor information centre** in Bodmin produces an inspired series of leaflets, titled *Leave the Car at Home Days*. These give you all the information you need to take public transport to various Cornish destinations and suggest a wide range of things to do once you get there.

CYCLING

On a sunny, wind-free day one of the nicest rides on Bodmin Moor takes you along the upper reaches of the **River Fowey** for six miles, from Golitha Falls (start in Liskeard if you prefer) right up to the Jamaica Inn at Bolventor; after a smart about-turn, head south along a tiny lane that runs between Colliford Lake and Dozmary Pool, all the way to St Neot, from where it's a pretty two-mile ride back to Golitha Falls.

North of the A30, I find the landscape **northwest of Altarnun**, heading towards Davidstow, quite entrancing. Narrow lanes and steep gradients make getting out of Altarnun a bit of a haul, but once on the lane to Bowithick it's all stream-fed moorland, close-cropped by sheep, and too many good places to stop, paddle and picnic to mention. Then, suddenly you're up next to the old Davidstow airfield, which can feel a bit creepy in less than perfect conditions and it's time to turn back through high open farmland to Altarnun.

Families with children may enjoy cycling around **Cardinham Woods** (just east of Bodmin), with gravelled and flattish routes through woodland in the valley bottom, and more challenging tracks on the slopes for mountain bikers. A very pretty section of the Camel Trail is also popular with families and can be picked up just west of Bodmin at Dunmere Halt. This is a great way to get to Blisland, which lies a mile off the trail close to where it terminates at Poley's Bridge, making a round trip of about 14 miles.

For those wanting a longer mission, you can pick up the thoroughly signposted **Sustrans NCN Route 3** (the Cornish Way) across Cornwall at Blisland and follow the western fringe of the Moor to Davidstow and onwards to Bude.

CYCLE HIRE

Cornwall Bike Hire ✆ 07950 774067 ⊘ cornwallbikehire.co.uk. Delivers high-quality touring bikes including electric bikes to individuals and groups anywhere in Cornwall. SUPs and sea-kayaks also available to hire. Suggested routes and maps are all part of the deal.

Explore by Bike Priory Car Park, Bodmin PL31 2DQ ✆ 07985 586586. Handy for joining the Camel Trail at Bodmin and discovering the less-populated end of the trail. Hybrid and mountain bikes only.

Snail's Pace Café and Bike Hire Camel Trail Car Park, Wenfordbridge, St Breward PL30 3PN ✆ 07398 700154 ⊘ snailspacecafe.co.uk. Electric bikes offered as well as the usual at this great family-run café, perfectly positioned for cyclists at the Bodmin end of the Camel Trail (page 87). Free car park.

Trailmunki Carminnow Industrial Estate, Bodmin & Cardinham Woods, PL31 1EP ✆ 01208 892758 ⊘ trailmunki.com. Specialist mountain-bike hire. Guided tours available.

HORSERIDING

For many people, the Moor is best viewed from between the ears of a friendly horse and several moorland pubs have places where you can

TOURIST INFORMATION

Bodmin Shire Hall, Mount Folly, Bodmin PL31 2DQ ✆ 01208 76616 ⬧ bodminlive.com

leave your mount safely tethered. Escorted rides across moorland or through wooded valleys at a pace you feel comfortable with are offered by the following companies:

HORSERIDING

Hallagenna Hallagenna Farm, St Breward PL30 4NS ✆ 07780 702704 ⬧ hallagenna.co.uk

Lower Tokenbury Equestrian Centre Caradon Town, Upton Cross PL14 5AR ✆ 01579 362747 ⬧ lowertokenburyequestriancentre.co.uk

WALKING

Bodmin Moor – on a fine day – is one of the best places in England for walking and exploring. On a rainy day, however, or when the mist comes down, the Moor can be fiendishly disorientating. Outside the villages, waymarkers tend to be few and far between, and opportunities for getting seriously – even dangerously – lost should not be underestimated. On a more positive note, the sense of personal discovery that such **wild and remote places** offer can be hugely rewarding. Even a Moor expert like Mark Camp reckons that he never goes out on to the Moor without discovering something new each time.

North of the A30, the Moor has various focal points – the twin summits of Brown Willy and Rough Tor (page 115) are easily reached from Camelford; the de Lank River close to Blisland (page 116) a less obvious but delightful destination. South of the A30, wild Bodmin walks tend to focus on the Cheesewring and the Hurlers stone circle (page 129), both an easy stroll from Minions, with a hearty extension up Kilmar Tor for the enthusiastic.

Rainy-day walkers wanting to avoid upland exposure might like to head for the well-marked **woodland trail** that follows the tumbling River Fowey to Golitha Falls (page 126) or the longer woodland trails of Cardinham Woods (page 124).

The Copper Trail

A century and a half ago, Bodmin Moor was alive with industry and criss-crossed with paths trodden by quarrymen, farmers and miners. As the abandoned mines sank back beneath the heather and gorse, many of the footpaths disappeared. Mark Camp, who spent his boyhood years roaming the Moor, had been mulling the idea of 'the best possible' circular walk around it for some time, and the 2000 Countryside and Rights of Way Act, enacted in 2005, provided the final impetus to join up the dots on his emerging route. In total the trail covers 60 miles, taking in Minions, St Neot, Bodmin, St Breward, Camelford and Alternun, along with many other good pit stops on the way. To help walkers get the most out of their walk, he has published a pocket-sized book, *The Copper Trail: Once around Bodmin Moor*, available in most TICs, brimming with the kind of information that Slow explorers will welcome. Mark is your man for guided walks (✆ 01503 262072).

THE NORTH MOOR

North of the A30, the Moor is characterised by craggy granite peaks and marshy flats; woodland is sparse and the sky in all its often-brooding glory dominates. Davidstow Moor in the north, with its wartime memories and forgotten history of Formula One racing, has a particularly haunting atmosphere. But follow the infant River Camel, from Camelford southwards along the northwest fringe of the Moor, and it's a different story: wooded, stream-fed valleys, cosy villages and a feeling that civilisation is not too far away.

1 ALTARNUN & TREWINT

Snuggled in a wooded valley, just a stone's throw from the A30, **Altarnun** scores top marks for its photogenic qualities. The church of **St Nonna**, the 'Cathedral of the Moors', with its high tower, sits prettily beside a babbling tributary of the River Inny, where a 15th-century packbridge leads to part two of the village. A village green, whitewashed, slate-roofed cottages, a village shop, a post office and a pub complete the picture.

The 80-odd carved bench-ends inside the church are an absolute knockout: there are jesters and jugglers, a piper, fiddler and bagpipe player, a sheaf of corn that is also a face, sheep on the hill and portraits of various characters from the village. They were carved in the early part of the 16th century by one Robert Daye, who proudly added his name to the carvings. You can also visit the holy well, in a field behind the vicarage. Pity the poor 'lunatics', who were immersed here backwards before being marched up to the church for complementary prayers.

The former **Methodist chapel**, next to the shop, is worth more than a glance for the bust of John Wesley over the door. **Neville Northy Burnard**, one of Altarnun's most gifted, yet saddest, sons, grew up in the cottage next door, and made this in 1836, at the age of 18. Once the darling of London society for his portrait busts, Burnard was slowly destroyed by private demons and the bottle. The death of a daughter finally tipped him over the edge and, abandoning his work, wife and other children in the capital, for years he drifted the lanes of Cornwall, ending up in a pauper's grave in Camborne.

Wesley Cottage

Trewint PL15 7TG ℰ 01566 880265 or 07754 558276 (curator) ◊ lamc.org.uk/wesleycottage2020 ☉ normally daily but ring to check if making a special visit

So close as to be almost a part of Altarnun, tiny **Trewint** has become something of a Methodist shrine, thanks to the kindness of stonemason Digory Isbell and his wife, Elizabeth, who gave hospitable shelter at what is now known as Wesley Cottage to Wesley and his companions as they scurried up and down Cornwall on a hectic round of preaching in 1743. The Isbells were so overcome by the Wesleyan style of praying from the heart, without recourse to a prayer book, that although they remained steadfast to St Nonna's in Altarnun (where their graves may still be seen), they became, without contradiction, Wesleyans too. The cottage became the focus of impromptu prayer meetings and Digory built a small extension to accommodate them, with a room above for lodging his new-found spiritual mentors. These two rooms and their Wesleyan memorabilia can be visited, and the Pilgrim's garden marks the spot where Wesley once preached to a gathering of around three hundred. Hospitality is still offered in the form of a help-yourself refreshments table.

¶¶ FOOD & DRINK

Kings Head Altarnun PL15 7RX ℰ 01566 86241 ◊ kingsheadlaunceston.co.uk. This is a traditional inn with a jukebox, local ales such as Skinners' Betty Stogs and generous helpings of pub grub. Four reasonably priced rooms make this a popular overnight roost for walkers.

1 A murmuration of starlings over Davidstow Moor. 2 Carved bench-end in St Nonna's Church, Altarnun. 3 Altarnun. 4 Wesley Cottage. ▶

2 LANEAST & AROUND

Head northwest out of Altarnun and immediately you're in a tangle of narrow lanes, dipping and rising at medieval bridges, inviting footpaths (frequently crossing six-foot stone stiles) and isolated farms. There are some lovely walks and bike rides to be done here, for which the OS Explorer map 109 is essential. **St Clether** and **Laneast** are the only settlements of any size – neither has shops or pubs, but they do offer a nice line in holy wells and St Michael's in Laneast has some striking medieval stained glass. The village shop in Altarnun has copies of the *Inny River Trail*, a six-mile circular walk which takes in the ruined manor at Trethinna, a medieval bridge at Gimblett's Mill and Laneast.

¶¶ FOOD & DRINK

Rising Sun PL15 7SN ✆ 01566 86636 ♿ therisingsuninn.co.uk ⊙ closed Mon & Tue. This stands alone at a rural junction of two lanes, midway between Altarnun and Laneast. A great pub, deservedly popular both for eating (Slow Food is taken very seriously here) and drinking. There is a small campsite beside the pub and tie-ups for horses, too.

3 DAVIDSTOW

From miles away you can see (and sometimes smell) the cheese factory here; gathered around it are the low buildings of an old pig unit and

THE SHY ASTRONOMER

Not many people can tell you who discovered Neptune, but more than usual know the answer in Laneast. John Couch Adams, whose bust – by his exact contemporary Neville Northey Burnard – can be found in the Lawrence House Museum (page 34), was a scholarship boy from a local farming family; a brilliant mathematician and thoroughly decent chap, as modest as he was brainy.

Using mathematics he proved the existence of the most distant planet in the solar system, whose orbit had hitherto been confused with that of Uranus, and in 1845 he passed his findings to the Astronomer Royal, Sir George Airy. In the weeks following, Adams and Airy managed somehow to avoid communicating, which was sad, because seven months after Adams made his discovery, Urbain Le Verrier, a French astronomer, published a paper in which he came independently to the same conclusion. But Adams had his supporters and eventually an honorable draw was declared. In any case, friendship with Le Verrier was more important to Adams than 'winning'. Later, the gentle polymath was offered the post of Astronomer Royal and a knighthood, both of which he shyly declined.

dairy farm which operated here before they were converted (though possibly not convinced) to become the wartime RAF base. This had always struck me as a sad and lonely part of the Moor (though I'm told that the old military buildings were a popular spot for raves during the 1990s), but things changed with the opening of two new military museums in the old buildings in 2006. Their deeply knowledgeable and hugely enthusiastic creators assembled two quite different collections and experiences, which complement each other nicely.

Davidstow Moor RAF Memorial Museum

PL32 9YF ⌀ 07796 556939 ⌖ davidstowmemorialmuseum.co.uk ⊘ closed Nov–easter

Davidstow Moor RAF Memorial Museum is curated by David Keast, who spent his boyhood years on the local farm; he and a small band of elderly volunteers are movingly dedicated to keeping the memory alive of those who served here during World War II. What you find is an intimate record of the men and women (and carrier pigeons) who lived, worked and, in some cases, died at Davidstow between 1942 and 1945: letters, uniforms, medals, photos ('the photos are the pride of this collection') and lots and lots of model aircraft as well. A family spanning three generations at least, the oldest of whom had known the airbase during the war, were visiting while I was there and exchanging stories with the affable Mr Keast. The youngest lad in the party was staring, wide-eyed, at a 1,000-pound bomb, his lips moving as he read the lettering on its side: 'For Display Purposes Only'. Admission is free; donations very much appreciated.

Cornwall at War Museum

PL32 9YF ⌀ 07799 194918 ⌖ cornwallatwarmuseum.co.uk ⊘ closed in winter; check website for opening times

Next door to the RAF Memorial Museum, in a scattering of Nissen huts, air-raid shelters and old accommodation blocks that would not disgrace a film-set for *The Avengers*, Steve and Sheila Perry have installed their formidable collection of military memorabilia, from a couple of unsmoked 'Blue Liner' cigarettes to a U-boat bomb. 'There are two myths about Davidstow,' grins Steve, ex-army, whose boundless enthusiasm for the place is matched by the kind of knowledge that should see him on *Mastermind*. 'One – it was built by the Americans, and two – it was too foggy to be operable. Wrong on both counts. Mind you, I

THE DAVIDSTOW STARLINGS

From mid-October to mid-March, at the onset of dusk, up to a million starlings take to the air and perform one of nature's most extraordinary spectacles: swooping and wheeling in perfect synchronicity, the flock resembles a vast black silk scarf being shaken out across the sky. Dozens of spectators drive up to the Moor on fine evenings to follow the performance, which closes with a sudden retreat to the woods around Crowdy Reservoir where the birds roost for the night.

feel sorry for the Canadian 404 Squadron, who came here in May '44 after being stationed on Shetland. Cornwall! They must have thought: "sunshine and beaches, our luck's in, boys!" Then they discovered it was Davidstow ...'

The latest exhibit the Perrys have assembled turns out to be an officers' mess in a restored Nissen hut. A score or more of mannequins in uniform and civvies fill the room – sitting, standing, smoking, drinking, chatting ... their frozen silence was quite unnerving, as though they were all playing musical statues and were waiting for the music to start again. Still more unnerving was the unexpected invitation to join a ghost-hunting party later that week. Investigations into the paranormal are frequent at the airbase; wimpishly I declined and retired to the NAAFI canteen for a cuppa and to browse the newspapers – dated from the war years, naturally.

Every Thursday from July until September, Steve drives a minibus on a guided tour around the deserted airfield, bringing it vividly to life with a commentary that blows away the years. He evokes not only the war (when the runways were camouflage-painted green and dotted with painted sheep) but the post-war years too, when for three glorious years in the 1950s, the airfield was home to British Formula One racing, and crowds of 25,000 witnessed the first triumph of Lotus.

4 CAMELFORD

Despite the golden camel that does weathervane duty on top of the old town hall's bright green clock tower, everyone knows that 'Camel' refers to the old Cornish word 'cam', meaning 'a winding stream', and 'Allan', which means 'fine-looking'. There's not a huge amount to do, but Camelford makes a great base for walkers. There are free car parks and toilets, and the footpath to the looming peaks of Rough Tor and Brown

Willy starts here. However, if striding out over high moorland is not for you, consider the gentle Riverside Walk that starts in Fore Street (under an arch where a plaque announces the route) and follows the Cam through a bucolic landscape to **Penteroon Bridge** – a lovely spot to pause and picnic – and beyond.

🍴 FOOD & DRINK

Four Seasons Café 1 Market Pl, PL32 9PB 🖉 01840 211779. Sit outside in the garden by the river if it's sunny and tuck in to breakfast, lunch or tea. Homemade soups and cakes are always on the menu and macaroni cheese is another favourite. Nothing pretentious here, just simple, good food and friendly service.

Mason's Arms Market Pl, PL32 9PB 🖉 01840 213309 🖉 themasonsarmscamelford.com. Just the job if returning from a leg-stretch over the Moor, with a good, friendly atmosphere, a pretty garden at the back and hearty home cooking. St Austell ales on tap and Cornish cider. Pub grub is served, much of it sourced as locally as possible.

5   THE TWIN PEAKS: BROWN WILLY & ROUGH TOR

From Camelford a ten-mile walk takes in the two highest peaks in Cornwall, or you can drive out along an arrow-straight lane for a couple of miles to the National Trust car park at the foot of **Rough Tor** and take it from there. Rough, by the way, rhymes with cow in these parts (one of the Penpont Brewery's nicest beers is called Rough Tor, but when I asked for a bottle of 'Rowter' in a pub in Wadebridge, I was met with raised eyebrows and had to point; getting your pronunciation not only right, but right in the right place, is something of an art in Cornwall). The proximity of

"Brown Willy, whose crook-toothed crown stands across the valley to the east, is the wilder, lonelier place."

the car park to the summit, less than a mile away, means there's usually company on your hike uphill – some walkers have even claimed the company of sad Charlotte Dymond, murdered on the hill in 1844; her lover, a farmhand named Matthew Weeks, was found guilty and hanged at Bodmin.

Brown Willy, whose crook-toothed crown stands across the valley to the east, is the wilder, lonelier place. The views from the summits of the two tors are both revealing and deceiving. Revealed is the buzzard's-eye contextual map of Cornwall: Bristol Channel, English Channel, Camel and Tamar, old farm field systems, new wind turbines, standing stones and claypit spoil. Deceiving, however, is the view east, over the source of the River Fowey. A mere stroll, by the look of it, down to Altarnun … but the low ground with its too-green grass is treacherous bog and should be avoided. Daphne du Maurier, in *Vanishing Cornwall*, gives a white-knuckle account of an attempt to ride across this seemingly innocuous plateau on a fine November afternoon, which disintegrated rapidly into rain and fog and darkness. 'Bogs, quarries, brooks, boulders, hell on every side … I had never known greater despondency.' And this was in the days before the Beast of Bodmin appeared. You have been warned.

¶ FOOD & DRINK

The Old Inn St Breward PL30 4PP ✆ 01208 850711 ⌂ theoldinnandrestaurant.co.uk. A lovely and very ancient village pub next to the village church, high on the Moor. A free house, serving Cornish ales and cider and good food to a jolly mix of the local football club, walkers and members of the St Breward Silver Band. It's dog friendly, and children are welcome in the restaurant and garden.

Snail's Pace Café and Bike Hire Camel Trail Car Park, Wenfordbridge, St Breward PL30 3PN ✆ 01208 851178 ⌂ snailspacecafe.co.uk ◷ April–Oct Tue–Sun. Filling a gap in every sense, this is a young family-run venture providing bike hire at the less-populated end of the Camel Trail (page 87). The off-grid eco-café serves lovely fresh, home-grown or local food for breakfast, lunch and tea.

6 BLISLAND

⌂ **East Rose Farm** St Breward (page 418), ▲ **South Penquite Farm** (page 418), **Yurtworks** Greyhayes (page 418)

After the bracing wilderness of the north moors, the descent into the wooded valley of the Camel brings a sudden and absolute change of mood and tempo, which reaches its most gratifying moments (for lowland softies at any rate) in Blisland. A huge, tree-fringed village green surrounded on all sides by handsome granite cottages and houses ('it has not one ugly house in it,' wrote Betjeman) and overlooked by one of the best pubs in Cornwall, and a Norman church, the Victorian restoration of which Betjeman said 'could hardly be bettered', are Blisland's high points. But more importantly, perhaps, it's a village with a beating heart that believes in the value of local identity: here's a community that has fought

"But more importantly, perhaps, it's a village with a beating heart that believes in the value of local identity."

to keep its school, that has raised funds and support to reopen its shop and post office and that is trying to keep its bus service going. If awards were given to Slow village of the year, Blisland would be high on the list of nominees.

A short walk north out of the village takes you back on to the Moor and the **Jubilee Rock** just east of Pendrift. This huge lump of granite was chosen by one Lt John Rogers to celebrate the 1810 golden jubilee of King George III. His elaborately chiselled graffiti was cleaned up in 2010 to celebrate its 200th anniversary and revealed the familiar profile of Britannia, the Royal and Cornish coats of arms as well as those of some local families, together with a plough and the Masonic symbols of compass and square. If you want to walk further, there's a magical spot on the de Lank River less than a mile away, where it rushes over granite boulders through dappled woodland, and there's rarely a soul in sight. To get there, go back to Pendrift and follow the marked footpath due north, down a steep wooded bank and across level rough pasture. At the river, a footbridge allows the trail to continue to St Breward. A superb circular route of 5.2 miles is offered by the app iWalk Cornwall; search for the walk titled 'Poley's Bridge to Blisland'.

¶¶ FOOD & DRINK

Blisland Inn PL30 4JK ℘ 01208 850739. Typically there will be seven or eight real ales on tap, all in perfect condition. Decent, basic pub food is served, but this is a place you go for grown-up drinking with the locals, not for gastronomy, and children are best left outside to entertain themselves on the green. Dogs, however, are given treats if well behaved. 'King Buddha', the larger-than-life landlord (it's tattooed on his tummy), knows what his devoted regulars like, and it has served him well in the form of more CAMRA awards over the years than you can shake a stick at.

7 PENCARROW

Washaway, Bodmin PL30 3AG ℘ 01208 841369 ⊘ pencarrow.co.uk ☉ garden: Mar–Oct daily; house: Apr–Sep Sun–Fri

Walk, cycle or drive very slowly up the two-mile drive. It's like woodland in a Tolkein story and at one point the drive actually passes through an Iron Age hillfort. The house, with its grand Palladian façade, and the Italianate gardens, are lovely, but for me, nothing surpasses that magical woodland arrival. The old walled gardens by the car park offer pick-your-own soft fruits, which is another good reason to visit.

Despite the external grandeur, there's absolutely nothing stuffy about Pencarrow. Children are encouraged to romp on the lawns, the affable head gardener produces cuttings of favourite plants for sale and the house has a distinctly lived-in atmosphere.

The Molesworth St Aubyns have lived here since the time of Elizabeth I and it's still very much a family home. Dogs, toys and family photos are surrounded by Sèvres porcelain, Chinese silk captured from a Spanish treasure ship and family portraits

"The Molesworth St Aubyns have lived here since the time of Elizabeth I and it's still very much a family home."

by Sir Joshua Reynolds – and there's a grand piano upon which Sir Arthur Sullivan composed the finale to the first act of *Iolanthe*. Another guest to stay at Pencarrow was Charles Austin, a parliamentary lawyer. He spotted a specimen of *Araucaria imbricata*, recently introduced to Britain from Chile, growing in the park and remarked 'that tree would puzzle a monkey'. And that was how, in 1834, the monkey puzzle tree acquired its popular name.

8 BODMIN

🏠 **Bodmin Jail Hotel** (page 418)

Once the county town of Cornwall, Bodmin has suffered mixed fortunes to say the least. The unlikely – though beautifully executed – transformation of the Bodmin Jail into a luxury boutique hotel in recent years has done much to upgrade the image of a place that seems to have lost out over the years to other Cornish towns. Truro, for example, won the spiritual and secular prizes of cathedral and county court, Penryn landed the university; meanwhile, in Bodmin, the prison closed, the Duke of Cornwall's Regiment moved out, the branch line from Bodmin Parkway into the town centre was axed and St Lawrence's Hospital, formerly Bodmin Asylum, which posed as a good candidate for Exeter and Falmouth universities' new campus in 2002, has been partly demolished. But hats off to the town for making the most of its history. Bodmin is full of museums with interactive visitor experiences, including a new science museum, especially aimed at children, and the ever-popular **Bodmin & Wenford Steam Railway**. The Duke of

◀ **1** Brown Willy. **2** Camel Valley Vineyard. **3** The monument to Sir Walter Raleigh Gilbert above Bodmin. **4** Bodmin & Wenford Steam Railway.

Cornwall's **Light Infantry Museum** (⊘ bodminkeep.org.uk ⊙ Tue–Sat) tells the story of the regiment's involvement in conflicts ranging from Waterloo to the American War of Independence to Northern Ireland.

There were no touch-screen experiences advertised at the tiny **Bodmin Town Museum**, housed in an ancient granite building on the site of an even older Franciscan friary (⊘ bodmin.gov.uk ⊙ May–Oct Mon–Sat). Instead, I found Reg and Sue Sheppard, passionate volunteer supporters of the museum as well as ardent right-to-roamers, and it was through the very interactive experience of chatting to them that I found out how Bodmin is currently charting its way from an affluent and interesting past to a heritage-laden future. The Sheppards and the excellent **tourist information centre** in the Shire Hall just opposite also pointed me towards some of the best walks in and around the town.

Besides all the museums, Bodmin is good for just pottering: shops are particularly strong on local food and everybody knows the way to **Barnecutt Bakery**, where the bar is set high for pasty aficionados.

"Besides all the museums, Bodmin is good for just pottering: shops are particularly strong on local food."

Granite Georgian buildings sweep up and down the hilly town centre, and although giving an overwhelming impression of greyness, are nearly all worth a second glance. But above all, Bodmin is about its people and the traces they have left for us to read. The victims of Bodmin's macabre gallows are listed in the town museum: Elizabeth Osborne, aged 20, for example, hanged for setting fire to a hayrick. The quality of mercy seems to have been noticeably absent in Bodmin Assizes. On the other hand, a solid granite **dogs' drinking trough** placed at the entrance to Priory Park, in the town centre, tells a strange, compassionate story. The exiled Prince of Siam, Chula Chakrabongse, who lived just outside Bodmin from 1938 until his death in 1965, had a great fondness for his canine companions, and this gift to Bodmin's thirsty dogs is dedicated to his terrier, Joan, and bulldog, Hercules.

Priory Park has recently added another gift to its visitors, and though principally aimed at the under-12s, the new science museum, **Discovering 42** (⊘ discovering42.co.uk) is interesting for all, offering a series of interactive artworks designed to 'ignite curiosity in science and sustainability'. Everything inside has been created from reclaimed materials and when I visited, it was filled with young children and their

THE BEACON

No prominent hill in Cornwall is complete without a monument of some kind, and Bodmin rises to the occasion at the Beacon, where a 144-foot-high spike on a plinth was erected as a monument to Sir Walter Raleigh Gilbert in 1857. Gilbert (whose distinguished lineage is reflected in his hybrid name) was born in Bodmin but spent most of his adult life in India, generally indulging in the sort of military gung-ho activity that resulted in the medals and monuments dished out to Victorian military heroes.

The hill on which the monument stands is an easy walk from the town centre; now a nature reserve, with a young community woodland and hay meadows where wildflowers are encouraged to self-seed. The deep dip beside the monument is an old cock-fighting pit and on the other side of the path you may just make out the lipped edge of a large circular enclosure that once was a Cornish wrestling ring. It makes a good picnic spot and the views over both town and moorland more than reward the (not too strenuous) climb.

parents immersed in play with mirrors and magnets, potato-powered electricity, bits of bike and marbles. Staff were on hand to explain and help as well as offering hot chocolate and coffee at the tiny bar. Visits are timed so that everyone gets a chance to make the most of the museum.

Bodmin has its fair share of interesting piles of stones. **Castle Canyke**, clearly visible looking east from Beacon Hill, is Cornwall's largest Iron Age hillfort, and a possible contender for the location of Arthur's stronghold, Killiwig. On the hilly northern fringe of Bodmin, close to the old jail, is **Berry Tower** – all that remains of a fine chapel, built in the early years of the 16th century. Together with the 300-year-old friary, it succumbed to the ravages of the Reformation – after just 30 years of service. But Bodmin's 15th-century church, **St Petroc's** (bodminchurch.com), survives, despite losing its tower to lightning in 1699 and succumbing to the inevitable Victorian restoration. Nevertheless, there are some real treasures inside, including an elaborately carved Norman font and a lectern made from carved bench-ends, which in one case shows a man sporting an extra finger. There's a painted German panel dating from 1501 and a fine slate memorial by Neville Northey Burnard (page 110). But the biggest treasure lies in a niche in the south aisle wall, where the reliquary casket that once contained the bones of St Petroc can be seen. The 6th-century saint's bones have had a rough time of it over the years. First they were interred at Padstow, but late in the 10th century the Vikings arrived and the relics were hurriedly moved to Bodmin.

Then they were stolen by jealous French monks in 1177 and taken to Brittany, where reluctantly (they managed to hang on to a rib) they were handed back to Henry II's justicier, Walter of Coutances, who patched things up by returning them to Bodmin in a fine casket made by Sicilian craftsmen in ivory and gold. Somebody thought it wise to hide the casket during the Reformation, and it was only rediscovered, walled up in the porch, during the 19th century, though empty of all relics. Almost unbelievably it was stolen again in 1994, only to turn up, 40 days later, in a field in Yorkshire. You will notice the improved security surrounding the casket.

The Bodmin & Wenford Steam Railway

Harleigh Rd, PL31 1AQ ✆ 01208 73555 ♂ bodminrailway.co.uk ☺ Feb–Oct; reduced service Feb–May & Oct

In the 19th century, Bodmin lay between two rival rail companies racing along the south (via Plymouth) and the north (via Launceston) of Cornwall to lay the fastest route from London to Wadebridge and points west. A connecting line, which curled into Bodmin just next to the regimental barracks, was eventually completed in 1895 and for almost 70 years, until Beeching's axe fell, Bodmin's residents could chug across Cornwall without having to walk more than a few hundred yards to their station.

The line and much of its steam and diesel rolling stock were rescued from dereliction in 1986 by a group of local enthusiasts, who formed a trust to preserve this colourful remnant of Cornish train history. Apart from the rides out west to Boscarne Junction (right next to the Camel Trail) and/or east to Bodmin Parkway, one-day driver-experience courses are offered (over-18s only), giving fellow enthusiasts the opportunity to work alongside the regular crews and experience the filth, sweat and the glory of the footplate.

¶¶ FOOD & DRINK

Courtyard Bistro Bodmin Jail Museum, Scarlett's Well Rd, PL31 2PL ✆ 01208 76292 ♂ bodminjail.org ☺ daily 10.00–22.00. Included in the multi-million pound transformation of the prison building into a luxury hotel, the café on the ground floor is looking pretty smart these days and has picked up a reputation far beyond the town as the place to go for a good lunch. It's inside the prison walls but outside the museum, so admission to the café is free.

Malcolm Barnecutt Bakery The Old Guild Hall, Fore St, PL31 2HQ ✆ 01208 73205.
Malcolm's grandfather, Percy, opened the first Barnecutt bakery in Liskeard in 1930, and
there are now eight branches scattered across Cornwall. A decent café behind the shop in the
restored 17th-century guildhall rooms serves the bakery's famous pasties as well as home-
cooked lunches and teas.

9 CAMEL VALLEY VINEYARD

Nanstallon PL30 5LG ✆ 01208 77959 ⌂ camelvalley.com ⊙ vineyards & shop: Mon–Fri,
also May–Sep Sat; tours 14.30 (not Sat), booking recommended

Back in the days when English wine was not something you mentioned
in polite conversation, Bob Lindo and his wife Annie were rethinking
their lives. Bob, a pilot with the RAF, had just emerged barely in one piece
from a spectacular crash with no option but to look for another career.
'We were doing a bit of sheep farming in Cornwall already, but it was
while trying to repair a fence – lying on my side because of my injuries –
that I realised how right this hillside would be for vines,' says Bob. 'Much
more appropriate than sheep.' Two decades on, Camel Valley Vineyard
is very much established at the top of the English winemakers, league
table, a strong Cornish presence in a niche industry so far dominated by
producers in Sussex and Kent.

Although the Lindos started with still red and white wines, their
runaway success has been the sparkling white 'Cornwall Brut', made by
the *méthode champenoise*, but with three grapes particularly suited to
the English climate – Seyval Blanc, Reichensteiner and Bacchus. 'It's not
champagne; that's what the French make,' says Bob. 'We make Cornish
sparkling wine that should be judged on its own merits.'

Those in a position to judge have heaped awards and accolades on
the product and the Lindos' son, Sam, has now won the Best British
Winemaker award no less than three times. Sam is justifiably proud
to display the new Royal Warrant, issued by the Prince of Wales in
2018, knowing that his bubbles are now served on royal tables all over
the kingdom.

THE MOOR SOUTH OF THE A30

The Moor east of Bodmin is greener, watered by the rivers Fowey and
Lynher, their tributaries and lakes where wildfowl gather. Wooded all
around its southern fringe from Cardinham to Dobwalls, and dotted

with villages linked by threading lanes, this is Bodmin Moor at its most accessible and picturesque. Further east, towards and beyond Minions, the Moor reasserts its wilder, more rugged self, among relics of an industrial mining past and Neolithic standing stones.

10 CARDINHAM WOODS

The Old Deer House Warleggan (page 418)
PL30 4AL 01208 78111 (café only) forestry.gov.uk/cardinham & woodscafe.co.uk

I must confess that on my first visit I didn't get much further than the superb little café in an old woodman's cottage by the river, but this broadleaf forest, owned and immaculately managed by the Forestry Commission, is a wonderful spot for walking, cycling and riding. There are well-kept tracks running all through the woodland, crossing streams and climbing into the hills. Only two miles from Bodmin, the woods are well used by locals and holidaying families who have discovered

"Trees, water and lots of space make a happy alternative to the beach at any time of the year."

that trees, water and lots of space make a happy alternative to the beach at any time of the year. Mountain-bike hire is available from Trailmunki (page 107) where, if you like, you can also hire a guide. David and Lara Spurrell run the deservedly popular café here, producing heartening soups, stews and homemade cakes, and keeping the fire going in cold weather. Perfect.

11 KERDROYA

 SX165720 goldentree.org.uk/projects/kerdroya & cornwall-aonb.gov.uk/kerdroya

On the western shore of Colliford Lake, an ambitious project to create a giant sevenfold labyrinth from stones laid in the manner of a 'Cornish hedge', is slowly taking shape. Launched in 2019, to mark the 60th anniversary of Cornwall's 12 AONBs (Areas of Outstanding Natural Beauty), Kerdroya celebrates the extremely ancient craft of Cornish hedge making – an art that demands years of apprenticeship to acquire the necessary expertise. The Cornish hedge is neither hedgerow nor dry-stone wall, but a solid construction of granite and soil and plant life, supporting its own ecosystem. Completion is due in the autumn of 2023, but if it runs late due to lack of funding, there are always the lovely lakeside paths to enjoy, and easy parking.

12 ST NEOT

🏠 **The London Inn** (page 418)

Like Blisland to the north, St Neot has everything going for it – a superb church with staggeringly beautiful stained glass, a thriving community with its own orchards and garden, a school, shop and the London Inn, a pub with a fantastic reputation for both eating and drinking that extends far beyond the parish.

The **church**, dedicated to St Anietus (the Latinised form of Neot), stands on a rise just next to the pub and is the chief glory of the village. On a sunny day, its early 16th-century windows, the subject of a sensitive Victorian restoration, outshine anything else in Cornwall. Bring binoculars if you want to catch all the high-up detail, but there's quite enough visible without them to keep even the idlest visitor completely entranced. It's the human detail (isn't it always?) that makes these windows so special. A respectful Noah doffs his cap as instructions for dealing with the Flood are delivered from on high; a fresh-faced young monk cranes his neck to see the diminutive Anietus (some accounts say he was only two feet tall, but this seems a little exaggerated) being received by the Abbot of Glastonbury; Anietus rescues a bewildered deer from a suitably grumpy hunter – there are scores of scenes and human faces to be savoured.

A nicely hand-drawn map outside the church suggests a walking route round the village, which clusters around the steep slopes of a tributary of the Fowey, the Loveny. My own map showed the oddly named Romano-British earthworks, **Crowpound**, just west of the village, where I was lucky enough to come across a family out for a walk whose youngest was able to answer my query. 'It's called Crowpound,' she piped up, 'because the saint made all the crows stay there while the farmers were in church.' There must have been an outcry in the village when, in AD974, the saint's relics, which had been laid to rest in the church a century earlier, were taken to St Neots in Huntingdonshire where a new abbey was being constructed and appropriate saintly relics required.

🍴 FOOD & DRINK

The London Inn St Neot PL14 6NG 🕾 01579 326728 🖑 londoninnstneot.com. A free house, serving local ales, ciders and very decent pub food, much appreciated by locals and visitors alike. There are also three lovely B&B rooms (page 418).

13 CARNGLAZE CAVERNS

Near St Neot PL14 6HQ ✆ 01579 320251 🖮 carnglaze.com

Liskeard is fortunately placed for access both to the sea and Bodmin Moor. An evening at the covered, outdoor theatre at Upton Cross six miles to the north (page 133), for example, is easily achieved from here. Even closer, on the Dobwalls to St Neot road, are the Carnglaze Caverns – an old slate mine where evening concerts ranging from Tibetan chanting to glam-rock tribute bands are held in a cathedral-like, acoustically superb subterranean space. By day, and armed with an information sheet and safety helmet, you can wander round the three caverns that make up the former slate quarry; the highest of the three vast chambers served as a rum store for the navy during World War II, the lowest is now filled by a spectacular, floodlit lake. Outside are six acres of woods and gardens on a whimsical fairy theme to explore.

14 GOLITHA FALLS

📍 SX225687

This is a popular spot on a sunny day and it's easy to see why: the car park at **Draynes Bridge** is large and the footpath wide and level, the shallow, rushing river is delightful, with the promise of otter-sighting, and the beech woods are mossy. Forty minutes is ample time to follow the river to where it disappears, tumbling over granite boulders into the woods, and to return on the higher woodland path. Don't expect a single great fall of water as at St Nectan's Glen (page 58); this is a gentle sequence of falls and splashy pools and a grand spot for children to lark about. In fact, the happiest people I saw on a wet and chilly August day, when the beaches were empty and the museum queues long, were a family who'd come here in wellies and found they had the streaming woods and water (nearly) all to themselves. If the thought of crowds is off-putting, you could try the woodland walk along the River Lynher below Cadsonbury Fort, which is likely to be much quieter (page 143) or the falls on the de Lank River north of Blisland (page 116), which are not so accessible and rarely troubled by visitors, but all the lovelier for that.

"The shallow, rushing river is delightful, with the promise of otter-sighting, and the beech woods are mossy."

---

1 Dozmary Pool. 2 Golitha Falls. 3 Cardinham Woods. ▶

⊗ FOOD & DRINK

Inkie's Smokehouse BBQ In the car park at Draynes Bridge, PL14 6RX ✎ 07849 488655. A wonderful café with saddles for seats and picnic tables outside. Its pit-smoke barbecues and homemade sauces have won a devoted, year-round local following. The coffee is pretty good, too. Dogs are very welcome and special ice creams for canine palates are available (cheesy old sock and carrot crunch are favourites).

15 DOZMARY POOL

From Golitha Falls, a narrow lane follows the River Fowey north along the length of its steep-sided valley. If you have brought a bike by car, leave the car in the Draynes Bridge car park and six miles of easy pedalling, provided the wind is not blowing from the north, brings you to this strangely atmospheric moorland pool. This is where, in the legend, Sir Bedivere came after Arthur's death at Camlann and, following instructions, threw Excalibur into the pool – only to see the sword rise from the water, held aloft by a lady's hand. Ladies of the Lake aside, the biggest mystery is where the water comes from; nobody seems to have worked this one out yet. Brave swimmers take the plunge here, perhaps hoping to find something more interesting than old beer bottles: on the one occasion when the lake is known to have dried up in the late 19th century, the bottom was found be littered with stone arrowheads. The hills surrounding the pool are rich hunting ground for archaeologists too. Hut circles, standing stones and burial mounds are marked on the map, and getting to them has become easier since much of the high moorland became subject to open access.

16 AROUND ST CLEER: KING DONIERT'S STONE & TRETHEVY QUOIT

Around St Cleer (the next good pit stop – with pubs and a shop – as you head east after St Neot) the Moor rises and trees fall away. **King Doniert's Stone** and its companion, known simply as the Other Half Stone, stand right next to the road to Minions, just before the turn-off to St Cleer. When I last visited, a bunch of jolly Dutch cyclists were enjoying a break in the little grassy enclosure that surrounds the two stones, both of which are broken chunks of what must have been imposing Cornish crosses. On one of these a Latin inscription begs prayers for the sake of Doniert's soul. Doniert is thought to be the Latinised form of Dumgarth, a 9th-century Cornish king who drowned while crossing the Fowey. Humbler than Shelley's fallen statue of King Ozymandias in the desert perhaps ('Look on my works, ye Mighty, and despair!'), but not lacking in poignancy.

At St Cleer, **Trethevy Quoit** on the east side of the village is the most likely feature to claim your attention. So hidden that it's easy to miss, the massive Neolithic dolmen is thought to date from 4500BC.

¶¶ FOOD & DRINK

Olive & Co Café Siblyback Lake, PL14 6ER ⊘ olivecocafe.com. When Roxy, Lee and their young daughter, Olive, moved their popular café from the centre of Liskeard to the shores of Siblyback Lake, out on the Moor, there were many who raised their eyebrows as they wished them well in their bold new venture. Happily, the lakeside café, serving breakfasts, lunches and teas – homemade soups, dhals, bulging wraps and cakes – has been a runaway success and is perfectly positioned for lakeside walkers, cyclists and watersports enthusiasts with hearty appetites.

17 AROUND MINIONS

Generous car parks on the outskirts of the village tell you all you need to know about the popularity of this part of the Moor with walkers. This is chiefly due to two spectacular sets of rocks, one a Neolithic stone circle known as the **Hurlers**, and the other a naturally formed pile of rocks on the south-facing slopes of Stowe's Hill called the **Cheesewring**. Coming from a cider-making background, it dawned on me as I stared up at the giant slabs of rock perched one on top of the other, that it resembled nothing so much as a stack of pulp-filled nets, waiting for the press, known in the cider world as a 'cheese'. There's more to discover in this brief amble,

"Generous car parks tell you all you need to know about the popularity of this part of the Moor with walkers."

though it may be more by accident than design that you come across the remains of the hillfort that surrounds the Cheesewring, or the Bronze Age track heading north from Stowe's Hill.

The well-worn footpath from the Hurlers leads past the **Rillaton Barrow**, where a Bronze Age gold cup, now in the British Museum, was uncovered (there's a copy in the Royal Cornwall Museum in Truro), before ascending the boulder-strewn slopes of Stowe's Hill and, with a bit of help, you may find **Daniel Gumb's cave**. In fact, the excitement of stumbling across the 18th-century cave-home of the enigmatic Gumb –

stonemason, mathematician and hermit (if you exclude his three wives and nine children) – is tempered by discovering that it is not Gumb's cave after all, but a replica made using some of the original stone by respectful quarrymen when the original dwelling was undermined by their activities.

Close to the car park on the east side of Minions, a restored mine building serves as a self-service **heritage centre**, as well as a useful shelter for rain-dodgers.

¶¶ FOOD & DRINK

Crow's Nest Inn Darite PL14 5JG ✆ 01579 345930 ♂ thecrowsnestcornwall.co.uk. A mile south of Minions, surrounded by the ruins of a mining past, this pub is hard to resist. A log fire welcomes wet walkers – and their children and dogs. There are sheltered tie-ups for those wanting to park their horses. St Austell ales and good food are served.
Minions Shop and Tea Room Minions PL14 5LE ✆ 01579 362926
♂ minionsshopandtearoom.co.uk. Minions can look rather forlorn in the rain, but the dog-friendly tea room behind the shop/post office is a cheerful refuge. Soggy walkers turning up before the official opening time of 10.00 are no rarity here, evidently. On sunny days outdoor tables and chairs overlook the village common.

18 THE LYNHER VALLEY FROM UPTON CROSS TO TREBARTHA

Upton Cross is a handsome granite village that has seen a lot of visitors over the years thanks to the popularity of Sterts, the unique covered amphitheatre and arts centre (page 133). The surrounding countryside of open moorland and plunging, wooded valleys offers a huge variety of routes for walkers and cyclists.

If you don't mind hills, try the lovely walk down to the valley of the River Lynher at the euphonic **Plushabridge**, where the footpath follows the river north to **Rilla Mill** and back up the hill to Sutton, where lanes take you back to Upton Cross.

As you trace the River Lynher north, either by the narrow road that wiggles along its eastern banks from Rilla Mill to Trebartha, or on foot, following the Copper Trail, the land is steep and wooded, with scattered villages and settlements hugging the sheltering shoulder

◀ **1** Trethevy Quoit. **2** King Doniert's Stone and its companion, the Other Half Stone.
3 The Cheesewring. **4** Rillaton Barrow.

LISKEARD & CARADON RAILWAY

At one time the railway ran right through Minions, transporting ore from Caradon Hill and granite from the quarries down to Moorswater, where it was transferred to barges for the last part of the journey to the dock at Looe on the Liskeard to Looe canal. That was in the mid-19th century, when granite quarrying as well as tin and copper mining were at a peak. But with the closure of the mines in the 1880s, granite was not sufficiently profitable to keep the railway going and the tracks were eventually ripped up and sent to France as part of the World War I effort. Now you just see the old granite setts that mark its snaking progress across the Moor: lonely trails to nowhere. A model reconstruction of the railway is displayed in the tea room at Trevallick's Farm Shop (see below) where, at the press of a button, a little train can be sent scurrying through the miniature landscape. Key moments in its history are listed below the display.

of Hawk's Tor and Kilmar Tor. High up, to the west also, looms Twelve Men's Moor, studded with prehistoric remains and fleeting traces of the old mineral railways. **North Hill** has some rather fine estate workers' cottages and farm buildings. The estate is **Trebartha**, mentioned in the Domesday Book and held by the same family until 1940. The 16th-century manor by this time was in ruins and a new one has been built; the gardens are occasionally open in the summer. Timber yards and sawmills are much in evidence; forestry is clearly the estate's main enterprise these days. Footpaths leading up on to the high tops of the Moor start from Trebartha, but are not always clearly marked. It's lonely and desolate on top and you need good visibility to get your bearings, even with a map. It's a very long way to the next village if you keep heading west.

¶¶ FOOD & DRINK

Caradon Inn Upton Cross PL14 5AZ 🖉 01579 364066 🖉 caradoninn.co.uk 🕓 Wed–Sun; food served Fri–Sun. Popular with drinkers (Doom Bar and guest ales), walkers (it's child- and dog-friendly too) and, traditionally, theatre-goers – the arts centre is just opposite.

Trevallick's Farm Shop & Tea Room Pensilva PL14 5PJ 🖉 01579 364061 🖉 trevallicks. com. What a find! I was so mesmerised by the catapult feeder that sends food flying into the pig paddock below the tea garden, much to the delight of the piggies (and tea drinkers), and then by the model railway in the tea room that tells the history of the Caradon Railway, that I almost forgot my soup. Everything here is delicious, and is enlivened with a dash of eccentricity. This tea room is not to be missed.

19 STERTS THEATRE & ARTS CENTRE

PL14 5AX ✆ 01579 362382 ⟨ sterts.co.uk

One of the Moor's happiest surprises was – until 2023, when the structure was condemned as unsafe – the tented outdoor theatre and barn-conversion gallery at Upton Cross on the eastern edge of the Moor, just a mile east of Minions. The setting may not be quite as spectacular as the cliffside Minack near Land's End, but the canvas canopy meant performances, which continued into winter, were never cancelled. Swaddled in blankets and often clutching hot-water bottles, audiences sat on a tiered semicircle of benches, and if the rain beating on the canvas sometimes drowned the actors' voices, nobody minded: it was all part of the Sterts experience.

"Swaddled in blankets and often clutching hot-water bottles, audiences sat on a tiered semicircle of benches."

Conceived in the 1980s by Ewart and Anne Sturrock, who spotted lots of untapped potential in the local community and in the old farm buildings next to their house, a small, community arts centre and outdoor theatre was born. This rapidly grew into an important venue for touring theatre companies, such as Cornwall's home-grown and much-loved Miracle Theatre Company. Ewart continued to direct the community plays, which remained the beating heart of the theatre, until his death in 2015.

At the time of writing things are looking positive: Sterts has survived the turbulence of closure and a new roof covering for the theatre is to be built. During an interview with BBC Cornwall in April 2023, Chairman of the Trustees Nick Hart said he was 'confident we will have a full season running in 2024'. While waiting for the new roof, performances continue at local venues. The present leadership team intend to continue to work not only on the design for the new roof construction, but also on the programme of events; you might catch an ABBA tribute band, a Shakespeare tragedy or an adaptation of Chekhov.

20 TRECARRELL MANOR

Trebullett PL15 9QG ✆ 01566 782286 ⊙ by appointment only

'If you're interested, you'll find your way here,' say Neil and Ruth Burden, who farm here and live in the unsignposted Grade I-listed manor house. It is indeed hidden, close to the River Inny, lost in a tangle of lanes between Higher Larrick and Trebullett. Those with a genuine interest will then have the privilege of making their own Slow discovery of the Great Hall and Lady Chapel which were built early in the 16th century on the site of a much older manor for Henry Trecarrell, mayor of Launceston. Or at least, that was the plan, for Trecarrell never finished his project. Too heartbroken to continue building a fine family home after the death of his wife and child, Trecarrell turned his attention instead to the construction of St Mary Magdalene in Launceston (page 32). Much of the wonderfully carved stone which decorates the church was originally intended for the manor. The story does not end with Henry Trecarrell, however. Guided by Neil, one of the best-informed and generous of local historians, the rich history of this part of Cornwall finds a voice through one of the most interesting buildings in the county. The Burdens are happy to welcome Slow visitors, but theft from the manor some years ago has made them understandably shy of publicity. Do telephone first.

"The rich history of this part of Cornwall finds a voice through one of the most interesting buildings in the county."

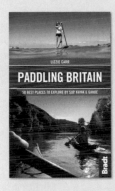  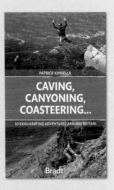

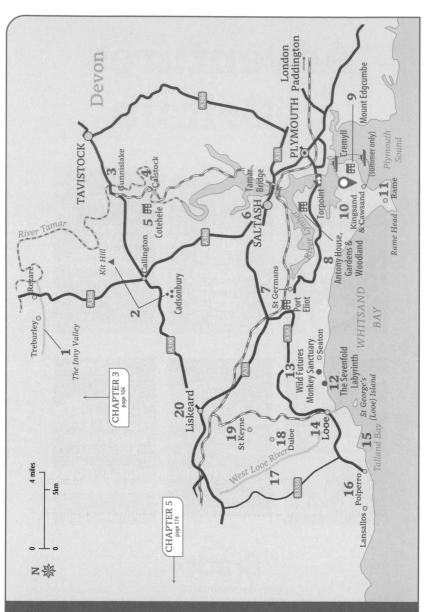

SOUTHEAST CORNWALL: FROM THE TAMAR
TO POLPERRO

4

SOUTHEAST CORNWALL: FROM THE TAMAR TO POLPERRO

The bridges that cross the Tamar have a special significance for those whose hearts lie on the western banks – especially for those who regard Cornwall as another country rather than another county. As the historian A L Rowse wrote, 'The Tamar is a decisive boundary such as no other county possesses – but, then, Cornwall is not an ordinary county …'. I've heard of all sorts of odd ritualistic behaviour by travellers on the bridges, but the story I enjoyed most came from a holidaying family where, said the parents, the children breathed out as the car joined the Tamar Bridge on the Devon side and refused to inhale until the Kernow *a'gas dynergh* (Welcome to Cornwall) sign on the Saltash side had been passed, 'so the air doesn't get mixed up'.

I've no great fondness for the blink-and-you've-missed-it Dunheved Bridge that the A30 rushes over at Launceston, and while I often use the impressively engineered road and rail bridges at **Saltash**, 20 miles to the south, it's the three medieval road bridges that lie in between which give the greatest sense of place. The medieval narrowness of Greystones, Horsebridge and Newbridge allow Slow travellers to savour the moment of arrival, to register the *exactness* of departure. My favourite is the 15th-century **Greystones Bridge**, three miles southeast of Launceston, so narrow you instinctively breathe in as you cross. Arriving on the Cornish side, a left-hand turn, highly unsuited to heavy vehicles, rises swiftly above river and water meadows and there, on a near-vertical slope is **Howard's Wood**, now in the care of the Woodland Trust, with 'Welcome' written on the gate. That's a good start to a county.

Artists and fruit growers have colonised the gentle banks of the Tamar. Despite Rowse's defiant assertion, I find the boundaries blurred in these parts. The **Tamar Valley** is its own world, neither especially Cornish nor Devonish, but happy with its own identity. Many on the Cornish side flit across into Tavistock for shopping or eating out; just as further south, many who work in Plymouth commute via the Torpoint ferry to homes on the **Rame peninsula**. It seems to me that there is less anxiety here than in other parts of rural Cornwall, less edginess; yet also less affluence and security than in the leafy creekside villages of the Helford, Fal and Fowey.

South of the River Lynher, Cornwall's 'forgotten corner' may be linked umbilically to Plymouth, yet in the remote farmland beyond **Torpoint**, its self-proclaimed obscurity is easy to appreciate. There are grand houses at every strategic estuarine juncture, their gardens lush in the mild maritime climate, and in the south, fishing villages with an almost Mediterranean air about them; to the west are desolate, storm-lashed cliffs, shanty-town chalets and long, empty beaches.

Westwards of Seaton, the Channel coast suddenly assumes its Cornish personality; fishing ports, hidden rocky coves and Neolithic stones bear names that speak an older tongue. This is the start of the Pens and Pols, the Lans and Looes; and instead of Johns and Michaels, churches are dedicated to semi-mythical Celtic saints. Inland, where wooded river valleys rise to meet the southern fringe of Bodmin Moor, there are some of the best walking and camping spots to be enjoyed in Cornwall, the county's smallest circle of standing stones, beech trees that are home to Amazonian woolly monkeys and, in **Liskeard**, the opportunity to discover a handsome market town with an equally engaging identity.

GETTING AROUND

One of the great pleasures of visiting southeast Cornwall is the public transport network of trains, buses and ferries that makes getting around without a car relatively easy, at least in comparison with other parts of Cornwall that are less well served.

TRAINS

Two thriving branch lines make travelling by train a real option. The hubs are **Plymouth**, from which you can take the arrestingly lovely ride north to Gunnislake, crossing the Tamar at Calstock – the perfect place to hop off and follow the riverside walk to Cotehele (page 147), and **Liskeard**, which sees the start of a single-track line down to Looe which follows the route of the old Liskeard to Looe canal. Both lines publish maps and timetables which also give details of 'Rail Ale Trails' (⌀ greatscenicrailways.co.uk), suggesting decent pubs within walking distance of the stations.

BUSES

Huge improvements to bus services mean you can connect with the main hubs at Callington, Saltash, Torpoint, Looe and Liskeard. Some, but not all of the **Rame peninsula** is covered by the 70 service, originating in Plymouth, while the 72 takes in Saltash, Looe and Polperro. Walkers will be pleased to learn that it is now possible to walk well into the afternoon along the coast and find buses that will take you back to your point of departure. Hooray. Check out routes and timetables at ⌀ firstbus.co.uk/cornwall.

FERRIES

Calstock Ferry Since Saxon times, Calstock has had a history of ferries linking the two shores of the Tamar. Now, the Tamar Valley AONB has plans to reinstate the iconic Calstock Ferry after receiving a funding boost from Defra. The proposed ferry service, which will link the Cornwall and Devon sides of the river, will run on a trial basis in the summer of 2023 to assess long-term sustainability and viability. Fingers crossed.

Cawsand Ferry ✆ 01752 253153 ⌀ plymouthboattrips.co.uk/cruising. A summer service that carries people, bikes, dogs and pushchairs from Cawsand Beach to Plymouth Barbican, with departures every 90 minutes from 09.30 until 17.00. The crossing takes 30 minutes.

Cremyll Ferry ✆ 01752 253153 ⌀ plymouthboattrips.co.uk/cruising. A year-round passenger service between Cremyll and Admiral's Hard in Plymouth. The 15-minute crossing runs every half-hour at peak times. Check the website for seasonal and Sunday variations.

Torpoint Ferry ✆ 01752 812233 ⌀ tamarcrossings.org.uk. A 24-hour, daily chain-ferry service that transports vehicles and foot passengers between Plymouth and Torpoint, with ferries every ten minutes at peak times.

CYCLING

So far, there are no specially designated cycle routes across this part of Cornwall, and you will need OS Explorer maps 107 and 108 to plot your own routes. Following the valleys of the **Tamar, Lynher**, or **East** and **West Looe** rivers is one of the best ways to plan a ride, but there's no escaping the steep hills and plunging valleys that characterise the

TOURIST INFORMATION

See also ✑ visit-southeastcornwall.co.uk.

Liskeard Foresters Hall, Pike St, PL10 1HZ ✆ 01579 349148 ✑ liskeard.gov.uk
Looe The Library, Millpool Car Park, West Looe PL13 2AF ✆ 01503 262255
✑ visitlooe.co.uk/visitor-information

region, and will test even the keenest adherents to the maxim that the views from the top of a long haul uphill reward the effort.

CYCLE HIRE

Edge Cycles Unit 8 Gallows Park, Torpoint PL11 3AX ✆ 01752 823433 ✑ edgecycles. co.uk. It used to be impossible to hire a bike on the Rame peninsula, but keen cyclists Adam and Anna have changed all that. Bikes for all ages and abilities are available to hire for three hours, a day or a week, with pick-up and drop-off available, too. Great for exploring Mount Edgcumbe's glorious acres and spectacular coastal scenery, or for roaming further afield.
Rame Riders The Barrow Centre, Mount Edgcumbe Country Park PL10 1HZ ✆ 07577 279928 ✑ rame-riders.co.uk ☉ closed winter. A family-run business offering guided e-scooter tours around the park as well as a family-friendly selection of bikes for hire.

WALKING

Rewarding areas for **circular coastal walks** include Rame Head and Mount Edgcumbe, where the peninsular character of the land means you can get waterside walking for much of the way (page 156), while a wildlife-spotting ramble round Looe Island is good for strollers rather than hikers; around Looe there's some impressive river scenery inland following the West Looe River. A 30-mile Discovery Trail follows the Tamar from Launceston to Plymouth; there's no continuous riverside route and planning circular walks isn't that easy, though the branch-line rail service from Plymouth to Gunnislake can be useful for return journeys. The trail can be linked to a route around Kit Hill – excellent for a blustery stroll and far-reaching views. The Rame peninsula offers some spectacular walks through landscape ranging from woodland creeks to windswept clifftops, accessible from Plymouth via the passenger ferries to Cremyll (close to Mount Edgcumbe Country Park) or Cawsand, further to the west.

Mark Camp, who devised Bodmin Moor's Copper Trail (page 108), offers **guided walks** specialising in local heritage or wildlife all over southeast Cornwall. For more information see ⏁ welcometolooe.com/explore/walk-about-west.

ALONG THE TAMAR

Once filled with fields of daffodils, market gardens and orchards, the Cornish banks of the Tamar in springtime now see field margins and woodland understorey splashed with floral memories of those years in cream, yellow and white, the bare canopy above enlivened with occasional clouds of apple, cherry and plum blossom.

The river below **Launceston** descends to Plymouth Sound in no particular hurry: a lazy ribbon of meandering loops joined by the swifter currents of the Inny and the Lynher. Egrets perch in oaks undercut by the water, kingfishers skim above the surface and, during the winter months in the tidal reaches, avocets and spoonbills stalk the shoreline. Salmon and sea trout start running the clear waters in April heading upstream to their spawning grounds, and the otter population is rising. With no small measure of justice, in 1995 both sides of the Tamar were together designated an Area of Outstanding Natural Beauty.

It's hard to fault the manmade additions to the landscape either. The soaring viaducts that span the river at **Calstock** and below **Saltash** seem only to enhance the beauty; and the same may be said of the great riverside houses at **Cotehele, Pentillie** and **Ince**. The relics of an industrial past – mines, engine houses, docks and warehouses – have crumbled with heroic grace beneath the meadow flowers and ferny woodland.

"The river below Launceston descends to Plymouth Sound in no particular hurry: a lazy ribbon of meandering loops."

It would be strange if such an inspiring landscape did not attract artists, but on my last visit to the valley I became aware that Tamar artists are gaining in number and recognition, thanks especially to the small, but influential Limekiln Gallery at Calstock. These artists are also gaining a stronger voice and – though not a school – a distinct identity is emerging. Cornish art, which for so long has been focused around Newlyn and St Ives, now has a counterweight in the east of the county.

1 THE INNY VALLEY

🏠 **Coombeshead Farm** Lewannick (page 418), 🏕 **Spring Park** Rezare (page 419)

Having discovered the infant River Inny while looking for Coombeshead Farm (see below) and later, while crossing a narrow medieval bridge in my hunt for Trecarrell Manor (page 133), I was curious to see more of this pretty tributary of the Tamar, particularly around Rezare, where it drops through mixed woodland to Innyfoot. Look at the OS map, however, and you'll see a marked absence of public footpaths, for this is fly-fishing territory and the sea trout and salmon spawning grounds are carefully protected. From March to mid-October, licences, day tickets and instruction are not difficult to organise, via Launceston Anglers' Association (⊘ gethooked. co.uk) or Lewannick Post Office (PL15 7QD ⊘ 01566 782269). Walkers who like to follow a river should head in the direction of Bodmin Moor and base themselves at Rilla Mill or Upton Cross, where the young River Lynher provides ample scope for rambles beside splashing water (page 131).

"This is fly-fishing territory and the sea trout and salmon spawning grounds are carefully protected."

🍴 FOOD & DRINK

Coombeshead Farm Lewannick PL15 7QQ ⊘ 01566 782009 ⊘ coombesheadfarm.co.uk. An idyllic working farm and on-site bakery supply this hidden gem of a restaurant, open to non-residents for Sunday lunch and evening meals. The set three-course menus might include marinated radish and broad bean tops with ricotta followed by home-reared beef with creamed kale and nettles, with malt ice-cream to finish. Home-grown vegetarian options are always available.

Springer Spaniel Treburley PL15 9NS ⊘ 01579 370424 ⊘ thespringerspaniel.co.uk. The watering hole of choice in these parts. Real ales come from Skinner's, Sharp's and St Austell breweries, the food is very good indeed and much thought has been given to both the sensitively restored interior and the garden. Children and dogs welcome.

Tre, Pol & Pen Lezant PL15 9NN ⊘ 01566 706527 ⊘ trepolandpen.co.uk. The Cornish name describes a farm, a hill and a spring; entirely appropriate for this wonderful farm shop plus café on the road from Callington to Launceston. Meat, as well as fruits and honey, come from the family farm, ales from Atlantic Brewery and wines from the Looe-based Cornish Wine Company. From locally caught sardines on sourdough to salads with Hogs Bottom's nettle, ginger and lemon dressing, the imaginative lunchtime menu is full of local treats. Look out for occasional evening openings.

2 KIT HILL & CADSONBURY

The close-up intimacy of river valleys is seductive, but there comes a point when you want to get up a hill and put the whole landscape into perspective. **Kit Hill** is the highest and most accessible peak between Bodmin and Dartmoor – and you can drive right to the top if you wish, which has the advantage of leaving you with lots of energy for exploring the 400 acres of granite heathland, quarries and ruins from a well-maintained network of tracks.

Kit Hill belongs to the people of Cornwall. It used to be Duchy land, but in 1985 it was handed over to Cornwall County Council to celebrate the birth of Prince William. The views from the summit are sublime and a happy half-hour can be spent doing nothing more than rambling about at the top, trying to identify places encountered at close quarters.

Go early in the morning and you may see novice balloon pilots and their instructors slipping upwards and south, drawn by the airborne currents of the Tamar.

"A happy half-hour can be spent doing nothing more than rambling about at the top."

The summit is quite clearly defined by an earth embankment, now covered in grass, which turns out to be the remains of a folly, built in the late 18th century by Sir John Call of Stoke Climsland, whose estate, Whitefield Park, is now occupied by the Duchy College. The folly resembled a five-sided Saxon fort, built in commemoration of a 9th-century battle, fought on the lower slopes of the hill, which brought Saxon rule to Cornwall.

Bang on the summit stands a chimney, though from a distance it has a distinctly monumental appearance. This is the most significant relic of the 19th-century mine workings that riddle the hill, serving a steam-driven engine that pumped water and lifted ore from the innermost workings of the mine. For some reason, the chimney was built on the site of a prehistoric burial mound. In 1858, archaeological sensitivity and mineral exploitation, it seems, did not shake hands too often. There are, however, some 18 other barrows scattered around the hill.

With such easy access – and a nice tea room (page 145) – Kit Hill is likely to be pretty busy at weekends and in the holidays. If you prefer your hilltops a little less populated, turn your gaze across the rooftops of Callington to the Iron Age hillfort that rises steeply above the River Lynher. **Cadsonbury** belongs to the National Trust and comes supplied with a car park but that's all. Enjoy the leafy solitude of the river walk

JIM WILEMAN/A

PJ PHOTOGRAPHY/S

IAN PETER MORTON/S

and – if you have the puff to cross the lane leading back to the car park and climb the hill – you can look across to Kit Hill with a smile. Parking is just off a lane beside the bridge at Newbridge, PL17 7HL.

FOOD & DRINK

Louis Tea Room Kit Hill PL17 8AX ℰ 01579 389223 ⌂ louistearooms.co.uk ☉ daily until 8pm. Right by the entrance to Kit Hill, and open all year, this friendly, steamy café is in just the right place and stays open in the evenings, serving homemade curries, pasta dishes and stir-fries along with burgers and fish and chips. Sadly the guinea pigs and llamas are no longer in residence. No dogs allowed.

3 GUNNISLAKE

Gunnislake is soaked in history, from the narrow 16th-century bridge at its foot, where Parliamentarians fought their way into Cornwall, to the rich tin, copper, arsenic and wolfram mines that gave the town its considerable size and importance in the 19th century. The steep, wooded landscape around the town was painted by Turner, whose magisterial *Crossing the Brook* was first exhibited in 1815, and Betjeman waxed lyrical about this part of the Tamar Valley.

The branch line from Plymouth terminates at the top of the hill above the town, and from here it's an easy walk to the **Tamar Valley Centre** (Drakewalls PL18 9FE ℰ 01822 835030 ⌂ tamarvalley.org.uk ☉ Tue & Thu 10.00–16.00; call ahead to check). Housed in an eco-friendly building, often used for art exhibitions and talks, this is a good place to pick up information about the latest heritage and leisure projects in the valley and maps of the valley trails. *Trails from the Track*, a collection of self-guided walks accessible from stations on the Tamar Valley line, suggests a particularly good (though steep and muddy) five-mile walk from Gunnislake station that takes in a canalised section of the Tamar and passes through woodland in which the relics of Clitters mine can still be seen.

4 CALSTOCK

Spirits rise in Calstock, for the village is full of life both on and off the river and is decidedly photogenic: whitewashed houses and cottages

◀ **1** The view across the Tamar Valley from Kit Hill. **2** Canoeing on the River Tamar. **3** Calstock.

DRAWN TO THE VALLEY

J M W Turner was not alone in finding the Tamar Valley a place of unique and inspiring beauty; there is now a large and diverse community of artists living, working and exhibiting here, rather in the way that St Ives drew artists half a century or so ago. Artists' group Drawn to the Valley (⟨ drawntothevalley.com) was formed in 2003, not only to promote the work of these creatives, but also to promote the Tamar Valley AONB and contribute to the regeneration of the area through exhibitions and Open Studio events. Look out for their work at the Calstock Arts Centre, the Tamar Valley Centre and the Ashtorre Rock in Saltash.

spill down steep banks to the shore of the Tamar, where the wide, free-flowing river is spanned by the lofty arches of the **railway viaduct** built by John Lang, a Liskeard engineer, and completed in 1907.

There's a lively arts centre, based in the old **Methodist chapel**; the **Limekiln Gallery**, exhibiting classy stuff by local artists; a well-supported village shop in an old library van; and two really good, distinctively different pubs, as well as a rich history of mining, shipbuilding and river-based activity to explore.

Despite the odd hermit (I enjoyed a cottage door signed 'I'm disturbed enough already'), Calstock's community spirit was clearly thriving when I last visited. The village was fundraising to buy a new pilot gig for the rowing club (A Gig for a Gig brought live music to the quayside) and the evening **May Revels** (held annually on May Day bank holiday) saw the whole village turn out to watch primary school children dance and parade with a papier-mâché river giant (symbolising the union of the Tamar and the Tavy) until the giant was released to float away down river.

"Hidden away down deep lanes, Calstock is a bit like an island, unique in its sense of remoteness and self-sufficiency."

Hidden away down deep lanes, Calstock is a bit like an island, linked by rail and river to the world outside, unique in its sense of remoteness and self-sufficiency. Arriving by train on the little branch line, you can walk swiftly down the steep hill to join a very pretty ten-mile footpath that runs along the river to **Cotehele** (page 147). Just out of Calstock, you'll pass a boatyard with a help-yourself honesty-box café, offering homemade cakes, cold drinks and a very good selection of teas and coffees. Amazing. I found myself liking Calstock even more.

🍴 FOOD & DRINK

Boot Inn Fore St, PL18 9RN ✆ 01822 481589 ⬦ thebootinn-calstock.foodndrink.uk. A cosy pub, with open fires – perfect for winter evenings and rainy days. Sunday roasts are a particular treat.

Lishe 6 Commercial Rd, PL18 9QT ✆ 01822 832323. Now a well-established part of Calstock's foodie scene, and located opposite the Limekiln Gallery, this café prides itself on sourcing local produce (some of the salads and veg are grown by the owner) and serving lunches and tea on old china. There is a friendly ambience, and dogs are made to feel welcome, too.

Tamar Inn The Quay, PL18 9QA ✆ 01822 832487 ⬦ tamarinn.co.uk. There are wooden benches both inside and outside this pub, overlooking the quay, and at least half of this community-minded village seem to gather here in the evenings with their dogs and kids. Locally brewed ales from both sides of the river and a reasonably priced, very good restaurant draw both a lunchtime and evening crowd.

5 COTEHELE

St Dominick PL12 6TA ✆ 01579 351346 ⊙ house closed winter; garden & estate open all year; National Trust

Cotehele is a proper working estate – only a handful of its 80 cottages are used as holiday lets – with a strong local identity that draws the neighbouring population to its food markets, boat jumbles, wassailing and rural-crafts workshops. The **Tudor house** at the heart of the estate is outstanding, virtually unaltered since its construction (on the site of an earlier family pile) for the Edgcumbe family, which began in the last years of the 15th century. Magically, there's still no electric light, so on gloomy days a torch is a good idea for examining the tapestries and furniture commissioned by the original Edgcumbes. An alcove in the chapel contains a complicated set of cog wheels and weights, and a winding mechanism – the working parts of a turret clock, the oldest of its kind in the world to be still striking the hour (a turret clock has no face to show the passing minutes) and in its original position.

The **walled gardens** hidden in the wooded slopes below the house are lush and almost subtropical, thanks to the sheltering walls and frost-impeding presence of the river below. A short walk from the gardens along a woodland path high above the river brings you to the 'chapel in the woods', built by Sir Richard Edgcumbe in the late 1480s, shortly before work started on the new house. Richard had been an outspoken critic of Richard III and at Plymouth joined a failed rebellion against

CANOEING ON THE TAMAR

From Easter to September inclusive, **Tamar Trails** offers three-hour guided trips in Canadian canoes, starting from Cotehele Quay (𝒮 01822 833409 𝒶 tamartrails.co.uk). Paddling with the tide, the pace is relaxed and unhurried, the peace and stillness of the river as important as the informal exchange of information en route, and the bring-your-own-picnic break. It's perfect for families looking for a Slow activity. Paul and Kate, who run the business, also offer mountain biking, bushcraft courses and 'tree-surfing' (at their base in Gulworthy, on the Devon side of the river).

the King. As a result, the King sent the notoriously brutal Henry Bodruggan to Cotehele to sort matters out. The chapel marks the spot where Edgcumbe, hidden among the trees, escaped his pursuers by weighting his cap with stones and casting it into the river below. While Bodruggan believed him drowned, Edgcumbe made his way to Brittany, joined forces with Henry Tudor and re-emerged on the battlefield at Bosworth, which saw Henry victorious and his brave supporter able, at last, to return to Cotehele. But Richard Edgcumbe did not live long enough to see the new house built; it was his son Piers who oversaw the construction. Despite the decision by Piers's son (another Richard) to relocate the family seat to Mount Edgcumbe, (page 154) ten miles downstream, in 1553, Cotehele remained part of the Edgcumbe estate until 1947, when it was handed over to the National Trust. Because it was only intermittently occupied for 400 years, no great reworkings of the building were undertaken (apart from a tower, added in 1627, which provided three extra bedrooms); take away the visitor signs, restaurant and gallery and there's very little that Piers or his father would not recognise. And they would probably appreciate it if the **Barn Restaurant** were not taken away, as it does an exceptionally good line in lunches, using produce derived from the estate and local farmers (𝒮 01579 351346).

A day is barely long enough to do Cotehele justice. Down by the river, on the quayside you can wander into the boatshed, where repairs are undertaken to the old craft which still occasionally ply up and down the Tamar. The *Shamrock*, built for sea and river duties in 1899, is permanently moored here, though was being given a complete overhaul

1 Cotehele gardens. 2 The Royal Albert Bridge at Saltash. 3 St Germans. ▶

under a tent when I called in. There's a small free museum, devoted to the days when the Tamar was an industrial highway, full of ketch-rigged barges like *Shamrock*, huge ore-transporting vessels and passenger ferries too. Next to the arches of old limekilns, a handsome granite house is now the **Edgcumbe Arms**, a daytime-only pub and tea room, perfect for riverside walkers with a thirst on. Cider made from apples grown in Cotehele's 'Mother Orchard' – home to dozens of rare local varieties of cider apple – and pressed in the ancient mill, is not to be missed.

Follow a gushing millstream, the Morden, for 15 minutes on foot through woodland and you find yourself at **Cotehele Mill**, which produces not only stone-milled flour (come on Thursdays and Sundays to see the miller in action), but also energy for the bakery and several workshops. It was here that I met Barry Mays, a greenwood furniture maker and long-standing resident of Cotehele. Pausing from his work, Barry gave me an insight into what it's like to live in or around Cotehele, and we both agreed that 'Slow' just about summed up the year-round enjoyment of local food and drink, tradition and skills encouraged by the estate. Opposite Barry's workshop, Zane Hazeldine's pottery deserves a special mention. Simple, rustic jugs and plates, in shades of palest blue and cream set the tone and prices are extremely reasonable. If arriving by car, make sure that you park at Cotehele Quay and enjoy the lovely 15-minute walk described above to visit the mill as there is no roadside parking.

6 SALTASH

⅄ Bush Farm Wild Camping (page 419)

Hosting the Cornish end of Brunel's triumphant railway bridge, 'The Gateway to Cornwall', as the town styles itself, rises from a picturesque harbour through some less than picturesque architecture to a busy high street, packed with shops that serve the local community rather than the tourist trade. One shop, however, has become something of a visitor attraction: **Elliott's Grocery Store** in Lower Fore Street (⬙ tamarprotectionsociety.org.uk ⊙ May–Oct Wed & Thu afternoons & Sat mornings) is a time-warp, with everything left just as it was when it closed in the 1970s.

Inside, I was instantly transported back to my childhood, and crikey, I thought – looking at the tins and packets – diets and packaging have changed a bit since then. The story is that Frank Elliott, who kept this

THE ROYAL ALBERT BRIDGE

Isambard Kingdom Brunel's swansong, an engineering feat of heroic problem-solving, remains the crucial link in joining Cornwall to the rest of England by rail. The Royal Albert Bridge took six years in the planning and six in construction, but the official opening by Prince Albert on 2 May 1859 was missed by Brunel due to ill health. Two days later, he was fit enough to make the crossing in an open carriage; four months on, he was dead.

What made the project so complex was the Admiralty's stipulation that the river must remain navigable without interruption to its high-masted shipping. There was also a lack of available bedrock in the riverbed for building piers on which high arches could be supported. Then, having come up with a clever solution, his contractor went bankrupt and Brunel was obliged to take on the construction contract himself. Brunel was probably what we'd call bipolar and his dark moods were not helped by these challenges.

But the single, mid-river pier was built and on 1 September 1857, watched by some 20,000 spectators, the first of the two oval-shaped, arched spans was floated out into the centre of the river between two barges. It took two hours, five navy vessels and 500 men to manoeuvre it through 45 degrees, working with the turning tide. The iron construction was gradually raised at a rate of six feet a week using hydraulic jacks until on 1 July 1858 it reached its final height, 100 feet above the water at high tide, as the Admiralty had prescribed.

On 10 July 1858 the second span for the Devon side was floated out into the river. Word had spread about the incredible spectacle and special trains were laid on to bring even more spectators from London. Less than a year later, Prince Albert walked across the bridge, while Brunel, bedridden and frustrated, could only imagine the applause.

The best view of the bridge is from the quay at Saltash.

grocer's shop and was vociferously anti-decimalisation, decided in 1973 to turn it into a museum, as a sort of protest (and also to avoid paying business rates on the property). Great fun for over-50s, even if you leave feeling slightly older than when you went in and possibly a bit queasy too. In addition to the Elliott Store, the Tamar Protection Society takes care of the delightful **Elizabethan cottage and garden** (48 Culver Rd, PL12 4DT) that once belonged to Mary Newman, first wife (apparently) of Sir Francis Drake. Opening times can be found on the society's website (⊘ tamarprotectionsociety.org.uk).

The views from Saltash over the estuary are pretty stunning, and one of the best places to enjoy them is from the windows or terrace of the **Ashtorre Rock**, a community-run café (⊘ ashtorrerock.co.uk), right under Brunel's Royal Albert Bridge. This is the heart of the arts community in Saltash, and there are always exhibitions, arts projects and classes going on in the studio upstairs.

FOOD & DRINK

The Rod and Line Tideford PL12 5HW ✆ 01752 851912 🖱 rodandlinetideford.co.uk. On the A38 close to the turning to St Germans, this doesn't look much from the outside and you could easily drive past and miss it, but it's a gem (of the diamond in the rough variety), both for eating and drinking. Lots of people recommended it to me, with Sunday lunch getting a special mention.

7 ST GERMANS

🏠 **The Old Luggage Van** and **The Travelling Post Office** (page 419)

A handsome estate village with a grand church that in Saxon times stood as Cornwall's cathedral frames the entrance to **Port Eliot** (✆ 01503 230211 🖱 porteliot.co.uk), a dreamy, castellated house, parts of which have stood here for over a thousand years, comfortable among green pastures in a meander of the River Lynher. Sir John Soane was involved in much of the late 18th-century remodelling, creating a spectacular round room and generally reorganising the architecture to flood the new and elegant living quarters with light.

Only in England would you find such a gloriously shabby and eccentric stately home, and for a few months in spring and summer it opens its doors to the public. Family portraits by Reynolds decorate the entrance hall, conventionally enough, but thereafter expect an eye-popping series of anachronistic, but much-loved possessions among the faded grandeur. A classic motorbike leans against an unfinished mural on the theme of good and evil, life, sex, love, drugs and rock 'n' roll by Robert Lenkiewicz; gigantic chandeliers are decorated with flowers and swan feathers in operatic opulence.

"Parts of Port Eliot have stood here for over a thousand years, among green pastures in a meander of the River Lynher."

The spirit of the place, however, is changing. Peregrine, the famously bohemian Earl of St Germans, died in 2016; it was his eccentricities and eclectic tastes that informed the surprising décor. After his death, his third wife Catherine moved out amid a monumental family row in order to make way for Peregrine's young grandson who was heir to the title. (The boy's mother was the widow of Peregrine's late son, Jago.) The tabloids had a field day. You'd never guess at the upheavals as a visitor, though. The gardens and park are beguilingly tranquil, the house still endearingly eccentric in its furnishings. Meanwhile, the new café in the stableyard serves a delicious breakfast and brunch menu, designed to suit contemporary tastes.

THE RAME PENINSULA

Across the River Lynher, a knobbly peninsula, dubbed 'Cornwall's forgotten corner', looks across the confluence of the Lynher and the Tamar, known as the Hamoaze, at the urban sprawl and dockyards of Plymouth. Two great gardens, **Mount Edgcumbe** and **Antony**, crown the eastern headlands; all else is empty hilly farmland and long beaches sheltering beneath crumbling cliffs on the Channel shore. All the people seem to have been shaken down into the picturesque conjoined villages of **Kingsand** and **Cawsand** that once stood on either side of the county boundary with Devon. Some villages are distinctly Anglo-Saxon in name – Crafthole, St John, Millbrook – and have a remote air about them, though none is quite so lost as tiny **Rame**, an inspiring destination for romantic souls, particularly on Christmas Eve when candles light the lonely chapel.

8 ANTONY HOUSE, GARDENS & WOODLAND

Torpoint PL11 2QA. House & gardens ✆ 01752 812191 ⊙ Apr—early Oct 3 or 4 days/week; National Trust. Woodland garden ✆ 01752 815303 ⊘ antonywoodlandgarden.com ⊙ garden Feb -Oct; woodland walk all year

The Carew Poles are a family of great gardeners to which the gardens and woodland at Antony, which has been their ancestral home for centuries, bear witness. The current owner, Sir Richard Carew Pole, was president of the Royal Horticultural Society from 2001 to 2006; his parents assembled important collections of camellias and day-lilies, and enjoyed the help and assistance of J C Williams of Caerhays, who gave his name to some of the greatest camellia hybrids (page 215). Earlier still, in 1792, Humphry Repton was called in to sweep away the lingering formality of the first gardens, created when a new house was built for the family between 1711 and 1721. Evidently the spirit of innovation and development remains strong: there is a thought-provoking collection of modern sculptures and surreal moments of recognition, for the topiary walk was used in Tim Burton's 2010 film of *Alice in Wonderland*.

Quintessentially Cornish, the **gardens** at Antony are perhaps best viewed in spring, when they are filled with the flowers of camellias, magnolias, rhododendrons and azaleas above the River Lynher with magnificent views of the estuary rich with wildlife.

The **house**, which opens to the public too, is rather splendid, though very much a lived-in home and not a museum. The **woodland garden** (which is not part of the National Trust property and requires a separate admission) overlooking the Lynher is a dendrologist's dream, and even if you can't tell your *Taxodendrons* from your *Metasequoias*, the sheer loveliness of the woods, walks and water – and a decidedly upmarket tea in the Broomhill Cottage Vintage Tea Room – will take care of the rest of the day.

⏸ FOOD & DRINK

Wilcove Inn Wilcove, Torpoint PL11 2PG ✆ 01752 812381 ⏷ thewilcoveinn.com. Situated on the tidal shoreline of Cangapool, overlooking the Hamoaze. Local ales, decent food and fine views; child- and dog-friendly.

9 MOUNT EDGCUMBE

⛰ **Hawkins Battery** Maker (page 419)
Cremyll, Torpoint PL10 1HZ ✆ 01752 822236 ⏷ mountedgcumbe.gov.uk ⊙ house & garden Apr–Sep Tue–Thu & Sun; grounds all year daily

So, I was wondering, what could possibly have induced the Edgcumbes to leave the loveliness of Cotehele? Here, ten miles south of Cotehele, they had a deer park and in 1547 work started on a new and very grand house. Perhaps by the late 17th century, when the move happened, Cotehele was looking rather dated and the new pile the more attractive residence of the two? A century earlier, Mount Edgcumbe had certainly caught the eye of the captain of the Spanish Armada, who declared that he would live there when the war was over.

The mid-18th century saw grand landscaping works as the grounds were brought up to date in the new Arcadian style, by which time both the façade and the innards of the house would have looked quite

---

1 Rame Head. **2** Antony Woodland Garden. **3** Mount Edgcumbe. **4** Kingsand on the Rame peninsula. ▶

A ramble around Mount Edgcumbe

✤ OS Explorer map 108 or Landranger map 201; start: free car park at Maker Church
♀ SX446520; six miles, shortened version: 3½ miles; moderate.

O ne of the best walks I've ever done in Cornwall (and it was raining much of the time) starts in the field by Maker Church (free car parking); you could also start at the Cremyll passenger ferry landing. The walk takes you on a looping circuit of the Mount Edgcumbe section of the Rame peninsula, through woodland, parkland, clifftop and deer park, with the almost surreal backdrop of Plymouth city and dockyards, and several good pit stops along the way.

Walkers looking for a longer route – this one is a pleasant two-hour ramble – can continue westwards on the coast path to Kingsand, where an inland path doubles back, along a high ridge and across farmland towards the start point.

During the summer months you can enjoy the best of both worlds – the rural peninsula as well as the shops, cafés and restaurants of Plymouth's waterfront development – by using the seasonal ferry service between Cawsand and Plymouth Barbican (page 139), in conjunction with the year-round passenger ferry from Admiral's Hard in Plymouth to Cremyll.

1 Park at **Maker Church** and follow the signed footpath northwest across the field to the B3247. Cross the road carefully and rejoin the footpath which descends through woods and open meadow to a narrow lane.

2 Cross the lane and rejoin the path, following the field edge, overlooking the muddy shores of Millbrook Lake to **Empacombe Quay**, an attractive cluster of houses overlooking the water. The path continues to Cremyll, where the passenger ferry from Plymouth lands. There are public toilets, a car park and pub.

3 Enter **Mount Edgcumbe** (free admission to the park) through the imposing gates on your right. Turn left and walk under the arch. Pass the Orangery café and continue through the gardens, keeping to the left. There are views across the water to Plymouth. Stay on the coast path as it winds through the park, following the contours of the cliff.

4 The path passes above **Fort Picklecombe** (built in 1848 to defend Plymouth from possible attack by the French, and converted into a residential complex some years ago) and forks:

For the short-cut back to the start: fork right, steeply uphill, through the deer park to reach Maker Church.

To continue the full walk: turn left at the fork, crossing the lane that leads to Fort Picklecombe and continue along the coast path for two miles to **Kingsand** – ensure you allow time to explore the village before returning. Remember also, that if you want to linger in the village, ferries run from neighbouring Cawsand to Plymouth Barbican during the summer months.

5 As you enter the village through a gate, turn right up the steep hill, keeping an eye out for the sign on the right indicating the footpath that takes you along the ridge.

6 Join a lane that leads to **Maker Farm**. Follow the lane as it curves first left then sharply to the right. Join the footpath at a stile in the hedge and cross the fields to **Friary Manor**. Pass behind the building and follow the footpath through the fields, using the tower of Maker Church to guide you back to the car park. The 15th-century church has a Norman font (pinched from St Merryn), carved with a virtuoso display of twirling, coiling snakes.

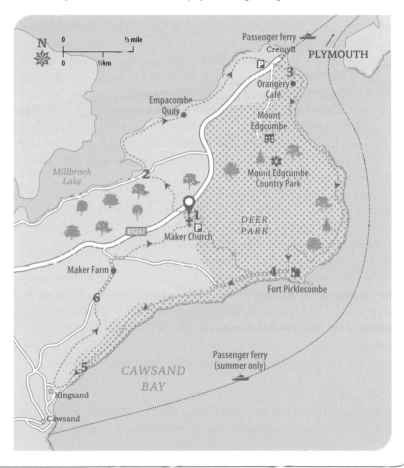

different from the original Elizabethan design. A stray incendiary bomb hit the house in 1941, destroying almost all of the interior fabric of the building, though astonishingly the external walls remained intact. Today, it's clear that the rebuilding, which began in 1958, proved the silver-lining theory, as modifications to make the house lighter and more comfortable to live in could be incorporated into the restoration plan. Many of the older pieces of furniture and paintings did not survive the blast, but there are some superb tapestries from Cotehele and a joyous painting of a Cotehele tenants' dinner, dating from the 19th century.

The Cremyll foot passenger ferry to Plymouth deposits walkers at the eastern approach to the 1,000-acre park, heralded by a grand slope of grassy, tree-fringed hillside sweeping up to the house and formal gardens. Just inside the Cremyll entrance gates are more formal gardens and the tea room, the latter in a huge classical orangery. Beyond here, unless you are following the coast path, which runs along the wooded fringes of the park, take the well-marked routes past lakes and camellia-clad slopes, through woodland and a wide-open deer park. Paying to visit the house also gives admission to the earl's garden, with its 400-year-old lime tree, cedar lawn and shell seat, decorated with shells reputedly provided by Captain Cook, whose voyages often began and ended in Plymouth harbour.

Since 2017, Mount Edgcumbe park has been home to Britain's first native **honey-bee reserve**, as the Rame peninsula was discovered to have one of the few populations of the diminutive black bee left in the country. DNA tests show the little chaps may have Breton ancestry, but that's not the point, is it?

Behind the house, the handsome old stable yard was given a new lease of life as the **Barrow Centre**, housing an attractive mix of art and craft studios and shops – I was particularly taken with Helen Round's hand-printed linens ($\oslash$ helenround.com) – as well as providing a base for survival adventure skills ($\oslash$ survivalwisdom.com). You can also hire a bike or tour the park on a mountain bike, Segway or e-scooter.

FOOD & DRINK

The Canteen at Maker Heights Millbrook, Torpoint PL10 1LA $\oslash$ 01752 659069 [f]. After Nick and Lisa Platts transformed two war-time Nissen huts into a gloriously light and airy café-restaurant, it deservedly became a runaway success – not only with the next-door campsite, but much further afield, as news of the top-notch cooking and friendly vibe spread to the wider community. However simple, everything is deliciously fresh and attractively presented: I had the best scrambled eggs on toast I've ever tasted here.

Farriers Café The Barrow Centre Mount Edgcumbe, Torpoint PL10 1HZ ℘ 01752 823823 ℘ thefarriers.co.uk. A nice line in home-cooked lunches and teas.

10 KINGSAND & CAWSAND

After the emptiness of the surrounding landscape, it can be a bit of a shock to find the peninsula's twin villages chock-a-block with visitors, enjoying the harbourfront views from the narrow streets and pavements, on to which, in Mediterranean style, tables and chairs spill. On my last summertime visit the place was filled with the buzz of holiday chatter (it's popular with the rich and famous; I overheard more people spotting celebrities than seals) and the aromas of grilling fish and garlic. (This turned out to be a man barbecuing his mackerel on the harbour wall, but might just as well have come from any one of the harbourfront cafés and pubs.) Come in winter, though, and the villages are almost empty; second homes and holiday lets have had a withering effect on the local community and, at the time of writing, there's a big push to encourage full-time residency among new buyers.

"On my last summertime visit the place was filled with the buzz of holiday chatter and the aromas of grilling fish and garlic."

The two villages run into each other almost seamlessly, but the distinction was once important, as the stream running between the two marked the division between Devon and Cornwall, first established in the 10th century by Athelstan and not pushed back to the Tamar until 1844. A wall-mounted sign on the appropriately named Boundary Cottage close to the Halfway House Inn marks the old division.

During the summer, a **foot passenger ferry** leaves Cawsand Beach for Plymouth Barbican every 90 minutes or so. If arriving from Plymouth, be prepared to paddle the last few yards at low tide. Car parking is expensive and space limited, which gives the place a special Slow appeal: 'It's the lack of parking that has saved us from becoming another Polperro,' grinned one local resident. 'We appreciate that here.'

¶¶ FOOD & DRINK

The Devonport Inn The Cleave, Kingsand PL10 1NF ℘ 01752 822869 ℘ devonportinn. com. Highly rated by locals, both for eating and drinking. All fish is caught locally by

Kingsand fisherman 'Bumps'. The mackerel sushi is especially recommended. Dog walkers are very welcome and blankets available for 'dogs who find our floor too hard'.

The Old Bakery Garrett St, Cawsand PL10 1PD ✆ 01752 656215 ♂ theoldbakery-cawsand.co.uk ◷ Fri–Sun (plus Mon–Wed eves in high season); closed in winter. Chris and Liz Gunn bake their own sourdough bread from organic flour and terrific pizzas on Monday, Tuesday and Wednesday evenings in high season.

11 RAME & THE CHANNEL COAST

Although only a mile up the hill from Cawsand, lonely **Rame** has a world's-end feel to it. A scattering of small houses and a 13th-century church make up the village, though the graveyard is filled to overflowing, there being no cemetery in the twin villages below. Drowned boy sailors, smugglers brought to justice, children, gig pilots and all their families, friends and enemies lie here: a fascinating and poignant record of social history, inscribed in stone and slate. Without electricity, the little church is lit by candles for services; the flickering candlelight, brave against the winter night and black sea, creates a very special atmosphere and ensures the Christmas Eve carol service is particularly well attended.

Out on **Rame Head**, you can park by the volunteer coastguard building and walk out on a spur from the coast path to a medieval stone chapel, close to the site of an Iron Age cliff-fort, so utterly isolated that Rame feels almost suburban by comparison. On a clear day, the headland just visible on the far western horizon is the Lizard; to the south and east there are closer views of shipping entering Plymouth Sound.

A clifftop road overlooking the sandy beaches of **Whitsand Bay** wiggles narrowly through scruffy chalet territory towards the MoD's Tregantle Fort firing range, where it joins the steadier B3247 to Looe. If the red flags are not flying, the beach below **Tregantle Cliff** is peaceful, wide and often empty; easier access is to be found at **Sharrow Point** close by, which has National Trust parking and steps down to the beach. The rip tides are ferocious.

¶¶ FOOD & DRINK

Cliff Top Café Tregonhawke PL10 1JX ✆ 01752 822069 ♂ clifftopcafe.co.uk. A gem of a café, perched on the cliff side of the road between Rame and Freathy. Great friendly atmosphere that extends to children and dogs. The coffee is excellent, the cakes and scones homemade and the breakfasts just the job after an early beach walk.

AROUND LOOE

The hinterland east of Looe, hilly and wooded along the stream-fed valleys, is a world apart from the busy streets and harbour of the town. Narrow lanes and footpaths can be knitted together to make up some fairly challenging walks between Millendreath, the valley of the River Seaton and Bucklawren, for which you will need either the OS Explorer map 107 or the 'Bucklawren Countryside' walks leaflet, available in Looe TIC. It was a warm August day when I walked through Treveria and Keveral woods, following the Seaton path, and I didn't see another person all morning, just rabbits, roe deer and buzzards circling overhead.

12 THE SEVENFOLD LABYRINTH

🏠 **Windsworth** (page 419)

In a field beside the old route of the coast path, midway between Looe and Seaton (♀ SX282542), local resident Caroline Pethcrick has taken it upon herself to cut this meditational turf labyrinth, some 60 feet in diameter, giving walkers the opportunity to stop and reflect. She identified the right spot by dowsing for the crossing of two ley lines and an appropriate blood sacrifice was made when her dog appeared with a freshly killed vole at the hole where the centre stone was about to be raised.

'You can go and sit there and realise the earth isn't such a bad place after all,' Caroline told me. 'It's just a gentle pleasure for people to enjoy. I live in a phenomenally beautiful place and I wanted to share it somehow.' The path that runs past the labyrinth has now been officially closed, due to landslips further east, so for access, leave your car on the roadside at the National Trust-owned Bodigga Cliff, and climb the gate to access the permissive path that takes you, up and down, as far as the labyrinth, with a branch path dropping down to the seashore.

If the place really takes a hold of you, you can stay in an off-grid, eco-friendly cliff-top house for holiday rental (🖱 windsworth.org.uk).

13 WILD FUTURES MONKEY SANCTUARY

Murrayton House, St Martins, Looe PL13 1NZ 🖉 01503 262532 🖱 monkeysanctuary.org
🕐 Wed–Sun; closed in winter

I'd really come to see the wildflower gardens and the sanctuary was swarming with children when I visited, but was immediately distracted by the affable keepers who were doing a grand job, getting the message across that monkeys are not pets. While all eyes followed the monkeys as they pottered about in their huge, tree-filled, netted enclosures, the story of Leonard Williams unfolded. Williams, a teacher of Spanish guitar (and father of guitarist John Williams), was bequeathed a pet woolly monkey during the 1950s, and as time went on, acquired a few more. The leap from living in London with five pet monkeys to living in Cornwall came in 1964: here, in the large gardens, he could accommodate more and more rescued monkeys. By this time, Williams had come to understand the terrible effects of social deprivation on Amazonian woolly monkeys and deplored the practice of slaughtering mothers in order to send their infants to pet shops and zoos. At Murrayton, the monkeys were allowed to live as close as possible to their natural state in colonies, with minimal human contact, and with the first births, Williams saw his emerging colony regaining lost, instinctive skills and patterns of behaviour. However, attempts to rehabilitate young monkeys in their natural Brazilian environment foundered, and now all the female monkeys are given contraceptive pills to stop the population growing beyond the means of the sanctuary, whose main responsibility – under the stewardship of Wild Futures, the primate welfare charity – lies in rescue and education.

"At Murrayton, the monkeys were allowed to live as close as possible to their natural state, with minimal human contact."

The sloping site makes for good viewing, even when the monkeys are moving about high up in their enclosures or on rainy days, when they seek the shelter of the leafy canopy. There's a film room and a very good shop, where you can sit out the showers happily in the adjoining café.

Much of the monkeys' food comes from the sanctuary's gardens and orchards; local residents are invited to recycle vegetable waste in the sanctuary's giant compost stacks which all ends up in the garden.

Very sadly, the sanctuary is facing possible closure due to loss of income during the pandemic, withdrawal of European funding post Brexit and the cost of living crisis. A massive fundraising effort is under way at the time of writing.

14 LOOE

Looe has everything you might expect of a Cornish seaside town: a sandy beach and fishing port, children crabbing off the harbour walls; quirky old buildings and steep narrow lanes oozing a history of smuggling and

ST GEORGE'S (OR LOOE) ISLAND

A mile out of Looe harbour, but only spitting distance from Hannafore Point to the north, the green, humpback form of St George's (or Looe) Island offers a tempting excursion for anyone looking for a quiet hour or two observing marine wildlife. The Cornwall Wildlife Trust runs a boat to the island from Easter to September (𝒸 looeseasafari.co.uk); check the information board by the lifeboat station in East Looe for sailing times. On arrival, there is a short briefing, given by one of the Trust's small team of volunteers who live and work on the island, about the kind of marine and island wildlife you might see

and then you set off on your own to explore. The main house, built in the 19th century for customs officers to keep an eye on smugglers, was later home to the Atkins sisters, Babs and Evelyn, who bought the island in 1965, with a loan of £22,000. Their love of nature, at a time when the island might have been vulnerable to development, preserved the local biodiversity, and when Babs died in 2004, she bequeathed it to the Trust.

The woods and maritime heathland cover only 22.5 acres, but these are some of the least spoilt acres in Cornwall, rewarding close-up and respectful observation.

fishing; shops variously selling pasties or ice creams or fish and chips; beamy pubs and fishermen offering boat trips. Not to mention (since 2023) a certain amount of TV notoriety, as *Beyond Paradise* – the BBC's *Death in Paradise* spin-off – looks set to do for Looe what *Doc Martin* did for Port Isaac. Dodging the film crew on my last visit, I enjoyed the busy activity of Looe's fish market, the fun of being able to take a boat across the river to **West Looe** or down the coast to **Polperro**; I loved the unexpected music and the friendliness in a tiny crêperie, and it was great to be able to walk into town from the railway station.

Some years ago, Looe was not the smartest of Cornish destinations; I remember watching, with embarrassment, a boat return ahead of schedule from a shark fishing trip, and disgorge its muscular, tattooed passengers, who were all grinning at the skipper's refusal to accept their 'Ungentlemanly Behaviour on the High Seas'. Now, however, the town is remarkable for its preponderance of seafood cafés and restaurants ('too many' grumbled one café owner), many supplied by the **Pengelly sisters**, whose wet-fish slab right by the harbour is supplied daily as the boats come in. It is as irresistible as anything you'd see in an Italian or French market.

The Old Guildhall Museum and Jail in Higher Market Street (𝒸 01503 263826 𝒸 looemuseum.co.uk) looks heavily restored from the outside, but this 15th-century building is still remarkably intact. The cells below and the magistrates' court above reveal an impressive stone and timber fabric, and the side rooms are stuffed with exhibits relating to Looe's boatbuilding, fishing and smuggling past. There is no room for storage, so everything's out on display – from a mastodon tooth to a grisly cat-o'-nine-tails.

A stroll along the harbour may, if you're lucky, offer a glimpse of the odd seal following the fishing boats, hoping for an easy morsel of fish. There's one seal, however, you can't miss.

"A stroll along the harbour may, if you're lucky, offer a glimpse of the odd seal."

Nelson, the one-eyed grey seal, who for 25 years made the sea around Looe his home and was much loved by local residents, became a kind of ambassador for all Cornish seals when his image and name were used in a successful campaign to increase awareness of Cornwall's fragile seal colonies. When Nelson died in 2003, the town did not forget him. His statue, cast in bronze, was unveiled by sailor Robin Knox-Johnston in 2008; it crowns the Pennyland Rocks, where the Looe River meets the sea.

¶¶ FOOD & DRINK

Looe's rising identity as a destination for foodies is marked by the presence of a timber building on the quay which houses the excellent **Quayside Fresh** (Buller Quay, East Looe PL13 1DX ✆ 01503 262838 ⊗ quaysidefresh.co.uk), a wonderful farm shop that stocks a complete range of foods from local growers.

Daisy's Café Castle St, East Looe PL13 1BA ✆ 07988 803315 ⓕ. A nice place to take children, and dogs are welcome too. Bright, cosy décor and luscious homemade cakes, daisy-shaped scones and spotty teapots.

Fisherman's Arms Higher Market St, East Looe PL13 1BW ✆ 01503 265800 ⓕ. Often packed with a jolly local crowd, this is one of Looe's more authentic pubs, with decent real ales, semi-spontaneous music nights and an open fire.

Larsson's 7 Buller St, East Looe PL13 1AS ✆ 01503 265368. Something of an institution in Looe, thanks to Martin Noble (favourite artist: Carl Larsson), who has jammed more tables, music, good conversation, coffee and crepes into a small space than you would think possible. At the time of writing Mr Noble is inviting would-be proprietors of this delightful place to contact him, as he's decided to put it up for sale.

1 Looe. 2 Polperro. 3 Talland Bay. ▶

Purely Cornish 18 Fore St, East Looe PL13 1DT ☏ 01503 262680 ⏚ purelycornish.co.uk.
Local produce, 'pick your own' hampers and mail order too.
Ye Olde Salutation Fore St, East Looe PL13 1AE ☏ 01503 262784. A locals' spit-and-sawdust pub, with low beams and a huge fire. Friendly staff, Doom Bar on tap and fish on the menu.

15 TALLAND BAY

⌂ **Talland Bay Hotel** Porthallow (page 418)

Two pretty, sheltering coves with beaches, rockpools, summer-only cafés and a quirky, award-winning boutique hotel and, further towards Polperro, tiny Donkey Beach, are predictably popular in the summer. In April sunshine I've had the emerald and cobalt waters and soft sand almost all to myself. One improbably narrow, steep lane leads in and out of Talland; the village must heave a collective sigh as the seasonal influx of cars causes predictable jams. But on foot, following the clifftop coast path, the beaches are only 45 minutes' walk from either Looe or Polperro; in summer there are, as one local resident put it, 'more skylarks than you can listen to with one pair of ears'. The church, wedged into a leafy shoulder of the cliff, stands almost alone (Talland is not so much a village as a cluster of scattered houses and farms) between the rising land and the open sea. The architecture is partly responsible for this feeling of self-containment: the tower, half buried in the grassy hillside, was built separately from the nave in the 13th century, but the gap was given a walk-through arch and roofed 200 years later, creating a narrow, cloistered approach between sheltering walls of granite.

⟘⟘ FOOD & DRINK

Talland Bay Hotel Porthallow PL13 2JB ☏ 01503 272667 ⏚ tallandbayhotel.co.uk. A one-off, luxury establishment with a very fine kitchen and quirky decorative surprises every step of the way in both the garden and the hotel. Light lunches and afternoon teas are a real treat, and there's a dog menu, too, featuring Kittow's sausages served cold and other such doggie delights.

16 POLPERRO

⋀ **Highertown Farm Campsite** Lansallos (page 419)

Seasonal boat trips venture from Looe to Polperro, a very enjoyable way to arrive in this picturesque fishing village, which has featured on more jigsaw puzzles and chocolate boxes than has been good for it. Alternatively, it makes sense to start in Talland Bay and walk a very pleasant mile or so along the coast path; otherwise you are more or less obliged to leave your car in the large Crumplehorn car park at the head of the valley and walk (or take the electric 'omnibus'-style transport on offer) into the village, which takes less than ten minutes.

Although undeniably charming, the approach is crowded with touristy shops, which may obscure its Slow appeal. Come very early on a summer morning, however, and the loudest noise is the River Pol, rushing beside the medieval lanes before disappearing under a 13th-century bridge and tumbling into the inner harbour. Hugger-mugger cottages and warehouses, threaded together by narrow paths around the stream and the harbour, where a small fish market still operates, and an unexpected encounter with a shell-encrusted façade of a fisherman's cottage, all make for enjoyable ambling. I couldn't help wondering how Polperro residents ever manage to get anything bigger than a medium-sized fish (let alone a fridge or sofa) into their houses.

The **Polperro Heritage Museum of Smuggling and Fishing** in The Warren (℘ 01503 273005 ⌖ polperroharbourtrust.org ☉ May–Sep) is, as you might expect, dedicated to fishing and smuggling. The smuggling exhibits, which include tales of 21st-century drug-smuggling activity, rather outdo the fishing ones in terms of excitement. Sadly, none of the exhibits address the vexing issue of furniture delivery.

Leaving Polperro by the westbound coast path, just a few yards on from the harbour and down a steep rocky path, you'll find a large semi-natural rock pool, big enough for grown-ups to take half a dozen proper strokes and small enough for youngsters to get a taste of a wild, splashy swim.

¶¶ FOOD & DRINK

The Blue Peter Inn Quay Rd, PL13 2QZ ℘ 01503 272743 ⌖ thebluepeterinn.com. A welcoming, gossipy pub, full of laughter and locals and well known for its regular music nights. Blues Best, brewed specially for the pub by Sharp's, is always on tap, beside the usual suspects, Doom Bar and Tribute, as well as cider from Cornish Orchards.

THE LOOE VALLEYS

The branch line to Liskeard follows the leafy contours of the East Looe River, its single track occupying much of the footprint of the 19th-

century canal that once ferried granite, copper and tin from the canal basin at Moorswater, just outside Liskeard, to the seaport at Looe. It's a peaceful journey, through broadleaf woods, shouldered by hilly farmland, serving a handful of small villages along the way. The West Looe River, muddily tidal and teeming with birdlife, is perfect for quiet woodland walks on either shore.

17 ALONG THE WEST LOOE RIVER

A little boat ferries passengers from the harbour at East Looe across the river to the town's westerly half, which is mostly residential. (You can walk across the bridge in half the time, but that's not the point.) The TIC will give you a leaflet, 'Explore Kilminorth Woods', or you can simply set off on the well-marked path to this oakwood nature reserve, which offers lovely views across the tidal shores of the West Looe River. Alternatively, look for the 'Kilminorth Woods and the Giant's Hedge' three-mile circular walk on the iWalk Cornwall app.

On the north side, **Trenant Wood** belongs to the Woodland Trust, but is far less frequented by walkers and nature lovers, as it's quite difficult to find the way in. The trick is to head to the fiveways crossroads at Trenant Cross (SX246543) and head up the lane towards Polpever Farm. As the lane swings right, carry straight on up the track, to where it opens on to a wide grassy spot, where parking is permitted. Thereafter there are discreet signs indicating the footpaths through the woods and new plantations of native broadleaf trees, with glimpses of busy Looe far below across the river. It's a very special place to visit, which I would not have discovered had not Jo from Treworgey Farm (page 419) told me that it was her favourite walk.

18 DULOE

 Treworgey Farm (page 419)

Jump off the train at **Causeland** and, after following the road south for about 400 yards, a footpath on the right leads through woods and fields to Duloe, passing the apple orchards at Westnorth Manor Farm on the way. This is the home of **Cornish Orchards** (01503 269007 cornishorchards.co.uk), one of Cornwall's most prestigious cider farms. Andy Atkinson (now retired) came here first as a cattle farmer

◀ **1** Duloe stone circle. **2** Liskeard town centre.

in the early 1990s, but took an interest in growing heritage cider apples and became a true master of the craft of cider-making. April, when the orchards are in blossom, is the prettiest month to visit, and late October when the pressing is in full swing is the working end of the season. Tours lasting a couple of hours are offered on Saturdays at 10.30am and juices and ciders can all be tried in the farm shop.

The footpath into Duloe spurs off beside the cricket pitch, and leads to a sheep-grazed paddock, where a Bronze Age **stone circle** (oval to be more accurate), the smallest of its kind in Cornwall, sits unobtrusively beside a hedge. On the other side of the main road into the village, the **church of St Cuby** occupies an almost circular graveyard, which has given rise to speculation that this was once the site of an Iron Age hillfort. Inside the restored medieval church, there are several carved slate memorials to the wives and daughters of local landowners, dating from the 16th century. The name of Maria Arundell is touchingly re-wrought as a mixture of 'marigold' and 'laurel' and her short life likened to the brevity and beauty of those plants: 'Both feed the eye, both please the optic sense/Both soon decay, both suddenly fleet hence.'

"A Bronze Age stone circle (oval to be more accurate), the smallest of its kind in Cornwall, sits unobtrusively beside a hedge."

¶¶ FOOD & DRINK

The Plough at Duloe Duloe PL14 4PN ℘ 01503 262556 ⌂ theploughduloe.com. Having won a good reputation for food locally, word has spread, and the village pub has become something of a destination for foodies. It's even scooped several awards for its seasonal, locally sourced menus. Real ales include the ever-popular Sharp's Doom Bar plus St Austell Tribute and Proper Job.

19 ST KEYNE

🏠 **Botelet** Herodsfoot (page 419)

There's a slight feeling of having entered a lost world if you hop off the train at St Keyne and start exploring. **Lametton Mill** is a gloriously un-wrecked remnant of rural Cornwall, where a waterwheel once turned to mill flour. From the 18th-century barn here, you may still hear the ghostly echo of an old Wurlitzer organ; Paul Corin's Museum of Old Music Machines closed in 2013, but I like to think that Mr Corin still takes to the keyboard occasionally.

A few minutes' walk along the road from the station is a leafy spot where a **holy well** (♥ SX248603) is supposed to confer marital authority on the first half of a newly wed couple to drink from it. You can almost hear the poet Robert Southey chuckling as he penned the last verse to his poem, in which he tells of meeting a local Cornishman who believed in the well's magic properties:

I hastened as soon as the wedding was done,
And left my wife in the porch
But i'faith she had been wiser than me,
For she took a bottle to church.

20 LISKEARD

'Fresh from the quaint old houses, the delightfully irregular streets, and the fragrant terrace gardens of Looe, we found ourselves, on entering Liskeard, suddenly introduced to that "abomination of desolation", a large agricultural country town,' wrote Wilkie Collins in *Rambles Beyond Railways,* when Cornish tourism was still in its infancy.

Collins must have been in a bad mood when he visited Liskeard, for good-looking towns that have resisted selling their souls to tourism are not thick on the ground in Cornwall, and handsome Liskeard is one of those I like best. Much of the town's good looks comes from the prosperity brought by the boom in mining during the 19th century, coupled with the Georgian vision of architect Henry Rice, who designed over a hundred houses in Liskeard for those who had grown rich on rising tin and copper prices. The **Liskeard Museum** (Forrester's Hall, Pike St ℘ 01579 559569 ♦ liskeardmuseum.com) has a small display devoted to the architect, while the arts and heritage centre at **Stuart House** (Barras St ℘ 01579 347347) has produced a Henry Rice Trail leaflet. This house is a real treasure; it was built 400 years before Rice first sat at a drawing board, and

"Much of the town's good looks comes from the prosperity brought by the boom in mining during the 19th century."

sheltered Charles I for a week during the Civil War. A couple of rooms are devoted to Civil War exhibits, but overall there's a warm and intimate feeling about the granite-and-timber structure, overlooking a courtyard garden filled with clipped box and roses. This feeling stems, I'm sure, from the way the house is made available to the community. You can pop in for tea and homemade cake (a donation is requested) or sit in the garden; there are lunchtime concerts and evening lectures, craft fairs and demonstrations.

In Stuart House and the museum, as well as elsewhere in Liskeard's public buildings, are some unusually beautiful doorknobs, made of blue glass. These are the work of local craftsman Liam Carey of **Merlin Glass** (Barn St ✆ 07877 230507 🔗 merlinglass.co.uk), whose workshop can be visited by appointment. The shop is like a gallery with its showcases of these jewel-like glass knobs.

Part of Liskeard's charm is the high number of small, independent shops, like Liam's, which make it such an enjoyable place for pottering. The flea-market-style shops and studios in the old cattle market further add to the attraction. Liskeard's agricultural show, held in July, and prime stock show in October remain key events on the calendar and continue to uphold the town's identity as an important centre for livestock sales.

¶¶ FOOD & DRINK

The Himalayan Spice 4 Castle St PL14 3AU ✆ 01579 208040 🔗 thehimalayanspice.com ☺ eves only. Friendly service and delicious food on a Nepalese theme, cooked from scratch in a town where Slow Food generally means a long queue at the kebab house.

The award-winning Slow Travel series from Bradt Guides

Over 20 regional guides across Britain.
See the full list at bradtguides.com/slowtravel.

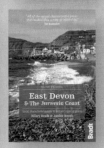
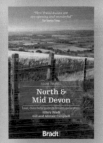

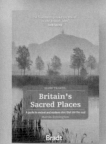

THE FOWEY VALLEY & THE CORNISH ALPS

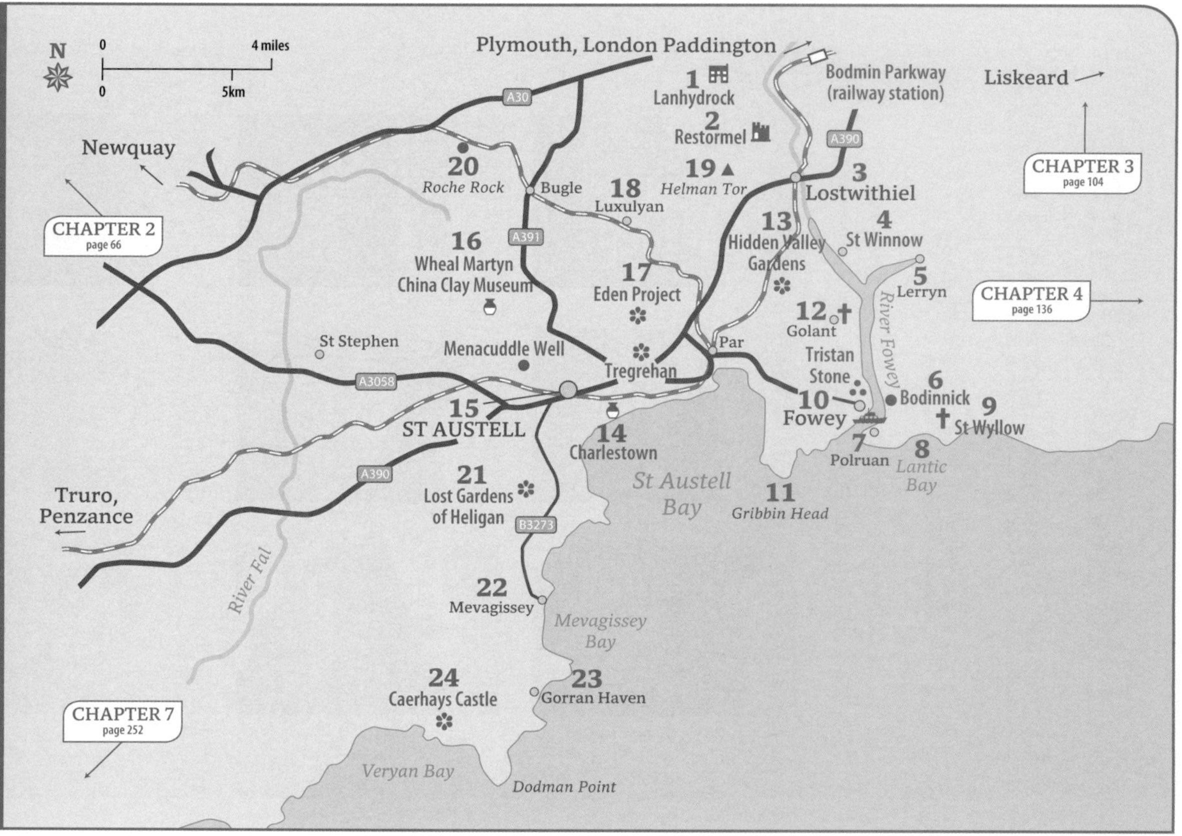

N
0
4 miles
0
5km
Plymouth, London Paddington
1
Lanhydrock
2
Restormel
Bodmin Parkway
(railway station)
Liskeard
A30
A390
Newquay
20
Roche Rock
Bugle
18
Luxulyan
19
Helman Tor
3
Lostwithiel
CHAPTER 3
page 104
CHAPTER 2
page 66
16
Wheal Martyn
China Clay Museum
A391
13
Hidden Valley
Gardens
4
St Winnow
17
Eden Project
5
Lerryn
CHAPTER 4
page 136
12
Golant
River Fowey
St Stephen
Menacuddle Well
Tregrehan
Par
Tristan
Stone
A3058
15
ST AUSTELL
6
Bodinnick
10
Fowey
9
St Wyllow
14
Charlestown
7
Polruan
8
Lantic
Bay
21
Lost Gardens
of Heligan
St Austell
Bay
11
Gribbin Head
Truro,
Penzance
B3273
22
Mevagissey
River Fal
Mevagissey
Bay
24
Caerhays Castle
23
Gorran Haven
CHAPTER 7
page 252
Veryan Bay
Dodman Point

5
THE FOWEY VALLEY
& THE CORNISH ALPS

Even by Cornwall's extraordinary standards of contrasts, you would be hard put to find a greater divergence in the landscape than in the few miles that separate the wooded, watery world of **the Fowey**, its towns and villages steeped in medieval history, from the almost lunar landscape of the clay pits above **St Austell**. Slow explorers will relish the individual characters of both – and gardeners (to whom the concept of Slow comes as readily as planting trees, I suspect), will discover here some of the most inventive and creative gardens in Cornwall, enjoying the dendrological delights of **Tregrehan** as much as a dazzling display of summer perennials in the **Hidden Valley Gardens**, or the ambitious **Eden** biomes and magnolia-filled slopes of **Caerhays**.

Industrial heritage is never far from view in Cornwall, but here the exploitation and export of china clay is current and active and still shaping the landscape. Rivers and streams run milky white around St Austell, cargo ships slip through the yachts and pleasure craft at Fowey to load up just out of sight at Carn Point; the conical white spoil heaps from the clay pits grow and change shape on the horizon. **Cornish alps**, indeed!

Researching this chapter gave me some wonderful excuses to take to the water: paddling a canoe up Lerryn Creek, in the wake of **Kenneth Grahame**, riding the little passenger ferries from Polruan to Fowey and Fowey to Mevagissey and swimming in the turquoise sea at Lantic Bay. It also encouraged me to start rereading **Daphne du Maurier**, whose lyrical descriptions of the Cornish coast around Fowey had first enthralled me as a teenager. Walking in her footsteps above the beach at Polridmouth or gazing across the water to Bodinnick from the chain ferry animated my reading, and gave added allure to an already romantic landscape. The great thing about this stretch of the Cornish coast and estuary is that you don't need your own yacht to experience the thrill of seeing the land from the magically altered perspective of the sea. Returning to Fowey on the ferry from Mevagissey, I scanned the trees behind the red-and-white stripes of the Gribbin Daymark, hoping to glimpse the rooftops of Menabilly, the house that had been the inspiration for Manderley in *Rebecca*. Then, like the novelist, cruising around the coast on *Ysdragil*, I saw 'the clay-hills hard and white on the western skyline. Then the slope of the Gribbin peninsula … bracken-covered, green, and beyond it, hull-down between its coverage of trees, two chimney tops and the grey roof of Menabilly.'

GETTING AROUND

The A390 and A391 converge on St Austell, linking the town to Cornwall's principal arteries, the A38 and the A30, and Lostwithiel and Bodmin along the way. Fowey, too is easily reached by road from Lostwithiel or St Austell (although it is unwise to even think of driving a car into its narrow, twisting streets). But east of the River Fowey, a tangle of tiny country lanes with desperately steep inclines make navigation a bit of an adventure; the six miles to Polruan from Lostwithiel could easily become 20 without a map. Similar adventures await those who venture into the cat's cradle of lanes south of Mevagissey, too.

TRAINS

Lostwithiel, Par and St Austell all lie on the **main line** from Paddington to Penzance and a **branch line** from Par runs northwest to Newquay, passing through the lovely Luxulyan Valley and, conveniently for walkers and cyclists, stopping at Luxulyan; Bugle and Roche are the next stops, more used by clay-industry commuters than visitors, but handy for cyclists accessing the Clay Trails or looking for the strangest of medieval hermitages at Roche.

BUSES

The narrowness and steepness of the lanes around the Fowey estuary are impossible for buses to navigate, especially on the east bank, which keeps the local taxi cabs busy. On the west bank, even the simple journey north from Fowey to Lostwithiel means heading west first, and changing buses at Par. Around St Austell, **buses run regularly** to the major attractions: Eden Project, Wheal Martyn, Mevagissey and

Heligan, though beyond Gorran Haven the narrow, twisting lanes mean no buses, making Caerhays particularly inaccessible unless arriving by car or bike. For more information see *⏣* firstbus.co.uk/cornwall.

WALKING

The southerly section of the **Saints' Way** bifurcates just north of Helman Tor before meeting up again at Fowey. Both routes offer lovely inland walking through woods and hilly farmland and form part of the circular walk described on page 196 around Gribbin Head. The western route just skirts the lower end of the wooded Luxulyan Valley (page 208), which offers intriguing glimpses of an industrial past, including Treffry's soaring viaduct. The train service from Par to Newquay, stopping in Luxulyan, is an invaluable service for walkers exploring these parts.

The best river and seaside walks are **well-beaten paths** – follow the Fowey from Lanhydrock to Lostwithiel or cross the river twice by ferry to complete the famous **Hall Walk** that skirts the river from Bodinnick to Polruan; a longer stride over the cliffs is rewarded by the sublime expanse of Lantic Bay at your feet.

FERRIES

There are no bridges across the Fowey below Lostwithiel, but a small eight-car ferry operates **between Fowey and Bodinnick** all year round. Queues for the ferry in the summer holidays are inevitable. The passenger ferry **between Polruan and Fowey** is a year-round service too; there are extra charges for dogs and bikes. Details of both services can be found at *⏣* ctomsandson.co.uk. During the summer months a passenger ferry crosses St Austell Bay **between Mevagissey and Fowey**, four or five times a day, depending on the weather (*⏣* mevagissey-ferries.co.uk).

CYCLING

A terrific section of the **Sustrans NCN Route 3** (the Cornish Way) passes through Caerhays, Mevagisssey, St Austell and Bugle and continues to Bodmin and Bude. Expect hills and clifftop views, plunging woods and white clay mountains. At St Austell, the route connects with the **Clay Trails**, offering off-road routes to Pentewan, Wheal Martyn China Clay Museum and the Eden Project (*⏣* claytrails.co.uk). The trails – particularly around Wheal Martyn – generally involve long inclines through spectacular wild country dramatically altered by industry:

TOURIST INFORMATION

Fowey 5 South St, PL23 1AR ✆ 01726 833616 ⟨⟩ fowey.co.uk
Lostwithiel Community Centre, Liddicoat Rd, PL22 0HA ✆ 01208 872207
⟨⟩ lostwithiel.org.uk
Mevagissey Hurley Books, 3 Jetty St, PL26 6UH ✆ 01726 842200 ⊙ closed Sun
St Austell By Pass Service Station, Southbourne Rd, PL25 4RS ✆ 01726 879500
⟨⟩ staustellbay.co.uk. Hidden behind the Texaco garage on the Liskeard road out of town,
this is convenient for drivers and cyclists on the Sustrans NCN Route 3 (the Cornish Way). A
second visitor information centre is in St Austell railway station.

clay pits, emerald pools and white spoil heaps, ruined chimneys and
engine houses line the trails which were originally constructed for the
transportation of clay.

 CYCLE HIRE

Freedom-e-Bikes 30 Beach Rd, Carlyon Bay PL25 3PH ✆ 07870 688646 ⟨⟩ freedom-e-
bike-hire.business.site. AJ's café-bar offers electric bike hire; local delivery offered.
Pentewan Valley Cycle Hire 1 West End, Pentewan PL26 6BX ✆ 01726 844242
⟨⟩ pentewanvalleycyclehire.co.uk ⊙ Easter–end Sep. Right on the Sustrans NCN Route 3
(the Cornish Way) and the gentle Pentewan section of the Clay Trails; bikes can be hired for
upwards of half a day.

THE FOWEY VALLEY

The River Fowey rises high on Bodmin Moor, in the shadow of Brown
Willy, trickling through impenetrably marshy moorland before gathering
pace in deep, wooded valleys on the southern fringes of the moor. Two
or three miles short of Bodmin the green river valley takes a southerly
turn, and overlooked by the grand old estates of Lanhydrock and the
ruins of Restormel Castle, winds on to Lostwithiel, the medieval capital
of Cornwall. Below Lostwithiel's ancient bridge the river becomes tidal,
and the last six miles to the sea are sheltered by a glorious landscape
of wooded hills and creeks, giving way to the purposeful movement
of china clay by rail and ship above the yacht-strewn haven that lies
between busy, popular Fowey and quieter, more self-contained Polruan.
There's plenty of scope for Slow exploration here: the narrow streets
of Lostwithiel, Fowey and Polruan make pottering a pleasure and the

villages that lie in between, hidden among the woods and deep lanes, have a largely unselfconscious charm, unusual in Cornwall. The walking is superb, both above and below Lostwithiel, with a good network of well-marked footpaths on both sides of the river, while some of the most enjoyable canoeing in Cornwall is to be found in the tidal creeks below St Winnow.

This is the part of Cornwall that Daphne du Maurier loved with a passion and described so eloquently in her novels; and other writers such as Sir Arthur Quiller-Couch and Kenneth Grahame drew inspiration from the woods and water, too. On the beach at Readymoney Cove I saw a teenager, her iPod discarded, deeply immersed in *Rebecca*; and what better place than the riverbank in Lerryn to introduce the younger members of the family to Ratty, Mole and Toad?

1 LANHYDROCK
Bodmin PL30 5AD ℰ 01208 265950; National Trust

Plenty of wow factor here, from the moment the pinnacled gatehouse comes into view, amid a great sweeping roll of parkland, bisected by a long avenue of beeches. More wows as you look up through the formal gardens to the grand house, the church on the rising slopes behind and – if you visit in spring – the clouds of pink, red and creamy blossoms as hundreds of magnolias, camellias and rhododendrons erupt into bloom in the woodland garden. The formal gardens are an exercise in Victorian perfection: box-framed beds packed with a seasonal succession of bright bulbs and annuals, clipped yews and lawns so trim they might

"Plenty of wow factor here, from the moment the pinnacled gatehouse comes into view, amid a great sweeping roll of parkland."

have been laid by a carpet-fitter. Inside the house, it's a bit like walking into the film-set for *Downton Abbey*: no fewer than 50 rooms are open to the public, furnished as they would have been in Lanhydrock's late Victorian heyday; the dining room is laid for dinner; the vast kitchens below reveal the colossal efforts of the 20 kitchen staff to keep the entire household fed and watered; and upstairs and well out of earshot, the nursery wing (designed to accommodate ten children and their nannies) and attics full of toys are as separate as the servants' quarters. Once when I visited, it was just before Christmas; a magic lantern show was in progress in the library and a wing-collared butler served me a tipple of mulled apple juice. All muddy from a wintry walk along the Fowey, I felt slightly underdressed.

Lanhydrock is without doubt a jewel in the National Trust's Cornish crown, but it is a museum rather than a family home; great wealth does not guarantee heirs. The memorial plaques in the church tell the sad story of the last generation of the Agar-Robartes who made Lanhydrock great: the toll taken by World War I, and the last two sisters who died unmarried and childless. The estate came into the care and management of the National Trust in 1953. The church warden, who showed me how the altar had curiously migrated from the north to the east aisle, was also able to fill me in on the chequered history of the house and gardens. John Robartes, a wealthy merchant from Truro, built the original house in the mid-17th century on the site of a Benedictine priory. Four wings met at the gatehouse from which an avenue of sycamores unfurled towards the Fowey (a couple still survive). A century later, the east wing was demolished, leaving the gatehouse to stand alone, but opening up the views over the landscaped grounds. Fast-forward another century to 1857 and the high priest of the Gothic Revival, George Gilbert Scott, was busily employed, designing additions to the house which re-incorporated the gatehouse into the new garden walls. But scarcely was his work finished when, in 1881, fire destroyed everything bar the north wing, entrance porch and gatehouse, and the job of rebuilding fell to a pupil of Scott's, Richard Coad. Which is what you see today. After the fire, the layout was retained but the latest in gadgetry and creature comforts appeared, including an electric lift for taking trunks upstairs, a capacious bathroom, central heating and electric light.

"John Robartes, a merchant from Truro, built the original house in the mid-17th century on the site of a Benedictine priory."

During the winter months most of the house is closed, except on special opening days, but there's always a good log fire burning in the Servants' Hall café, a good pit stop if you've been exploring the woodland gardens (which remain open) and walks along the Fowey. The woods here take some beating: pass through the wooden gate (to your left as you approach the Servants' Hall) and the world suddenly changes. The Great Wood is criss-crossed with paths, each so inviting it's hard to know which way to turn, though the broad track that runs downhill to the river, known as the Lady's Walk, is perhaps the most popular –

LANHYDROCK TO RESTORMEL CASTLE ON FOOT

The train service between Lostwithiel and Bodmin Parkway is the key to making this a fine, car-free day's walking. (It's only seven miles, but hours can be spent exploring the house and gardens at Lanhydrock, and there's a tempting diversion to the Duchy Nursery for refreshment, too.) The footpath to Lanhydrock starts right by Bodmin Parkway and tracks the Fowey as far as the great beech avenue that leads to Lanhydrock House, a mile distant. Follow the Lady Walk through the Great Wood, taking the right-hand path at the fork and exit, turning right on to the lane. After 100 yards, a left turn indicates the footpath. Turn right across a stream, crossing the fields and reed beds leading to the waterworks. A quiet lane runs to Restormel Castle, passing the handsomely restored Duchy headquarters. Continue to Lostwithiel, where there are lots of possibilities for refreshment (or follow the signs to the Duchy Nursery and café). Trains from Lostwithiel back to Bodmin Parkway leave roughly every hour.

partly because it's the start of a lovely walk that takes in a stretch of the Fowey and brings you back to the house via the long beech avenue. In May, bluebells carpet the woodland floor beneath an emerging canopy of beech, oak and ash. And if you take one of the less-travelled paths, you'll discover an orchard of Britain's rarest tree, the Plymouth pear, established here, far from the danger of cross pollination, as part of a rare species recovery programme.

2 RESTORMEL CASTLE

Lostwithiel PL22 0EE ✆ 01208 872687 ⏱ Apr–Oct; English Heritage

His father, Richard, Earl of Cornwall, had built castles at Launceston and Tintagel, but young Edmund had his eye on his father's latest acquisition: a motte and bailey hunting lodge overlooking a deer park and close to a little town, quaintly called 'The Place at the Tail End of the Woodland' (Lostwithiel in Cornish) that was rapidly prospering on tin, with its own port on the Fowey. Edmund's new castle, begun in 1271, was a circular edifice, built to impress. In fact it would have been dazzling: the high walls built of slate were rendered and limewashed white. Inside, there was even piped water. Edmund died in 1300, but Lostwithiel's glory years as a medieval Klondike City were already numbered; tinning activity upriver was causing the river to silt up, and by 1400 the port was available to only the flattest-bottomed craft. The

castle was stripped and abandoned after the death of the Duchy's first duke, the Black Prince, and by the time of the Civil War it was already a ruin. Today, because there are so few vantage points from which the castle is visible, it's easy to visit Lostwithiel or even walk the path that skirts the hill on which it stands without a glimpse, but the walls still stand – and from their battlemented heights the views over the Fowey Valley are sublime.

3 LOSTWITHIEL

It's not difficult to be seduced by Lostwithiel. History oozes from its medieval stones and the river flows prettily beside Brunel's handsomely restored railway-carriage works (now flats and offices) and past invitingly grassy picnic places where you can dabble your toes in the shallows. Pottering comes easily here: antique and bric-a-brac shops, delis and cafés throng the main street; there's a free museum, dedicated to the town's far-from-dull history; and a cluster of characterful pubs serve locally produced food, ciders and ales.

But you'd miss an awful lot without some inkling of Lostwithiel's status and importance in the 13th and 14th centuries, and its Civil War history. The best place to start is at the **medieval bridge**, which has spanned the Fowey for seven centuries. The Norman foundations of the first crossing are now buried under the road on the west side of the river, so what you see are 13th- and 14th-century arched additions, necessitated by a rapidly silting river altering its course.

The **Old Duchy Palace**, on the corner of Fore Street and Quay Street, is instantly recognisable by its solid buttresses and Gothic arched windows, suggestive of medieval ecclesiastical architecture. This, however, was no church. The original building, constructed around 1292 – just as the paint was drying on the walls of Restormel Castle – was a vast administrative centre for the tin industry, for the Duchy and for Cornwall. Tin was brought here to be assayed, weighed and stamped; licences were granted for sale and export; stannary courts administered tin-related justice, the county court covered the rest; and wrongdoers were held in its prison. The oldest recorded strongroom for business activity was contained within its walls too, together with counting rooms – in effect, a prototype bank. In total, the complex covered two

◀ **1** Restormel Castle. **2** The kitchens at Lanhydrock. **3** Lerryn.

acres, overlooking the busy port. Like Restormel Castle, however, its glory was transient, ironically curtailed by the same industry that had created its wealth and prestige. Silt washed down by tinning activity blocked the port and Fowey, at the mouth of the river, prospered instead. By Elizabethan times, new wealth from tanneries rescued the sagging building, but it had lost much of its status. In 1644 some of the bloodiest and most destructive fighting during the Civil War took place in Lostwithiel, where a besieged Parliamentarian army fell to Royalist forces. The Duchy Palace was burned and in the slow reconstruction of the town, parts were dismantled to make way for new buildings in which much of the old stone was recycled. So although substantial, the building left standing today is just a fraction of the old palace, and though in the safe hands of the Duchy, which oversaw a meticulous restoration in 2013, it has yet to find a new purpose.

The free **museum** on Fore Street (⊘ **lostwithielmuseum.org** ⊙ Apr–Oct Mon–Sat) is housed in the Georgian corn exchange and run by local historians. Betjeman is reported to have said that there is history in every stone in Lostwithiel and his words are borne out here with a fascinating series of exhibits that runs into the old jail at the back of the building. One of the star exhibits though, pre-dates the town's glory days under Edmund. It's a small, gilded figure of Christ, dating from the late 12th century, found in a field near the town in 1894 and then lost again. It turned up exactly 100 years later, hidden in a desk. The museum organises **guided walks** around the town every Wednesday between April and September at 11.00, starting from the community centre, in the park just off Liddicoat Road.

"Betjeman is reported to have said that there is history in every stone in Lostwithiel."

The tower of **St Bartholomew's**, the parish church, was probably built in Edmund's time, and the Black Prince would have seen the nave under construction, during his periods of residence at Restormel in 1353 and 1365. (The Breton-style octagonal spire which neatly tops off the tower was added at the same time.) But like the palace, it suffered at the hands of the occupying army during the Civil War, when it was used as a garrison and stables. Records of 1644 tell of a horse christened at the font by Parliamentarian troops, who jeeringly called it 'Charlie' and of a barrel of gunpowder that was deliberately exploded beneath Royalist prisoners, cowering in the belfry.

It seems appropriate that a town with so much ancient history should have become the 'antiques capital' of Cornwall, and there's a bit of a buzz when the popular **antiques market**, held in the community centre, comes to town ($\mathscr{O}$ lostwithiel.org.uk).

A bit of a buzz was also generated when plans to give new purpose to the old Lostwithiel golf course and adjoining former dairy farm were submitted in 2019, and local feelings have run high in recent times. Sir Tim Smit, the man behind the Eden Project and the Lost Gardens of Heligan, bought both farm and golf course a few years ago, and created **Gillyflower Farm** ($\mathscr{O}$ gillyflowerfarm.com), replanting much of the land with heritage orchards, an experimental market garden, wildflower meadows and an environmentally friendly nine-hole golf course, where each of the nine holes is surrounded by 'a unique crop of edible or wildlife encouraging plants'. Nothing too controversial about that; it was the application to construct a residential educational centre where innovation and sustainability in growing edible plants (agronomy and horticulture) could be practised and taught, that caused the upset. Local objectors claimed it would damage rather than support the local economy and landscape. It's not clear at the time of writing what the outcome will be, but Smit's passion and determination have yet to see him fail in something he sets his mind to.

¶¶ FOOD & DRINK

Lostwithiel has a name for promoting local food and drink producers and counts as one of the top **Slow Food** destinations in Cornwall. The food shops – butcher, baker, deli – are outstandingly good and on the fourth Saturday of each month the Cornish Guild of Smallholders runs a terrific local produce market in the scout hut (in the main car park).

Bellamama Deli 24 Fore St, PL22 0BL $\mathscr{O}$ 01208 872524 $\mathscr{O}$ bellamama.biz. A great spot to pick up picnic items or – if it's free – perch in the window seat to consume your coffee and buns.

Canoeing down the River Fowey

Lostwithiel is not a place to hurry through and that suited my friend Hugh and me, because we were planning to leave in a canoe, on the outgoing tide. By the time we were done exploring the medieval backstreets and alleyways, it was clear that the tide had been ebbing for some time, which was good, but not having canoed the river before, we had no degree of certainty about how long it would take to paddle ourselves clear of the muddy junction with Penpol Creek, three or four miles downstream and into the broader, deeper waters of the Fowey below Golant.

But it was a bright October morning and with the river flowing fast and shallow we put in on the slipway by the gateway to Coulson Park, with hopes that we would not find ourselves stranded on a mudbank, halfway to Fowey. The current took us gently out of the town and within minutes we were gliding past the rushy margins of **Madderly Moor** on our left and **Shirehall Moor** to the right: saltmarsh vegetation, stalked by herons and egrets. The water was very shallow now, and our paddles brushed the shingly riverbed more often than was comforting. And, as the morning grew warmer and the tower of **St Winnow** appeared through the trees, the mid-river channel we were following dwindled to a winding trickle; on either side the receding tide had exposed huge mudbanks, making landfall impossible.

"We were advancing at the pace of a slow shuffle, but it was none the less magical."

From time to time I would hop out and push the canoe along, the water barely covering my ankles. It was hardly the stuff of epic canoe journeys, and we were advancing at the pace of a slow shuffle, but it was none the less magical. Waders and gulls poking about at the muddy shoreline barely glanced at us, the oak woods as we approached **Lerryn Creek** were the colour of tawny marmalade, and a slow locomotive pulling a seemingly endless string of trucks overtook us on the western bank. Our mid-river trickle forked between great mudbanks; we took a guess and paddled on, heartened by the deepening water and the rooftops of **Golant**, rising on the hillside ahead.

The tidal outflow had reached its lowest point as we finally emerged into deep water, rounded a bend and were then suddenly dwarfed by a container ship; the train that had just passed, which had been carrying china clay, was unloading its freight. We passed, slightly awestruck by the sudden industrialisation of the landscape, and then it was behind us and we were passing between yachts at their moorings and **Fowey** was just ahead … and so we landed, leaving the canoe in the car park by the chain ferry and, carrying the paddles, set off to explore the narrow streets of Fowey on foot.

We were thinking of returning to Lostwithiel by bus to collect the car, but spotted an empty table in Sam's (page 195) and gave in to a late lunch. It turned out to be one of those lingering meals you don't want to end. Fish was on our plates and we enjoyed a conversation with the cook, who came and sat with us for a while and talked about their new venture on the beach at Polkerris. By the time we had finished, it was clear the tide was rushing back upstream and all thoughts of catching a bus evaporated. This was a different river! Swept along by the tide, we only needed the paddles to steer, weaving our way back through the yachts and past the china clay dock; both ship and train had vanished. Lerryn Creek was rapidly approaching and after a minute's discussion we swung right, allowing ourselves to be propelled into the creek, between woods, muddily undercut by the water. For a mile we paddled and stalled and paddled, travelling as slowly as possible, to allow time for the swelling tide to carry us through the woods as far as Lerryn. We had wet feet for the last 50 yards and left the canoe on the grass above the landing beach for collection the following day. The three-mile walk back to Lostwithiel along narrow, hedged lanes was filled with dusky birdsong all the way.

⚓ CANOE HIRE

Encounter Cornwall Golant PL23 1LN ✆ 01726 832451 ⌂ encountercornwall.com. Guided canoe trips on the Fowey plus SUP and canoe hire for those with recent experience of independent paddleboarding or kayaking. They also offer lessons for novices.
Fowey River Hire The Alcove, 47 Fore St, Fowey PL23 1AJ ✆ 01726 833627 ⌂ foweyriverhire.co.uk. Experienced paddlers can hire a kayak, SUP or boat here for independent days or half-days out on the river. Accompanied trips for the less experienced are available too.

4 ST WINNOW

A rural backwater hidden among the woods and cider orchards on the east bank of the Fowey, St Winnow is almost too lovely to be true. There's too little of it to be spoiled, just a tiny rough-and-ready farm campsite in an orchard you can sail or paddle to with your tent. There's a shed full of old tractors and agricultural memorabilia, calling itself a museum; tea and cakes, locally made sausages and bacon are sold from Angie's caravan; and an ancient church stands on the riverbank. The narrow lane that ends at the farm is not easy to negotiate by car; far better to arrive on foot or by bike, or by canoe, when the tide is high enough to land.

TIVOLI GARDENS REVISITED

The famous Tivoli gardens in Copenhagen were the inspiration for a local china clay millionaire, Frank Parkyn, to create his own pleasure park just outside Lerryn, the village where he was born. Work began in 1920 and soon a delightful public space emerged from the hitherto inaccessible woodland above the creek, offering shaded walks and fountains, a plunge pool, arcade and small bandstand which in its heyday provided a base for the annual Fowey regatta, last held in 1968. The site began to revert to nature in the 1980s and now is largely ignored; visited only by intrepid explorers with a sense of adventure and good imagination. Finding your way in is far from easy, but if you use the What3words app, search for drips.helm.lordship, which will take you to a point of entrance. Alternatively, search for 'Lerryn River and Tivoli Lost Gardens' on the iWalk Cornwall app.

5 LERRYN

⋏ Lombard Farm, Mixtow (page 419)

Straddling the uppermost reach of Lerryn Creek, where the diminishing water is crossed by a Tudor bridge – and stepping stones at low tide – Lerryn is one of those magical places that those in the know hug quietly to themselves in the hope that it will always stay the same. Kenneth Grahame loved Fowey and often visited Lerryn by water; it's nice to think that the creek is reflected in the leafy, watery world of *The Wind in the Willows*. (Ethy Manor, hidden in the woods above the village, some like to say, could have been Grahame's inspiration for Toad Hall.) This is a blissful place for children, with plenty of safe opportunities for messing about at the water's edge, or in boats or canoes, though the tidal ebb and flow is not to be messed with.

Although it swells with holidaymakers in the summer, the village is a real community, with a school, top-notch shop and pub. Around Christmas, it dons fancy dress for the annual Seagull Race. Seagulls (lest your imagination be taking flight in the wrong direction) are a spluttery type of low-power outboard motor; lashed to pretty much anything that floats, the result is a water-borne type of pram race that would set Toad's heart racing.

⁑ FOOD & DRINK

Ship Inn Fore St, PL22 0PT ☎ 01208 872374. A perfect village pub: friendly, beamy and slate-floored, serving a good range of Cornish ales and above-average pub food. Children and dogs are made to feel very welcome.

6 BODINNICK

Daphne du Maurier's name will always be linked with Bodinnick, whose pretty cottages and ancient pub cling to an impossibly steep hill that terminates abruptly on the slipway of the small chain ferry that links the village to Fowey. Ferryside, the big white house with the blue paintwork, built against the cliff face to the right of the slipway, is where the 19-year-old fell in love with this part of Cornwall. She persuaded her parents, who had bought the house for holiday visits, to let her use it as a writer's retreat. Soon after, she wrote in her diary: 'The lights of Polruan and Fowey. Ships anchored, looking up through blackness. The jetties, white with clay. Mysterious shrouded trees, owls hooting, the splash of muffled oars in lumpy water ... All I want is to be at Fowey. Nothing and no one else. This, now, is my life.'

Four years later, in 1932, Major 'Boy' Browning sailed into the Fowey estuary, looking for her. He had read her first novel, *The Loving Spirit*, and fired by her descriptions of the Cornish coast, was determined to meet the woman behind the prose. A few weeks later, they were married – at the lonely church of St Wyllow, high in the hills behind Polruan. Her husband's military career often took her away from Bodinnick, but Ferryside remained their base until 1943, when they moved into the grand house at Menabilly (Manderley in *Rebecca*) on the other side of the Fowey.

Ferryside was restored by her son, Christian Browning, who lives there; the house is not open to the public.

The small chain ferry runs cars, bikes and foot passengers to and from Fowey, all year round. (The alternative is to cross the river at Lostwithiel, six miles upstream.)

THE HALL WALK

Despite being well known and well signposted, this four-mile riverside and creekside walk from Bodinnick to Polruan can be made to feel like an adventure by using the all-year ferries to cross the river. You can start at Fowey, take the chain ferry to Bodinnick then follow the Hall Walk, high above the River Fowey and up the creek known as Pont Pill then back on the other side of Pont Pill to Polruan, where the passenger boat takes you back to Fowey. The woods touch the water all along the shore and the path rises and falls, with the odd well-placed seat along the way. Allow yourself three hours, which will leave enough time to make the short (well-signposted) detour to St Wyllow; allow longer if planning to explore Polruan and Fowey.

LEADING TO
SYDNEY HILL &
TINKERS HILL

7 POLRUAN

Polruan looks across the estuary to fashionable Fowey with its packed streets and pubs, smart restaurants and celebrity residents and just seems to shrug, for it has the one thing that Fowey can't have: a picturesque view of Fowey across the water. Polruan's isolation from any main road (it's at least 45 minutes to Fowey on narrow lanes, via Lostwithiel) has given the village a quiet, self-contained character, much appreciated by its resident population of boatbuilders, artists, writers and retired folk and a community spirit that was described with great warmth by the volunteer coastguard I chatted to. While his gaze swept the sea and the estuary below his clifftop vantage point, beside the ruins of the 13th-century **St Saviour's Chapel**, an hour or more passed easily, as he told me of his concern that the volunteer coastguards, while offering an incredibly important service 'might put professional chaps in coastguard stations threatened with closure out of a job'.

We also talked about the community's passionate regard for its heritage. This was something I had already noticed, down

"Polruan has the one thing that Fowey can't have: a picturesque view of Fowey across the water."

at the harbour, where a plaque proudly announces that the Old Coal Wharf had been acquired in 1963 'on the initiative of Polruan people supported by public subscription (and) administered by Polruan Town Trust since 1973'. The 14th-century **blockhouse** has been preserved by local initiative, too. Originally, there had been a similar building on the Fowey side of the estuary (which, with a sad shake of the head, they will tell you in Polruan, was allowed to crumble beyond hope of repair) and chains slung between the two buildings could be raised to prevent pirates or worse still, the French, from entering the harbour.

On another occasion, I was talking to a former resident of Fowey, who explained that Polruan's exceptionally nice character 'was largely due to its high proportion of female residents'. In days gone by, he remarked, widows of sea captains moved from Fowey to Polruan. 'Now,' he added with a twinkle, 'it's the place of choice for Fowey's divorced wives.'

Community spirit is to the fore again on the first Sunday in September, for the annual swim to Fowey and back again (◼ FoweyHarbourSwim),

---

◀ **1** Aerial view over Lantic Bay. **2** The narrow streets and old stone cottages of Polruan.
3 Ferryside in Bodinnick where Daphne du Maurier wrote her first novel.

in support of the local lifeboat; a feat matched by the village primary school, whose brave pupils from years five and six swim the river each July, cheered on by parents and tourists alike.

¶| FOOD & DRINK

There are two cheerful pubs in Polruan, both owned by the St Austell Brewery: the **Lugger** (✆ 01726 870007) next to where the ferry lands is well placed for harbour-watching; the **Russell Inn**, up West Street, is smaller and full of character (✆ 01726 870292 ⌖ russellinn. co.uk). Both serve food and are child- and dog-friendly.

8 LANTIC BAY

This is one of Cornwall's best south-coast beaches, and the effort of getting to it from the Pencarrow car park (♥ SX149513) a mile away ensures it's never overcrowded. A wide horseshoe of pale sand, studded with outcrops of rock, and turquoise sea is the reward for those prepared to walk the sloping fields and plunging final descent. At low tide, a succession of smaller, sandy coves are revealed towards Polruan, often visited by boating families out of Fowey. The cove is known, however, for its occasional rip currents, and great care should be taken if you're contemplating a swim. From Polruan, the 1½ miles of clifftop walking eastwards to here gets choice views all the way.

9 ST WYLLOW
♥ SX145515

Restored with no loss of character in the 19th century, the tall-towered church at Lanteglos-by-Fowey is buried quietly among the woods and fields, high above Polruan. Daphne du Maurier was married here and it's as romantic and lonely a spot as a novelist could wish for – but a long walk for the faithful of Polruan and the surrounding hamlets (though handy for the farm next door). Inside, the woodwork is particularly special and the Tudor bench-ends, showing fish and faces, birds and animals, are among Cornwall's finest, which is saying something.

10 FOWEY
🏠 **Fowey Hall Hotel** (page 419), **The Dwelling House at Fowey** (page 419), **Foye Old Exchange** (page 419)

The steep, narrow streets lined with jostling cottages, shops, cafés, pubs and restaurants are great fun to explore, though you may find

LITERARY FOWEY

Fowey seems to exercise a particular hold over writers, in the same way that St Ives continues to draw artists. Daphne du Maurier is the most famous of these, but the town also celebrates the work of Sir Arthur Quiller-Couch, poet, novelist, critic and likeable eccentric who lived on the opposite shore, just above Bodinnick. It was 'Q', as he styled himself, who penned the following memorable ditty:

Oh the harbour of Fowey
Is a beautiful spot
And it's there I enjowey
To sail in a yot;
Or to race in a yacht
Round a mark or a buoy –
Such a beautiful spacht
Is the harbour of Fuoy!

… leaving readers no excuse for mispronouncing the name of his adopted home town.

The **Fowey Festival of Arts and Literature** (⊘ foweyfestival.com), held each May since its inception in 1997, has gone through several changes of direction and scale, and now encompasses a week of films, exhibitions, guided walks, boat trips, and an Art and Secret Gardens Trail.

yourself flattened against a wall each time a car attempts to squeeze past. Tantalising views of the glittering estuary are glimpsed through tiny passages, like windows on to the busy river. Enjoying Fowey from the water is an altogether different experience; in the early morning, for instance, when mist still hangs over the river or at dusk, with lights glimmering, the town rises enchantingly from the shore.

Like Falmouth, at the mouth of the next river to the west, Fowey's waters are deep and wide, allowing heavy shipping passage for a mile or so upriver, where they lurk unseen from the town. But whereas on the Fal the container ships are merely heading to deep-water anchorage, on the Fowey they are heading to meet the china clay train at Carn Point dock. The incongruous mixture of huge freighters, pleasure boats and ferries is one of the special features of taking in the scenery from Fowey's waterfront: there's such a mixture of commercial and leisure activity to watch. Fowey's architecture is equally fascinating: by turn Elizabethan, Edwardian, Georgian and Victorian, reflecting the non-stop development of the port from medieval times as it gradually took over from Lostwithiel, right up to the present day. The long and colourful history of Fowey is told in the **museum** in the town hall (⊘ fowey.co.uk ⊙ Easter–mid-Oct Mon–Fri), full to bursting with model ships, nautical memorabilia and other curiosities, such as the contents of a medieval 'garderobe' (or toilet), of particular fascination to social anthropologists investigating the diet of Fowey, c1400. Children obsessed with pirates will be impressed by the exhibits relating to the 'Fowey Gallants', a band of privateers licensed to attack French shipping in the Channel during the Hundred Years War, who got rather above themselves and saw any ship, friend or foe, as fair game. Privateers usually ended up as an embarrassment to those who had granted their licences in the first place and this lot of pirates was no exception. They were eventually tricked into a trap at Lostwithiel and several hangings took place to make the point. Nevertheless, you'll still see plenty of Fowey Gallants on the water today – it's the name of the local sailing club.

When you look across the water to Fowey, two buildings stand out, high on the hillside above the lesser rooftops: the church of **St Finbarrus** and behind it, the grey tower and castellated walls of **Place House**, home of the Treffry family since the 13th century. Sadly, it's not the original building: the house was rebuilt in the first half of the 19th century to suit the grandiose taste of mining tycoon Joseph Treffry. The architectural historian Nikolaus Pevsner described it as 'elephantine'; a little harsh,

JOSEPH TREFFRY

The Treffrys have stamped their name indelibly on Fowey's history and the surrounding landscape. In 1457, when the French broke through the defences at the mouth of the harbour and ransacked Fowey, Place House was the prize they were denied thanks to the efforts of Elizabeth Treffry, who organised her household to repel the invaders by pouring molten lead, collected from the roof, onto the heads of the French. But it was Joseph Treffry, born three centuries later, who claims the greatest attention. Nicknamed the King of mid-Cornwall, he built a mining empire that encompassed the harbours he built at Newquay and Par, confronting engineering problems that even Brunel was reluctant to address. Copper, tin, granite and clay from his mines were funnelled through railways conceived and built by Treffry – and water, so necessary to the industry, was channelled through miles of leats, including one that ran over the ten-arch Treffry Viaduct in the Luxulyan Valley.

perhaps. It's not open to the public, as the Treffrys, who value their privacy, still live in it.

Readymoney Cove begins where the town ends, so it's a predictably busy little beach, but nonetheless perfect for paddling tired feet if walking the hilly peninsula. Sheltered by the encircling wooded hills that rise above, it faces east – great for breakfast on the beach with the sun rising behind Polruan on the far shore of the estuary. **St Catherine's Castle**, on the rocky headland above the beach, was built around 1530 at an early stage of Henry VIII's plan to boost coastal defences against French invasion. (Pendennis and St Mawes, built a decade later, seem much more sophisticated by comparison.)

¶¶ FOOD & DRINK

Fowey is packed with places to eat and drink; the ones with good views of the harbour get very busy in the summer.

The Dwelling House 6 Fore St, PL23 1AQ ✆ 01726 833662. An elegant Georgian merchant's house – beautifully furnished inside and with a delightful courtyard garden at the back. You'll not find a better cup of tea (there are dozens to choose from) or a more perfect bacon roll (featuring bacon from Kittows) in Fowey. Bread, savouries and cream teas all homemade with organic, local produce.

Kittows Deli South St, PL23 1AR ✆ 01726 832639 ♂ kittowsfowey.co.uk. Something of a legend in these parts – wonderful bacon, sausages, scotch eggs and breads.

The Lifebuoy 8 Lostwithiel St, PL23 1BD ✆ 07715 075869. A tiny café with a nice, old-fashioned feel that does spectacularly good breakfasts. Everything on the menu comes from named, local suppliers. The fish fingers are homemade and best appreciated in the Lifebuoy's signature dish, the fish-finger butty.

Pinky Murphy's Café 19 North St, PL23 1DB ✆ 01726 832512 ♂ pinkymurphys.co.uk. Inside, it's all colourful, mismatched furniture and quirky displays of seaside retrobilia; upstairs squashy sofas, newspapers and magazines – and a log burner. The menu is big on soups, smoothies and 'fatboy' hot chocolates; just the thing after a morning on the river.

Sam's 20 Fore St, PL23 1AQ ✆ 01726 832273 ♂ samscornwall.co.uk. Specialises in local seafood, caught in the morning and dished up at lunchtime. There's a big choice of homemade burgers too. It's much loved by locals and, with a no-bookings policy, the queues in the summer can be daunting.

Ship Inn Trafalgar Sq, PL23 1AZ ✆ 01726 832230 ♂ shipfowey.co.uk. The long history of this pub, built in 1570 by John Rashleigh, is displayed on the walls beside the open fire and oak panelling. It's now a St Austell Brewery pub, with a good seafood menu.

11 AROUND GRIBBIN HEAD

A demanding circular walk of 6½ miles, starting and finishing in **Readymoney Cove**, takes in the cove and beach house immortalised in Daphne du Maurier's *Rebecca*, the 84-foot-tall red-and-white-striped Gribbin Daymark, a choice of delicious pit stops on Polkerris Beach and the last two miles of the Saints' Way.

The first mile and a bit to **Polridmouth ('Pridmouth') Cove** follows the clifftop coast path before descending steeply through woods to a sandy beach, separated from an ornamental lake by a raised walkway. The lake is the lowest of three created during World War II as a decoy to the gathering military activity in Fowey harbour during preparations for D-Day: the US 29th Division were loading ammunition for the Omaha Beach landing and lights were floated on the lake to distract approaching enemy aircraft. Out of sight, among the trees is **Menabilly**, the seat of the Rashleigh family since the 16th century. Daphne du Maurier lived in the house for the last 25 years of her life, enthralled by the secret spot which she had transformed, years before living there, into Manderley.

The coast path swings back up the cliff towards the **Daymark**, which is open on Sundays throughout the summer. The views from the foot of the stripy tower are impressive enough, but if you climb to the top, the views over inland Cornwall as far as Bodmin and the Tamar Valley to the east are outstanding. It was a Rashleigh of Menabilly who granted the land and materials for the building of a 'very handsome Greco-Gothic square tower', designed to ornament his view as well as contributing to 'the safety of commerce and … the preservation of mariners'. History does not record what the inhabitants of Lanlivery, up near Lostwithiel, thought about the Daymark. For centuries their church tower had been the landmark for ships entering Fowey, and in medieval times an annual coat of whitewash to the south face was paid for by the Crown.

Beyond the tower, the path follows the west-facing cliffs northwards to **Polkerris** with its views from the beach of the docks and sands of Par across St Austell Bay. The Rashleigh Arms ($\mathscr{d}$ therashleighinn.co.uk) is a much-loved pub almost on the beach – the food and ales are excellent. Next door an upmarket café, Sam's on the Beach (an offshoot of Sam's in Fowey; page 195) attracts a youngish crowd, and there's also a third

1 Golant. 2 Gribbin Head. 3 Hidden Valley Gardens. 4 Fowey. ▶

café, selling more conventional beach snacks. The trouble is you can get too comfortable in Polkerris, nicely placed for the afternoon and evening sun, and the walk back over the hills to Readymoney Cove starts with a bit of a climb out of the village to pick up the Saints' Way trail. But the walk back through **Tregaminion Farm**, crossing fields and streams, is lovely and the last stretch along **Love Lane**, which follows an old packhorse route, is downhill and wooded. The iWalk Cornwall app suggests this route too, starting and finishing at Polkerris.

12 GOLANT

An old pilgrim route (now a long-distance footpath), the Saints' Way passes the sequestered church of **St Sampson**, high above the picturesque village of Golant, which hugs the tidal shoreline of the river below (this is the only access point on foot to the west bank of the river between Lostwithiel and Fowey). Legend has it that King Mark married Isolde here; I was transfixed by the exhibition in the church in which the Tristan legend was retold in a series of creative floral arrangements, which thankfully, have been recorded for posterity in photographs. Despite some sympathetic renovation in 1842, the building has hardly been changed since it was consecrated in 1509, the date carved on the arched roof timbers overhead. Three original box pews survive and both pulpit and stalls are clad in old recycled bench-ends.

THE TRISTAN STONE

The tragedy of Tristan and Isolde unfolds between Ireland, Cornwall and Brittany, but much of the action centres around the court of King Mark, who was probably a genuine historical figure – a 6th-century Cornish chief and possible contemporary of Arthur.

If you are approaching Fowey by road, just after the turning to the Bodinnick ferry, a large granite stone appears on the left, inscribed in Latin. The stone was moved here from Castle Dore (a rather self-effacing Iron Age hillfort just above Golant, which has had a long history of association with King Mark).

The stone marks the death of 'Drustanus', a Latinised form of Tristan, and names him as the son of Cunomorus, a Latinised form of Kynvawr, who was identified in the 9th century as Marcus Kynvauwr. There's no proving anything, but if the sad story of Tristan, Isolde and King Mark (so reminiscent of the Arthur-Lancelot-Guinevere love triangle) is the sort of thing you enjoy, then the roadside appeal of the Tristan Stone will be limited, but there are worse places than the mossy churchyard of St Sampson's to mull over the evidence.

Golant is the closest village to the idyllically isolated **Old Sawmill Studios** (⊘ theoldsawmills.co.uk), a residential hideaway that has attracted some heavyweight names from the music industry over the past four decades.

¶¶ FOOD & DRINK

The Fisherman's Arms Fore St, PL23 1LN ⊘ 01726 832453. Golant's much-loved pub is a proper local, unpretentious and welcoming to dogs and children. Traditional pub food, sourced locally wherever possible, includes terrific Sunday roasts. Given the proximity of the recording studios, there's no knowing who you might bump into.

13 HIDDEN VALLEY GARDENS

Treesmill PL24 2TU ⊘ 01208 873225 ⊘ hiddenvalleygardens.co.uk ⊙ late Mar–mid-Oct

Tucked away in a fold of the landscape, below the railway line from Lostwithiel to Par, Peter and Tricia Howard have created a four-acre garden of intimate and intense beauty, filled with a rainbow palette of perennials, which lingers late into the season. It's unusual, in this part of Cornwall, to find a garden that isn't dedicated to spring flowering trees and shrubs; the Howards have done well to establish themselves at the forefront of a new breed of smaller Cornish gardens that really sing throughout the summer and autumn.

AROUND ST AUSTELL & THE CORNISH ALPS

The white peaks and plateaus of the clay spoil heaps can be seen from 40 miles away, and suggest a lunar desert when seen in satellite images. It's a powerful, manmade landscape, crossed by roads and cycle trails where you feel a million miles from the leafy creeks and picturesque coves that decorate the Fowey, just a handful of miles away, or the rich seam of gardens that lie on either side of St Austell.

14 CHARLESTOWN

St Austell was served by several ports in its industrial heyday, but none prettier than Charlestown, named after Charles Rashleigh, who funded the entire project in order to provide the infrastructure to his clay and copper exports. There was a foundry and tin-smelting house as well as dry-stores for clay; the level of activity during building (1790–1810) and after completion must have been phenomenal. It gets distinctly busy these days too: with its film-set looks (and frequent appearances in the *Poldark* TV series), Charlestown has become a sort of open-air museum, thanks to the permanent presence of at least one or two splendid square-riggers, moored in the narrow harbour and the well-preserved terraces of Georgian houses and cottages. In 2018, the harbour was acquired by Tim Smit, the man behind the Eden Project. Smit had already bought the **Shipwreck Treasure Museum** (✆ 01726 69897 ⅋ shipwreckcharlestown.co.uk) in 2016, as a sister attraction to the Lost Gardens of Heligan (page 210). Situated above the Inner Harbour in a former dry store for china clay, the museum concentrates on diving, salvage and rescue stories and exhibits, and you can explore the underground tunnels where clay was stored. Quite what Smit's plans for the photogenic harbour, listed as a World Heritage Site, will involve remain to be seen, but a food festival first held in 2022 looks likely to be repeated and seasonal food-related pop-ups are proving popular. One shopkeeper I spoke to told me she hoped more would be made of the harbour's history and heritage than its TV and film appearances. Despite this I couldn't help grinning to myself at the sight of a gaggle of young men queuing to pose behind a life-sized, stripped-to-the-waist, cut-out figure of Ross Poldark; a hole for the face completed the ridiculously silly picture.

⅋ FOOD & DRINK

Charlestown's prominence on Cornwall's foodie map is largely thanks to **The Longstore** (The Harbour, Charlestown Rd ✆ 01726 68598 ⅋ thelongstore.co.uk). 'Locally sourced from the land and the sea' is what is says on the outside and the inside delivers just that in a friendly, loft-like upstairs restaurant. I've not heard one bad word about the food, service or ambience. The downstairs café and deli, **Short and Strong** (⅋ shortandstrong.co.uk) specialises in Cornish produce.

15 ST AUSTELL

⅄ Court Farm Camping St Stephen (page 419)

St Austell is surrounded by so many good gardens, museums, walks and bike trails that it seems to have forgotten to look after its own identity, which has been a tad squashed by the large modern shopping

1 Charlestown. **2** Menacuddle Well. ▶

centre occupying the heart of the town. Followers of the architect Silvanus Trevail will have a field day though, peering up at sumptuous Victorian façades, and there's been a local sigh of relief that the lovely old **Market House**, dating from 1844, has been given a new lease of life, with a café and small, specialist shops as well as a local produce market on Saturdays.

It's true too, that St Austell is acquiring a slightly different identity as a centre for green technologies, which is partly due to its proximity to the Eden Project but also to the five 'eco-villages', heralded as models of sustainability, which are envisaged to occupy disused clay-mining sites around the town. Detailed plans for the first of these, **West Carclaze Garden Village** (⊘ westcarclaze-gardenvillage.co.uk), unveiled in 2018, proposed 350 new homes – 40% of which were to be classified as 'affordable' in line with Cornwall Council's housing criteria – together with a new school and extensive community facilities including a library, allotments and orchards. The website looks enticing, but the current reality shows a mixed reaction to the development: inevitably there is dispute about what constitutes 'affordable' in an area where wages are typically at the lower end of the scale. The library has been axed and the school opening delayed – although a fine (if temporary) venue was found at the Eden Project for the village's youngest arrivals. Watch this space.

"It's true too, that St Austell is acquiring a slightly different identity as a centre for green technologies."

There's also a determination to make more of the town's beautiful location above the bay and transform old 'Snozzle', as it is affectionately known after a pint too many of Tribute, into a model of green Cornish desirability. This is a three-stranded approach which involves planting trees and wildflower-lined routes on a massive scale to, first of all, visually reinforce the connection of the town to its bay, the landscape and the extraordinary beauty of gardens close by – Heligan, Eden, Tregrehan and Caerhays. The second aim is to encourage the kind of business that will attract green technology graduates, while the third objective builds on the importance of china clay to the town, making it a focus for ceramic art. Although the pandemic was a major hiccup in making this vision reality, it is starting to happen. Check ⊘ studiofelt. com/work/austell-project to get an idea of what is going on.

St Austell Brewery

63 Trevarthian Rd, PL25 4BY ✆ 0345 2411122 ⌖ staustellbrewery.co.uk

Industry needs its ale (especially in an area where temperance was being vociferously preached) and Walter Hicks was the entrepreneur who saw the business opportunity. His family had been farmers for over 400 years, but he mortgaged the farm and set himself up as a maltster, then a wine-and-spirit merchant, before building his first brewery in 1869.

By 1893 the business had outgrown the building and the Walter Hicks Brewery moved to Trevarthian Road, where the family business has become something of a local institution, employing generations of the same families and, up until 2014, still using the 1890 belt-driven barley mill and heating mash in even older cast-iron tuns. The company is revered locally for other reasons too: as a supporter of local charities and because it makes a point of using Cornish barley and spring water. All this is good news, because the brewery owns a huge percentage of Cornwall's nicest and most historic village pubs.

"All this is good news, because the brewery owns a huge percentage of Cornwall's nicest and most historic village pubs."

And I've never heard a bad word said about its best-selling ale, Tribute. In fact, it's thanks to the success of Tribute that the company has somewhat reluctantly upgraded all its brewing equipment and sales now extend well beyond the Tamar.

The brewery has a museum, shop and bar and runs entertaining guided tours throughout the year.

Tregrehan

Par PL24 2SJ ✆ 01726 814389 ⌖ tregrehangarden.uk ⊙ mid-Mar–May Wed–Fri & Sun; Jun–Oct Wed afternoons

One of Cornwall's finest, yet least-known gardens, with its own specialist appeal and character, lies within easy reach of the train station at Par, on the eastern side of St Austell. **Tregrehan** has been home to the Carlyon family since 1565, and its 20 acres of woodland, Victorian kitchen gardens and greenhouses are evidence of the family's deep and knowledgeable affection for plants, particularly trees and shrubs from the southern hemisphere. Tom Hudson, the latest family member to take on the estate, is no exception: his collection of high-altitude Asian trees, brought back from recent expeditions, complement his cousin's camellia hybrids and Jovey Carlyon's superb pinetum. Tregrehan may be stuffed with glorious examples of unusual trees that will excite dendrologists, but the gardens (which are only open for a limited number of days in spring and summer) are quiet and unshowy; Tom Hudson likes to keep it that way.

Menacuddle Well

♀ SX011533. Pass under the viaduct on the Bodmin road out of St Austell, & after half a mile take the small turning on the left, signed Brake Manor.

It's almost impossible to spot the entrance first time round, and the road past is fast and turning off it dangerous, but perseverance pays off: in a peaceful green dell, sheltered by old laurels, a clay-coloured stream bubbles and falls past a mossy granite shrine. The original building dates from the 15th century, but was heavily restored in 1922. Inside, the water runs crystal clear, unlike the milky stream outside, which is perhaps why so much faith has been attached to its curative powers for so many centuries. No matter whether you believe in this or not, it's a delightfully unexpected and secret place with a gentle atmosphere – on the grassy slope a granite Druid's seat is the spot from which to contemplate the well, and parking space has thoughtfully been provided for a couple of cars, too.

⑪ FOOD & DRINK

Polgooth Inn Ricketts Lane, London Apprentice PL26 7DA ⌀ 01726 74089 ⌂ polgoothinn. co.uk. A family-run, community pub that overlooks its own kitchen garden, supplying most of the herbs, salads and vegetables that appear on the menu. A really good find.

16 WHEAL MARTYN CHINA CLAY MUSEUM

Carthew PL26 8XG ⌀ 01726 850 362 ⌂ wheal-martyn.com

The lady on the ticket desk sighed: 'People go to the Eden Project, because it's the big must-do and then they don't come here – despite being so close, it's too much to visit both in one day – and [although there's a reduction in ticket price if you've been to Eden] too expensive.' Which is a shame, because Wheal Martyn is a wonderful surprise, both inside and out, and helps to put Eden (which was created in an abandoned china clay pit) into its historical and environmental context.

Inside the museum, an animated portrait of William Cookworthy describes his discovery of china clay on Tregonning Hill (page 250) and the revolutionary impact this had on porcelain production in England.

There are examples of some of the earliest experimental pieces of English porcelain here and surprising examples of other uses to which the clay is put today, such as the manufacture of toothpaste, cosmetics and paints, while paper manufacturing scoops up around 70% of production.

Outside, looping paths through 26 acres of woodland take you on a journey past waterwheels and trickling leats, drying yards and kilns, sheds full of engines and the odd art installation. What I liked was the freedom to explore without feeling overly directed or bombarded with information – discretion and fun appearing more important than overt pedagogy.

Unlike tin and copper mining in Cornwall, the china clay industry is very much alive and is still Cornwall's biggest industry; at the farthest end of the woods, the ground rises and opens on to a viewing platform, from which you gaze down over a vast pit, currently being worked by

SILVANUS TREVAIL

As he had such a wonderful name, and such a vast legacy of civic, commercial and domestic buildings all over Cornwall, you'd think everybody would have heard of the prodigious and talented architect and entrepreneur from Luxulyan. Not a bit of it: when he died in 1903 (he put a gun to his head in the ladies' lavatory on a train leaving Bodmin) his name died with him.

Nine of the Cornish buildings funded by the philanthropist Passmore Edwards (page 228) were designed by Trevail, and nearly 50 schools in the county as well as cottages and mansions, banks and churches. St Austell and Truro are stuffed with his buildings, but the coastal resorts are where he made a controversial name for himself. Trevail saw that tourism was about to boom in Cornwall and was determined to cash in on the top end of the market. In 1890, he formed the Cornish Hotels Company, with the idea of attracting wealthy visitors to Cornwall. He'd got it all cleverly worked out: the well-heeled would be able to travel the entire coastline, moving at their pleasure between the chain of upmarket hotels he had planned. The enormous and castellated Camelot Castle Hotel at Tintagel is his work, as is the imposing Headland Hotel in Newquay, which sparked riots among locals when it was built on supposedly common land overlooking Fistral Bay. He realised that infrastructure was important too, and fought local councils to improve (or in some cases, create) services for drinking water and sewage, attempted to push through rail connections between emerging resorts – and made a lot of enemies in the process. Following his suicide at the age of 52, Trevail was buried in Luxulyan churchyard, a few yards from where he was born; his grave is marked by a granite cross he had designed the year before.

the Goonvean China Clay Company and Imerys Minerals Ltd, which between them produce 4,500 tons of clay a week. So huge is the scale of the operation that the diggers and bulldozers look like Dinky toys working the pit bottom. But having come up through the museum, all the activity going on below makes sense: the digging, the washing, the separation of the liquid sludge, the growing conical mountain of spoil … it's an absorbing spectacle. I knew what Oscar Wilde meant: 'I love work,' he said. 'I can watch it all day.'

17 THE EDEN PROJECT

Bodelva, St Austell PL24 2SG 🖉 01726 811911 🖸 edenproject.com; reduced entry fees for those arriving on foot, by bike or by bus

Eden never stops adding to its cornucopia of attractions – but, to me anyway, it gets more interesting as you strip away each layer of crowd-pleasing novelty. Beneath the dizzying ingenuity of the vast, honeycomb-inspired, dome-like greenhouses, constructed from steel-framed inflated plastic cells, and the two plant-filled biomes (climatically defined ecosystems) that draw in visitors by the thousand each day; beyond the awe-inspiring exhibitions and the terrifying zip-wire that hurtles the courageous from one end to the other of this extraordinary place, there are deeper issues at stake. Eden is all about supporting healthy plant communities – in the rainforest biome, heated to tropical temperatures and humidified by a giant waterfall; in the warm, dry Mediterranean biome (as well as in the local Cornish biome outside the domes) – and pushes the message hard that we disrespect the plant world at our peril.

"People come to Eden for 'Neighbourhood Event Planning' workshops and 'Creative Community' ideas."

The less visible but wider project here is a creative response to such perils: by encouraging healthy, sustainable human communities, too, where people are interested in where they live and find ways of sharing and celebrating local identity. People come to Eden for 'Neighbourhood Event Planning' workshops and 'Creative Community' ideas, while social and environmental projects include helping young offenders back into work with outdoor training initiatives. Other ideas dreamt

◀ **1** Helman Tor. **2** Wheal Martyn China Clay Museum. **3** Treffry Viaduct, Luxulyan Valley. **4** The Eden Project.

up at Eden travel the globe – from relatively small-scale projects, like creating a garden in Kosovo or helping a village in Thailand reclaim local rainforest, to full-scale 'New Edens' in the making in China, New Zealand and Costa Rica (as well as closer to home in Morecambe and Dundee).

Eden gets predictably packed in the school holidays. The rope-bridge walkway, high up in the tree canopy under the dome, offers a wobbly initiation into the science behind cloud formation and rainfall, and is great fun for bouncy children (less so for nervous adults). The health warnings on entering the rainforest biome during the summer months are not to be taken lightly (carry drinking water; remove warm or heavy outer layers of clothing). But I remember a visit to Eden on a freezing day in January, when the hot, humid atmosphere of that biome was a haven: blackbirds were singing their hearts out among the ripening papayas and their tropical cousins were scuttling about in the lush undergrowth; robins perched on the stumpy vines in the Mediterranean biome and the scent of wild thyme and lavender among the olive trees transported me back to a happy year spent on a Spanish island.

I talked to Tim Smit when Eden was still on the drawing board, back in 1995; the Lost Gardens of Heligan was already an established success and his creative ambitions were leaping ahead: 'I can't begin to describe what the biomes will look like,' he said. 'It's tempting to think in terms of pyramids or Christmas puddings, but I don't want to influence or prejudice the architects working on the design. But this is fundamental: so often man is seen as an accretion in the environment, as somehow extraneous to it. My aim is to place the environment in the context of man.' And then, after a pause, he added, 'I must seem incredibly arrogant …' He didn't. Determined, passionate, thoughtful and – almost three decades later – vindicated.

18 LUXULYAN VALLEY

I have a soft spot for this wooded valley, with its tumbling river and soaring viaduct; hidden and self-contained, yet barely a mile from the Eden Project and the busy beach at Par Sands. Climbers come here to test themselves on the granite cliffs; industrial historians to potter among the relics of tin and clay and granite exploitation, and seek out the 650-foot, ten-arch viaduct built by Joseph Treffry (page 194). Walkers on the coast-to-coast Saints' Way find this the leafiest and most peaceful part of the long trail and children scramble for the odd rope swing to be found among the branches on the slopes of the river.

The train station at Luxulyan, at the head of the valley, is handy for exploring the valley on foot; by picking up the Saints' Way markers, you can continue downhill to Tywardreath and Par (the next station on the branch line) and return to Luxulyan by train.

¶¶ FOOD & DRINK

Kings Arms Luxulyan PL30 5EF ℰ 01726 850202 ⓕ. A great pit stop offering decent pub grub: cosy and traditional inside, welcoming children and dogs, damp walkers and cyclists.

19 HELMAN TOR

📍 SX062615

Northeast of Luxulyan and southwest of Lanhydrock, tucked away in a maze of tiny lanes, Helman Tor is one of the very special viewpoints of central Cornwall, with a path taking you up from its car park. From the top you look across to the Hensbarrow Downs, the Lanhydrock estate and the Gilbert Monument looming over Bodmin. A prized wildlife habitat and nature reserve managed by the Cornwall Wildlife Trust, with wetland, heath, woodland and acid grassland, it includes **Red Moor Memorial Nature Reserve**. If the Cheesewring at Minions (page 129) seems a little overcrowded at times, come here: you are likely to find it deserted.

20 THE ROCHE ROCK

Some 270 million years ago, in the late Carboniferous period, when great shifts underground were occurring, fluid borosilicates separated from molten rock and bubbled up towards the surface, finally cooling and solidifying into a crumpled rock formation, which rises broodingly over Roche (pronounced 'Roach'), on the Clay country's northern fringes.

A ruined hermitage, consecrated in 1409, crowns its craggy skyline, which can be reached by a wooden ladder. Some come here hoping for a glimpse of the rock's famous ghostly inhabitants. Chief among these is the 17th-century corrupt magistrate, Tregeagle, who after his death jumped a particularly nasty kind of demonic bail and was cornered here by a pack of hellhounds; there's also St Gundred, whose leprosy-stricken father removed himself to the rock to spare the other inhabitants of Roche from his affliction. Brave little Gundred stuck with her father to look after him, occasionally taking him down to rinse him in a local holy well, but ultimately perished with him on the rock. Parts of the horror film *Omen III* were filmed here, too. On a summer's day, however, with butterflies springing from the rough pasture at the foot of the rock, and a local group of climbers attempting to scale the sheer rock face, it's hard to see its presence as anything but benign and it's good to recall that in the Tristan and Isolde legend this is where the lovers were hidden from the wrath of King Mark by the friar hermit, Ogrim.

21 THE LOST GARDENS OF HELIGAN

Pentewan, St Austell PL26 6EN ℮ 01726 845100 ⇩ heligan.com

I first visited Heligan in 1997, when the newly restored gardens were just starting to hit the headlines and TV screens. Everybody seemed to be talking about someone called Tim Smit who, with his friend, John Nelson, had stumbled across a forgotten Cornish garden and fallen in love with the mystery and melancholy. Hothouses and potagers lay in the tangled embrace of briars and a jungle of tree ferns and rhododendrons had swarmed over rockeries and terraces, hiding Victorian bee boles, borders and pineapple pits.

I remember admiring Smit's bold approach to the project: 'It's unhealthy to think that if something is old it must be good,' he said. 'And as Heligan was made at different times, over a number of centuries, it's impossible to be completely authentic.' What Smit envisaged was a living, lively restoration, with a team of eager, expert gardeners working to exacting Victorian standards of horticultural practice, as well as exchanging information and ideas with other gardening teams. I remember him saying that he wanted Heligan to make people say 'Wow!', not 'How nice'. He likened the experience to being at a rock concert: 'We're doing this garden for the people dancing and having a good time, rather than the sober theorists standing at the back.'

"I remember Tim Smit saying that he wanted Heligan to make people say 'Wow!', not 'How nice.'"

Now, more than two decades later, the gardens are fulfilling that early ideal with conviction: it's a brilliant, dramatic place, immaculate in the

---

1 Roche Rock. **2** Caerhays Castle gardens in spring. **3** Gorran Haven. **4** Mud Maid living sculpture, Lost Gardens of Heligan. ▶

PAUL MAGUIRE/S

CAERHAYS CASTLE GARDENS

SS

CHRISDORNEY/S

Victorian kitchen gardens where it should be immaculate, wild and jungly in the ravine where wild and jungly are required; all is designed to wow the crowds that visit in great numbers. And I see no reason why Slow visitors should not be there at the front of the dancing crowd; 26 years after that first conversation, I was.

22 MEVAGISSEY

🏠 **Bodrugan Barton** (page 419)

The picturesque harbour and constant comings and goings of the colourful fishing boats are the stuff of Cornish dreams; no wonder Mevagissey is popular and its narrow maze of backstreets crowded with gifts shops and cafés. **Hurley Books**, on Jetty Street, right in the thick of things, is a lovely independent bookshop that doubles up as the visitor information centre, and is a great place to start a bit of Slow pottering. On the east wharf of the inner harbour, the free **museum** (✆ 01726 843568 ⊘ mevagisseymuseum.co.uk ☉ Easter–Oct) is a gem. In the best tradition of local museums it contains a lovingly assembled mixed bag of exhibits relating to its residents: local boatbuilding exploits rub shoulders with a fondly remembered Mevagissey milkman with a penchant for motorbike racing; Andrew Pears, the man who invented the first bar of soap you would actually want to wash yourself with, is given a hero's corner;

"The picturesque harbour and constant comings and goings of the colourful fishing boats are the stuff of Cornish dreams."

a Mevagissey pound note from the village's family-owned bank is sadly exhibited beside news of its bankruptcy in 1824; and there are quirky 20th-century ceramic models of surprised fishermen and a rapturous couple sharing a bath, by Bernard Moss. The **aquarium**, housed in the old lifeboat shed, is a treat too, stocked and regularly added to by Mevagissey's fishermen.

I had my bike with me, and found Mevagissey made a great base for cycling trips along the off-road trail to St Austell, seven miles distant (following the Sustrans NCN Route 3 – the Cornish Way), where it linked with the Clay Trails which pass through Wheal Martyn and the Eden Project. The steepest section followed a branching track to Heligan, which (mercifully) is less than two miles from Mevagissey.

Model railways were the last thing on my mind as I cycled back towards the harbour, but I wasn't in a hurry and in the spirit of Slow research I parked the bike outside a small wooden building, advertising itself as the **World of Model Railways** (Meadow St ⏾ model-railway. co.uk ⊙ Apr–Nov). What a treat: beyond the shop, which stocks everything a model railway enthusiast – including owner and top enthusiast Paul Catchpole – could hope to find, a miniature Cornish landscape unfolded, complete with stone circle, china clay pits, tin mine, gardens (including a Glendurgan-ish maze), harbour with a film crew, bike race, wedding and engineering works. No fewer than 30 trains quietly threaded their way through the extraordinary landscape, which I followed, rapt, up one side of the room and down the other, until the landscape gave way with unexpected abruptness to an alpine village. 'Ah, well, you see,' said the knowledgeable Mr Catchpole, 'the man who built this liked to spend his winter holidays in Grindelwald.' There can't be many other places where you can travel from the Cornish alps to the Swiss Alps in a dozen paces.

⏉ FOOD & DRINK

There's no shortage of places to refresh yourself in Mevagissey: the **Central Café** (3 Market Sq, PL26 6UD ⏾ 01726 843109 ⏾ centralcafemeva.co.uk) is a decent fish and chip shop; **Cofro** (14 Fore St, PL26 6UQ ⏾ 01726 842249 ⏾ cofro.co.uk) is an art and craft gallery (Cofro means 'keepsake' in Cornish) with a café, doing a nice line in locally made cakes and biscuits; the **Fountain Inn** (Cliff St, PL26 6QH ⏾ 01726 842320) is a characterful pub, one of the first to be bought by Walter Hicks of the St Austell Brewery (page 203), with a well-earned reputation for real ales and a good fish menu; and **The Sharksfin** (The Quay, PL26 6QU ⏾ 01726 842969 ⏾ thesharksfin.co.uk) is a bar-restaurant right on the harbour, managed by the same team as the deservedly popular Longstore in Charlestown (page 199), featuring lots of bare wood, superb seafood and burgers.

23 GORRAN HAVEN

Like many Cornish fishing villages, Gorran is in two parts: a cluster of cottages and houses built around the harbour, and higher inland a 'churchtown', where the streets are broader, the houses bigger and the smell of fish (in the past) less invasive. Because of its relative inaccessibility by road, Gorran is one of the few picturesque places on the Cornish coast that seems to have escaped commercialisation – it's a community rather than a commodity, and while its family-friendly beaches and cottages receive their fair share of families who return here year after year, it's not yet been overwhelmed.

¶¶ FOOD & DRINK

Barley Sheaf PL26 6HN ✐ 01726 843330 ⬦ thebarleysheafgorran.co.uk. An upmarket, friendly pub, with a reputation for good eating, local ales and an excellent cider produced at Cotna Barton, an organic smallholding (which also supplies the salads and vegetables), just outside the village.

24 CAERHAYS CASTLE

Gorran PL26 6LY ✐ 01872 501310 ⬦ visit.caerhays.co.uk ☉ mid-Feb–mid-Jun
🏠 **Caerhays Estate** (page 419)

Nothing quite prepares you for the loveliness of that first view of the castle in spring, standing massive and at ease behind its lake and velvety green pastures grazed by Highland cattle, against a rising backcloth of a thousand trees enriched by clouds of cream and pink magnolia blooms and scarlet bursts of rhododendron. Visitors arriving by car or bike (the entrance is on the cross-Cornwall Sustrans NCN Route 3) are directed down a narrow country lane to park at **Porthluney Cove**, so arrestingly beautiful in itself that it is quite a shock to turn your back on the sea and find the castle and its grounds dragging your gaze towards an altogether different kind of beauty. The next shock is the discovery that this view (known as 'the Cut') was only made possible by dozens of unemployed miners hacking away with picks and shovels at the interposing hill during the mining doldrums of the late 19th century.

Completed in 1813, Caerhays was built by John Nash for the Trevanion family, but bankruptcy ensured their enjoyment of the palatial building was short-lived; since 1853 this has been home to the Williams family, who still live here and occasionally open the house to visits. Its 100 acres of gardens are open from mid-February until early June, giving visitors the opportunity to see the wonderful collections of magnolias and camellias at the height of their flowering season. The steeply pitched slopes make for a lot of legwork, but create their own rewards, offering unusually close-up views of the blooms from above as well as below. Although of historic and national importance, the collection of plants at Caerhays is far from being preserved in aspic. The current owner, Charles Williams, and his head gardener, Jaimie Parsons, respond with astute commitment

"Nothing quite prepares you for the loveliness of that first view of the castle in spring, standing massive and at ease behind its lake."

DEMOCRATISING THE CAMELLIA

Gardeners who love camellias have good reason to be grateful to the Williamses of Caerhays, in particular to J C Williams (great-grandfather to the present owner) who produced the hardy, free-flowering and easy-to-grow camellias we enjoy in our gardens today. J C funded a number of expeditions to China by the great plant hunter George Forrest and turned the wooded slopes of Caerhays into a giant experimental nursery. But his real breakthrough came in 1923, when he crossed *Camellia saluenensis* and *Camellia japonica*, producing the first of the *williamsii* camellias. (The original parent plants can be seen growing either side of a green door on the entrance façade of the castle.) At last there was a camellia that was tough enough to withstand a British winter with the additional bonus of producing flowers that dropped off after flowering, instead of collapsing in an ugly mess while still attached to the plant. It seems the camellia gene has been passed on through the generations – the famous Burncoose nurseries at Gwennap were established by the Williams family and the passion for raising new hybrids remains as vigorous as ever.

to the annual challenge of replanting slopes denuded by the ravages of phytophthora (all the old *ponticum* rhododendrons have had to go) or by old beeches and Monterey pines sent crashing by strong winds; some of the replacement planting consists of young hybrid magnolias – the result of Jaimie Parsons's careful selection and patience. It can take up to ten years before a seed-grown magnolia produces a flower, and several more before its garden-worthiness can be established. (Fierce debate still rages over the greeny-yellow blooms of Caerhays-bred Tropicana – 'looks like the result of a bad night out' say its critics.) But what a moment it is when those black, downy flower buds appear for the first time on a home-bred hybrid – you can hear Mr Parsons's joyful exclamations down on Porthluney beach.

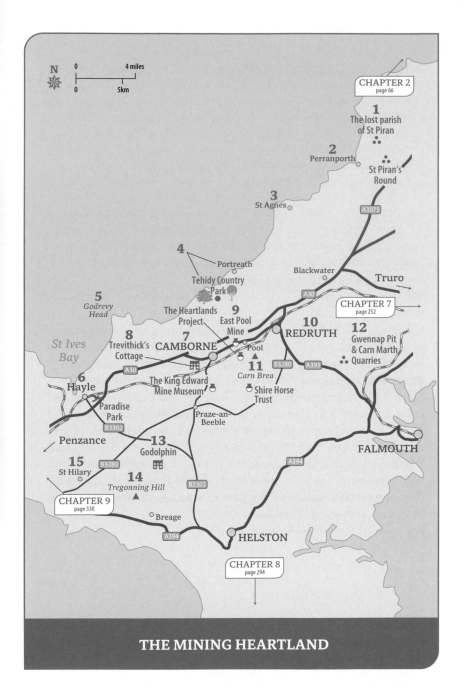

CHAPTER 2
page 66

1
The lost parish
of St Piran
∴

2
Perranporth

St Piran's
Round
∴

3
St Agnes ○

Blackwater ●

Truro

CHAPTER 7
page 252

A3075

4
Portreath

Tehidy Country
Park

5
Godrevy
Head

The Heartlands
Project

9
East Pool
Mine

10
REDRUTH

12
Gwennap Pit
& Carn Marth
Quarries
∴∴

St Ives
Bay

8
Trevithick's
Cottage

7
CAMBORNE

Pool

6
Hayle

A30

The King Edward
Mine Museum

11
Carn Brea ▲

Shire Horse
Trust

B3280

A393

FALMOUTH

Paradise
Park

B3302

Praze-an-
Beeble

Penzance

13
Godolphin

A394

15
St Hilary

B3280

14
Tregonning Hill ▲

B3303

CHAPTER 9
page 330

Breage ○

A394

HELSTON ●

CHAPTER 8
page 294

THE MINING HEARTLAND

6

THE MINING
HEARTLAND

Cornwall's industrial heritage is stamped indelibly on the landscape, towns and coast over the whole county, but with no greater density – and pride – than in the region of **St Agnes**, **Redruth**, **Camborne** and **Hayle**. I've extended the ground covered in this chapter southwards, to include the **Godolphin estate** and **Tregonning Hill**, as they form the largest of the ten separate areas which together create the World Heritage Site, established in 2006 in recognition of the importance of the Cornish mining landscape. There's enormous beauty here, not just in the wild and natural beauty of the north-coast dunes and cliffs or the wooded hills and farmland valleys of the interior, but in the decayed industrial architecture, softened by the steady encroachment of nature. You'll encounter a sense of place that grows on you and intensifies, especially after visiting one of the many museums dedicated to mining heritage, where the colossal human endeavour, which at its peak saw Cornwall meet two-thirds of the world's demand for tin and copper, is brought vividly to life. You really don't have to be an industrial archaeologist or have Cornish mining in your blood to appreciate the extraordinary inventiveness that went into extracting the shiny metals from lumpen ore, buried in wet ground, where efficient pumping was crucial to success and safety – nor the tales of courage, comradeship and survival that bound communities together.

The closure of the mines in the last century and the dispersal of the Cornish mining population to new, more profitable areas around the world was reflected grimly in the towns that had once prospered, but times are changing. Affordable housing and studio space have brought an influx of artists to Redruth and Camborne; **Kresen Kernow**, the recently completed Cornish Studies centre, is now housed (thanks to an £11-million investment) in the magnificently restored Redruth Brewery building; and a multi-million-pound development of housing, offices and studios continues to rise from the post-industrial wasteland of **Pool**; while Hayle, with its historic waterfront, is busily pursuing a Docklands-style revival.

These days, Cornish mining is in the news again as exploratory projects reveal significant quantities of lithium, both in hard rock and deep-level brine. But many Cornish eyes rolled when Boris Johnson declared Cornwall to be the 'Klondike of lithium' at the 2021 G7 summit in St Ives. Environmental concerns offset the emission-saving promises of lithium batteries. Hard-rock mining and extraction processes are far from carbon friendly and keeping toxic waste from adits (discharge channels) away from rivers is almost impossible to guarantee.

But it's not all about mining and its aftermath. The north coast is studded with safe, family-friendly beaches, and the giant dunes above Hayle and **Perranporth** conceal all sorts of treasures, from glow-worms and butterflies to buried explosives works, churches and sites of pilgrimage; among the dunes of **Perran Sands** you can lose yourself exploring the lost world of St Piran.

GETTING AROUND

The A30 provides a fast link from 'upcountry' to Redruth, Camborne and Hayle, from which it's just a short hop on spur roads to Perranporth, St Agnes and Portreath. Heading south of Carn Brea into Godolphin country can lead into a muddle of tiny lanes, which all seem to tie up at the gloriously named Praze-an-Beeble, whence it's a straight, short run to Leedstown before plunging into small-lane territory again around Godolphin Cross.

TRAINS

Redruth, Camborne and Hayle are all served by the **mainline service** from London and Plymouth, making this one of Cornwall's most accessible regions by train.

BUSES

Taking Redruth, Camborne or Hayle as your starting point, it's pretty easy to get around by bus, and the north coast resorts are served by **spur routes**, although some of the remoter places, such as Godrevy, have summer-only services. A **coastal route** links Perranporth to St Agnes. For more information, check ⌀ firstbus.co.uk/cornwall.

CYCLING, RIDING & WALKING

Given its industrial legacy, this may seem unlikely territory for walkers, but thanks to the well-signed routes forming the **Mineral Tramways Mining Trails**, centred on Camborne and Redruth and linking the north to south coast, from Portreath to Devoran on the Fal estuary, there is some very enjoyable exploring to be done. The circular route around Carn Brea (page 242), named after the Great Flat Lode, is one of the best places to explore the relics of the region's industrial past – and the views from the summit of Carn Brea are well worth the climb. The walks around St Agnes take some beating too, rolling together a fabulous mix of coastline and beach, desolate moor and everywhere the atmospheric ruins of engine houses, chimneys and mine shafts. A map showing all the trails, heritage attractions and places for refreshment as well as bike and horseriding centres is available at visitor information centres, and there's an exhibition room dedicated to the trails at **King Edward Mine**. The map is also available to download at ⌀ visitcornwall.com.

The **coast path** offers some pretty spectacular highlights along the way, too. Godrevy Head (page 228) is particularly suitable for wildflower enthusiasts or seal-spotters, while further north, the sand dunes above Perranporth (page 220) conceal the hidden remnants of early Christian places of worship.

CYCLE HIRE

The popularity of the mostly flat and well-marked Mineral Tramways has encouraged a good network of cycle-hire places and riding centres close to the routes.

Elm Farm Bike Barn, Camp and Café Nancekuke TR16 5UF ⌀ 01209 891498 ⌀ elmfarm. biz. Not just a cycle-hire and -repair place, but a farm with a café/shop selling local produce (real ale too, from Skinner's) and a field for camping. B&B is also offered in the farmhouse, four miles from Portreath on the coast-to-coast trail.
St Piran Bike Hire (Bike Chain Bissoe) Old Conns Works, Bissoe, Truro TR4 8QZ ⌀ 01872 870341 ⌀ bikechainbissoe.co.uk. Just outside the range of this chapter, but right on the north–south coast route and offering a large car park and café too. Bikes are hired on a daily basis, though longer hire periods can be arranged.

TOURIST INFORMATION

Hayle Hayle Library, 43 Commercial Rd, TR27 4DE ✆ 01736 754399
Redruth Visitor Information Point, Redruth Civic Centre, Alma Pl, TR15 2AT ✆ 01209
216760 ⌂ discoverredruth.co.uk

The Hub Portreath TR16 4NN ✆ 01209 844666 ⌂ thehubportreath.com. Fergus heads this excellent bike-hire venture, attached to a great café, just 200 yards from the beach. The perfect start/finish to a coast-to-coast ride, exploring Tehidy Country Park or the mineral trails network. Trek hybrid, mountain and electric bikes available for minimum rental of four hours.

HORSERIDING

Sandy beaches and the Mineral Tramways network make this area particularly suitable for both long and short rides, with cafés and pubs on the network offering tie-ups for mounts.

Goonbell Riding Centre St Agnes TR5 0PN ✆ 01872 552063 ⌂ goonbellridingcentre. co.uk. Picnic and pub rides in the summer; horses and ponies for all ages (including the very, very young) and abilities.
Reen Manor Riding Stables Reen, Perranporth TR6 0AJ ✆ 01872 573064
⌂ reenmanorstables.com. Perfectly placed for exploring the sandy dunes above Perran Sands, or longer rides inland, with a stop for lunch at a local pub.

FROM PERRANPORTH TO THE HAYLE ESTUARY

South of Holywell Bay, the windswept north coast is not short of variety: craggy cliffs, towering sand dunes and vast beaches alternate with tiny coves, accessible only to seal colonies and the most intrepid beach-lovers. Harbours once dedicated to mining exports now cater to the surfing industry, while in the hilly, wooded or heathy hinterland you are never far from the skeletal remains of an engine house or chimney stack.

1 THE LOST PARISH OF ST PIRAN

Behind the wide sweep of Perranporth Beach, the largest sand dunes in Britain, tufted with marram grass, rise to a height of 90 feet. The coast path dips and rises along the safer margins of the shifting sands, giving a seagull's-eye view of scudding sand-yachts and surfers far below. Turn the clock back 1,500 years or so, and you might have glimpsed an Irish monk, riding not a surfboard, but a slab of granite through the breakers and on to the beach. This would be Cornwall's popular Celtic hero, St Piran, lashed to a millstone and slung into the sea by a heathen Irish king, fearful of Piran's reputation for performing miracles. Legend has it that the millstone-cum-miraculous raft landed on the beach that still bears his name, and on the level plateau above the beach Piran built a small oratory. The story continues that Piran, having lit a fire on a black stone hearth, observed a bubbling trickle of silvery metal rise to the surface and thus discovered the existence of tin in Cornish granite. Which explains why Piran is the patron saint of tinners, and why the Cornish flag is a white (tin) cross (discovered by a Christian saint) on a black (granite) background.

How different the landscape must have looked in Piran's day, before the dunes took over. The 6th-century oratory – most probably a structure of wattle, daub and thatch, later replaced by stone as its importance grew – would have stood among fields and farms. However, blown in on north winds, the sands encroached and parishioners were forced to abandon it during the 10th century and build a new church, 300 yards further inland, across a stream. But, like the oratory, this church was eventually engulfed by sand and in 1804 it was removed, stone by stone, and rebuilt *"The oratory is believed to be the oldest building dedicated to Christian worship on mainland Britain."*

at Perranzabuloe, three miles to the south. Today, it's a good walk – two miles from Perranporth – over the dunes to find the remains of both **church** and **oratory**, neither of which is particularly easy to locate. Until 2014, all that could be seen of the oratory was a small, humpy dune (among many, many other humpy dunes), marked only by a discreet information plaque and surmounted by a simple granite slab, inscribed with the name of the saint. Beneath the dune was an astoundingly ugly blockwork structure, built in 1910, to protect the oratory remains; it was deliberately buried in 1980 as a response to flooding and vandalism. Locals, however, were well aware of the absurdity of such obscurity for a site of national importance – the oratory is believed to be the oldest building dedicated to Christian worship on mainland Britain – and a charitable trust was set up with the aim of uncovering and reopening the oratory. Following excavations in 2014–15, the oratory, like the church, is now exposed and most of the blockwork has been removed. The eight-foot **Celtic cross**, a short distance away, speaks of the vast medieval graveyard that lies beneath the sand. From time to time, bones are revealed, including the skeleton of a mother holding an infant, found close to the entrance to the oratory. The museum in Perranporth (page 223) has a permanent display dedicated to the excavations.

Some walking options

Don't expect easy-to-follow waymarkers to guide you here; the best option is to pick up a walking-route map in the **museum** (page 223), follow the coast path north from Perranporth as far as the MoD fence and turn right, keeping the fence to your left and ignoring the huge concrete cross on a dune to the south. After half a mile, the oratory (♀ SW768564) becomes visible. Continue in the same direction (skirting the deep stream bed) – looking out for St Piran's Cross to guide you to the church, which, like the oratory, lies close to the MoD fence.

St Piran's Round

♀ SW779545

On the edge of Rose hamlet is a remarkably well-preserved **circular earthwork**, which may or may not have started out as a fortified Iron Age farm. What is sure, however, is that the Perran Round was used for centuries as a theatre for Cornish mystery plays as well as wrestling matches, fairs and preaching. A medieval pilgrims' road once bisected the circle and it's possible that Miracle plays were laid on here to reward and educate travellers approaching the oratory. The depression in the centre marks the place of a pit from which the devil would spring – to predictable gasps and jeers.

These days, Cornwall's (secular) **Miracle Theatre** puts on plays here for one evening each summer and local and visiting **Mummers** will occasionally stage an event here too; it seems very little use for what is probably Britain's oldest 'Playing Place'.

2 PERRANPORTH

Once a mining village, Perranporth now appears to be dedicated to beach and surf, both in glorious abundance. At low tide, the level sands are a huge playground for sand-yachters, skimming the beach as swiftly as the wheatears and stonechats skim the tufty heights and hollows of the dunes above. But Perranporth really comes alive and bares its soul for the weekend closest to 5 March when the village celebrates the arrival of its saint, and kicks off with a giant model of St Piran arriving on the beach (in a rigid inflatable), followed with pageants, plays and a procession across the dunes to the site of the ancient church and oratory. A thorough dash of Cornish nationalism is thrown in too, with lots of flag waving and lusty renditions of 'Trelawney' along the way.

The **Perranzabuloe Museum**, attached to the library in the Oddfellows building (Ponsmere Rd, TR6 0BW ♪ 01872 573321 ♂ perranzabuloemuseum.co.uk ☉ Easter–Oct Mon–Fri) does a grand job of keeping Perranporth's identity from being submerged by holidaymaking traffic. Fans of *Poldark* will be gratified to discover the display dedicated to author Winston Graham, who lived at Nampara Lodge in Perranporth and found inspiration for his best-selling novels in the surrounding landscape. Surfers, meanwhile, should note the exhibit that reveals how the local coffin-maker, Tom Tremewan, spotting the new enthusiasm for riding the waves, sold coffin lids to tourists for this purpose in the 1920s. Perranporth was used as a training ground for the D-Day landings and wartime memorabilia includes the tiny uniform made for Jacqueline Fewins, the three-year-old mascot of an American battalion that was based here. And I liked the story of the shipwreck, that – for once – had a happy ending, when the skipper, who survived with his humour intact, commented: 'I have been wrecked in different parts of the world, even the Fiji islands, but never among savages such as those of Perranporth.'

A short walk through the village to the southern end of the beach takes you up the cliff to **Droskyn Point**, where on a grassy ledge an enormous granite sundial was installed to celebrate the millennium. True to the spirit of Perranporth, the gnomon has been set to show Cornish time: 20 minutes ahead of GMT.

￥¶ FOOD & DRINK

Bolingey Inn Penwartha Rd, Bolingey TR6 0DH ♪ 01872 571626 ♂ thebolingeyinn. co.uk. Less than a mile from Perranporth, and accessible by a footpath that starts opposite the Co-op car park, Bolingey is a pretty hamlet with a lovely old pub, great for both eating and drinking. Local ales are well kept, vegetables come from the pub's allotment garden, lamb from a nearby farm and ice cream from Callestick Farm, just up the road. Dog- and child-friendly.

3 ST AGNES

Å **Beacon Cottage Camping** (page 420), **Mount Pleasant Eco Park** (page 420)

The relics of an industrial past – chimney stacks and engine houses – crowd thickly around the steep and narrow valley that shelters St Agnes on its plunging descent to Trevaunce Cove. But this is no grim mining village: St Agnes is a flowery, cottagey sort of place, with good shops selling local produce, galleries that reflect an established arty community and busy little beaches, popular with surfers. **Wheal Kitty**, a short but steep walk out of town, is a beautifully restored cluster of mining buildings, now housing a film production studio, the iconic Finisterre outdoor clothing retailer and the HQ of its close ally, the magnificent Surfers Against Sewage (SAS) charity. (The charity's shop has closed and is now online.) In addition to its work holding the water companies to account over sewage-release issues, SAS is currently leading the campaign to eliminate plastic detritus from our oceans, beaches and lives, and have valuable resource material for those wishing to spread the word (page 20).

"This is no grim mining village: St Agnes is a flowery, cottagey sort of place, with good shops selling local produce."

Back in St Agnes, the **St Agnes Museum** (Penwinnick Rd, TR5 0PA ✆ 01872 552301 ⚲ stagnesmuseum.org.uk ☉ Apr–Oct), located at the top of the village and housed in a former Chapel of Rest (divided neatly in half with one entrance for Conformists and another for Nonconformists), likens itself to 'a Victorian Cabinet of Curiosities'. From the stuffed leatherback turtle at the entrance to the collection to the hideously curling, six-inch (Edwardian) toenail, collected by William Whitworth, one of five generations of Whitworths to serve as doctor to the community, you can see what they mean. There are minerals and models (including one of the harbour which once occupied Trevaunce Cove), a painted ship's figurehead and dozens of photos of village scenes and characters. Upstairs, beside an impressive display of surfboards, a whole cabinet is lovingly dedicated to the railway that once connected St Agnes to the rest of the world. (For those unable to

---

1 A surfer's paradise: Perranporth Beach. **2** Trevaunance Cove, St Agnes. **3** Skylarks, seen (and heard!) in the duney vegetation around the Towans. **4** A curious grey seal at Godrevy Head. **5** St Piran's Day parade at Perranporth. ▶

use the stairs, the disabled access is supplemented by a touchscreen illustrating the collection.)

A special exhibit contains the paintbox of the Georgian society painter John Opie (see below), who grew up in St Agnes, and pride of place is given to the recently acquired portrait of the artist's sister, Betty, together with one of Opie's 20 self-portraits. Edward Opie, who like his role-model great-uncle, became a Royal Academician, is also represented by a portrait of his father. All three portraits are arrestingly frank, but it is the intensity of John Opie's self-querying gaze that commands the attention longest.

If you don't mind hills, there are some great **walks**, starting and finishing in the village, that take you up St Agnes Beacon, or along the wooded Jericho Valley or out on to the wild coast at Chapel Porth. Whichever route you take, the tin industry is never out of sight and – if the lonely, lofty ruins intrigue you – it's best to go armed with the series of locally produced walking maps (*Ten Walks in and around St Agnes*) which tell the stories behind the relics and can be downloaded at ⏣ stagnesforum.com.

JOHN OPIE RA

John Opie (1761–1807) was just ten when he sold his first portrait, much to the disgust of his father, who was determined his son would follow him into the carpentry trade. But in 1776, aged 15, the St Agnes boy was released from his apprenticeship and delivered into the hands of Dr Wolcot, a Truro dilettante, who had spotted not only talent but the possibility of high earnings in the teenage prodigy. For six years, Wolcot touted Opie round Cornwall's big families, organising portrait commissions; then, encouraged by his protégé's rapidly developing artistic maturity, took his 'Cornish Wonder' to London. Opie was introduced to Sir Joshua Reynolds and from that moment his career, but decidedly not his sense of fulfilment, took off. Opie started to resent Wolcot's constant and exploitative presence and broke off their partnership; he then rushed into marriage with one of his prettiest and sadly, most immature sitters, and spent 13 years regretting everything and painting everyone. History subjects, especially the dramatic slashfest titled *The Murder of Rizzio*, painted in 1787, brought him wide acclaim and it can only be hoped that painting it brought him some kind of cathartic release from his marital troubles too. He died aged just 45, but not too unhappily: in his last decade he was made a Royal Academician (largely thanks to the Rizzio picture), divorced his wife who had mercifully eloped – and found blissful companionship in a second marriage. When he died, he was buried beside Reynolds in St Paul's Cathedral.

¶¶ FOOD & DRINK

St Agnes is enjoying a quiet foodie revolution – with the old post office rising from the ashes as a delightful café (**The Old Sorting Office**), the **Trunk Deli** specialising in Cornish produce and artisan cheeses from all over the world, the tiny but perfect **St Agnes Bakery** (♂ stagnesbakery.co.uk) and the **Cornish Pizza Company** (♂ thecornishpizzacompany. co.uk) – you really are spoilt for choice these days.

Locals tell me that the **St Agnes Hotel** (♂ stagneshotel.co.uk) is a very nice place to eat and drink. Lots of people also recommended **Schooners** in Trevaunce Cove (♂ schoonerscornwall.com) – for its fabulous food and ambience – and there's the **Taphouse** (♂ the-taphouse.co.uk), too, popular for its lively music scene on Thursday nights. Up-to-date information on all these places can be found at ♂ visitstagnes.com.

The Driftwood Spars Trevaunce Cove, TR5 0RT ✆ 01872 552428 ♂ driftwoodspars. co.uk. A friendly pub, beamy and full of character, close to the beach, with its own microbrewery in the blue timber shed across the road. Local ales and ciders, and a terrific menu of locally sourced dishes. Popular with everyone: locals, surfers, families and hairy bikers.

4 PORTREATH & TEHIDY COUNTRY PARK

Between Camborne and the sea, the Bassetts of Tehidy, a wealthy and influential mining family, built a succession of increasingly lavish houses, surrounded by gardens, lakes and a deer park. They built a harbour, too, at **Portreath**, from which copper and tin could be exported, while coal to drive the mine engines arrived on incoming vessels. But thanks to the profligacy of the last Bassett to reside at **Tehidy**, in 1916 the house and park were divided and sold. The house reopened as a TB sanatorium, but was destroyed by fire just two weeks after receiving its first patients. A new hospital and houses were built around the core of the ruins and, although the hospital has closed, this part remains a private residential area. Since 1983, however, the wooded grounds have been a public space, much appreciated by residents of Redruth and Camborne. It's a fine place for a morning or afternoon's sheltered ramble. A bike route runs through the park and if you follow it from east to west, you'll enjoy a gentle downhill slope. The café at the gate entrance on South Drive is open all year but closed on Mondays.

"Since 1983, however, the wooded grounds have been a public space, much appreciated by residents of Redruth and Camborne."

JOHN PASSMORE EDWARDS (1823–1911)

There's scarcely a town of any size in Cornwall that did not benefit from the generosity of the poor boy from Blackwater, who hauled himself out of poverty through education and made language a weapon for liberating others from oppression and injustice. Libraries and institutes where the poor could advance their education without payment were his legacy to Cornwall – as well as other towns across the south of England – and he also built orphanages and art galleries, convalescent homes and hospitals, earning himself the title 'the Cornish Carnegie'.

As a young man, Edwards was a bit of a firebrand and abandoned work as a solicitor's clerk to write for a radical newspaper, where he earned peanuts, but fought for the abolition of hanging and flogging, spoke passionately against war, rallied to the cause of the trade unions and opposed all forms of social injustice. By the age of 28 he was owner of his own paper, *The Public Good*, but his enthusiasm outdistanced his means and he was bankrupted. For ten years Edwards slaved to repay every penny owed to his creditors, and was rewarded by better fortune in the form of a happy marriage and the clever purchase of London's first evening paper. Notwithstanding libel actions (as when, for example, his paper lashed out at a parliamentary candidate for being more suited to representing Sodom and Gomorrah than Rochester) Edwards made a mint, and that was when the busy philanthropy started. His first project was to build an institute with a library in his home village, Blackwater, offering village boys and men an alternative to the pub. Few lives are lived better than this: there was never any trace of Victorian smugness, and even towards the end of his life, something of the young radical in Edwards led him to refuse a knighthood.

¶¶ FOOD & DRINK

The Hub Portreath TR16 4NN ✆ 01209 844666 ⊘ thehubportreath.com. Attached to an excellent bike-hire centre (page 220). The Hub's team of young, dedicated staff serve up top-notch coffee, light lunches including vegan specials, and local beers and ciders. Summer evening suppers are advertised on the website.

5 GODREVY HEAD & THE TOWANS

🏠 **Driftwood Beach Chalet** Gwithian Towans (page 420)

In summer, the two National Trust car parks are packed to overflowing and the three miles of west-facing sandy beach between Godrevy Head and Hayle freckled with bucket-and-spading families and surfers. **The Towans** (Cornish for sand dunes) are dotted with chalets and caravan parks, but alive with butterflies and skylarks among the duney vegetation.

It's hard to believe that a large part of the Upton Towans was the site of a dynamite factory in the early 1900s, but a scattering of ruined buildings and parts of the old tramway can still be seen. The dunes hide other secrets too: further north, close to **Gwithian**, a pre-Norman oratory, dedicated to the Celtic saint Gothian, was rediscovered when a local farmer decided to dig out a pond in 1827. It's since been reclaimed by the sand but Gwithian's 13th-century church, built on safer ground, has survived despite being almost entirely rebuilt in Victorian times. The Methodist chapel in Gwithian, built in 1810, is one of the few thatched buildings in this part of the county.

Tread softly in the dunes at dusk around midsummer and you may see glow-worms, too. Between Godrevy Head and Navax Point you can look down the sheer cliff to seal colonies, who come here to breed and raise their young. It's a long way down and access (even if it were possible) is prohibited, so a pair of binoculars is a good idea. Out of season, it's a lonely wilderness, visited by migrant birds and the walk to **Godrevy Head**, with its island lighthouse and views across the bay to the bright lights of St Ives, is a good way to work up a feeling of Romantic melancholy, or at least, following in the footsteps of Virginia Woolf, whose novel *To the Lighthouse* was drawn from memories of childhood holidays spent here, a Mrs Ramsay-ish type of introspection.

¶¶ FOOD & DRINK

The Jam Pot Gwithian Towans TR27 5BU ☎ 01736 755811 ☐ ☺ closed winter. A much loved beach café (the homemade cakes are legendary in these parts) in a historic building shaped something like a jam pot, which was in fact a coastguard lookout built in the early 19th century.

Red River Inn Gwithian TR27 5BW ☎ 01736 753223 ☐ red-river-inn.co.uk. Named after the stream close by that used to run red with the run-off from iron ore in the mining areas upriver, this is a free house with a jolly atmosphere and fine menu of local ales and dishes. Family- and dog-friendly.

THE COPPER & TIN TOWNS: HAYLE, REDRUTH & CAMBORNE

The real joy of going Slow is the way that the unlikeliest of places reveal themselves, heart and soul, and often in a most unexpected fashion. In fact, it was harder to find the beating heart of some of Cornwall's more fashionable resorts than it was in this trio of post-industrial towns that are working with passion and integrity towards a distinctive and sustainable future.

6 HAYLE

These are interesting times for Hayle, and much has changed since the first edition of this book appeared in 2012. The old harbour area continues to be the subject of a multi-million-pound redevelopment plan, intended to give it a mini-Docklands kind of facelift, with residential property and shops joining a supermarket housed within an award-winning building (honest) on South Quay, linked by a footbridge over Penpol Creek to the town centre. More housing is also springing up around the Marine Renewables Business Park on North Quay. You can see the thinking – Hayle is built around water: pools, creeks, wharves and the River Hayle itself; then there is the town's wealth of Victorian industrial architecture, just right for offices, loft apartments and artists' studios; and plenty of brownfield space, ripe for adventurous, eco-sensitive architecture. It is highly unlikely, though, that the slightly scruffy harbour and Penpol Creek, with its faded boats tied up along the narrow wharf, faced by a row of characterful shops and the odd café, will ever become a marina for the jet set; long may it continue to suit those who enjoy pottering and nattering and watching the dabchicks scuttle about the banks or the gig team scooting across the harbour at high water. Hayle is big on watersports as well as lifeguard training, and one of the gig-rowers grimaced pointedly as we discussed the buildings: 'Whatever they end up doing here, it would be nice if all the watersports could have a clubhouse.'

In the 19th century, Hayle developed rapidly, thanks to its booming copper industry, into a town of two tribes and two halves, which is why it's not very obvious today where the town's centre lies. One tribe consisted of the Harvey's Foundry workforce, who had their own commercial and residential centre, known as **Foundry**, in the region of the White Hart Hotel on the west side of town, while the other tribe was the Cornish Copper Company, which occupied the town to the east, known as **Copperhouse**. The Passmore Edwards Institute sits diplomatically between the two on the waterfront, but there are still granite posts dotted about the town, marked with H or CCC, which were erected to settle territorial disputes by formalising the tribal boundaries.

Copperhouse territory is also identifiable by the use of shiny black blocks in the construction of many of the older buildings. The material is scoria, the slag waste produced from smelting copper ore; it was a brilliant piece of recycling, but unless it has acquired a patina of lichen, not terribly attractive.

On the other side of Copperhouse Pool lies **Phillack**, a rural outpost of Hayle, with its back to the grassy dunes that give it some protection from northerly gales. Heads swivel as they pass Phillack's St Austell Brewery-owned pub, on account of its name, the **Bucket of Blood**. The once dark and beamy pub no longer plays up to its reputation of being haunted (long ago, the landlord let his bucket down into the well and drew up the blood of a murdered customs man) and has become a light and bright, family-friendly sort of place, much to the despair of some locals. Phillack's Victorian church, **St Felicitas**, built on the remains of a Norman church and even older Christian Celtic site, is granite, but the churchyard's retaining wall is built of scoria. St Felicitas, in Copperhouse territory, was Hayle's only Anglican church, so the Foundry tribe tended to go to the church in St Erth, until the decision was taken to build a church in Hayle to cater for them. This was the imposing St Elwyn's, completed in 1888, which stands on a rise overlooking the junction of harbour and Copperhouse Pool. Needless to say, there were two Methodist chapels; the Copperhouse one has been demolished, but the Foundry chapel is now a galleried indoor shopping and gallery space, known locally as **Pratt's Market**, specialising in crafts and antiques (⌂ oldfoundrychapel. co.uk). Just around the corner, in a nicely

"Heads swivel as they pass Phillack's St Austell Brewery-owned pub, on account of its name, the Bucket of Blood."

converted range of old foundry buildings, **Foundry Farm**, where horses were once stabled, has been sensitively converted with a mixture of studios and craft workshops. Meanwhile, **Foundry Yard** is due to be redeveloped as residential and office space. For more information, check ⌂ harveysfoundrytrust.org.uk.

With much history to celebrate, **The Hayle Heritage Centre** in Foundry Square (✆ 01736 757683 ⌂ hayleheritagecentre.org.uk) is steadily expanding to fill the old Harvey foundry with exhibitions covering the town's long industrial (and pre-industrial) history. You can also pick up a *Hayle Discovery* map from here, where the best walking routes around the town are well laid-out with helpful illustrations and historical notes.

A stroll up **Foundry Hill** takes you into Millpond Gardens and into the wooded fringes of the Millpools – manmade pools fed by the Penpol Creek which once provided power for the watermills below. The return journey through Foundry Yard gives an impressive overview of the once-mighty engineering works.

To get a better idea of how Copperhouse and Foundry sit together, cross over the iron bridge by the harbour and follow the **George V Memorial Walk**, fragrantly lined with subtropical planting, from the open-air swimming pool all along the back of Copperhouse Pool, from which Hayle's grander buildings stand out with clarity. Returning to the town over the Black Bridge, it's a straight run down through shops and terraced houses to St Elwyn's Church, where the harbour joins Penpol Creek. I've already mentioned the row of interesting shops and cafés along Penpol Terrace, but there's a good reason to cross the road to the grassy wharfside: here is the memorial to Hayle-born Rick Rescorla, who died while helping more than 2,700 people to safety from New York's World Trade Center on 11 September 2001.

Hayle's birds

Hayle's watery environment and tidal exposure of marshy mudflats is an important overwintering ground for all sorts of wildfowl and visiting migrants. The whole estuary, much of which is owned by the RSPB, is hugely popular with birdwatchers, from those who enjoy the avian spectacle from the comfort of the car by **Copperhouse Pool** (there's free parking space by the outdoor swimming pool on the Phillack side of the water) to seriously tooled-up photographers, crouched silently behind zoom lenses in the hide at Ryan's Field, close to the A30. Copperhouse Pool is famous for its rarities, often spotted flitting between the pool and the main estuary. For most people though, just observing the resident population of shelducks, redshanks, curlews, herons, egrets and gulls going about their business, or enjoying the seasonal influx of pattering dunlins, sandpipers and turnstones, and the flocks of plovers and lapwings, is quite enough.

---

1 Hayle estuary. **2** & **4** Dunlins (below) and curlews (above), seen at Hayle estuary. **3** East Pool Mine. ▶

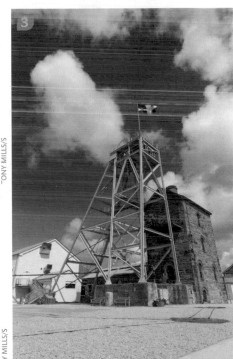

With all this free and natural bird entertainment on hand, a trip to the bird sanctuary at **Paradise Park** (16 Trelissick Rd, Hayle TR27 4HB ✆ 01736 751020 ⌨ paradisepark.org.uk), a natural wetland and protected site, might seem an unnecessary expense, but behind the gaudy advertisements are seven gorgeously planted acres of serious conservation at work and children seem to love it, especially on dry afternoons, when some of the birds are allowed out of their huge and imaginatively designed aviaries and fly freely. Like the Monkey Sanctuary near Looe (page 161), Paradise Park was created by a single individual, whose hobby developed into a passionate cause. It began with a pair of parrots, kept as pets. Mike Reynolds (who, in his professional life, led the Milky Bar Kid advertising campaign in the 1960s and 1970s) soon saw his love for the birds advance into a concern for the threat to wild populations; in 1989 he set up the World Parrot Trust, a charity which supports conservation and education projects around the world.

"Paradise Park was created by a single individual, whose hobby developed into a passionate cause."

One of the trust's greatest successes was a project to save the rare echo parakeet of Mauritius, whose numbers in the wild had dwindled to around 15 known individuals by 1990 but can now be measured in hundreds. Reynolds, who died in 2007, also set up the world's first ever Parrot Action Plan, which has become a blueprint for conservation programmes around the world. His family still runs the conservation centre at Hayle and one of the latest projects is to re-introduce the red squirrel to Cornwall.

I went, because I wanted to find out more about their chough breeding programme. David Woolcock, the head keeper, explained that the relatively recent wild population of choughs in Cornwall (page 302) has been traced genetically to a very small number of breeding pairs, who arrived on the Lizard, blown off course from their native Ireland. 'Imagine if the human population of Hayle were descended from just one couple,' he said, keeping a perfectly straight face. 'You'd hope for some blood to strengthen the gene pool, wouldn't you?' Indeed you would. Which is why at Paradise Park they have been breeding Welsh choughs, with the future aim of introducing them to the wild, but purely Irish, population. However would you do that? 'A straight egg swap,' replied David. 'We simply swap our Welsh chough eggs with eggs from the nests of the wild birds. The parent birds should not notice a thing.'

¶¶ FOOD & DRINK

The Big Green Shed Sunrise Farm, TR27 6AL ✆ 07380 165858 🖰 thebiggreenshed.co.uk ☉ closed Mon & Tue. Ben Prior (of the much missed Ben's Cornish Kitchen in Marazion) and wife Lisa (formerly of the Peppercorn Café in Perranuthnoe) have a devoted following and their venture overlooking a bucolic valley just outside Hayle is a very welcome addition to the breakfast and lunch scene in these parts.

Bird in Hand Trelissick Rd, TR27 4HY ✆ 01736 753974 🖰 birdinhandhayle.co.uk. At the entrance to Paradise Park, and run by the same family, this pub is big on music nights with local bands often performing. The pub brews its own speciality ale, Paradise Bitter.

Richards of Cornwall Carwin Farm, near Hayle TR27 5DG (just off the A30, close to the West Cornwall Retail Park roundabout at Loggans Moor) ✆ 01736 757888 🖰 richardsofcornwall. co.uk. This is a fantastic farm shop, selling fruit, vegetables and salads direct from the farm and daffodil bulbs in the autumn. Lots of organic Cornish dairy and meat and a superb frozen counter, where you can buy fruit and vegetables by the scoop.

Salt Kitchen Bar 25 Foundry Sq, TR27 4HH ✆ 01736 755862 🖰 salt-hayle.co.uk. At the Foundry end of town, Salt looks like the shape of things to come in Hayle: industrial architecture close to the water and a contemporary Mediterranean-style menu based on local ingredients.

Trevaskis Farm Gwinear TR27 5JQ ✆ 01209 713931; shop 01209 714009 🖰 trevaskisfarm. co.uk. An awful lot of good stuff happens at Trevaskis: it's an organic farm and kitchen garden with an educational as well as a productive mission; there's a comprehensive farm shop with a huge deli counter, and a café-restaurant that opens daily for breakfast, lunch and dinner.

7 CAMBORNE

Outsiders to the region tend to lump neighbouring Camborne and Redruth (and Pool which lies between) together, often with a shudder of horror at the thought of visiting the urban centre of Cornwall's post-industrial heartland. It's a rather outdated attitude, though, typified by S P B Mais in his 1950 book *We Wander in the West*, where talking of Camborne-and-Redruth, he writes: 'neither of which … has much to offer the stranger in search of beauty except some very virile Rugger'. He was right about the rugby though: Camborne and Redruth have distinct identities and a history of rivalry, played out with concentrated ferocity on the rugby pitch. And Pool in the middle is in the process of receiving a multi-million-pound development scheme, just as South Crofty, the last mine to close, in 1998, is the subject of much speculation as a 2020 drill programme successfully demonstrated the presence of lithium-rich lodes.

It's true that Camborne doesn't go out of its way to entice visitors; most of the signposted attractions are to mining heritage centres in the vicinity, but I like it all the more for its self-contained reticence. A visit to the public loo just off Commercial Square, for example, brought me face to face with a pair of beautifully carved, clearly contemporary, wooden gates. 'The Outlaws Hide in the Forest' ran the lettering, above a man in a tree looking at a fox and holding his finger to his lips. There was no plaque, no explanation, just the carved words 'Beunans Meriasek' ('The life of Meriasek' in Cornish). I found part of the answer in Camborne's church, the other in the Driftwood Spars, a St Agnes pub (page 227). Standing in a large and leafy churchyard, **Camborne's parish church** is a lovely amalgamation of Norman, Tudor, Georgian and Victorian building. It's dedicated to St Martin and St Meriadoc, Meriasek in Cornish. The 16th-century mystery play *Beunans Meriasek* tells the story of the saint coming to Camborne and founding the church. And in the Driftwood Spars I discovered that the brewer, the late Peter Martin, had been a most talented and versatile chap as it was he who had carved the gates. The church revealed some other surprises, too: in the main sanctuary, the panelling and seating along the walls are made from 15th-century bench-ends showing a mermaid, a unicorn and other mythical creatures, but the best treasure lay under the altar cloth in the Lady Chapel. There, with the help of the church warden, I looked at the 10th-century altar slab, inscribed in Latin with its sponsor's dedication and five Norman reconsecration crosses, originating from the chapel of St Ia, near Troon, a couple of miles away.

"Camborne is stuffed with grand Victorian architecture that speaks of prosperous times and Victorian benevolence."

Camborne is stuffed with grand **Victorian architecture** that speaks of prosperous times and Victorian benevolence. As you might expect, there's a Passmore Edwards Library, designed – as so many of Edwards's donations were – by Silvanus Trevail (page 205). A statue of Richard Trevithick (page 238), with a model of the Camborne locomotive tucked under his arm, stands outside looking up the hill on which he tested the full-size version of the machine to destruction in 1801. By the time the library was built, Camborne already had a literary institute, complete with classical portico and lecture room, on the edge of Commercial Square, and two enormous Wesleyan chapels. All these

THE NATIONAL DAHLIA COLLECTION

Kehelland, Camborne TR14 0DD ✆ 07753 959856 ⬛ nationaldahliacollection ⊙ during flowering season (Jul–Oct Wed 17.00–dusk, Sat 10.00–16.00)

Even if dahlias are not your thing, an evening visit in August or September, when flowering is at its peak, is a soul-stirring experience. Some may remember when, from 1998 to 2020, the National Dahlia Collection was on display in a field at Varfell, looking out towards St Michael's Mount and part of a commercial venture. Louise Danks, who had once been production manager of the Varfell dahlia collection, was teaching horticulture at the Duchy College when she learned that the business was closing and the dahlias were about to be lost. She managed to secure the site at Kehelland, a horticultural learning centre, and with the help of her dad and a mass of volunteers, replanted the entire collection of 40,000 plants during the Easter holiday of 2021. By late summer that year Louise and the many visitors who came to see these colourful natives of Mexico were rewarded with a staggering display of floral bravado.

are still standing, but no such respect was shown for the internationally renowned **Camborne School of Mines**, which was demolished in 1974 and replaced with a supermarket. It's no exaggeration to say that Camborne was the Oxbridge of the mining world; from 1888 anyone associated with minerology, mines and mine engineering *anywhere* in the world would have heard of Camborne. (The school still exists, as part of Exeter University, located at the Penryn Campus.)

🍴 FOOD & DRINK

The Kehelland Trust Shop Kehelland, Camborne TR14 0DD ✆ 01209 718 975 🌐 kehellandtrust.org.uk ⊙ closed Sun. Kehelland is a horticultural centre that gives adults with learning and/or physical special needs the opportunity to learn how to grow and sell plants and produce. The shop is the nicest place in Camborne to buy groceries, supplemented by high-end dairy and bakery goodies.

8 TREVITHICK'S COTTAGE

Penponds, Camborne TR14 0QG ⊙ pre-booked tours only, Wed afternoons between Apr & Oct; National Trust

Lois Humphrey invited me to enjoy the small, but colourful garden while she took a couple who had arrived just ahead of me inside the whitewashed, thatched cottage in Penponds.

RICHARD TREVITHICK (1771–1833)

Camborne salutes its favourite son each year on Trevithick Day, on the last Saturday in April, with steam-engine displays, street parades and dancing along the route of the inventor's most famous steam-driven experiment 'up Camborne Hill and down again' (as the song goes).

Trevithick was every bit as brilliant as (and probably more versatile than) his contemporary, Sir Humphry Davy, but his genius did not extend to capitalising on what his fecund mind produced and his adult life was spent lurching from one financial pit to another. In the highly profitable and hugely competitive world of Cornish mining in the late 18th and early 19th centuries there was endless demand for technology to solve the problems of deep-shaft flooding and transportation, and steam was seen as the way forward.

But whereas everyone has heard about James Watt and George Stephenson, outside Cornwall, Richard Trevithick's name has got lost along the way. He may have been unworldly and open to exploitation, but his vast and eclectic record of achievement is none the less impressive: pumping engines, steam locomotion, lifts, turbines and floating docks – there was clearly something of the Leonardo in him.

His one real stroke of good luck and judgement came in his marriage to Jane Harvey, a daughter of the Hayle Foundry empire. Throughout his frequent and financially disastrous trips away from home, which included 11 unprofitable, danger-filled years in South America, and a last, desperate year in London, where he died a pauper, she never faltered in her fondness or support.

It's been extended since the Trevithicks lived here and quite how Richard, a local mine captain, and Anne Trevithick raised Richard junior and his five sisters in such a confined space is hard to imagine.

Only the parlour on the ground floor can be visited by the public and this is only on Wednesday afternoons between April and October (just as well for the Humphreys, who live here, by arrangement with the National Trust). What you see is a tiny, but perfectly unspoiled Georgian living room, which has been panelled and carefully decorated with portraits, memorabilia and photographs that give flesh to the Trevithicks and the way they lived. The small size of the space means overcrowding is easy; booking a visit is therefore essential.

Richard left home in 1797 when he married Jane Harvey, but the couple returned to live here with their own children in 1810, for a brief period, when ill health and bankruptcy forced them out of London. Lois and I looked at the portrait of the steadfastly loyal Jane, who waited 11 years for her husband to return (empty-handed) from South America. And we looked at the portrait of Trevithick, a big man with gentle, unworldly eyes, gazing back at the small room that can barely have contained his restless energy or her enduring patience.

9 EAST POOL MINE

Trevithick Rd, Pool TR15 3ED ✆ 01209 315027 ⊙ pre-booked tours only, Tue–Sat; National Trust

You'll know when you're getting close: the northern site of the museum is easily identified from a distance by its towering chimney stack, with EPAL (East Pool and Agar Ltd) picked out in white bricks.

I can imagine the great steeplejack Fred Dibnah being very happy here (and I'm sure he must have visited because I saw his signature in the Trevithick Cottage visitors' book), watching the great, oiled shafts of the two enormous beam engines in action. The museum is split between two sites, one on each side of the main road that links Redruth and Camborne. The engine at Taylor's shaft, on the north side, was manufactured by Harvey's of Hayle, and designed to pump water from the deep mine; the engine on the south site, at Mitchell shaft, was engineered by Camborne's dynastic family engineering firm, Holman's, and designed to work a winding mechanism, or 'whim'. Although no longer powered by high-pressure steam (electricity does the job now), the two great beasts, pumping away to their own steady rhythm, are none the less impressive.

🍴 FOOD & DRINK

The Bakery Café Wilson Way, Pool TR15 3RT ✆ 01209 218989 ⊘ bakertom.co.uk ⊙ closed Sun. Artisan baker Tom Hazzledine is pre-eminent among Cornwall's breed of speciality bakers; you'll find his sourdough, focaccia and plenty of cakes flying off the shelves of his bakeries in Falmouth, Penzance and Wadebridge. Here in Pool, despite being somewhat lost among the industrial estate buildings, the bakery – with some outdoor seating – is famous for its hearty breakfasts and lunchtime specials, and has a loyal and enthusiastic local following.

The Heartlands Project, Pool

The road uniting Camborne and Redruth used to offer a disheartening prospect of abandoned, scrappy mining buildings and retail trading estates. There's still some of that on offer, but a huge development, powered by photovoltaic energy and fuelled by a biomass boiler, has risen from the industrial ashes, and is determined to give Pool a fresh start and a wildly different image. Beside the beautifully restored Robinson mine, which houses a free mining-heritage centre, as well as a large café and shop, an eco-friendly cluster of houses, artists' studios, offices and community buildings now stands around a marketplace. The rest of the 19-acre site is slowly filling with more houses, trees, pools and grassy places for play. I was taken with the concept of the **Diaspora Gardens**, filled with plants native to the Americas, South Africa, Australia and New Zealand, and representing the spread of Cornish miners and Cornish mining technology across the globe. In reality, a lot of the southern-hemisphere plants would be a lot happier in more southerly parts of the county, but it's still decently maintained and a nice place for a pause on a sunny day. The biggest complaint I heard was the cost of the parking, but that's something you hear all over Cornwall.

"A huge development has risen from the industrial ashes, and is determined to give Pool a fresh start and a wildly different image."

10 REDRUTH

Once the financial capital of the mining world, Redruth is chock-full of history, written all over its handsome Victorian architecture. The town leans out in three hilly directions from its centre in Fore Street, where since 2008 a bronze sculpture of a miner, arms flung out wide, feet firmly on the ground, appears to be on the point of launching into flight. It's a striking image for a town which saw both boom and bust, when two-thirds of its mining population were forced into emigration as their industry collapsed. I like the ambiguity of the miner's gesture: the artist, David Annand, seems to have caught both the heroism and the suffering, the rootedness and the eventual flight of the Cornish miner.

Every one of the old buildings in Redruth has a story to tell, but none more poignantly encapsulates the rise, fall and emerging restoration of Redruth than the preserved ruins of **Druid's Hall** in Penryn Street. This was built in 1859 as a cultural centre of commensurate grandeur for such an important town, containing a library, vast assembly room and theatre. In 1910, as Redruth's fortunes were on a downward roll, and the cultural centre closed, it was given a lease of life as a cinema. In post-war years the building, which had once represented the civic pride of

Redruth, was transformed into the Zodiac Bingo Club, destroyed by fire in 1984. Only the intriguing shell of the structure remains and this now encloses a small garden, planted in 2000, symbolic of the Redruth, rising not so much from, as within, the ashes of its past.

Walk through the garden and you emerge on a small street, next to a 14th-century stone cross, which marked the entrance to **St Rumon's Chapel**. The medieval chapel was demolished in the 17th century and replaced with a modest house, where William Murdoch (see below) lived (with the Trevithicks as neigbours, for a brief period) for the last two decades of the 1700s. Today, at **Murdoch House** on Cross Street (✆ 01209 213807 🖧 murdochhouse.org.uk ◷ Fri mornings), trustees are available to chat to visitors about the inventor over coffee and cheese scones, in a room filled with exhibits describing Murdoch's life and inventions.

The best place to start exploring Redruth's past is the **Kresen Kernow** Cornish studies facility, housed in the beautifully restored and converted Redruth Brewery (✆ 01209 614430 🖧 kresenkernow.org). This is where anyone interested in tracing their Cornish roots or anything to do with Cornwall or Scilly's past will eventually find themselves. The archives are vast, so visits need to be carefully planned and appointments are

OLD RIVALRIES

Not to be outdone by Camborne's Richard Trevithick, Redruth has its own hero of steam invention: the Scot, William Murdoch, whose life and works are celebrated in mid-June on Murdoch Day, with a similar blast of noise and colour to that of Camborne's Trevithick Day. Murdoch was James Watt's most ambitious and creative employee, but Murdoch's interest in 'strong steam' engineering (where the steam rather than the vacuum created produces energy) cut no ice with Watt, who saw it as risky and experimental. So when Trevithick showed up on Murdoch's Redruth doorstep, the frustrated Scot was delighted by the young man's curiosity and enthusiasm and gave him a demonstration, using a little model engine that ran round his drawing-room floor.

When Trevithick married, he and Jane moved into Redruth, taking accommodation next door to Murdoch. Redruth partisans are in no doubt that Murdoch was the victim of industrial espionage, perpetrated by Trevithick, who went on to claim 'strong steam' as his own invention. Secure in this knowledge, visitors can move about the streets of Redruth safely (unless that is, you're wearing the cherry-and-white colours of Camborne rugby club on the day of the derby match).

necessary. But the library and exhibition spaces need no appointment to visit and it is hoped that tenants for the café on the ground floor will soon be found. Meanwhile, the Redruth visitor centre has been replaced by a comprehensive website, ◈ discoverredruth.co.uk. A useful heritage trail map that explains the significance of all of Redruth's important buildings and makes for enjoyable ambling is to be found at ◈ chycor.co.uk/redruth/map.htm.

Redruth's mining history is important, but it hasn't consumed the town's identity entirely. Artists and creative businesses are increasing in numbers to the point where the **Krowji studios**, just off Blowinghouse Hill (West Park, TR15 3GE ✆ 01209 313200 ◈ krowji.org.uk) can describe itself as 'Cornwall's largest creative hub'. Krowji is housed in an old grammar school that has been converted into dozens of artists' studios and offices and substantially expanded. The studios open for a Christmas weekend in December and again in May/June for the Open Studios Cornwall week, and in between there's usually at least one exhibition or event to visit, and occasional music at the centre's café.

ⵖ FOOD & DRINK

Stones Café Krowji West Park, Redruth TR15 3GE ✆ 07903 324324 ◈ stonesbakedgoods. com ☉ Mon–Fri. Wholesome breakfasts and lunches.

11 CARN BREA & THE GREAT FLAT LODE

Just to the south of Camborne and Redruth, the humpback ridge of **Carn Brea** is one of the great landmarks of west Cornwall, crowned as it is with what looks from a distance like a giant chess piece, and a little lower down embellished with a fortress-like building. You can drive up to the village of Carnkie, just short of the summit, but it's infinitely more interesting to walk, bike or ride the eight-mile track that loops around the hill, through gorse and stunted thorn, taking in the many vestigial remains of engine houses, smelting works, mineshafts and chimneys along the way: basilica-like wrecks of a lost civilisation. It's funny sometimes how nature and the ruins of industrial architecture work so well together – the landscape would not be half so interesting without the ruins and the ruins would not look half so appealing without the soft, green wrappings of nature.

The monument on top of the hill was erected in 1836 to honour Sir Francis Bassett of Tehidy. It's known as the Dunstanville rather than the

Bassett monument in recognition of the title bestowed on the bravest and most popular of the Bassetts, who marched 65 miles with his miners to reinforce Plymouth's woefully inadequate defences from the threat of a combined Spanish and French invasion in 1779. A little way down the hill, the restored castle, one room of which perches on top of a colossal outcrop of granite boulders, was originally built by a medieval Bassett, more as a hunting lodge than as a defensive fortress. It now contains what has to be one of Cornwall's least expected delights: a Jordanian family-run restaurant (page 246).

The well-marked trail around Carn Brea is known as the **Great Flat Lode** (GFL), a reference to the rich vein of tin-bearing ore (lode) underground, which while not exactly horizontal, was far from vertical, as most tin lodes tend to be. This accounts for the proliferation of shafts along the trail: how much easier it was to hit the lode with a sequence of short shafts than the single deep shaft that most lodes required, with galleries off, from which the ore could be hacked. The mine owners had other reasons to be grateful to the GFL: the copper-bearing ore above had been exhausted by 1870, and the discovery of tin below kept the mines open for several decades longer than expected, finally closing in 1917.

"It's funny sometimes how nature and the ruins of industrial architecture work so well together."

To make a full day of the walk, there are a couple of worthwhile places to stop at on the way: King Edward Mine and the Shire Horse Trust, both on the southern section of the trail.

The King Edward Mine Museum

Troon, Camborne TR14 9DP ℘ 01209 614681 ⊙ kingedwardmine.co.uk ⊙ seasonal variations: check website for details

'What we have here is either priceless treasure – or a pile of junk, depending on your point of view,' grinned the man on the admissions desk, 'but none of it can ever be replaced.' I am no industrial archaeologist, but one of the real pleasures of researching this chapter has been the opportunity to engage with some of the characters who keep Cornish mining history alive and accessible. The engineering principles may be roughly the same, whichever mine you visit, but each mine has a different story to tell, and the voices that tell the story are worth listening

to. In this case, it was Ian, a volunteer at the museum, who explained the history and machinery of the mine and set the enormous dipper wheel into action. Since 1901, when the mine was refurnished with the latest in mining equipment for training purposes, all students of the Camborne School of Mines have done their practical training here, both above and – until 1921 – below ground. There's some lovely footage on the museum website of students here in the 1930s, all tweed-suited and Brylcreemed, learning surveying techniques and playing a game of impromptu football among the old buildings.

Meanwhile, the exhibition within the old boiler house is designed to put the mine in the context of Carn Brea's long history. There's an excellent café, **The Croust Hut**, just outside the entrance (page 246).

Shire Horse Trust

Lower Gryllis, Treskillard TR16 6LA ⌀ 01209 713606 ◼ Shire Horse Trust and Carriage Museum ⊙ Easter–end Oct Sun–Fri 10.00–16.00

There's a serious conservation issue being addressed at this bucolic, if slightly scruffy, farm southwest of Carn Brea, where nonagenarian Harry Gott has been breeding Suffolk Punches a breed of heavy horse on the verge of extinction – all his adult life. As a boy, Harry was evacuated during the war to a farm where horses were being used as draught animals, and he's never looked back, though it saddens him to have witnessed the rapid decline of the breed in post-war years. 'We hope to see a foal born here every year,' he says, 'but that doesn't alter the fact that more Suffolk Punches die than are born in the UK each year.' Geronimo, a splendid stallion bought from an Amish community, is Harry's pride and joy and several of Geronimo's offspring can be seen on the farm. He keeps Clydesdales and shire horses here too, and there's a working forge where you can see the horses being shod.

"Harry Gott has been breeding Suffolk Punches – a breed of heavy horse on the verge of extinction – all his adult life."

At 90-something, Harry lets his staff of young women (who clearly love working here) show visitors around, but if you happen to catch the old rascal – and he likes you – the stories will come tumbling out. Wear sensible footwear and do not expect a visit to be a theme-park

◀ **1** Carn Brea and the Great Flat Lode. **2** Gwennap Pit. **3** Interior of the King Edward Mine.

experience; this is an unforgettable slice of rural history, which won't be around forever. Note that the carriage museum is permanently closed.

FOOD & DRINK

Carn Brea Castle Carnkie, Redruth TR16 6SL ✆ 01209 218358 ⏥ carnbreacastle.co.uk ☺ eves only. Very hard to find and get to (it's down a pot-holed track, somewhere near the summit of Carn Brea), especially on a dark evening, but the reward for intrepid and determined diners is pure magic: candle-lit granite walls that are 700 years old, a Jordanian welcome (you will meet the Sawalha family, who had the imagination and courage to set up a family restaurant here in 1990) and simple Middle Eastern food. See if you can persuade one of the staff to let you climb up to the roof; the views across Cornwall are sublime.

The Croust Hut Newton Rd, Troon TR14 9HW ✆ 01209 612635 ⏥ thecrousthut.co.uk ☺ closed Mon; see 🅵 for variations. Just by the entrance to the King Edward Mine Museum, this independent café does a roaring trade in traditional breakfasts and lunches – including dishes on an Asian theme – throughout the year. In warmer months there is plenty of outdoor seating, but in winter, when indoor space is limited, booking is advised.

12 GWENNAP PIT & CARN MARTH QUARRIES

Three miles south of Redruth, on the edge of Gwennap, TR16 5HH ♥ SW741400 ✆ 01209 822770 ☺ visitor centre: spring bank holiday to end Sep

Gwennap Pit is one of the most important places on the Methodist map. In 1762, John Wesley wrote, 'The wind was so high that I could not stand at the usual place at Gwennap; but at a small distance was a green hollow capable of containing many thousands of people. I stood on one side of this amphitheatre towards the top and with people beneath on all sides, I preached.' He returned on no fewer than 18 occasions, once (reportedly) attracting a crowd of 32,000, which seems a slight exaggeration: the pit is impressive enough, but surely not that big. The grassy tiers were cut out by local miners in the early 19th century, to make seating easier for the crowds which continued to flock to the site; today the annual Whitsun service (as well as regular summer services) continues to draw large audiences. There's an indoor chapel next to the entrance and a small visitor centre.

A lovely six-mile walk, which starts at the visitor centre, takes you up quiet tracks – from where the views become increasingly spectacular as you climb – to and around the **Carn Marth Quarries**. Granite from these quarries was once used to build the Redruth Viaduct and the clear water is popular with anglers and swimmers alike. If you have a spare

CORNISH METHODISM

There's nothing like an industrialised, working-class community for generating a feeling of 'Us and Them', and by the middle of the 18th century mining communities across Cornwall were feeling about as far removed from the mine-owning 'Thems' as was possible. Even on Sundays, there was no getting away from the feeling of alienation, shuffling into a church which seemed to represent a similarly distant, incomprehensible authority, accessible only to the toffs in the front pew.

So when the Wesley brothers, Charles and John, arrived in Cornwall in 1743 (it was the first of 32 whirlwind tours of preaching by John), preaching personal rather than institutionalised faith and salvation, it was taken up by the working classes with gusto. What's more, it meant not being restricted to worshipping in church with the local toffery; services could be held in cottage parlours, farm buildings or even woods and quarries. Chapels began to spring up, but that didn't change the basic fact that Methodism was comforting, comfortable and spoken in everyday language.

But as the numbers of chapels increased, many of the old Anglican churches in Cornwall were falling to pieces and watching their congregations dwindle. This in turn generated its own dynamic response: by the mid-1800s, a huge rebuilding initiative to preserve the old parish churches was launched and dozens of Victorian architects rolled up their sleeves.

hour or two and the right shoes, do give it a go. Details of a shorter walk as well as this one can be found on the iWalk Cornwall app.

FOOD & DRINK

Portreath Bakery Lanner TR16 6HJ 𝒫 01209 314613 𝒸 portreathbakery.com. Lots of gluten-free options as well as traditional pasties and saffron buns. Good place to pick up a picnic.

GODOLPHIN COUNTRY

South and west of Camborne, a maze of roads winds through undulating farming country, dotted with small villages and hamlets, littered not only with remains of the mining industry, but relics of older activity too, in the form of isolated barrows and standing stones, earthworks and abandoned settlements. Bassett mines give way to Godolphin estates and less than five crow-flown miles from Camborne, the trickling beginnings of the River Hayle have been crossed and the wooded entrance to the headquarters of the once-powerful Godolphins lies ahead.

13 GODOLPHIN

🏠 **Godolphin House** (page 420)

Godolphin Cross TR13 9RE ✎ 01736 763194; National Trust

An entry in the visitors' book compares the gardens at Godolphin most unfavourably with Lanhydrock's manicured acres, which gives everybody who loves the place a good giggle.

Parts of Godolphin's gardens are more than 700 years old and much of the special atmosphere derives from the feeling that time and horticultural fashion have slipped past, leaving a sort of leafy, self-contained lushness, just on the right side of unkempt, that the 17th-century poet, Andrew Marvell, would have recognised and loved: 'Society is all but rude,/To this delicious solitude.' The head gardener was moving on to another position when I visited, but she assured me that the National Trust, which acquired the property in 2007, has no intention of 'improving' the gardens, despite massive renovations to the buildings that have seen the creation of a discreet **visitor centre** and **tea room** in the old piggery and conversion of the main house into an upmarket holiday let. (The house can still be visited on selected dates; it is worth checking the National Trust website in advance and following the links to house open days.)

Originally the gardens were laid out as eight squares, enclosing in the ninth square a small castle, erected in or around 1300. The castle was pulled down in the late 1400s, and a house built, set around two courtyards, embellished by generations of Godolphins, until by the mid-1600s, it was ranked as one of the biggest houses in Cornwall. Just one **courtyard** survives today, with its chief glory intact: the double-height, colonnaded north façade, an idiosyncratic blend of Tuscan classicism and English battlements. The Civil War halted the building programme and although the Royalist Godolphins recovered their wealth and influence the house was left increasingly unoccupied and ultimately more or less abandoned until 1937, when Sydney and Mary Schofield bought it from a local mining man and initiated a loving and sensitive restoration of what remained of the **house**.

Beyond the gardens are 550 acres of National Trust-owned estate **woods** to explore, beneath which lies the source of Godolphin wealth: tin- and copper-mine workings, some dating back to the 16th century.

◀ **1** The gardens at Godolphin. **2** View from Tregonning Hill.

The **old engine houses**, engulfed now by trees, reminded me of those ruined jungle temples you find in Cambodia or Peru; those of a more prosaic temperament might find the allusion a little far-fetched and suggest a head-clearing stroll up Godolphin Hill, which pushes its bare crown above the treeline and offers bracing views of both north and south coasts and everything in between.

¶¶ FOOD & DRINK

The Queen's Arms Breage TR13 9PD ✆ 01326 564229 🖰 queensarmscornwall.com. You're not far from Helston (page 304) or Porthleven (page 300) by the time you get to Godolphin or Tregonning, but there's this decent pit stop on the way. It's a big, friendly pub, with a couple of B&B rooms, serving home-cooked, locally sourced food and local ales; it's dog- and child-friendly, too. At the back there's parking and hook-ups for camper vans, and when I asked about putting up a tent, I was shown across the road to a delightful grassy spot, in a walled enclosure adjoining the churchyard.

14 TREGONNING HILL

Several footpaths lead to the summit, but the shortest and most accessible route starts in Balwest, where there's free parking in a field during the summer months (park on the grassy triangle at the start of the track at other times) and an information board and map by the gate. The views from the top are stupendous, a huge reward for an easy climb of well under a mile, along a track that is well used by mountain bikers too. From the **war memorial** that stands close to the trig point, you can see both the north coast and the great, glinting arc of Mount's Bay, St Michael's Mount dwarfed by distance and height. Godolphin Hill, a mile away to the north, though just lower by 30 feet, is similarly reduced to molehill proportions. A short walk southeast along the summit ridge leads to a **Wesleyan preaching pit** in a disused quarry and a plaque commemorating William Cookworthy's discovery of china (kaolin) clay here in 1746. Cookworthy, a young chemist from Plymouth, had spotted local miners were using Tregonning clay to repair their furnaces, and guessed that if it could withstand such high temperatures without cracking, it must have similar properties to kaolin-type clay, from which porcelain was made. He was right: Tregonning Hill was full of it and British porcelain-

"The views from the top are stupendous, a huge reward for an easy climb of well under a mile."

makers' dependency on imported kaolin from China was about to end. The reason why Tregonning Hill bears no resemblance to the 'Cornish alps', is that the clay here turned out to have a high mica content, and the pits were abandoned as 'kaolin fever' spread east and purer kaolin was found around St Austell. Cornwall's most profitable industry ever had been launched.

15 ST HILARY

Roadside parking is very limited in this tiny, picturesque village, but it's a pleasant walk of less than a mile along farm lanes from its slightly larger neighbour, Goldsithney. Although very much off the beaten track, the **church** at St Hilary repays the effort of getting there by virtue of the astonishing collection of paintings by members of the Newlyn School – Dod and Ernest Procter, the Garstins, Harold Knight and Harold Harvey – that decorate the walls, pulpit and choirstalls. There's also a full-length image of St Francis by Roger Fry, and pieces by Annie Walke, the wife of St Hilary's (in)famous vicar, Father Bernard Walke. His notoriety derived from his High Church insistence on Anglo-Catholic ornament, and he was faced with a Protestant pitchfork mob in 1932, which had taken the trouble to drive up from Plymouth in two hired coaches for the sole purpose of raiding the church and smashing its Catholic artefacts. The poor churchwarden was imprisoned in the tower while the mob wrought its havoc. Next door, a small **heritage centre** (⊘ sthilarypc.org.uk ⊙ May–Sep Wed & Fri 11.00–16.00), staffed by knowledgeable members of the community, has more tales of its turbulent priest.

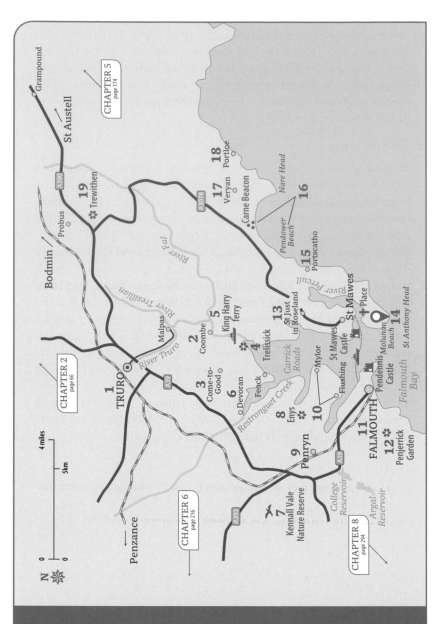

TRURO & THE FAL ESTUARY

7
TRURO &
THE FAL ESTUARY

From Truro to Falmouth by river, there is not one inch of unloveliness, the estuary shores designated in their entirety an Area of Outstanding Natural Beauty. Herons, silent and still, observe the water, egrets gather in oak trees and oystercatchers sweep down to the muddy banks at low tide. And the sorrowful cry of the curlew echoes around the tidal creeks, epitomising the soft, green loneliness of these very special hidden places.

Although it's common to refer to the whole estuary as **the Fal**, the Fal is just one of several rivers that flow into the deep, wooded ria – or flooded estuarine valley – below Truro, where the Allen and Kenwyn flow into the **Truro River**. The Truro is joined by the Tresillian at Malpas, and it's not until further downriver that the Fal cuts in from the east. On the west bank, the Carnon and Kennal join in at **Restronguet Creek** and the Penryn River merges with the generous embrace of Falmouth harbour. Here, with the sea in sight, the estuary widens hugely and becomes known as the **Carrick Roads**, narrowing only marginally where Falmouth and St Mawes face each other across a yacht-filled mile of sea. It's a busy estuary, populated not only by sailing boats and passenger ferries, but also towering container ships, heading to the deep moorings above the **King Harry ferry**, where they sit out the lean times, surrounded by dense oak woods, absurdly out of place beside the red-sailed oyster boats, dredging the riverbed the traditional way, through the autumn and winter months.

The western banks of the estuary are the busiest, with a student population at Falmouth and Penryn contributing to the youthful, arty buzz that distinguishes both these towns from other Cornish harbours. There's a heady mix of culture here, encompassing music and the visual arts, gardens and regional cuisine that erupts into a summer-long series of festivals against the backdrop of the river. While not so much goes on across the water, the **Roseland peninsula** has an idyllic waterfront, both riverine and coastal, fringed with sandy, secluded beaches, busy harbours, bright with yachts and dinghies – and some of the smartest hotels in the county. Inland, it's quietly pastoral and dotted with well-heeled little villages, farms and harbours all the way down to its remote, southernmost tip at St Anthony Head.

GETTING AROUND

It's no fun driving through Truro or Falmouth during the morning and evening rush hours, and as the university campus at Tremough expands Penryn gets busier and busier in term-time, too. If arriving by car in Falmouth during the summer months, take advantage of the **Park and Float** scheme, which is more expensive than Park and Ride (both operate out of the Ponsharden car park), but gives you the joy of arriving in the middle of Falmouth by boat.

Summer brings a concentration of cars to the narrow lanes of the Roseland peninsula, and long queues for the King Harry ferry. This is a lovely way to cross the river at its narrowest point – and it cuts miles off the road trip around the head of the estuary, but at peak times can end up being the slower option. However, getting around on public transport is easy, and there's every reason to dump the car and arm yourself with an integrated ferry, bus and train pass.

The **Fal Mussel Card** (it should have been called the Fal Oyster Card, but London Transport objected) comes in two forms. The Local card is valid on ferries only (particularly useful for car drivers commuting on the King Harry ferry); the Visitor card covers travel on the Maritime branch line, local buses and all the classic ferry routes, up, down and across the river (⊘ falriver.co.uk/mussel).

TRAINS

A two-carriage train shuttles up and down the west bank of the estuary every half-hour between Truro and Falmouth Docks, stopping at Penryn and Falmouth Town (The Dell) on the way. The **Maritime branch line** has proved a phenomenally successful service: packed with students and commuters on weekdays and only marginally quieter at weekends.

BUSES

Walkers on both sides of the river are well served, with buses from **Truro** covering the main villages on the Roseland peninsula and linking

TOURIST INFORMATION

Falmouth Fal River Visitor Information Centre, Prince of Wales Pier, TR11 3DF ℰ 01326 741194 ⌀ falmouth.co.uk

St Mawes The Roseland Visitor Centre, The Square, TR2 5AG ℰ 01326 270440 ⌀ stmawesandtheroseland.co.uk

Truro Boscawen St, TR1 2QQ ℰ 01872 274555 ⌀ visittruro.org.uk

with the passenger ferry from Falmouth to St Mawes. **Falmouth**, which is anathema to cars in the summer, has a great round-the-town service departing every 20 minutes from the Quarry car park. The free *Fal River Cornwall Area Guide Book*, published annually, shows how it all fits together and includes suggested bus- and ferry-linked walks. All bus routes and timetables are to be found on ⌀ firstbus.co.uk/cornwall.

FERRIES

The **King Harry ferry** from Feock to Philleigh is the only means of getting a car across the river below Truro, but is much used by walkers and cyclists, too. The service runs all year and is staffed by a very friendly crew. In summer, there's often a chap selling bags of Fal mussels on board.

The other year-round service is the **foot passenger ferry** between Falmouth and St Mawes. In addition, from the beginning of April to early November a small, open boat (fuelled ecologically by old chip fat) ferries walkers from **St Mawes** across the Percuil to Place Creek, on the southernmost tip of the Roseland peninsula.

Other summer services link **Falmouth** to **Truro** and points in between, such as Flushing, Mylor and Trelissick – go to the ferry kiosks on Town Quay in Truro or Prince of Wales Pier in Falmouth.

Details of all ferry services can be found online at ⌀ falriver.co.uk.

CYCLING

There's good cycling to be had on both sides of the estuary and you can take bikes cheaply on all the passenger ferries. The Sustrans NCN Route 3 (the Cornish Way) crosses the Fal on the King Harry ferry and winds pleasantly down to the beach at Pendower (where you'll have to carry your bike over a footbridge) and rejoins the coast again at Portloe. Steep hills and twisty, single-track lanes are the price to be paid for pursuing inviting detours to the remoter shores of the Fal around Lamorran woods.

CYCLE HIRE

St Piran Café & Bike Hire Old Conns Works, Bissoe, Truro TR4 8QZ ✆ 01872 870341. ⎙ bikechainbissoe.co.uk. Well placed for exploring the network of Mineral Trails which fan out west and south of Truro; bikes can be hired by the day or week and there's a café too, beside a large car park.

WALKING

The wide mouth of the Fal estuary, known as the Carrick Roads, offers gentle walking along its shores, where the easy, level footpaths make this area popular with families and those who prefer a leisurely stroll to the undulating rigours of the coast path. The walk from **St Mawes** to **St Just in Roseland** is delightful, but you'll probably end up coming back on the same path as there are only a few inland routes. A notable exception is the figure-of-eight route that loops around **St Anthony Head**, described on page 287. For more rugged, remote and challenging terrain, head north to **Portscatho** and pick up the coast path to Nare Head and Portloe. There is a joined-up bus service from Veryan that is very helpful to walkers on this section of the coast path.

1 TRURO

Cornwall's only city may not have the tourist-pulling power of Falmouth or Padstow, but it is a rewarding destination for Slow explorers, especially if time is spent discovering its gentle riverine setting.

A city with lots of Slow attributes, that looks prosperous and well cared for, Truro is a place to be enjoyed on foot and at a leisurely pace. Truro is small by any city standards, with a population of around 21,000, but that serves to make it all the more approachable. It looks good from a distance, settled snugly in its shallow valley, the three pale towers and spires of the neo-Gothic cathedral soaring high above the surrounding rooftops; it's hard to believe that such a defining landmark has stood there for only a little more than 100 years.

You don't get much of a sense of Truro's strategic position as a riverhead port, however, unless you take to the water (Enterprise Ferries runs a boat from Town Quay to Falmouth during high tides in the summer months) and get a view of the docks and warehouses that line the approach to the quay and a glimpse of the two small rivers, the Kenwyn and the Allen, that flow through the town to meet at this point. The Kenwyn disappears almost immediately beneath the piazza-like expanse of Lemon Quay, but the Allen can be followed on foot, through the Memorial Gardens and car park beyond to the leafy lanes behind the cathedral.

Truro's Celtic and Norman origins were modestly built on fishing, farming and tin; it was Penryn, a few miles downstream, with its internationally important Glasney College, that became the happening place in medieval times. But Truro had stannary town status and a safe port and its prosperity as a commercial and industrial centre grew to heady heights in the 18th and 19th centuries, under the stewardship of one family in particular, the intriguingly named Lemons. William Lemon (1697–1760) was a self-made mining tycoon who married well, invested shrewdly and was twice mayor of Truro. Known locally as 'The Great Mr Lemon', he had great visions for building and improving the town, but it was his grandson, also named William, who put the plans for the creation of a grandly terraced avenue in place and thoroughly revamped the layout of Truro. By the time he died in 1824, the town was frequently compared to Bath in terms of architectural and social scenery. Important Cornish families came to Truro to 'do the season' – it was in the fashionable Assembly Rooms that dynastic unions were forged by anxious Georgian mamas and papas, intent on securing family

RICHARD LANDER (1804–34)

Truro's hero is the boy who grew up in the Fighting Cocks Inn listening to seafarers' tales and walked alone to London aged nine, looking for adventure. By the age of 14 he had spent three years in the West Indies and within five years he had seen something of Europe too, earning his keep as odd-job boy and servant to a succession of wealthy employers. Aged 21 he joined the Scottish explorer Hugh Clapperton's expedition to chart the course of the Niger from source to sea; all the expedition members died of fever, apart from Lander, who received a hero's welcome when he eventually returned home to write a hair-raising account of his adventures.

Two further expeditions to Nigeria followed, partly fuelled by the dangerous mission of attempting to eliminate human slavery; the first, on which he was accompanied by his younger brother, John, was counted a success. The second ended with his death, after a gunshot wound turned gangrenous.

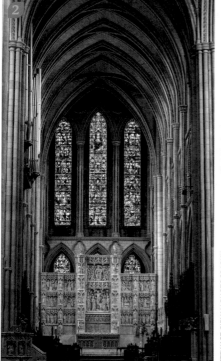

wealth. The name of Lemon is everywhere you look in Truro: Lemon Street is still grandly Georgian, Lemon Quay is the city's festival- and marketplace, Lemon Villas is just as it sounds; a local barbershop calls itself Lemon Heads. But the man on top of the tall Doric column at the head of Lemon Street is not who you might imagine; this is Truro's other hero, Richard Lander – equal (and contemporary, had he lived longer) of David Livingstone, in charting the heart of Africa.

TRURO CATHEDRAL

St Mary's St, TR1 2AF ℰ 01872 276782 ℰ trurocathedral.org.uk

Truro's Victorian masterpiece was the first Anglican cathedral to be built on a new site since Salisbury Cathedral began to rise from the ground in 1220. It needed to be impressive: for 800 years Cornwall had been denied its own bishop, and decades of intense lobbying finally paid off when, in 1877, the diocese of Cornwall (which had last been held at St Germans, in the 10th century) was finally re-established on Cornish soil, at Truro. There were other contenders for the honour – St Germans, naturally, put up a good case; Bodmin too. Even St Columb threw its hat into the ring.

Truro had a parish church in the town centre, but it was in a shabby state by the 1860s and it was assumed that it would have to be pulled down to make way for the new building. But the architect, **John Loughborough Pearson**, made a very convincing case for incorporating the south aisle of the old church into the new structure and won further approval by putting an unobtrusive bend in the main axis, thus avoiding the cost of purchasing an extra block of land to the south. It's cleverly done: you have to stand in the centre of the nave and look up and down to register the six foot difference in alignment between the nave and chancel. Pearson's extravagantly Gothic vision, topped off by three spires, was completed in 1910, 30 years after the first stone was laid.

Inside there's a lot to admire. Pearson worked closely with the sculptor **Nathaniel Hitch**, a man with the ability to make stone seem like butter in his hands. The vast stone reredos behind the high altar is by Hitch, and as you look around, other intricately detailed relief carvings by the

◄ TRURO: **1** Truro Cathedral, dominating the city's skyline. **2** The interior of Truro Cathedral. **3** The newly renovated Hall for Cornwall. **4** A cheese stall at Truro farmers' market.

A WANDER THROUGH THE CITY

Orientation in Truro is fairly straightforward, with the compact historic centre lying around and immediately south of the cathedral. **High Cross**, by the cathedral entrance, is dignified by the 1780 façade of the **Assembly Rooms**, decorated with handsome Wedgwood plaques representing Thalia (the Muse of actors), Shakespeare and actor David Garrick. But the façade is all that's left: the splendid theatre-cum-ballroom that lay behind has long gone, and the arched Georgian windows now display pasties. A few steps away, **Millpool** is a quiet, leafy spot beside the River Allen and overlooked by the cathedral café; there's a 1930s police box by the bridge over the river, which occasionally lends itself to an extremely small art exhibition or installation.

A wander down St Mary's Street takes you past the **Old Grammar School**, founded in 1597; Humphry Davy, the inventor of the miners' safety lamp, went to school here, shortly after the retirement of its legendary headmaster, George Conon, who described the establishment as 'the Eton of Cornwall'.

William Lemon (the elder) enrolled himself here as an adult; having missed out on education in his early years, the mining tycoon humbly decided to make a start on his Latin and Greek. Whether or not he was allowed to bring his pet chough into the classroom (until it was accidentally shot by one of his junior classmates) is a matter for conjecture.

Just around the corner, the many gabled and chimneyed building known as **Coinage Hall** (built as a bank in 1848) contains a marvellously old-fashioned tea room on the first floor with grand views of the Italianate **town hall** and the shops along **Boscawen Street**. Between Coinage Hall and the town hall, **Princes Street** (how can you resist entering via Squeezeguts Alley?) was clearly the place to build your house if you were anyone in the mid-18th century. **Princes House**, designed by Thomas Edwards, was built in 1739 for the chough-loving Lemon, and the **Mansion House** was the town residence of Lemon's chief assistant, Thomas Daniell. Edwards was once again the

same hand stand out with clarity. While I was admiring the **reredos**, an elderly Truronian nudged me and pointed up at a tiny bit of blue glass, evidently a repair, in the stained-glass windows, high above the altar. 'That's the only bit of wartime damage,' he chuckled, 'but it's not what you think. A bored boy chorister with an air rifle did that, and the emergency repair hasn't been replaced.' He was gone before I thought to ask him how he knew.

I was in for another surprise. A large painting, titled *Land of the Saints*, caught my attention. It's a heaven's-eye view of the entire county, painted with astonishing topographical virtuosity, with every one of its parish architect, but his brief was different in one important respect: the house was to be built of Bath stone. Thomas Daniell had married Elizabeth Elliot in 1754; as a wedding gift, Elizabeth's uncle, Ralph Allen, a Cornishman living in Bath, gave them the stone extracted from quarries he owned for the house. The gift had a secondary purpose: Allen had spotted a market in Truro and wanted to showcase Bath stone as cheaper, paler and altogether more desirable than the local Newham stone. The Mansion House took seven years to build – from 1755 to 1762 – at a cost estimated to be in the region of £8,500. And as an advertisement it worked; even the cathedral, when it came to be built just over a century later, was constructed partly of Bath stone. The problem though, is that Bath stone is not as resistant to the Cornish weather as the local stuff, resulting in some major restoration work to the cathedral between 2010 and 2018.

The completion of the Daniells's house meant an earlier grand residence, started in 1706 for mining magnate Samuel Enys in neighbouring Quay Street, quickly became known as the **Old Mansion House**, a fine example of early Georgian town house architecture. On a more domestic scale, **Walsingham Place**, a perfectly preserved crescent of Georgian cottages, set Betjeman's heart racing with relief that it had not been lost to the post-war building boom. And you can almost hear the Poet Laureate muttering 'Proportion, proportion, proportion' to himself, wandering the length of **Lemon Street** with a smile on his face.

Among all this Georgian splendour, the concreted-over harbour known as **Lemon Quay** is something of an anomaly. The extended and massively refurbished **Hall for Cornwall**, unveiled in 2020 with its new entrance on the quay, gives the place a lively buzz on theatre or music nights, but the quay really comes to life during the city's jamborees, which include the multi-arts Truro Festival in late April. Guided walking tours of the city, which take in many of the sights listed above, can be booked at ⊘ visittruro.org.uk.

churches lit by a tiny beacon of light, painted in 1980 to help celebrate the cathedral's centenary. The surprise for me was the artist: my first-ever visit to Cornwall had been to meet **John Miller** in his garden studio at Sancreed in 1993. I knew him then for his almost abstract – now iconic – images of Cornish sea and sky; I had not guessed at the sacred in his work, but in front of the immense and lighted panorama it now made sense.

If you can make it to the cathedral for Friday lunchtime there's a free world-class recital on the magnificent **Father Willis organ**, which is raved about by visiting organists. Recitals start at 13.10 and are deservedly well attended. The choir too has an international reputation and can be heard at evening prayer daily at 17.30 or at 10.00 and 16.00 during Sunday services. The cathedral shop sells CDs of their music and there's a terrific coffee shop, too.

THE ROYAL CORNWALL MUSEUM

25 River St, TR1 2SJ ✆ 01872 272205 ⌂ royalcornwallmuseum.org.uk ◷ Tue–Sat

The Royal Institution of Cornwall – the organisation that still owns and manages the Royal Cornwall Museum and Courtney Library in River Street – was founded in 1818 for 'the promotion of knowledge in natural history, ethnology and the fine and industrial arts, especially in relation to Cornwall'. The exhibits, spread over two floors, are some of Cornwall's finest: the Rashleigh collection of minerals (collected by Philip Rashleigh of Menabilly between 1760 and 1811) is of international importance; the most valuable finds from Cornish Bronze Age settlements are on display; and the gallery contains the best collection of paintings by the Newlyn School outside Penzance's Penlee Gallery as well as a superb self-portrait by Opie (page 226). Perhaps the least Cornish of the exhibits is an Egyptian mummy.

"The gallery contains the best collection of paintings by the Newlyn School outside Penzance's Penlee Gallery."

There is an admission fee, as well as a café and shop. Activities for children in the school holidays and the occasional lunchtime lectures are rated highly by those with a finger on the pulse of Truro's cultural agenda. It seems unthinkable that the museum would be forced to close due to lack of funding, but in 2022 that almost became reality. At the time of writing the museum is being kept open thanks to a transitional support fund while a sustainable future for the museum is debated.

¶¶ FOOD & DRINK

The **farmers' market** (⌂ trurofarmers.co.uk) on Lemon Quay is held every Wednesday and Saturday and is one of the best around – it's the sort of market you'd be proud to show to a visitor from France or Italy. The stalls found here are ever-changing, differing from one season to the next, but there's usually street food and often a bit of street entertainment, too.

Skinner's Brewery, close to the docks (Riverside View, Newham ✆ 01872 245689 ⌂ skinnersbrewery.com) produces Truro's much-loved ale, Betty Stogs, among other favourites, such as Cornish Knocker and Heligan Honey, found all across the county. A huge sigh of relief could be heard when – having gone into administration in 2022 – a new buyer was found for this cornerstone of Cornish brewing. There are daily tours of the brewery (and tastings), which has won more awards than any other brewery in the West Country – not bad going with St Austell Ales and Sharp's just down the road. For a taste of Skinner's outside the brewery, go to the **Old Ale House**, one of Truro's oldest pubs, with an atmosphere to match; it's on the corner of Quay St (✆ 01872 271122 ⌖ theoldalehousetruro.co.uk).

There's no problem finding a place for a bite around the cathedral and city centre, though if you're after an old-fashioned (indeed, Victorian) tea room, with uniformed waitresses and leaf tea served in proper china, you should head up the stairs of Coinage Hall, and squeeze past an enticing second-hand bookshop to **Charlotte's Tea House** (✆ 01872 263706 ⌖ charlottes-teahouse.co.uk).

Just out of town, the **Great Cornish Food Store** (Tregurra Park, Newquay Rd, TR1 1RH; next to Waitrose) ✆ 01872 306060 ⌖ greatcornishfood.co.uk) is exactly what it says, and more. In addition to the well-stocked Cornish deli and fabulous vegetable, meat and fish counters, there's a café, and it's open seven days a week. Hats off to Ruth Huxley (page 17) who got the whole thing off the ground – in 2022 it became the first employee-owned business of its kind in the country.

Sam's in the City 2 Newbridge St, TR1 2AA ✆ 01872 228187 ⌖ samscornwall.co.uk. Having acquired a devoted following in Fowey and Polkerris, Sam added a diner in the centre of the city to the delight of Truronians. Fish of the highest quality and a relaxed, informal atmosphere.

ALONG THE RIVER FROM TRURO TO FALMOUTH

To appreciate the estuarine setting of Truro, it's worth exploring the river scenery that's close by. One of the best ways to approach the city is by river from Falmouth; **Enterprise Ferries** runs boat trips when there's a high tide in the summer months, with a stop at Malpas on the way (⌖ falriver.co.uk).

The journeys by road and river between Truro and Falmouth paint two entirely different pictures: the A39 is a rather featureless artery, frequently clogged with rush-hour or tourist traffic, which gives no hint of the true beauty of the riverside harbours, gardens and wild, marshy creeks busy with wildfowl that lie within a mile or two of its austere path.

2 COOMBE

The cottages clustered around the shore of the creek were once home to oystermen and dredgers, their incomes and larders supplemented by the orchards of cider apples and local speciality plums that rose behind their houses. Generations of children grew up around the creek, learned to sail or row out into the deep waters of the Fal and returned with the tide to the lighted windows along the shoreline. It's all very different now. At least seven of the 19 cottages in the estate-owned hamlet have been transformed into smart holiday lettings; more are planned as the ageing tenants disperse – the community is on the verge of extinction. This was the story I heard from one elderly resident of Coombe, who felt keenly the loss of the community he had raised his children in. He had just returned from committing the ashes of a neighbour to the creek, early one morning at high tide, observed by a circle of old friends in their rowing boats. Later he sent me the following lines:

> No tears, no outward signs of grief;
> Perhaps a long, soft sigh as the ashes spill into the creek.
> A moment of love and profound memory.
> The glassy calm of the mistbound morning tide.
> The melting sun just warming through.
> Oars paused dripping and then slowly dipped as all the boats
> Disperse and make for home.

I have a feeling it was not just his neighbour that he was mourning, and his words stayed with me as I walked the footpath through the woods above the creek and found myself looking across the river to **Smugglers Cottage** on the quayside at Tolverne; you can still imagine the scene here in 1944, when General Eisenhower addressed 27,000 American troops before they embarked for the D-Day landings. It is not open to the public.

3 COME-TO-GOOD

Come-to-Good Farm, Feock (page 420)

There's a footpath over the fields from Coombe to Come-to-Good, a lovely name for this cluster of houses and beautifully restored Quaker meeting house, built of whitewashed cob and thatch, dating from 1710, making it one of the earliest to be built in Cornwall after George Fox's travels (and travails) in Cornwall in 1656. The village's name is still the subject of some debate. One theory is that it derives from Cwm-ty-coit meaning 'the coombe by the dwelling in the wood'. Others think that because the name does not appear before the late 17th century, by which time the community's Quakers were gathering for meetings in a local disused building, it may well be an ironic reference to the meeting house.

Inside, the interior has hardly changed since it was built: light streams through the lattice windows on to the wooden benches and plain, limewashed walls. It's a place of absolute peace and serenity; the grassy garden around the building is awash with snowdrops in February.

4 TRELISSICK

Feock TR3 6QL ✆ 01872 862090; National Trust

From Easter to September, ferries from Truro, Falmouth and St Mawes (⌂ falriver.co.uk) drop off and pick up passengers from the pontoon at the bottom of the garden – which would get any garden visit off to a flying start, and in this case invests the whole experience with a kind of poetic quality. It's a steep climb through the densely planted slopes, but the stupendous views on all sides and the rich diversity of exotic trees and shrubs make it all the more worthwhile. And all along the main path are inviting diversions: grassy glades, shaded by the pick of the world's most beautiful trees, now grown to maturity; little summerhouses and a footbridge over the sunken lane which leads to the King Harry ferry invite you to discover yet more acres of handsome specimen trees and shrubs. You encounter vivid herbaceous borders too, designed to extend the colour in the garden through to autumn, national collections of photinias and azaleas, and closer to the main buildings, walls swarming with roses and wisteria. One of the best-known images of Trelissick –

THE KEA PLUM

Take the footpath from Kea to Cowlands and Coombe during late July and August and you'll see orchards laden with small red or black fruit, more like damsons than plums. The salt- and wind-resistant Kea plum is native to this valley, and the fruit highly prized for its high pectin content, which makes it eminently suitable for jam or chutney. People say the plums are too sharp to be enjoyed as dessert fruit, but the ones I tasted, at the end of August, were sweeter than I'd been led to believe – the red ones were especially good. You'll find produce made from Kea plums on sale in local farm shops, the jam and chutney labels sporting the badge of the Tregothnan estate which has the only commercial Kea plum orchard in the valley.

especially visible on the road approach – is a round tower, capped with a steeply pitched conical slate roof, as though it had been lifted from a French chateau or fairy tale. It was a cleverly disguised water tank, built in 1865, and used for irrigation and fire control; now it's an unusual National Trust holiday cottage.

By contrast to the Rapunzelesque tower and romantic gardens, the house, when it finally comes into view, is a model of classical restraint: Nikolaus Pevsner described it as 'the severest neo-Greek mansion in Cornwall'. It was built in 1824 for Thomas Daniell (whose mining-magnate father was known as 'guinea-a-minute' Daniell). Daniell junior, however, had a gift for losing the money his father had earned and 30 years later, he was forced to sell the family pile. Trelissick's next owner, Carew Davies Gilbert, added to the house and planted many of the fine collections of trees, but the gardens really came to life in the last century, when the new owners, Ronald and Ida Copeland, began to fill the grounds with the rich variety of plants seen today. Ronald Copeland was a director of Spode and the gardens provided many of the floral models for the famous porcelain designs. Sadly, the collection was sold and dispersed in 2013. Since 2014, the National Trust has opened the house to visitors and frequently changing exhibitions give a glimpse into the lives of those who lived here. Volunteers from the Trust play the grand piano in the drawing room, but anyone is welcome to tinkle the ivories.

5 THE KING HARRY FERRY

⊘ falriver.co.uk

The clickety-clank of heavy chains is part of the soundscape on this stretch of the Fal, and the current ferry, launched in 2006, has glass panels allowing you to see the impressive chains in action. The 300-yard crossing is all too brief – there's just time to take in the mussel beds and birdlife, get a glimpse of an incongruous container ship or two, mothballed while their skeleton crews wait for commercial activity to resume – and then the cars are rolling off again, cyclists prepare for a steep uphill exit and walkers shuffle their maps and look hopefully up at the sky. There's been a crossing here for more than a thousand

---

1 View across the river towards Malpas and Truro. 2 The water tower at Trelissick. 3 The Quaker meeting house at Come-to-Good. 4 Kea plums. 5 King Harry ferry. ▶

years, as it's on an old pilgrim route to St Michael's Mount and the name refers to pious Henry VI, to whom a chapel in the woods on the east bank was once dedicated. The first chain ferry rumbled across in 1888, saving travellers' (and their horses') legs 26 miles of road via Truro and Tresillian. As green statistics go, the ferries are pretty impressive: each year five million car miles are saved, which equates to 1,870 tons of CO^2 emissions.

6 DEVORAN

At the head of Restronguet Creek, Devoran's cottages sprang up as a result of an initiative to recover tin from the mud at the end of the 18th century, and as its quay facilities and tramway into the mining areas west of Truro expanded, so the population increased to the point where a church was called for. Devoran's church is Victorian, and its claim to fame lies in its architect, J L Pearson, who went on to design Truro Cathedral some years later. The churchyard turns out to be a treat for garden-minded people: wild meadow flowers and Cornish hedgerow plants are clearly encouraged, but there's also evidence of careful planting – there are camellias, palms, roses and escallonia, berberis and even a crinodendron. This is no accident, for Devoran is where the great plant hunter, Thomas Lobb, was buried in 1894, and Carclew Manor (just across the creek) is where he and his brother William (who also became a renowned plant hunter) worked as boys before being taken on by the great Veitch nurseries in Exeter. (Carclew Manor was destroyed by fire in 1934, but the gardens where the Lobbs worked have been restored and open occasionally for charity.)

¶¶ FOOD & DRINK

The Old Quay Inn St John's Terrace, TR3 6ND ✆ 01872 863142 ⬥ theoldquayinn.co.uk. Devoran's pub is a gem: inside are log fires, old wooden tables and papers and magazines to read. The food is exceptionally good, the local ales are well kept and there's a friendly feel to it all. At the back, a steeply terraced garden has pockets for seating while benches at the front overlook the creek.

7 KENNALL VALE NATURE RESERVE

♥ SW753375; the entrance is off the road past the post office – the approach appears to be the private driveway of the last house on the right, but keep to the right & the entrance is clearly marked ⬥ cornwallwildlifetrust.org.uk

I am indebted to Falmouth resident Glyn Winchester, who introduced me to a short but fascinating circular walk through this peaceful wooded valley, watered by the fast-flowing River Kennall, among the deeply atmospheric relics of an old gunpowder works. From 1812 until the decline of the Cornish mining industry forced its closure in 1910, the Kennall Gunpowder Company was Cornwall's foremost manufacturer of explosives. There's a map and information board at the entrance to this self-contained and secret valley, a mile or so north of Penryn on the Redruth road, on the outskirts of Ponsanooth. Tragic accidents were not uncommon, and though the birdsong in the leafy canopy and the splashing rills and spouts that jet across the path provide a deliciously melodic background to the mile long, looping path, there is no denying the sense of sadness that haunts the mossy ruins.

¶¶ FOOD & DRINK

Dynamite Valley Brewery Beer Café Viaduct Works, Ponsanooth Viaduct, TR3 7JW
✎ 01872 864532 ⚲ dynamitevalley.com. Occupying the sheds beneath the Ponsonooth Viaduct, this is a 9–5 shop-cum-café producing a great range of craft ales, which you'll find in most Falmouth pubs and delis these days, and further afield, too.

8 ENYS

St Gluvias, Penryn TR10 9LB ✎ 01326 259885 ⚲ enysgardens.org.uk ☺ Apr–Sep Sun & Mon, plus some days in school hols

Cornwall is not short of places where each May bluebells steal the show, giving the rhododendrons a run for their money, but Enys must come near the top of the list. Although the gardens are open from April to September, the majority of visitors come to witness the extraordinary blue phenomenon in the tree-fringed part of the grounds known as **Parc Lye**, believed to have been undisturbed since medieval times. The house and gardens, which have been home to the Enys family since 1272, however, have undergone great transformations: the Elizabethan manor

"Cornwall is not short of places where each May bluebells steal the show, but Enys must come near the top of the list."

was destroyed by fire in the early 1820s and the old walled garden was pulled apart to make way for a less formal design. In 1833 John Samuel Enys engaged Henry Harrison, a London architect, to produce designs for the garden as well as the house. He created the Ladies' Garden (now

called the **Flower Garden**), which leads through a stone arch into the **Colonel's Garden,** named after Colonel Enys (1757–1818). Colonel Enys had an unusually large nose, and I was delighted to discover that this beautiful enclosure, brimming with colour and happy insects, was deliberately replanted as a scented garden, a befitting tribute to the Colonel's great conk. (Many of the scented plants have now ceded their place to more showy individuals.) But it was J D Enys (1837–1912) who made one of the biggest contributions to the planting; he was a great traveller and regularly sent seeds and plants home from New Zealand and Patagonia, which have now grown to splendid maturity. The huge gardens and grounds are cared for by head gardener Danni (Danielle) and a band of volunteers. If you call in advance, Danni will take a brief break from her heroic labours to show you around.

9 PENRYN

I've completely fallen for Penryn; its history and its future seem to have found a nice balance, and while the huge influx of students at the university campus have ruffled a few feathers of the indigenous population ('you can't get a seat on the bus these days') shops are busier, cafés are flourishing and a number of creative businesses have established themselves beneath the wind turbines in the zero-carbon buildings of **Jubilee Wharf**.

"Penryn's chief glory, before the Reformation saw its decline and ultimate destruction, was Glasney College."

Penryn's history is not dissimilar to that of Lostwithiel – it was a town of enormous significance in medieval times, which dwindled with the loss of its port as silt made it increasingly difficult to navigate. And just as Lostwithiel found itself superseded by Fowey, so Penryn lost out to Falmouth, with its deep, accessible harbour. But Penryn's chief glory, before the Reformation saw its decline and ultimate destruction, was **Glasney College**, known throughout Europe as a centre of learning. It was built in the late 13th century, on the instructions of the Bishop of Exeter (whose diocese included the whole of Cornwall) and the collegiate church was nothing less than a slightly scaled-down replica of Exeter Cathedral. Virtually nothing is left of its remains today

◀ **1** Devoran. **2** Jubilee Wharf at Penryn. **3** Bluebell display at Enys. **4** Kennall Vale Nature Reserve. **5** Flushing.

– just a grassy playing field and a few bits of architectural masonry – but there are several houses in Penryn, notably in **Easom's Yard**, that clearly benefitted from pieces of the ecclesiastical pile.

The free **museum** (⊘ penrynhistory.co.uk ⊘ Mon–Fri), housed in the early 19th-century market house, bang in the middle of Penryn's main street, tells the story – with a model, maps and drawings – and the complex of cloisters, chapter house, refectory, infirmary, mills, houses, deer park and fish pond, as well as the cathedral-like church, makes a powerful impression.

As the local ditty goes: 'Penryn was a flourishing town/When Falmouth was a furzy down.' Despite the loss of Glasney, Penryn continued to grow rich, exporting granite, tin and copper from its port and its streets filled with the handsome houses of its prosperous merchants. Falmouth may have snatched the lucrative customs house away from the port in 1650, but the town continued to hold its own, until the general decline in mining and quarrying took a grip and decay set in during the last century. But Penryn was lucky – incredibly lucky – to have its many handsome Tudor, Jacobean and Georgian buildings saved in the 1970s by a mammoth listing and restoration project, in which 200 buildings were rescued from near dereliction. No other Cornish town has as many listed buildings and it all makes for very pleasant ambling around the streets, opes (alleyways) and squares. The museum has put together a **heritage trail** (no mere leaflet – it's the size of a small book) that takes you through the town's architectural and social history.

"No other Cornish town has as many listed buildings and it all makes for very pleasant ambling around."

What saves Penryn from being just a heritage town is the lease of life it's been given by the groundbreaking eco-architecture on Jubilee Wharf, the Innovation Centre at the **Penryn Campus** and resident or working population of artists and designers – many of whom are graduates of Falmouth University, just down the road. A wander up or down the hill from the museum, for example, often reveals temporary or seasonal exhibits of contemporary local fine and applied art at affordable prices in vacant shop premises. There's more to see on Jubilee Wharf, where you can look through the windows at printmaking in action – it could be a class of novice woodcutting students or experienced copperplate engravers – at **John Howard Print Studios** (⊘ johnhowardprintstudios.com).

But it was only while chatting to the volunteers in the museum that it dawned on me how much contemporary Penryn, full of new ideas and buildings and students from far beyond the Fal, in a curious way, is reliving its medieval past.

Jubilee Wharf

⊘ jubileewharf.co.uk

What an intelligent and brave piece of town planning this is. Completed in 2007 to the designs of Bill Dunster, a pioneering hero of zero-carbon urban housing, the **two linked buildings** (which bear more than a passing resemblance to an old riverboat, with an upturned hull for a roof) sit comfortably in their slightly scruffy harbour surrounds, surrounded by tall ships' masts, beside which the four, almost silent wind turbines look quite at home. (These are now coming to the end of their life and will be replaced by solar panels, designed to resemble a basic tree shape). Local labour built the project and, wherever possible, local and reclaimed materials found their way into the construction, which has all been given a cladding of Cornish cedar and larch.

There are flats, workshops, offices, a busy café and a nursery, all nicely mixed so that the wharfside community feels properly integrated, helped along by the **ZedShed** – a community space, so called because Zed stands for zero energy development.

¶¶ FOOD & DRINK

The Famous Barrel St Thomas St, TR10 8JP ⊘ 01326 373505. In one of the most picturesque backwaters of Penryn, the pub is named after the huge barrel you walk through once inside. Sharp's Doom Bar is the local ale and there's usually a guest ale too. There's no food, but you're welcome to bring your own and sit by the log burner or outside in the leafy walled garden. Family- and dog-friendly.

Stargazy Cucina and Pantry 24 Lower Market St, TR10 8BG ⨍. I continue to hear lots of good things about Penryn's friendliest café, which dishes up imaginative takes on classic breakfasts and lunches.

10 MYLOR & FLUSHING

The novelist Katherine Mansfield and her husband John Murry fled Zennor for **Mylor** in 1916, after a short-lived attempt at braving the wild, north coast of Penwith in the company of D H Lawrence and his wife, Frieda. Lawrence wrote 'it is too bleak and rocky for them. They want the south side, with trees and gardens and softness'. The world (at least the world that comes to Cornwall) is still divided into those that come for the wildness, the remoteness and austerity that characterises so much of the north coast and those that come for the gentle, leafy rivers and creeks, sheltered harbours and lush gardens of the Fal estuary (as well as the easy access to the cosmopolitan civilisation of Truro and Falmouth). And it doesn't get cosier than Mylor, with its snug, whitewashed cottages, green riverbanks and tree-fringed churchyard. If you want to get on the water, head down to the harbour, where little motor launches, sailing dinghies and punts can be hired. And where nicer to tie up than outside the picturesque **Pandora Inn** (Restronguet Creek, Mylor Bridge TR11 5ST ⊘ pandorainn.com), where the food and drink is as good as the setting?

Mylor's close neighbour, **Flushing**, has terraces of pretty Queen Anne houses and cottages built by Dutch immigrants from Vlissingen in the 17th century. The small harbour is busy with local fishing and sailing boats, and has retained a lot of character; other parts of the village have been so smartly renovated that you could be in a Kensington mews.

11 FALMOUTH

Falmouth must rate as one of the most appealing places to live in England; it's the sheer diversity of what it has to offer that makes it so fortunate. There's the sparkling beauty and almost Mediterranean glamour of the wide estuary and harbour, the grit and guts of a large, working dockyard, a Victorian-style seafront with beaches, hotels and exotic gardens, a ribbon of old streets, packed with good shops and art galleries – and a rich history of maritime adventure written all over its engaging quays and alleyways. The population of art students adds another dimension too: there's a youthful liveliness about the town that brings guitars and campfires to the beaches on summer evenings, art to the foreground at summer show time and a buzz to the cafés and bars. Rainy-day visitors wanting an alternative to beach and boats are well looked after in Falmouth, too. The **maritime museum** and **Pendennis Castle** make a special effort to woo children and the free **Falmouth Art Gallery** has been a winner of *The Guardian* Family Friendly Museum competition.

"There's a youthful liveliness about the town that brings guitars and campfires to the beaches on summer evenings."

You can circumnavigate Falmouth in a couple of hours on foot and get a good feeling for all the different faces of the town. Pendennis Castle, high on the headland beyond the docks, calls for a bit of extra time and effort; a shuttle bus from the town centre loops around Falmouth, taking in the beaches and castle.

The Killigrews of Falmouth

Falmouth wouldn't be the place it is today without the Killigrews, who took up residence on the muddy shores of the estuary towards the end of the 13th century. A wander down Grove Place towards Discovery Quay and the Maritime Museum takes you past their handsomely restored manor, **Arwenack House**. It was converted during the 1980s into private accommodation, but in its medieval and Elizabethan incarnations was home to 16 or so generations of this enterprising and occasionally scandalous family. (Everyone in Falmouth has heard of Lady Mary Killigrew, a throat-slitting pirate, whose death sentence was commuted by a frankly admiring Elizabeth I to a spell in prison.)

"Falmouth wouldn't be the place it is without the Killigrews, who took up residence towards the end of the 13th century."

In 1598, when Sir Walter Raleigh visited Arwenack, the house stood alone on the shores of the river; the nearest church was at Budock, a good mile away over the hills, and all the boats went to Penryn or Truro. Raleigh couldn't help pointing out what a great spot for a harbour lay before the house; the point was taken, but by the time of the Civil War, the Killigrew fortune – built largely on piracy and abuse of government posts – was starting to evaporate. John Killigrew bankrupted himself trying to found the new town and build a lighthouse on the Lizard (page 318); and while his divorced wife stayed on at Arwenack, Parliamentary troops seized the house and set fire to it. His brother, Henry Killigrew (whom Elizabeth I described as 'dull'), was forced to abandon his new home at Ince Castle on the River Lynher and rally to the Royalist cause: Henry was one of the heroes of the terrible siege of Pendennis Castle. Loyalty to the Crown did the family – and Falmouth – no end of good; Charles II granted the town its charter (despite furious opposition from Penryn) in 1661 and within a decade a church had risen in the new town centre, ingratiatingly dedicated to 'King Charles the Martyr'.

RAINY-DAY FALMOUTH

Falmouth's art galleries are a joy. The **Falmouth Art Gallery** (The Moor ☎ 01326 313863 ⚲ falmouthartgallery.com ⊙ closed Sun), with its wonderful collections of Cornish impressionists, prints, portraits and very funny automata, knows how to put on a good exhibition. It's the attention to detail that counts: placing exhibits that children will enjoy at the right height for them; using humour in interpretation that even grumpy teenagers can't resist – I've never been in and not seen children (and adults – often their grandparents) enjoying themselves. And it's free.

The gallery **Beside the Wave** (Arwenack St ☎ 01326 211132 ⚲ beside-the-wave.co.uk) exhibits and sells big-name contemporary Cornish art – landscapes by Richard Tuff, Andrew Tozer and Paul Lewin all feature there regularly. And it's always worth a look to see who else is up-and-coming; exhibitions change every month.

The Royal Cornwall Polytechnic Society, known simply as **The Poly** (24 Church St ☎ 01326 319461 ⚲ thepoly.org) is Falmouth's much-loved arts centre, fuelled by local support and enthusiasm. There's always an exhibition on the ground floor, featuring work by local artists, and the annual Summer Exhibition showcases some of the best emerging and established local talent.

Since the award-winning **National Maritime Museum** (Discovery Quay ☎ 01326 313388 ⚲ nmmc.co.uk) opened in 2003, every inch of its imaginatively designed space has had the ability to engage you instantly, from the moment you enter the main hall where a flotilla of iconic boats are suspended overhead, to the underwater viewing chamber where you can see what's really going on in the harbour – a cormorant diving for a fish, perhaps. Year-long exhibitions focus on the epic and sensational treasures in the collection, which often achieve national impact. Falmouth's maritime history was given tremendously lucid exposure by the publication of *The Levelling Sea*. The author, Philip Marsden, who lives close to Falmouth, is well known at the museum and his occasional talks sell out rapidly, but do get a ticket if you can.

There's a lot to be said for visiting a subtropical garden in summer rain: the air smells fresh and damp, the dripping foliage acquires a lush intensity and often it's just you and the blackbirds, sheltering under the same palm. The **Fox-Rosehill gardens** are very discreetly hidden on the beach-facing slopes of the town, beside the buildings of the **Falmouth School of Art**. The Quaker shipping magnate, Robert Were Fox (who retired to Penjerrick, page 281), lived in the house that the school now occupies, and started to fill the gardens with exotic plants in the mid-19th century. His family continued to fill the gardens, introducing Australian gums and New Zealand cordylines (this mild, south-facing pocket of Falmouth is often referred to as 'Little Australia'), until handing it over to the town in 1974. The open day, held over the first weekend in June, is a lovely event, with plant sales, talks and picnics, well supported by locals, whatever the weather.

With royal favour riding high, and Killigrews pushing hard for the geographical superiority of their port to be recognised, the packet ships were transferred from London to Falmouth in 1669. This was a prize worth having – packet ships carried mail and gold bullion to all corners of the empire and the rewards for controlling the service were immeasurable. The Killigrews should have prospered enormously, but through accident and heirlessness they managed the exact opposite.

The **Killigrew Monument** opposite Arwenack House is a strange sort of memorial to such a colourful clan; the tall granite pyramid was erected in 1737 on the instructions of Martin, the last Killigrew of Arwenack, and was deliberately left without any kind of inscription. Oddly, when the pyramid was taken apart and moved to its present position, two empty glass bottles were found inside, creating even more of a mystery. A stroll through the pretty terraces of Regency, Georgian and Victorian houses on the slopes above Arwennack reveals the decline in the family fortune, as the land behind the manor was sold off piecemeal.

The seafront

The three connected beaches, **Gyllyngvase, Tunnel** and **Castle**, on Falmouth's south-facing shores, get very busy with students 'revising' at the first hint of sunshine; it takes a few more minutes, walking west, to find the quieter shores of **Swanpool Beach** and its brackish pool, just across the road, a scruffy but essential haven for wildlife and waterfowl.

Several of the grand Victorian hotels that once lined the seafront have been converted into luxury flats, saving the prom from losing its dignified charm; Gyllyngdune Manor, set back from the prom on the clifftop, was sold after just two generations of occupancy by the Coope family to Frederick Horniman (who was later to found the Horniman Museum in south London). The gardens had a tunnel entrance to their own private beach, both of which became open to the public when the house was bought by the town in 1907.

Gyllyngdune Gardens are approached by steps opposite Tunnel Beach; one surprise leads to another. First there's an extraordinary quarry garden with shell grottoes and a fernery – then, around a corner, a beautifully restored Edwardian bandstand sits in the immaculately planted centre of an elegant, glass-roofed cloister. Beyond lies the old mansion, converted to a concert hall in 1911. (Now too, the lovely old building continues to host a varied programme of concerts and entertainment.) Opened by Princess Alexandra, it has since then been known as **Princess Pavilion**. The café serves delicious home-made lunches and cakes and is a destination in itself.

¶¶ FOOD & DRINK

Falmouth celebrates its centuries-old oyster harvest in mid-October with the **Falmouth Oyster Festival** (⊘ falmouthoysterfestival.co.uk) held on Events Square (in front of the maritime museum). The Fal is the only place in the country where oysters are dredged by traditional methods – by the last oyster fleet working under sail or oar – and deserves its celebration. If Falmouth were in France, they wouldn't be hand-dredged, but there would be stand-up oyster bars up and down the town, crowded with locals; here, it's a little different. My favourite seafood restaurant, **Hooked on the Rocks** (page 280), serves oysters (albeit from Porthilly on the north coast) from a converted horsebox in the car park.

    Falmouth farmers' market is held every Tuesday on the Moor, a lovely, traffic-free square, bringing together a particularly rich seam of farm shop producers around the Fal, many of whom you'll find at the Truro farmers' market on Saturdays. The **Natural Store**, just around the corner from the Moor (⊘ 01326 311507 ⊘ naturalstorecornwall.co.uk) sells everything organic, and **Stones Bakery** (35 High St ⊘ 07791 003183 ⊘ stonesbakedgoods. com ☺ closed Sun), just a step away, make their own muesli and crackers as well as superb breads. The flapjacks and focaccia are in a league of their own and the bakery has added a small number of tables so that a coffee or tea can be enjoyed with the cakes.

Beacon Coffee 28A High St, TR11 2AD ⊘ beaconcoffee.co.uk ☺ closed Sun. For true coffee connoisseurs. Alex and Sam offer a choice of blends in a pared-down, stylish bar.
Beerwolf 3 Bells Court (just off Church St), TR11 3AZ ⊘ 01326 618474 ⊘ beerwolfbooks. com. Free house incorporating a secondhand bookshop in the upstairs bar, much favoured by Falmouth's students. Always a cheerful vibe and regular music nights.
The Cornish Bank 34 Church St, TR11 3EF. My Falmouth friends love this place and I can see why: not only is the food and drink – and evening music – on offer quite the best, it has a social responsibility to the poorer members of the community, too. Everything is sourced locally and profits go back into the community Canteen lunches.
The Dog and Smuggler Pasty and Tuck Shop Custom Hse Quay, TR11 3JT ⊘ 07866 215963. A highly rated venture from the owner-cook of the late lamented Pea Souk. Pasties here come with a range of fillings in three categories: vegan, vegetarian and carnivore.

---

1 St Mawes Castle faces Pendennis Castle across the mouth of the Fal estuary.
2 Falmouth Art Gallery. **3** Falmouth waterfront. **4** Penjerrick Garden. ▶

Espressini 39 Killigrew St, TR11 3PW ✐ 07890 453705. This friendly café, very close to the farmers' market, does terrific breakfast and lunchtime food inspired by what's local and seasonal at very reasonable prices. Rupert, the owner, who pioneered Falmouth's exceptional coffee scene, takes great interest in all his suppliers and can give you chapter and verse on the origins of the coffees he blends himself and hot chocolates, too. The special leaf teas are also excellent.

The Front Custom Hse Quay, TR11 3JT ✐ 01326 212168. The barrels are lined up on the wall as you walk in, giving the impression that a real ale festival is taking place. But this is everyday: Max the new landlord keeps a terrific range of local and guest ales and ciders and regularly scoops up awards from CAMRA. The sign outside says: 'we're a pub, so bring your own grub!' and lots of people do. It's handily next door to the highly rated **Harbour Lights** fish and chip shop, and opposite The Dog and Smuggler Pasty and Tuck Shop (page 278). Note the brick chimney directly opposite, known as **The King's Pipe** – a witty nickname, as contraband tobacco was once incinerated here.

Good Vibes Café 28 Killigrew St, TR11 3PN ✐ 01326 211870. A choice of home-blended coffees on the menu and a delicious range of breakfast bagels and lunchtime treats, made with the freshest local ingredients. Lovely Sunday brunches.

Hooked on the Rocks Swanpool Rd, TR11 5BG ✐ 01326 311886 ⌨ hookedontherocksfalmouth.com ☺ closed Mon. Just yards from the beach, an informal crowd gather here for fresh, local seafood, with, as the menu says, minimal 'fripperies and embellishments'.

Picnic Cornwall 4 Church St, TR11 3DR ✐ 01326 21165 ⌨ picniccornwall.co.uk. There's a real celebration of Cornish produce in this small café and deli. You can order a picnic online or by phone (the motto here is eat-drink-explore), delivered in jute bags or recycled card boxes; a luxury wicker hamper is also available.

Provedore 43 Trelawney Rd, TR11 4RE ✐ 01326 314888 ⌨ provedore.co.uk ☺ Wed–Sat. Off the beaten track and much cherished by locals – a tiny but brilliant café-cum-tapas bar, with an olive tree in the courtyard garden to sit under and drink coffee made by Tim, a proper barista in true Mediterranean style. Thursday and Friday evenings, when Tim produces his favourite Spanish dishes or Venetian cicchetti, are worth getting to early as there's no booking and a cheerful queue stretches down the street. The Facebook page gives weekly updates. Cash only.

The Seven Stars 1 The Moor, TR11 3QA ✐ 01326 312111. A legendary pub run by five generations of the same family. Legendary for its perfect pints of Bass, Sharp's and Skinner's, legendary for refusing to serve food other than crisps and legendary for its unchanging décor. Its loyal, burping, dry-witted regulars would rather die than be seen with a mobile phone at the bar and there would be a riot if anything was ever altered.

Stones Bakery 35 High St ✐ 07791 00318 (page 278).

12 PENJERRICK GARDEN

Budock, near Falmouth TR11 5ED ✆ 01872 870105 🖥 penjerrickgarden.co.uk ⏱ Mar–Sep
Sun, Wed & Fri

If you're the sort of person who is put off visiting a garden by the sight of huge car parks and visitor centres at the entrance, or find you have little enthusiasm for crisply edged lawns and immaculate borders, Penjerrick will be your kind of place. There's no car park – you just park carefully on the grass-edged drive – and the entrance fee goes into an honesty box. The owner, Rachel Morin, is unrepentent: 'Penjerrick Garden has got everything a garden enthusiast needs: plants, plants and more plants, secret corners, winding paths, thriving shrubs, towering trees, lush green. Do not visit Penjerrick, however, if you prefer neatly laid out flower beds or if you are looking for a cup of tea – you will not find either of them here. It is "just" a garden – and that's all we could wish for.' A pair of gumboots, she adds, is highly advisable.

The gardens were planted by Mrs Morin's Victorian forebears, a branch of the Fox family, who were also responsible for creating great gardens at Trebah and Glendurgan (pages 311 & 313). Robert Were Fox, whose enthusiasm for exotic plants led to the creation of the Fox-Rosehill gardens (page 276) in Falmouth, retired to Penjerrick in 1872 and spent the next five years filling the gaps in the gardens that his son, Barclay Fox, had laid out 20 years earlier. Barclay's sister carried on planting after her father's death, working with Samuel Smith, Penjerrick's head gardener, who was thoroughly caught up in the contemporary craze for rhododendron hybridisation. Today, the garden is a lush jungle: wildly overgrown, but not unloved, and best visited in a spirit of romantic adventure.

¶¶ FOOD & DRINK

Argal Farm Shop TR11 5PE ✆ 01736 372737. A lovely place to buy high-quality local produce or pick up a pasty for lunch. Family-run, friendly and in a good spot, with parking.
Wild Vibes Café Argal & College reservoirs (Water Park) TR10 9JD ✆ 01736 702105. A great lakeside spot for fishing enthusiasts and families, and much appreciated by dog-walkers. The two-mile circuit around the lake and reservoir can be rounded off with breakfast, brunch or tea from the newest branch of the Good Vibes Café in Falmouth (see opposite). Wholesome, delicious soups, salads and specials are all on the menu. In the next hut, a remarkable outdoor fitness programme run by Fitness Wild (🖥 fitnesswild.com) offers bespoke training for individuals and groups in lovely lakeside surrounds.

THE ROSELAND PENINSULA

South of the Fal, the Roseland peninsula licks the gateway to the estuary with a long tongue of land, cleft by the Percuil River, unbridged for the length of its 20-mile journey inland. The two neighbouring headlands thus created could not be more different: north of the Percuil is fashionable, upmarket **St Mawes**, much favoured by the yachty crowd and linked all year to Falmouth by the to-ing and fro-ing of the passenger ferry and to Truro and St Austell by the much-improved A3078. For garden lovers, the climb up the hill to **Lamorran Gardens** (⊘ lamorrangardens.co.uk ☉ Apr–Sep Wed–Fri) is rewarded by an elegant and exotic sequence of garden 'rooms' which cascade down the steep hillside above the Tresanton Hotel, with carefully contrived glimpses of the pretty harbour below. St Mawes is also the gateway for

CORNISH TEA LEAVES

TR3 6AR ⊘ tregothnan.co.uk

Camellias and Cornwall have been enjoying each other's company for almost 200 years, and their end-of-winter blooms herald the start of the Cornish garden season. On the Tregothnan estate, however, the species *camellia sinensis* has been planted for more than its ornamental value: it's harvested (rather romantically, at dawn during the summer months) for tea. The thinking was this: for centuries in cool, damp, hilly regions of China and India, the growing tips and buds of this obliging species have been picked and carefully dried to make tea; why should not this favoured corner of Cornwall, with its microclimate so like the foothills of the Himalayas, produce tea of equal value? The first tentative experiments were made at Tregothnan in 2000 and proved so successful that you now see the Tregothnan label all over Cornwall and further afield.

Three culinary experts from Darjeeling were being filmed among the rows of tea bushes in the old walled garden when I last visited, their bright saris looking a little incongruous against the glittering backdrop of the Fal. You can take a private tour of the gardens which takes three hours and reveals a botanic collection of exhilarating diversity, assembled by several generations of Boscowans, whose seat this has been for the past 600 years, and the current garden director, Jonathon Jones. Each tour concludes as you might expect with a pot of home-grown tea (it is very good) and scones in an Edwardian summerhouse at the head of a glade fringed with giant rhododendrons. The spring weekend when the gardens open for charity is exceedingly popular and tickets are snapped up very quickly.

DIVINE GRAFFITI

An elderly lady I know described a visit she had made years ago with her husband to the little church at **St Anthony**. 'We were enchanted by the antiquity and deep sense of peaceful seclusion,' she said, 'and then the verger appeared, anxious to show us a pillar. He claimed a young Jesus had scratched a cross on a piece of quarried stone, later used in the building of the church.' Local legend has it that Joseph of Arimathea, accompanied by his young nephew, landed on the Roseland peninsula and stories abound of the traces left on their journey from Cornwall to Glastonbury. 'Well, we peered at the pillar,' she continued, 'but it was hard to make out anything in the gloom. I think the verger must have been disappointed by our reaction.' Locals look sceptical when I asked, but one woman in Portscatho said her mother had told her there's a cross carved by the divine hand on one of the beams in Place House, next to the church.

walkers heading to St Just in Roseland, with its picturesque church in a garden at the water's edge. To the south, **St Anthony headland** is remote and wild, accessed only by a single-track lane or, in summer months, by the open boat that crosses the Percuil from St Mawes. The coastal shoreline of the peninsula conceals a string of harbours, coves and beaches of quite immoderate loveliness all the way to Nare Head.

Inland are deep, quiet woods, threaded by spindly lanes, the fingertips of marshy creeks and a scattering of hamlets and farms. The vast **Tregothnan estate**, which produces the only tea grown in England, occupies a large and leafy chunk of the east bank of the estuary; the gardens – built up by several generations of botanically minded Boscawens – can be visited by appointment (page 282). Provided you're not in a hurry, the Roseland is a lovely place in which to get lost.

One of the things that gives the Roseland its rather grown-up air is the absence of commercial entertainment on offer; visitors come here for boats, beaches, walks and good eating. The annual **Roseland Festival** ($\mathcal{O}$ roselandonline.co.uk/roseland-festival) delivers an elegant programme of literary, artistic and musical events, held in pubs, hotels and churches around the peninsula.

It's not unusual to see families braving the winter chills and cooking up a Christmas lunch or New Year's day picnic on the well-heeled beaches of the Roseland; I met someone who had spent a Christmas Day walking from Nare Head to Portscatho and been invited to share more than one glass of champagne and venison sausage (as well as a heap of

A FAMILY OF PLANTSMEN

🖉 treseders.co.uk

John Garland Treseder's father was a Truro nurseryman, but young John Garland and two of his brothers had fancied their chances as gold prospectors and took off for Australia in 1853. Plants, however, proved more lucrative than gold for J G, who over the next 40 years founded a small empire of plant shops and nurseries as well as designing gardens in Victoria and New South Wales. He returned to Cornwall in 1895 to take over the family nursery, laden with seedlings and seeds of subtropical plants, as well as the first *Dicksonias* (tree-ferns) that were to find their way into all the great Fox gardens around Falmouth and Trewidden, near Penzance. The garden would just be starting to look established in the 1920s when H V Morton wrote 'I have blundered into a Garden of Eden that cannot be described in pen or paint ... I would like to know if there is in the whole of England, a churchyard more beautiful than this ... You stand at the lychgate and look down into a green cup filled with flowers and arched by great trees. In the dip is the little church, its tower level with you as you stand above. The white gravestones rise up from ferns and flowers.'

Inevitably, by the late 1970s, the garden had reached a point where it needed to be restored and replanted; Neil Treseder, J G's grandson, who was running the family nursery at the time, took on the task. More recently, a memorial garden was added to the higher slopes above the lane to the church. All the planting was carried out by none other than James Treseder, one of the seventh generation of Treseders to be running a nursery.

Treseders nursery is situated at Lockengate, a few miles north of St Austell, and is open daily except Wednesdays (🖉 treseders.co.uk).

mince pies) along the way. This cheery outdoor gathering is typified by the crowd that gathers at the Hidden Hut (page 289), on the coast path just north of Portscatho, overlooking Porthcurnick Beach.

13 ST JUST IN ROSELAND

I count myself lucky to have made my first visit to the creekside village by sailing dinghy, zigzagging across the glittering blue expanse of the Carrick Roads from Mylor. Nothing quite prepared me, as we dodged through the thicket of masted craft moored in St Just Creek, for that first glimpse of the 13th-century church at the water's edge, and the lush canopy of exotic tree ferns, fan palms, monkey puzzle and Western red cedars, vast rhododendrons and magnolias that rises behind. Maybe if you live there you get used to its beauty, though it's hard to believe you would. Arriving on foot from St Mawes, some months later in winter, the approach from the slopes above the church was no less magical: the lychgate framed the short, grey tower below, camellias bloomed, fuzzy magnolia buds looked ready to burst and even the periwinkle was in flower, sheltered by the mild microclimate of the creek and protective shoulders of the hill behind. It was John Garland Treseder, a Victorian nurseryman, recently returned from Australia, who spotted the potential of the site for exotic, subtropical plants, and he was lucky to find the rector of St Just an enthusiastic plantsman, willing to co-operate. The Reverend Humfrey Davis had ideas too, for embellishing the churchyard. The path from the lychgate to the church is lined with 55 small granite tablets, each bearing a pious quotation. Most of the ankle-height words of wisdom are taken from the Bible or hymns, but one or two are of his own composition.

￦ FOOD & DRINK

Miss V's Cornish Cream Teas TR2 5JD ⌀ missvs.co.uk. A car park takes the strain off the narrow lane that descends towards the church and, on a grassy slope to one side, this wonderful café hits all the right spots. Sit outside and enjoy the views with a cream tea or a light lunch. Perfect.

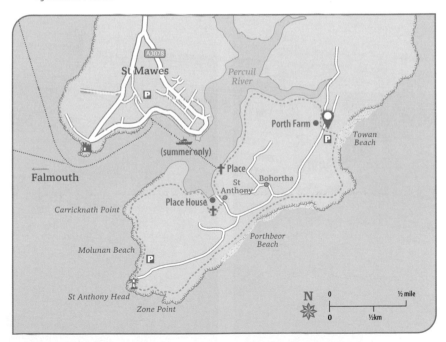

14 ST ANTHONY HEAD

🏠 **St Anthony Head Cottages** (page 420)

You can undertake a rewarding circular walk (❋ OS Explorer 105 or Landranger 204) that is almost entirely coastal, around a peninsula-within-a-peninsula; it takes about three hours at an ambling pace. The walk starts at Porth Farm, near the head of the Percuil River, then goes either way – clockwise or anticlockwise – southwest to St Anthony Head and its lighthouse, heading back on the other side of the peninsula. In summer, the passenger ferry from St Mawes lands a short, leafy walk away from Place (which consists of a grand stuccoed house and delightful old church), close to St Anthony, and there are National Trust car parks at Porth Farm and St Anthony Head, both just yards from the coast path. Three hours, however, will not be enough for Slow explorers or secret beach addicts: there is the **ancient church** in St Anthony to explore, tucked away behind the imposing **Place House** and built in 1840 for the Spry family, and the three gloriously sheltered coves, known collectively as **Molunan Beach**, to discover.

A short, uphill detour, through gorse and craggy Monterey pines, brings you to the top of the headland, just above the **St Anthony lighthouse**. The views of Falmouth and the mouth of the estuary are sublime from this lonely, windswept vantage point, which served as a World War II observation post, where traces of 1904 gun emplacements can still be seen. It's now owned by the National Trust, who have restored the observation offices and let them as unconventional holiday cottages. From here, **St Mawes** and **Pendennis** castles, built each side of the estuary mouth as part of Henry VIII's coastal defences against the French and Spanish, stand out clearly on their headlands.

> "The views of Falmouth and the mouth of the estuary are sublime from this lonely, windswept vantage point."

There's another superb beach on the cliff path that tracks the Channel-facing coast of the peninsula. **Porthbeor** cove is all soft gold sand and craggy rocks that seem to slither down to the shoreline, while a mile further north, though less than 200 yards from the car park at Porth Farm, **Towan Beach** feels as perfectly remote as any of the less accessible coves along the way.

◀ **1** The 13th-century church seen from St Just Creek. **2** Portscatho. **3** St Anthony Head.

The footpath back to St Anthony crosses a stream, woodland and meadows before finding Porth Creek on the shores of Percuil and the ferry landing at Place. You'll find both the long and short versions of this walk on the iWalk Cornwall app.

🍴 FOOD & DRINK

Porth Farm Café TR2 5EX ✆ 01872 580773 ⟨⟩ thethirsteacompany.co.uk. Starting with a converted van parked at the National Trust-owned Porth Farm above Towan Beach, Seth and Jodi Richards have gone from strength to strength. Their café in the farm stableyard opened in 2020, offering a simple menu of cakes, sandwiches and homemade soups. Eric (the van), is now to be found at Carne Beach, a two-hour hike north along the coast path, for drinks and ice creams at weekends and during school holidays.

15 PORTSCATHO

⚲ **Treloan Coastal Holidays** Gerrans (page 420)

Simon, a retired builder and native of Portscatho, crossed his arms and rolled his eyes, 'like bleddy Chelsea in the summer round here,' he grinned. It's the **Hidden Hut** effect – Simon Stallard and Jemma Glass's wildly successful clifftop café (see opposite) – that brings visitors flocking to the little village. ('Keeps the Sunday colour supplements in business, too' added local artist Chris Insoll.) Jemma grew up in Portscatho and met Simon while he was cheffing at a local hotel. It was a huge step to pack in their jobs and take on the tiny café in a hut. The evening feasts started when Simon had a load of spare mackerel that needed eating. The rest is runaway-success history.

Second homes and holiday lets outnumber the houses owned by locals in Portscatho. 'But doesn't that just help to boost the local economy and keep the village shop going?' I countered. Simon (the builder, not the chef) snorted. 'You'd think so, but five minutes after their huge tinted-window 4x4s arrive, the supermarket delivery vans turn up. So no, I don't think so.' Chris Insoll, who I'd run into at the Gerrans Heritage Centre at the top of the hill, was indignant for other reasons. 'People think the Hidden Hut is all there is here, and leave without bothering to find out what makes Portscatho and its surrounds so special.' I know I'm preaching to the converted – because you have bought and are reading

"The evening feasts started when Simon had a load of spare mackerel that needed eating. The rest is runaway-success history."

this book – but more converts to Slow travel are needed to heal this kind of rift. Enjoy what Simon Stallard has created here (it's truly good food cooked by good people, and very much in tune with Slow Food), but stay a while and get to know the village. The **Gerrans Heritage Centre** is a good place to start (⊘ gerransheritage.co.uk ☉ currently by appointment; ✉ gerransheritage@gmail.com), or drop into the **New Gallery** (⊘ thenewgalleryportscatho.co.uk ☉ Thu–Sat) to see Chris's work, and give a firm nudge to anyone who shies away from shopping in the village shop. It will be noticed and appreciated.

⫪ FOOD & DRINK

The Hidden Hut Above Porthcurnick Beach, TR2 5EW ⊘ hiddenhut.co.uk. Very decent picnic food is served out of its modest hatch during the daytime and amazing campfire feasts are cooked up on sell-out summer evenings. Sit on the grassy slope overlooking the beach or share a rustic, convivial table, long enough to accommodate 20 people. There's an ample car park on the road into Portscatho from the A3078, a five-minute walk away.

The Standard Inn Treloan Lane, Gerrans, TR2 5EB ☏ 01872 719232 ⊘ standardinn. co.uk. Simon Stallard's (see opposite) latest venture is this locals' pub, between Gerrans and Portscatho. Dated furnishings have been stripped out and the menu reflects Stallard's creative use of carefully sourced Cornish produce. A wood-fired grill in the pretty garden completes the attractive picture.

Tatams The Slipway, TR2 5HQ ⊘ tatams.co. An outdoor coffee bar (converted from the public loo) with a tremendous seafront view. Behind it is **Tavola** (⊘ tavolaportscatho.co.uk ☉ Thu–Sat eves), an Italian bar-restaurant specialising in pizza. Both belong to Stallard's stable of great eateries in this part of the Roseland.

16 PENDOWER BEACH & CARNE BEACON

A mile of south-facing, firm golden sand, sheltered from east winds by the bulky presence of Nare Head: **Pendower Beach** (which runs seamlessly into **Carne Beach** to the east) is long and deep enough to absorb everyone. Families come here because it's safe and easily accessible; the proximity of the Nare, one of Cornwall's most upmarket hotels, idyllically positioned just above the beach, is a bonus for those who like their beach life to be tempered with a bit of luxury. Even in summer there's a feeling of wide-open space, and in winter it's a huge playground for dogs and their owners.

Keen walkers will want to carry on along the coast path to the heights of Nare Head and on to Portloe, a stiff three miles further on. A very

useful bus service from Truro connects Portloe with Veryan, Portscatho, St Just and St Mawes.

While you're down on the beach a tumulus is visible on the skyline to the east. Having heard that **Carne Beacon** was one of the largest Bronze Age burial barrows in England, possibly containing the relics of the 5th-century King Geraint, I set off to find it. Surrounded by sheep and sugar beet and approached by a short wooden ladder, the tumulus gave nothing to indicate its significance; in fact, it looked like nothing more than a turfed-over reservoir. Despite local objections that it was a historic site, the mound was used during World War II as an enemy aircraft lookout post, and kitted out with observation equipment – but all that remains now is a concrete plinth.

¶¶ FOOD & DRINK

Nare Hotel Carne Beach TR2 5PF ℰ 01872 501111 ⊘ narehotel.co.uk. For a spot of sybaritic refreshment, the hotel's Quarterdeck restaurant does an afternoon tea that includes a glass of champagne, smoked salmon sandwiches, local strawberries and homemade scones.

17 VERYAN

🏠 **Hay Barton** Tregony (page 420)

Veryan is a village of two halves: Veryan Churchtown and Veryan Green, the road at each end flanked by a pair of small round cottages, topped with thatched conical roofs; entering the village is rather like passing through the stubby towers of a solid medieval fortress. The five **roundhouses** (the fifth is in the village behind the school) were the idea of the Reverend Jeremiah Trist, who had them built in 1817. Quite why he chose to build them this way is a matter for speculation: many guidebooks like to say they were built to house each of his five daughters or that no corners leave the devil no place to hide, but the likelihood is that the Reverend just had a leaning towards the picturesque and liked round buildings. There's no evidence either that any of his daughters lived in them. In fact, documentation reveals that he was captivated by a round cottage built for £42 at St Winnow, near Lostwithiel, by his friend Charles Vinicombe Penrose. In 1811 Penrose published its floor plan as

◀ **1** Family-friendly Pendower Beach. **2** Two of Veryan's roundhouses. **3** Trewithen. **4** Portloe.

suitable for a workman's home. History does not record what the first tenants thought of their circular accommodation as they struggled to find a suitable place for granny's dresser.

The village is as picturesque as the quaint roundhouses guarding the road in. Immaculate whitewash and neat thatch, a trickling stream and flowery gardens decorate the area around the church, which was heavily restored in the mid 19th century, but sits no less attractively for that in its leafy surrounds beside the village green. With a pub, a shop and an art gallery, Veryan poses no problems for potterers and it's a perfect base for exploring the safe beaches in Gerrans Bay, the

> "The village is as picturesque as the quaint roundhouses guarding the road in."

summer gardens at **Poppy Cottage** in Ruan High Lanes or the nearby village of **Ruan Lanihorne**, tucked away in the backwoods of the Fal, and for watching oystercatchers stalk the tidal creek.

¶¶ FOOD & DRINK

Da Bara Bakery in the Garden Café Roseland Plant Centre, Ruan High Lanes TR2 5JR ✆ 01872 211206 ⌂ dabara.co.uk ⊙ Mon–Sat. Famous for its cinnamon buns, the da Bara Bakery has gone from strength to strength and now has three cafés (see their website for details), all serving fabulous breakfasts and lunches – and clearly with an eye on the top pasty spot, too.

King's Head Ruan Lanihorne TR2 5NX ✆ 01872 501263 ⌂ kings-head-ruan.co.uk. In a tiny, tucked-away village, beside a tributary of the Fal, the pub is a treat for those who are serious about enjoying their food and drink. Skinner's of Truro supply the ales, some of the wines come from a friend's vineyard in France and the food is a constantly changing menu based on fresh, local ingredients. There's no children's menu.

18 PORTLOE

Remarkably remote, Portloe is approached by tiny lanes that twist their way along a convoluted course for several miles; even on foot, it's a hefty walk along the cliff path to the next outpost of civilisation. However, this is no forgotten backwater: a boutique hotel, a cluster of freshly painted cottages and an art gallery scattered around the prettiest of harbours tell you that – although catches of lobster and crab are hauled up its narrow beach almost daily, Portloe no longer relies on fishing for its main income. It's so picturesque it could easily be a film set, so there's no surprise to discover it is often used for just this purpose.

19 TREWITHEN

Grampound Rd, near Truro, TR2 4DD ⊘ trewithengardens.co.uk ⊙ Mar–Sep

Great things are happening at Trewithen; by 2025 the approach to the historic estate – in every sense – will have changed out of all recognition. There's no cause for alarm: the beautiful Queen Anne manor house, gardens, woodlands, park and surrounding farms remain in the safe and capable stewardship of the Galsworthy family, ten generations of whom have lived here since 1715. However, the sale of the wildly popular Sipsmith gin, of which young Sam Galsworthy was a founder-director, has given the family the opportunity to invest hugely in the estate. With his wife Kitty and the continuing involvement of his father, Mike, Sam has set the wheels in motion for the old home farm to be turned into a rather beautiful farm shop and restaurant supplied with estate produce, a working kitchen garden and permaculture orchard together with a museum for Trevithick's threshing machine. (This was Richard Trevithick's first engineering commission and the splendid machine will be going back into the building that was originally built to house it in 1812.) Gary Long, Trewithen's long-standing head gardener, who was explaining all this to me, sounded pretty excited. Meanwhile the main vista of the garden from the house is being returned to the original 1747 plan with a straight-edged long lawn drawing the eye over the ha-ha to the park and farmland beyond, where a new herd of longhorn cattle will graze beneath stands of holm oak.

Starting in 2024, a camellia festival will be held in late February, just as the gardens burst into flower with a tremendous show of magnolias and spring bulbs. Gary can hardly wait and his enthusiasm is palpable.

The Cornish historian A L Rowse wrote: 'Trewithen as an ensemble is unquestionably one of the most perfect and pleasing places anywhere in Cornwall … As a whole, quite unforgettable'. I think it's fair to say that he would heartily approve of the new goings-on.

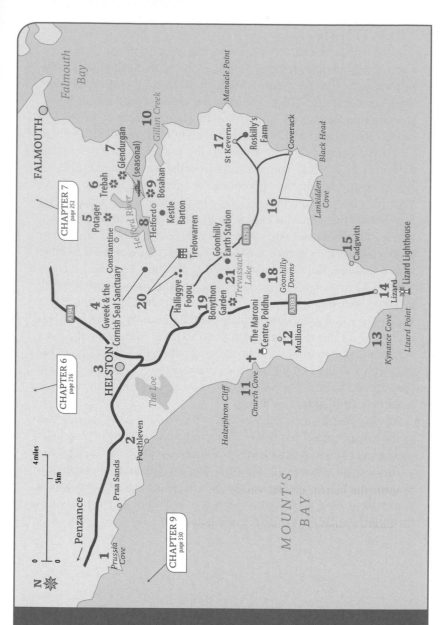

N

0 4 miles
0 5km

Penzance

FALMOUTH

Falmouth Bay

Gillan Creek

Manacle Point

Coverack

Black Head

Roskilly's Farm

CHAPTER 7
page 252

10

7 Glendurgan

6 Trebah

9 Bosahan

5 Potager

Constantine

8 Helford (seasonal)

Helford River

Kestle Barton

Trelowarren

17 St Keverne

Lankidden Cove

4 Gweek & the Cornish Seal Sanctuary

Goonhilly Earth Station

B3293

16

15 Cadgwith

20

Halliggye Fogou

19 Bonython Garden

21 *Trevassack Lake*

18 *Goonhilly Downs*

Lizard lighthouse

CHAPTER 6
page 216

3 HELSTON

The Loe

The Marconi Centre, Poldhu

A3083

14 Lizard

Lizard Point

2 Porthleven

11 Church Cove

Halzephron Cliff

12 Mullion

13 *Kynance Cove*

1 Prussia Cove

Praa Sands

A394

A3083

CHAPTER 9
page 330

MOUNT'S BAY

SOUTHWEST CORNWALL: THE LIZARD PENINSULA

8
SOUTHWEST CORNWALL: THE LIZARD PENINSULA

The Slow lane starts here: away from main roads, crowded beaches, jammed harbours and busy towns, this part of Cornwall is perfect for quiet exploration and unhurried hours spent just looking, listening and absorbing the very diverse character of the peninsula. More of an island, in fact, than a peninsula, the **Lizard** has a coastline that faces not only west and east, but south for a few miles as well, while the **Helford River** carves a broad path through the hilly, wooded landscape to the north.

Lush and lovely gardens face each other across this wood-fringed river and footpaths ramble past muddy boatyards, secluded beaches and leafy creeks that can only be glimpsed or guessed at from tarmac roads. Tiny, unspoiled coves lie far below the southern cliffs where, if you search, pebbles of red or green serpentine rock that sit smooth and heavy in the hand can be found. Gaze skywards and you may be lucky enough to see a pair of choughs – Cornwall's emblematic bird – tumbling overhead.

In stormy weather, the furious sea breaking over the harbour wall at **Porthleven** from the safety of a pub window is compelling viewing; but beneath the lichen, coastal village churchyard tombstones remember the victims of the many shipwrecks on the Lizard's unkind reefs and bars. Inland, miles of **heathland** teeming with butterflies are criss-crossed by tracks passing ancient tumuli, half-hidden beneath the gorse and heather. Westwards, the empty heath gives way to an aquamarine sea, embraced by

"This part of Cornwall is perfect for quiet exploration and unhurried hours spent just looking, listening and absorbing."

rocky coves, where pale sandy beaches are revealed as the tide recedes. When a couple of friends from New Zealand who had been working in London asked me where they could find the kind of barefoot, natural maritime world they were pining for, I knew they would be happy here, staying at **Henry's Campsite**, a haven for lovers of a wild and simple way of living under canvas by the sea.

The remote exposure to the Atlantic has proved irresistible to the pioneers of communications technology. Marconi built his famous transmitters on the promontory at **Poldhu**, from where the first transatlantic radio messages were sent in 1901. Six decades later, the biggest satellite station in the world rose from the abandoned radar station at **Goonhilly Downs**, and now plans are advancing to turn the redundant station into a space-science centre, fulfilling the prophecy (for some) that Arthur will rise again.

Enjoying local food and drink forms a vital part of Lizard life. Organic ice cream, made by the Roskilly family, is hard to miss, and pasties from Gear Farm or Ann Muller in Lizard village are, like Vicky's Bread (originating in Helford but now based in Helston), legendary in these parts; freshly caught crab is a harbourside treat, and Helford Creek cider and apple juice will go down well with fans of real cider. Micro-breweries include Lizard Ales and the much-loved Spingo, brewed at the Blue Anchor in Helston. Trelowarren and Porthleven are rapidly establishing themselves as places where Slow Food is championed, and on the eastern side of the Helford, the vegetarian menu is supplied from the veg patch at the Potager Garden.

GETTING AROUND

Helston sits midway between Falmouth and Penzance on the A394, which is not the fastest of roads, particularly in the summer holidays, but the A3083, which branches off at RNAS Culdrose on the outskirts of Helston, offers a swift route south to Lizard village.

The B3293 swoops off this to St Keverne in the east and Coverack, a little further to the south. Beyond these roads you'll need a map and a good sense of direction to get around the tangle of narrow lanes that link the remote villages around the Helford River or inland from the coast.

TRAINS
Getting about by rail is not an option in this part of Cornwall; the branch line from a junction near Camborne that once served Helston closed in the early 1960s.

Penzance and Redruth are the nearest mainline stations; the busy line from Truro to Falmouth links up with bus routes that take in the big gardens on the north side of Helford River.

BUSES

Your options for getting about by bus are much better these days. **Helston** is the hub, with services to Penzance, Falmouth, Truro and Camborne. As for the peninsula, the L1 and 34 cover the west coast via Mullion to the Lizard with branching options to Ruan Minor. The 36 will take you via Goonhilly to Coverack and St Keverne, while the 33 covers the south shores of the Helford. All is made very clear on the maps page of ⊘ firstbus.co.uk/cornwall.

At Helford you can catch a seasonal foot ferry to the north bank of the river, where Glendurgan and Trebah gardens are easily reached on foot, or connect with the 35 service which runs between Helston and Falmouth via Gweek and Mawnan Smith.

CYCLING

There are no official bike routes through the peninsula, so the OS Explorer map 103 is the best tool for planning a ride. The biggest question left unanswered by the map, however, is the problem of crossing Loe Bar with a bike.

It can be done, though pushing a bike over 400 yards of shingle is not much fun, and crossing in wild weather, when waves smash across the bar, is extremely dangerous. The picturesque solution is the five mile, largely level detour around the Loe, through the National Trust's **Penrose estate** and **Helston** (there is a bike path on the short stretch of main road past RNAS Culdrose).

On the east side of the peninsula, the little boats that offer a seasonal foot passenger service between Helford and Helford Passage will do their best to accommodate a bike or two; and as there are hardly any riverside lanes or tracks upstream from here, it's great for cyclists and walkers wanting to see a bit more of the **Helford River**.

 CYCLE HIRE

Lakeside Cycle Hire Lakeside Coronation Park, Helston TR13 0SR ⊘ 07368 996058 ⊘ lakesidecycles.co.uk. Daily and weekly cycle hire, suggested routes and guided rides are available. Perfect for exploring the Penrose estate or accessing Porthleven during the Food

Festival when narrow roads and limited parking can lead to long delays. Free collection and delivery; helmets, locks and toolkits part of the deal.

Lizard Bike Hire The Square, Lizard TR12 7NZ ℰ 07951 934604 ⟨ lizardbikehire. co.uk. Local lads Alex, Josh and Matt, who set up the business in 2022, offer heaps of local knowledge together with e-bikes, hybrids, trailers and tandems. Delivery or collection.

Shipyard Cycles Porthleven TR13 9JY ℰ 07462 411664 ⟨ shipyardcycles.co.uk. New family business offering e-bikes, hybrids and lots more, available for both long- and short-term hire.

HORSERIDING

If the sight of horseriders cantering across the beach at low tide fills you with longing, the place to go is **Newton Farm** (ℰ 01326 240388 ⟨ newton-equestrian.co.uk), between Poldhu and Mullion. Rides can be arranged for both novice and experienced riders, ranging from one to five hours. Hats can be borrowed, and boots hired.

WALKING

Inland, the Lizard peninsula is very flat and most walkers will gravitate towards the coastal and riverside footpaths for the outstanding views and varied terrain. However, anyone with an interest in birds, butterflies or wild flowers will enjoy rambling across the empty and expansive moorland of the **Lizard National Nature Reserve**, which adjoins the desolate satellite station on Goonhilly Downs (page 327).

Walkers pursuing the **coast path** are in for some rare old treats, even by Cornish standards: Church Cove, Kynance Cove, Mullion, Coverack and Cadgwith invite even the keenest hikers on timed schedules to slow down and explore. The **Helford River** is no less entrancing, from the river mouth at St Anthony to the secret wooded creeks inland. For solitude as well as splendour, Gillan Creek is unbeatable and low tide stepping stones from St Anthony to tiny Flushing make a circular route possible.

FROM PRUSSIA COVE TO THE HELFORD RIVER

A journey across the north of the peninsula takes you from some of Cornwall's most glorious – and treacherous – coastal scenery to the secret, leafy creeks and beaches of the Helford River, taking in handsome old Helston and busy RNAS Culdrose on the way. Unlike the rivers Fal and Fowey to the east, the Helford has no large towns or harbours facing each other across the yacht-filled estuary: here are creekside hamlets, subtropical gardens, broadleaf woodland and marshy banks strewn with dinghies and canoes pulled up above the muddy tideline.

1 PRUSSIA COVE

The small but free private car park is a generous gift to visitors anywhere on the Cornish coast, and much appreciated here. The track from the car park to the coast path reveals a cluster of totally unspoiled houses and cottages, all part of the **Porth-en-Alls estate**. The Tunstall-Behrens family, who own the estate, host an annual international gathering of musicians, giving the opportunity for both the young and the experienced to learn and perform together. It's an inspiring place – the sea is cobalt and turquoise, the coves sheltered and the rocky shoreline as ruggedly picturesque as anything you might find on a remote Aegean island. No wonder the music is inspired. Concerts held in local churches are listed on ℗ i-m-s.org.uk.

Prussia Cove is a generic name for this small stretch of coast, rather than belonging to an individual inlet. The name derives from Cornwall's most famous 'free trader' (smuggler if you must), John Carter, who since boyhood had taken Frederick the Great of Prussia as his hero and role model. During the last decade or two of the 18th century, the self styled King of Prussia and his brother, Harry Carter, lived here and used the shelter of Bessy's Cove to land contraband, in days when dodging the excise man was considered an honourable trade. The cliffs are riddled with underground passages and tunnels leading from coves to cottages; it's all pure Daphne du Maurier.

SPRING BLOOMS ON THE COAST PATH

Walkers following the track from the car park to the coast path at Prussia Cove will notice the stone-built 'Cornish hedges' have been planted with tamarisks: the new feathery foliage and sprays of pink flowers in May look delicate, but are particularly suited to the salty, maritime climate. The clifftops are carpeted in pink thrift, yellow bird's-foot trefoil, purplish-blue tufted vetch and white sea campion at this time of year, but one of the oddest sights is dodder, which forms a tangled mat of pinky-red stems and attaches itself parasitically to gorse and heather, looking as though a careless passer-by has been chucking out pocketfuls of string.

To the west, a lovely two-mile stride along the cliffs leads to **Perranuthnoe** (you can return by an inland route across the fields); to the east, the coast path takes you past **Kenneggy Sands**, a quieter, less-visited beach than the hugely popular **Praa Sands**, a little further on. If you decide to make it a circular walk and follow the footpaths from Praa Sands back to Prussia Cove, you pass through the yard of **Lower Kenneggy Farm**. Look out for the descendants of Oxo and Marmite, two gentle, hefty oxen who made the news in 2008 when they replaced the tractor here.

2 PORTHLEVEN

Porthleven has become something of a foodie destination, and its annual **Food Festival** in April is so popular that parking has become a real issue. Visitors are well advised to cycle – or even walk – from Helston if at all possible. But beyond the upmarket restaurants, the working harbour and often violent seas give the town a rather gutsy identity, and keep the small fishing community visible among the restaurants, art galleries, delis and cafés. Not many harbours face – open-mouthed as it were – the prevailing wind, but this one, built in the early years of the 19th century, was designed specifically as a safe haven for boats driven by southwesterlies into this corner of Mount's Bay. The decision to build the harbour came after the loss of the frigate, HMS *Anson*, wrecked on Loe Bar, a mile to the south, with catastrophic loss of life. It was just a few days after Christmas in 1807, and the ship had been on her way to Brest to support the blockade of the Napoleonic fleet. It was with a grim sense of justice, perhaps, that French prisoners of war were used for the dangerous work of clearing the shingle bar that held the sea back from the marshy valley that lay behind. Two of the *Anson*'s canons, dragged up from seabed, now face each other across the harbour. Another can be seen outside the folk museum in Helston.

Storm-watching is Porthleven's answer to theatre. On the south side of the harbour mouth the road narrows and twists around a granite-built clock tower on the corner of the town hall and the beach, punctured with jagged rocks, is revealed below. In really bad weather, this road is closed as waves crash right over it and dash against the clock

---

1 Prussia Cove. **2** Looking down over the Loe. **3** Cornish chough. **4** White sea campion and sea thrift. **5** The clock tower at Porthleven. ▶

THE CORNISH CHOUGH

Cornwall's emblematic bird – a crow with a long, curved red beak and red legs, given to aerobatic displays – disappeared from the county in 1949, as post-war agriculture became increasingly intensive and reliant upon pesticides. Choughs, which feed off the kind of insects found on grazed pasture close to their cliff nests, such as woodlice, spiders, ants and beetles, didn't have much of a chance. But a general change in land management on the Lizard tempted the first breeding pair to return to the cliffs at Lizard Point in 2001 and a small colony, closely watched and guarded by local volunteers, has re-established itself. Choughs are also gaining in numbers on the south Penwith coast and the chough breeding programme at Paradise Park in Hayle envisages chicks hatched in the wild in the near future (page 234). For up-to-date news of sightings and hatchings, ⌀ chough.org has all the latest chough gossip.

tower. But it's a marvellous show when seen from a position of safety, when the massive incoming waves offer an awe-inspiring spectacle of unstoppable energy.

The Loe & Penrose estate

Between Porthleven and Helston, one of the best spots locally for walking and cycling follows the contours of the freshwater lake, known as **the Loe**. Fed by the River Cober, but blocked from running into the sea by a huge (and growing) dam of sand and shingle, the Loe is one of those geography-textbook examples of lagoon formation. Not everybody can agree, however, when Loe Bar was formed. The idea was made popular in Victorian times that the Cober was navigable as far as Helston at the time of the Norman invasion and that the site of the current boating lake was once a busy port; it's a likeable theory, but sadly lacking in evidence. A more probable explanation is that the bar was formed at least 6,000 years ago, deposited by rising sea levels as ice melted across the globe.

No matter: the lake is stunningly, silently beautiful and lies within the **Penrose estate**, owned and managed by the National Trust. The route through the estate passes a mock-Roman bathhouse, at the foot of a great sweep of immaculate, landscaped pasture that falls away below the Georgian façade of the house, hidden on either side by woods and water. It's a good idea to bring binoculars: there's a birdwatchers' hide by the lake which is a haven for wildfowl – widgeon, teal, mallard, shoveler, pochard, tufted duck and coots are common – and there were a pair of crested grebes the last time I visited.

You can follow the Cober through the woods (carpeted with bluebells in May) to Helston and catch a bus back to Porthleven or cross the marshy junction of river and lake on wooden boardwalks, emerging by the derelict remains of Lower Nansloe mine, and do the complete six-mile circuit of the lake, crossing the shingle of Loe Bar to return to the starting point. There's a car park and map board at the entrance to the Penrose estate or limited parking where the road from Porthleven comes to an end on the cliff above Loe Bar. On the eastern side of the bar, a memorial to the lives lost when HMS *Anson* ran aground here in 1807 serves as a stark reminder of the maritime dangers of this coast.

HENRY TRENGROUSE

While virtually everybody has heard of Sir Humphry Davy and his invention of the safety lamp that saved so many miners' lives, few people outside Helston remember Henry Trengrouse, inventor of the ship-to-shore rocket-fired safety-line, forerunner of the 'breeches-buoy', that has helped to save thousands of mariners' lives across the globe. Born and bred in Helston, where his father was a builder, Trengrouse was among the number of appalled bystanders that watched, helpless, as HMS *Anson* foundered and broke on Loe Bar and more than a hundred men drowned just yards from the shore on the morning of 29 December 1807. The catastrophe made a profound impact upon him, and over the next ten years he poured £3,000 (which, as a cabinetmaker, was more money than he could afford) into developing his rocket-propelled lifeline.

The prevailing design, submitted to the government by George Manby in 1808, was for a mortar that fired a line from shore to ship – which was proving neither accurate nor practical. (Who, in the confusion and distress of a shipwreck, is going to catch a snaking line and attach it to the right part of a breaking ship?) But whereas Manby received £2,000 from the government for his troubles, Trengrouse was given merely a royalty of £50 as he relinquished manufacture to the Admiralty. (The Tsar of Russia, rather embarrassingly for the Admiralty, sent Trengrouse a personal letter of thanks and a diamond ring.) For the rest of his life, Trengrouse continued to design safety equipment for ships, including the 'Bosun's Chair' and a prototype life jacket.

There's an exhibition dedicated to his life's work beside a painting of the *Anson* shipwreck in the **Helston Museum of Cornish Life** while the **Trengrouse memorial stone** in St Michael's churchyard honours a man who died, unjustly, in poverty.

¶¶ FOOD & DRINK

Whether it's humble fish and chips or locally caught lobster, standards are high in Porthleven when it comes to eating, and never more so than in April, when the **Food Festival** (⌀ porthlevenfoodfestival.com) draws in producers and chefs from all over Cornwall. Its popularity makes car parking – or even getting close to Porthleven by car – a bit of a nightmare. Come by bicycle from Helston – or on foot if you can. (I know I'm repeating myself but I think it's important!)

Corner Deli 12 Fore St, TR13 9HJ ⌀ 01326 565554 ⌀ thecornerdeliporthleven.co.uk. If the lovely shop windows don't draw you in, the delicious aromas will. A couple of window seats allow you to enjoy terrific coffee, and there are wood-fired pizzas to take away in the evenings as well as an incredible array of comestible Cornish and Italian goodies on the shelves.

Kota Harbour Head, TR13 9JA ⌀ 01326 562407 ⌀ kotarestaurant.co.uk ⊙ Tue–Sat; check online for seasonal variations. A New Zealand couple with a passion for fresh seafood (Kota is Maori for shellfish) and organic, local produce have done much to put Porthleven on Cornwall's gastronomic map.

Kota Kai TR13 9JY ⌀ 01326 727707 ⌀ kotakai.co.uk ⊙ Wed–Sun; check online for seasonal variations. Kota's sister venture, just a short step away, on the top floor of Celtic House, is a more relaxed affair, and much enjoyed by local families; there are lots of sofas, a children's room, film nights and live jazz every Sunday lunchtime. The menu features delicious nibbly things and dishes on an Asian theme.

Nauti but Ice Commercial Rd, TR13 0SR ⌀ 01326 573747 ⌀ nautibutice.co.uk. Serving Origin coffee and Roskilly's ice cream, popular with locals as well as visitors.

Ship Inn Mount Pleasant Rd, TR13 9JS ⌀ 01326 564204 ⌀ theshipinnporthleven.co.uk. Built into the rocks on the north side of the harbour, this is the ideal spot to sit out a storm and watch the waves breaking – over a pint of Doom Bar, so to speak. Upmarket pub grub served daily, lunchtime and evening.

Stables Café Penrose estate, TR13 0RD ⌀ 01326 562882. A cosy café set within the old coach house courtyard of Penrose house, offering lovely views over the parkland. Just right for a tea, sandwich or soup lunch break – or an ice cream – when cycling or walking around the estate or the Loe.

3 HELSTON

Helston's identity is a complex one these days; on the one hand, the town leans heavily on its old buildings and traditions, while on the other, it's home to RNAS Culdrose, where 3,000 military and civilian personnel are employed in training, defence and air-sea rescue.

Helston's prosperous past is written all over the splendid houses that line the streets between St Michael's Church and the old shops, pubs and civic buildings on Coinagehall Street. This was one of Cornwall's five stannary towns, where ingots of copper and tin from the surrounding stannary had to be brought to be assayed, weighed and stamped in the Coinage Hall before they could be sold. Each ingot had a small corner – a 'coin' – cut off for assaying its purity, a task which brought phenomenal commercial activity to the town. It wasn't just the loss of 1,200 miners' jobs when Wheal Vor was threatened with closure in the early 19th century; it was the knock-on effect to other trades in the town that filled Helston with

"This was one of Cornwall's five stannary towns, where ingots of copper and tin had to be brought to be assayed, weighed and stamped."

fear. Small wonder that the Helston banker and lawyer, Humphrey Millett Grylls, who used his personal wealth to keep the mine open, was revered: the **Grylls Arch**, an imposing castellated gateway to the ancient bowling green at the bottom of Coinagehall Street, was erected in his honour when he died in 1834.

The town had faced a different kind of shock and salvation a century earlier, when **St Michael's Church** was struck by lightning and had to be demolished after the ensuing fire. Lord Godolphin, whose family had grown rich on local tin since Tudor times, sprang into action and personally funded the building of the new church, completed in 1763. Though built of local granite it's hardly Cornish in character; the architect employed by Godolphin was Thomas Edwards of Greenwich, a keen admirer of Nicholas Hawksmoor – which is why some elements of St Michael's are reminiscent of St Alfege's, a Greenwich church, designed by Hawksmoor in 1718.

It's not just the buildings in Helston that speak of stannary wealth: deep granite channels, or '**kennels**', bubbling with running water, play an important part in defining the town's character (as well as punishing careless roadside parking). These kerbside rills are channelled into the town by a sophisticated system of leats and sluices, some of which date from medieval times, from the infant River Cober, across the Wendron Valley a couple of miles north of Helston. Their purpose is not known for certain, but the usefulness of a continual supply of running water for maintaining street hygiene, particularly around the tanneries, can be imagined. From the top of the town the kennels branch out (invisibly in some streets, where they have been covered over) sending a constant trickle of water through the town, which eventually ends up back in the Cober at **Coronation Park**. When I called in at the bike-hire hut beside the revamped Lakeside Café (see opposite), it was clear that the park – at this slightly neglected end of Helston – had received something of a facelift, with improvements to the boating lake, paths, play park and general repairs as well the creation of a skate park. It is undoubtedly one of the town's greatest assets and the gateway to some of the most enjoyable walks and cycle rides in Cornwall.

Helston is perennially associated with its ever-popular and ancient **Flora Day** celebrations held in May to celebrate the feast day of St Michael. From early morning until late afternoon, the streets are thick with dancers, flowers, foliage and spectators, chasing out the winter and singing in the spring. It's an exhausting business, which involves the whole community, lots of Cornish flag waving, joyful renditions of 'Trelawney' and 'Hal-an-Tow' as well as ritual dragon slaying, but the key event is the midday Furry Dance. Led by the Helston silver band, couples dressed as though they are going to Royal Ascot parade and twirl through the streets to the well-known tune, which – be warned – stays in your ears for hours, if not days, afterwards.

For over 70 years, Helston has also been synonymous with helicopters, thanks to the busy presence of **RNAS Culdrose**, one of the biggest naval air stations in Europe, which swelled the population and brought energy to the town. The station is the search and rescue base for the whole of the southwest and you can watch the Sea King helicopters swing into action and other airborne activity from a small viewing car park, outside the perimeter fence. The café here is open in the summer only.

Helston Museum of Cornish Life

Market Pl, TR13 8TH ✆ 01326 564027 ⏾ museumofcornishlife.co.uk ⏱ Mon–Fri 10.00–16.00, Sat noon–16.00; free, but donations gratefully accepted

Housed in the old butter and meat market, the exhibits are arranged where the stalls once stood, like mini-museums on either side of the sloping, granite thoroughfare. It's all very engaging and the volunteers and staff are happy to chat knowledgeably as they polish the brass. As you enter, an enormous granite runnelstone and 18th-century cider press, both from the Trelowarren estate, take centre stage. Thereafter, an eclectic mix unfolds of Edwardian uniforms, chapel china, pre-war groceries, Marconi memorabilia and Victorian domestic equipment, until level ground indicates you have arrived in the old drill hall. Here, highlights include a costume gallery, a horse-drawn hearse and a Victorian schoolroom. Upstairs in the loft are displays of toys, garden equipment and bicycles, and an exhibit that tells the story of champion boxer, local lad Bob Fitzsimmons.

¶¶ FOOD & DRINK

The Bell Inn 35 Meneage St, TR13 8AA ✆ 01326 562965 🖥 bellinnhelston.co.uk. Locals tell that this family-friendly pub is a bit of a gem. There's a pleasant garden, way-above-average pub food, well-kept ales and a friendly vibe.

The Blue Anchor 50 Coinagehall St, TR13 8EL ✆ 01326 562821. A thatched pub at the lower end of Coinagehall Street – there's even a thatched anchor on the roof – that appears hardly changed since monks lived here in the 15th century. Fireplaces, cosy snugs, wooden settles and flagged floors, and four strengths of Spingo beer, brewed at the back, make this a place of pilgrimage for aficionados of real ale and lovers of proper old-fashioned pubs. Bring a pasty if you're hungry, as no food is served.

CAST (Cornubian Arts and Science Trust) Café 3 Penrose Rd, TR13 8TP ✆ 01326 569267 🖥 c-a-s-t.org.uk. Housed in the old Passmore Edwards school, behind the Helston Museum of Cornish Life, this initiative to provide local artists with studio and workshop space sports a good café, serving homemade lunches and cakes. In summer, the outdoor seating offers outstanding views over the rooftops of Helston and rolling farmland, as far as Sithney to the northwest.

Lakeside Café Coronation Park, TR13 0SR ✆ 01326 569969 🖥 nautibutice.co.uk. Local produce is championed at this café from the Nauti But Ice team in Porthleven. Lovely views over the lake.

4 GWEEK & THE CORNISH SEAL SANCTUARY

The oddly named village of **Gweek** (derived in fact from 'creek') slopes down to its bridge at the tidal limit of the Helford River, where there's a busy boatyard, much smarter these days due to massive investment by its new owners. One or two classic yachts undergoing restoration are reason enough to stop and stare. There's an excellent café beside the boatyard and a decent pub, the Black Swan (✆ 01326 221502), that does good food. There are lovely wooded lanes leading to the village of Mawgan, and the Trelowarren estate; anyone planning a bike ride or walk through the Lizard should make sure they make this route part of the itinerary.

Apart from its thriving boatyard, Gweek is best known for the **Cornish Seal Sanctuary** (✆ 01326 331261 ⬨ sealsanctuary.sealifetrust. org), which does valuable work rescuing and rehabilitating injured or orphaned seals found on the Cornish coast, before releasing them back into the wild. It's not a zoo or theme park, and visitors may baulk at the cost of admission, but the centre relies on entrance money and donations for its survival. There's a permanent community of old-timers, deemed unsuitable for release, and a constantly changing population of pups and older seals in various stages of recovery. Tender-hearted adults and children will want to dig deep into their pockets once they spot the sanctuary's adoption programme.

⫚ FOOD & DRINK

The Boatyard Café TR12 6UF ✆ 01326 702157. Under dynamic new ownership, the Gweek boatyard has enjoyed a huge revival of fortunes in recent years and includes a café with lovely riverside views and an indoor woodburner. The menu ranges from delicious breakfasts to falafel wraps and sandwiches.

5 POTAGER GARDEN

High Cross, Constantine TR11 5RE ✆ 01326 341258 ⬨ potagergarden.org ⦵ Thu–Sun & bank hols

This is one of my favourite places in Cornwall: not only is the garden inspiringly well planted, staggeringly productive and managed on organic principles, the whole place – including the café, workshops and all who work here – seems to exude happiness and creativity.

The influence of Falmouth University is clearly felt here. Peter Skerrett, co-founder of Potager, taught at the Falmouth School of Art and I recognised his name from the contemporary altar of yew and glass in a side chapel of Truro Cathedral. The architectural and sculptural elements of the garden are handled with true artistic vision; Dan Thomas, who originally planted the gardens had a terrific eye for colour.

But it's not always been like this. What Dan and Peter found in 1999 was an abandoned nursery, thick with brambles, nettles and self-sown trees, bursting through glasshouses. They cleared and planted, salvaged and repaired; some of the trees and shrubs remain, now smartly clipped

◀ **1** The upper reaches of the Helford River close to Gweek. **2** Potager Garden. **3** Helston Museum of Cornish Life. **4** Limpet the seal, a resident at the Cornish Seal Sanctuary.

or pruned, giving structure to the otherwise billowy planting. Then, in 2006 they opened a café in a mended glasshouse and started renting out some of the old buildings as workshops. Local boat builder Mark Harris took one on and built a superb 20-foot sailing boat in it. Since 2008 Mark and his partner Saffa have taken a major part in the running of Potager and it is going from strength to strength, attracting plantspeople, artists and anyone who just wants to escape for a bit and relax. The garden is equipped with hammocks as well as games to play. A superb **vegetarian café** uses produce straight out of the garden which is served at rustic tables in an eco-efficient greenhouse the team have designed and built themselves. The gardens have more recently been extended and now include orchards which sit above a long, sloping approach from the car park

"A superb vegetarian café uses produce straight out of the garden which is served at rustic tables."

Just down the road is **Constantine**, one of those well-heeled but equally dynamic rural communities where the arts are placed high on the agenda. **The Tolmen Centre** (Fore St, TR11 5AA ✆ 01326 341353 🔗 tolmencentre.co.uk) is where it all goes on, from classical guitar festivals to film, contemporary dance and drama, occasionally fresh from the Edinburgh Festival.

⅓ FOOD & DRINK

The Potager Garden Café High Cross, Constantine TR11 5RE ✆ 01326 341258 🔗 potagergarden.org ⊙ Thu–Sun & bank hols. Lovely vegetarian breakfasts and lunches, using produce either from the garden or sourced locally. The occasional evening meals are deservedly popular with locals and sell out fast.

THE SHORES OF THE HELFORD RIVER

It's wood-fringed riverside beaches and lush gardens all the way between **Helford Passage** and **Mawnan Smith**. Swimming is safe, the south-facing shoreline sunny, and an undulating coast path joins it all together. The further east you walk, the more secluded the beaches become: **Porth Saxon** and **Porthallack** are particularly seductive and perfectly placed for shelter and late afternoon sunshine. Both **Trebah** and **Glendurgan** gardens can be approached from their beach entrances.

South of the river, the lush dairy pastures, woods and coves give discreet shelter to some of Cornwall's most desirable real estate. And, where the river meets the sea and tidal Gillan Creek, the ultimate backdrop is offered to those who are happiest messing about on a boat.

¶¶ FOOD & DRINK

There are good pubs at either end of the walk – the **Ferryboat Inn** (☎ 01326 250625 ⌂ ferryboatcornwall.co.uk) at Helford Passage and the dark and cosy **Red Lion** (☎ 01326 250026 ⌂ redlioncornwall.com) in Mawnan Smith, with locally caught fish and game on the menu.

6 TREBAH

Mawnan Smith TR11 5JZ ☎ 01326 250448 ⌂ trebahgarden.co.uk

The Falmouth branch of the Fox family were hugely into their gardens. Quaker businessmen and women of enormous wealth, with ships at their disposal, the Foxes were able to fund plant-hunting trips around the world and the sheltered narrow valleys south of Falmouth proved ideal conditions for creating gardens of colourful exoticism that have since become identified as a particularly Cornish style of garden.

Dazzling collections of camellias, rhododendrons, magnolias, palms, pines and tree ferns, a stream-fed valley and, beyond a clump of craggy Monterey pines, a glimpse of a blue cove: this is the stereotype, and no garden pulls it off quite so magnificently as Trebah. Charles Fox, whose elder siblings were busy making gardens at Glendurgan next door and Penjerrick (closer to Falmouth), moved here in 1838 and spent the next 40 years developing the garden. Successive owners (who included car designer, racing driver and orchid breeder Donald Healey) continued to enhance the planting, but perhaps none more so than Tony and Eira Hibbert, who bought a rather run-down Trebah in 1981, intending to make it their retirement home. Within days of arrival, instead of sipping gins on the terrace as intended, they found themselves drawn into an exciting programme of restoration and replanting and opened the garden to the public in 1986. Everyone who met Major Hibbert, a much-decorated war hero, remembers his charisma and enthusiasm. Well into his 90s when he died in 2014, he was fond of saying, 'I would have died of gin and boredom if it wasn't for this garden'.

"The Foxes were able to fund plant-hunting trips around the world."

TREBAH GARDEN

PHILIP BIRD LRPS CPAGB/S

SS

PAUL NASH/S

7 GLENDURGAN

Mawnan Smith TR11 5JZ ☎ 01872 862090; National Trust

While Charles Fox was busy at Trebah, his elder brother Alfred and sister-in-law Sarah had been hard at work making a garden (and producing 12 little gardeners to help them with the weeding) in the next-door valley, above the miniature fishing village of Durgan. The brothers' shared passion for plants must have proved of mutual benefit to both gardens, but despite this and very similar geographical features, the two gardens are quite distinct in character today. Glendurgan's squishy-contoured laurel maze and wilder, looser planting on the valley slopes is more romantic in its appeal; Trebah is busier, both in plants and visitors, and has a distinctly commercial aspect. Charles Fox, who lives in Glendurgan House, is a great-nephew of Alfred. Artist, poet, plantsman, professional flower-arranger and garden designer, Charles remains the soul and spirit of Glendurgan, although this modest man would no doubt raise his eyebrows at the suggestion and remind you that this is a National Trust garden.

8 HELFORD & AROUND

'Just stand on the quay and wave – the ferry will soon come,' said the village postwoman as I quizzed her about crossing the river from Helford to the north shore. Sadly, my lonely waving was to no avail; it was a day or two before Easter and the ferry service had not yet resumed. So I went for a walk instead. The village – just a clutch of whitewashed and thatched cottages, surrounding a tiny harbour – is inaccessible to cars (there's a compulsory car park on the outskirts), ridiculously pretty and quite clearly holidayed in rather than lived in.

Kestle Barton

🏠 **Kestle Barton** (page 420)

Manaccan TR12 6HU ☎ 01326 231811 ⊘ kestlebarton.co.uk ⊙ Tue–Sun

Kestle Barton turned out to be a 20-minute stroll from Helford, on a wooded circular walk that takes in the densely wooded shores of Frenchman's Creek, immortalised by Daphne du Maurier's eponymous historical novel. An exciting conversion of farm buildings has resulted

---

◀ **1** The valley gardens at Trebah. **2** The maze at Glendurgan. **3** A thatched cottage in Helford. **4** Bosahan Woods.

in a very attractive and thoughtfully planned arts venue that reflects the affluence of Helford, with a gallery, a help-yourself café, a delightful garden filled with a very up-to-date mix of grasses and perennials, wildflower meadows and stunning, eco-sensitive accommodation.

¶¶ FOOD & DRINK

Shipwrights Arms Helford TR12 6JX ✆ 01326 231235 ⅋ shipwrights-helford.co.uk. Good food, local ales and the location, close to the river in the middle of the village, is idyllic. There's a lovely garden that is much enjoyed by children and dogs.

9 BOSAHAN

Manaccan TR12 6JL ✆ 01326 231351 ⊙ Mar–Jul Mon–Fri; closed bank hols

With a trio of great gardens on the opposite side of the river, unsung Bosahan is the kind of place you need to know about, rather than stumble upon, as although visitors are welcome, the opening times are limited and the entrance is not easy to find. (From Manaccan head for Helford, but turn right at the crossroads, following the sign to St Anthony. Take the first road on the left where, after a sharp bend, the gates to the Bosahan Estate are on your right.) There's a kind of lost-valley feeling here, among the giant tree ferns and podocarpus, metasequoias and cork oaks; in fact, most of the very distinguished tree planting, carried out in the 19th century by the owner of Bosahan, Arthur Pendarves Vivian, has now reached monumental proportions in the benign, riverside climate. Under the stewardship of a new generation of Graham-Vivians, the two valleys are being gently, though extensively restored.

The nearest village is Manaccan, where the church has acquired status locally due to the 200-year-old fig tree growing from the wall of the tower.

¶¶ FOOD & DRINK

It's gloriously uncommercialised here; the only offering is **Sid Rosevear's Fish and Chip Van**, which comes to Manaccan on Tuesday evenings throughout the year.

10 GILLAN CREEK

There can be few nicer ways to spend a Slow morning or afternoon than pottering or paddling around Gillan Creek. **Sailaway**, a small family-run shop on the beach at St Anthony (✆ 01326 231357 ⅋ sailawaystanthony. co.uk), hires out kayaks, toppers, dinghies and motor launches: the rest is up to you, though tuition is available for the inexperienced. Whichever way you point your craft, the views are sublime. Turn seawards and thread through the moorings to Dennis Head, braving the swell to enter the wide mouth of the Helford; turn inland and find yourself gliding through a green world, where kingfishers flash through the leafy shadows and swans patrol the margins of their watery world. The tide is everything: at low tide the creek becomes a muddy expanse of beached boats, crossed by stepping stones at its narrowest point. Turn your back for an hour and the sea has slid in, doubling the depth of the view in the upside-down reflections of boats, woods and cottages.

THE PENINSULA

The 20 miles or so of Lizard coast are rich in gorgeous beaches, often tucked away far beneath the high cliff path; great fun for Slow explorers, hunting for serpentine, shells or seclusion. Inland, among the heathery downs to the west and gentle woods and farmland to the east, there are equally sequestered discoveries to be treasured: a standing stone or fogou, an ice-cream farm, the saddest of churchyards and a garden filled with South African exoticism.

11 CHURCH COVE

A golf course, a sandy beach and a church with a separate tower, half-buried in the cliff, make incongruous neighbours, but these are the ingredients of Church Cove. There's been a chapel here since the 5th century, but what you see today is a Victorian restoration of a storm-damaged 15th-century church; the bell tower dates from the 13th century.

There have been terrible shipwrecks here and it's easy to imagine a desperate seafaring population building their church at a little distance from the village of Gunwalloe, right on the beach, where everybody would cluster for news or hope when a fishing boat or (fingers crossed) treasure-laden galleon went down on the rocks. Inside the church two surviving parts of a rood screen made from wreckage of the Portuguese ship, the *San Antonio*, can be seen. She was wrecked at Gunwalloe in 1527, en route from Lisbon to Antwerp, on a wild January night. Dollar Cove, just below the church, is still visited by treasure-seekers, and the odd gold or silver coin might yet be found.

¶¶ FOOD & DRINK

Halzephron Inn Near Gunwalloe TR12 7QB ℐ 01326 240406 ⏣ halzephron-inn.co.uk. An excellent pit stop if you are exploring the coast between Gunwalloe and Church Cove. This 500-year-old free house overlooks the sea on the lane south out of Gunwalloe, and has local ales and top-notch, locally sourced food.

12 MULLION

Busy Mullion is one of the few places on the peninsula with shops and banks, and the picturesque cove and harbour, preserved by the National Trust, is an absolute magnet for artists. It's not for those wanting to escape the crowds, but the church of **St Mellanus** right in the centre of Mullion itself is too interesting to miss. The hugely studded south door, through which you enter, is 13th century and contains a dog-door, which operated much like a cat-flap. It's nice to imagine the shepherds sitting quietly in the congregation, while their conscientious dogs popped in and out, keeping an eye on the flocks in the fields outside. The carved bench-ends are a real delight: you can see caricatures of clergymen and drinkers as well as more sober Christian imagery and an intriguing rendition of Jonah in the belly of the whale. They were preserved from destruction during the Reformation by local carpenters, who covered them neatly in plain pine boards. Not so fortunate was the carved rood screen; although one of the most eye-catching things in the church and a brilliant piece of 20th-century craftsmanship, only the tiniest bit of the 15th-century original remains. The barrel-vaulted roof is even more recent, completed in 1987, but faithful to the Cornish style and built of pegged oak and lime-and-horsehair plaster.

"The picturesque cove and harbour, preserved by the National Trust, is an absolute magnet for artists."

The Marconi Centre, Poldhu

TR12 7JB ℐ 01326 241656 ⏣ marconi-centre-poldhu.org.uk ⊙ Sun 13.30–16.30; free, though donations are welcome; National Trust

The year 1901 was a significant one for Guglielmo Marconi: in January, when he received a wireless communication from the Isle of Wight at his experimental station close to Lizard village, he proved that radio signals could travel well over the horizon. By December he was on the other side of the Atlantic in Newfoundland, celebrating the arrival of a Morse signal from the transmitter he had erected on Poldhu Point. To mark the centenary of this event in 2001, the Poldhu Amateur Radio Club opened the Marconi Centre, close to the spot where Marconi's four transmitters had stood. It's run by volunteers, whose enthusiasm is infectious; even teenagers wedded to their mobile phones find it hard to remain aloof here, among the headsets, dials, frequency static and radio chatter, where the everyday marvel of long-distance communication seems somehow more real than a digital tweet.

"Even teenagers wedded to their mobile phones find it hard to remain aloof here."

Marconi's experimental station, close to Lizard village, may look like a wooden hut in a field, but it is from here that he was able to begin trial radio transmissions to the Isle of Wight. It's no longer open to the public, but worth a respectful glance if following the coast path, or looking for a post-prandial stroll from the village. To find it, follow signs to the Housel Bay Hotel, which is half a mile east of Lizard village. A path runs out from the hotel to the cliff top at which point you turn left – you'll soon spot the dark wooden hut ahead.

The story of wireless transmission is picked up with a slightly different slant at the Telegraph Museum in Porthcurno (page 358). By 1929, Marconi's profitable network, which had been sold to the Post Office, was causing concern to those who had invested heavily in the overland and undersea cable-laying projects. Competitive wireless communication was deeply unwelcome and, with something approaching skulduggery, Marconi's invention was appropriated by the new Cable & Wireless Company.

13 KYNANCE COVE

🏠 **Kynance Cottage** (page 420)

📍 SW685134

Beaches don't come any lovelier than this, and the long walk and steps down to the cove from the huge National Trust car park on the cliffs is busy with families for whom the trudge is amply rewarded. What makes it so special are the pinnacles and islets of serpentine rock that create loose divisions and sandy niches around the cove, which as the tide recedes, add a naturally sculpted architecture to the crescent beach – and create pockets of shade, a thousand rock pools and vantage points for children playing pirates.

Just above the beach, a grassy slope offers a broad view of the cove, the emerald and turquoise water and the entertainment of beach activity.

¶¶ FOOD & DRINK

Kynance Cove Café TR12 7PJ ✆ 01326 290436 ☞ kynancecovecafe.co.uk ☉ Mar–Nov. Roofed with photovoltaic tiles, this eco-friendly place on the grassy shelf above the beach seems almost too good to be true; the loos are fed by spring water and waste treated by a 'bio-bubble'. And that's not all: the toilet-block roof is a mixture of turf and meadow flowers, helping the structure blend into the hillside.

14 THE LIZARD

🏠 **Housel Bay Hotel** (page 420), 🛖 **Henry's Campsite** (page 421)

The most southerly village in mainland Britain has a lot more charm than the westernmost point at Land's End. Both are busy and attract lots of tourists especially in the summer, but the Lizard is no theme park and the village has a lived-in feel and a warm community spirit. A 15-minute walk from the village takes you to the **Lizard Lighthouse** (see below) and, just beyond, to the drama of **Lizard Point** – a perfect spot for observing all kinds of wildlife. A noticeboard by the helpful information hut tells you what's been observed so far that day and there are often National Trust rangers on hand to help point your binoculars in the right direction.

Lizard Lighthouse

✆ 01326 290202 ☞ trinityhouse.co.uk ☉ tower & visitor centre open throughout the summer & school hols

The story goes that protests from local villagers, actively caught up in wrecking and looting ships, prevented a lighthouse from being built on this dangerous part of the coast until 1619, when Sir John Killigrew poured his own funds into building a beacon tower on Lizard Point. The poor man seems to have been hated both on land and at sea; resentful local builders dragged their heels and Killigrew's attempts to recoup his investment by collecting voluntary tolls from passing ships was met with derision, to the point where King James I imposed a levy of a halfpenny per ton of ship safely passing the light. The response from shipping agents was so aggressively negative that the idea was dropped

1 Church Cove. 2 The Devil's Frying Pan, Cadgwith. 3 Kynance Cove. ▶

and only four years after its beacon was lit, the first Lizard lighthouse was demolished and Killigrew was declared bankrupt.

For over a century, the idea was debated and rejected until finally winning the support of Trinity House, and a twin-towered building, linked by the keeper's cottage, was built by a private entrepreneur, Thomas Fonnereau, in 1751. With a coal-fired lantern burning in each tower, the bellows men had their work cut out. The keeper, positioned between them in his cottage, would give a blast on a cow-horn if he saw them relaxing their efforts.

It's all a bit different today, where just one of the towers is used and an automated white electric light flashes every three seconds.

FOOD & DRINK

The Lizard has a proper butcher's and nice deli (and **Ann's Pasty Shop**, see below, which is probably the most famous pasty shop in Cornwall); the pubs and cafés make the most of locally produced food and drink.

Coast Coffee Bar and Bistro The Lizard TR12 7NJ ✆ 01326 290400 ♿ coastthelizard. co.uk. Very highly rated by locals and justly so. The fish dishes were given particular mention (no surprise, as the owner's dad is Cadgwith's celebrated fisherman, Nigel Legge; page 321). **Polpeor Café** Lizard Point TR12 7NU ✆ 01736 290939 🅵. A splendid, traditional café (and Britain's most southerly one, to boot) with sublime views from both inside and out on the terrace. Great for lunches, teas and coffees. Everything is fresh, homemade and generously portioned. Dogs welcome, too.

PASTY QUEEN

The acknowledged queen of the Cornish pasty is **Ann Muller**, whose bright yellow house on the edge of Lizard village is almost a place of pilgrimage for pasty aficionados. Ann's mother taught her how to make a perfect pasty during a sailing festival in Brittany in the late 1980s, at which Ann was helping out with the catering. Soon afterwards she began making pasties for neighbours in the village, who paid with fresh fish they'd caught or home-grown vegetables. The cottage kitchen was soon outgrown, so Ann's husband converted the garage to make a professional kitchen to supply Ann's new shops (also bright yellow) in Porthleven and Helston. The family recipe continues to live on through Ann's son Fergus, who now works beside her. Seek out **Ann's Pasties** (♿ annspasties.co.uk) in Lizard (The Square, TR12 7PB), Porthleven (Fore St, TR13 9HQ) and Helston (Tresprison Business Park, TR13 0QD).

15 CADGWITH

There's something deeply seductive about Cadgwith: everybody wants to be a part of this tiny, world's-end community, wedged into a cleft in the serpentine rock, where tractors haul fishing boats, laden with crab and lobster, up the beach and sea shanties are sung in the beamy pub in the evening. Cadgwith's cosy, salty loveliness burnished even brighter in *Ladies in Lavender*, the 2004 film about two unmarried sisters (played by Judi Dench and Maggie Smith) who rescue a shipwrecked young musician and bring him into the community. A more realistic portrait of the community and the hardships faced by the dwindling number of fishermen was painted in the popular 2012 TV series, presented by Monty Halls, *The Fisherman's Apprentice*. There's no room for visitors'

"Everybody wants to be a part of this tiny, world's-end community, wedged into a cleft in the serpentine rock."

cars in Cadgwith, which have to be left in the car park on the hillside behind the village. The walk down takes you past thatched cottages, with minuscule gardens brimming with colourful exotics and a very small church, made out of corrugated tin and painted bright blue.

Nigel Legge, who makes traditional lobster pots out of withies, and helps to keep the pub supplied with fresh crab and lobster, runs boat trips out of the harbour and knows how to tell a story or two (⊘ lobsterpots. co.uk). But the tallest fishy story from Cadgwith is true: when pilchard fishing was at its peak, the Cadgwith fleet held the record catch for Cornwall, with 1.3 million pilchards landed in a single day.

On the south side of the harbour, the cliff path rises steeply, and what looks like a huge, sea-filled crater is revealed far below. Known as the **Devil's Frying Pan**, this is a collapsed cavern, and in wild weather, the sea swirls menacingly through an arch into this cauldron-like hole. However, it's only fair to point out that on a calm day, at low tide, with a seagull or two bobbing about, it's clear that the heat under the frying pan is not always turned up high.

🍴 FOOD & DRINK

The Cadgwith Cove Inn TR12 7JX ✆ 01326 290513 ⊘ cadgwithcoveinn.com. Adjoining an old pilchard cellar, where the fish would have been salted and pressed; pilchards are no longer on the menu, but the crab sandwiches are rather good and there's singing in the bar on Tuesday and Friday evenings.

16 LANKIDDEN COVE & COVERACK

⅄ Penmarth Farm (page 421)

On my OS map, I see my daughter has written 'not for the faint-hearted'. It was indeed a bit of a scramble to get down to **Lankidden Cove**, though ropes had been thoughtfully provided to help with the last section. Getting back up to the coast path took ages. This is probably one of the loveliest and most secluded beaches on the Lizard coast, which disappears completely at high tide, so unless you have studied your tide timetable, you may have to wait to gain access – and then work extremely hard for the pleasure such beauty and remoteness offers. Which is as it should be.

The narrow promontory that forms the western cliff behind the beach is the site of an Iron Age cliff-fort, known as Carrick Luz, Cornish for Grey Rock. But unlike other parts of the Lizard where serpentine is predominant, the grey rock in question here is crystalline gabbro. Going back about 380 million years, as continents advanced and collided, the earth's mantle and crust were shoved up to the surface, appearing as serpentine and gabbro respectively. Carrick Luz appeared where a fissure in the serpentine forced the gabbro to rear through. If this sort of thing interests you, go to Coverack Beach at low tide, where the exposed rocks offer a textbook geology lesson in igneous rock formation. In fact, **Coverack** is one of just a handful of places in the world where you can actually see the junction of mantle and crust exposed on the surface of the planet. As the information board by the car park in Coverack explains, 'as you walk south across the beach, you're travelling to the centre of the earth'.

On the cliffs above Coverack, coast path walkers encounter an unexpected – and free – treat. The **Terence Coventry Sculpture Park** (⌀ terencecoventry.com) opens directly off the path and the three huge, grassy fields are filled with the late artist's joyful output. Like giant pieces of origami, animal, bird and human forms populate the five acres between the sea and sky; glorious hymns to Coventry's years spent farming. The pieces on display are made from steel plate and ferrous cement, in order to withstand the onslaught of the weather. All have also been cast in bronze and may be found in private and public collections throughout the world. It's a very steep hike up the school

---

1 Looking towards Lizard Lighthouse. **2** Terence Coventry Sculpture Park, Coverack.
3 Cadgwith. **4** Roskilly's Farm, St Keverne. **5** Merlin, Goonhilly Downs. ▶

STEVE MEESE/S

OBS70/S

CLARE LOUISE JACKSON/S

STEVE DEE PHOTOGRAPHY/S

55

lane from the village car park to join the coast path, but the reward repays the effort many times over.

¶¶ FOOD & DRINK

Archie's Loft TR12 6SX ✆ 01326 281440 ⊙ closed winter. Overlooking the harbour at Coverack, Bryanna Roskilly produces terrific take-away homemade lunches (there's very limited seating) and cakes – and of course, also serves Roskilly's ice creams.

17 ST KEVERNE

🏠 **The Old Temperance House** (page 420)

It's hard to believe now that the thatch-and-whitewash village of St Keverne, surrounded by fields and woods, has had a such a sad history of burying the victims of shipwrecks. No fewer than 500 men, women and children who perished on the notorious Manacles, a submerged reef about a mile offshore, lie in the churchyard. Even today, there are some in the village who can remember their grandparents talking about the day the *Mohegan* went down in 1897 and 106 people drowned. Everybody in the village was involved in some way, giving shelter to those who survived, acting as pall-bearers, creating wreaths or digging the mass grave that eventually received more than 50 victims.

The village hero, however, is Michael Joseph, the blacksmith ('An Gof' in Cornish) who, with the Bodmin lawyer, Thomas Flamank, led a peaceful uprising against an unpopular new tax levied by Henry VII in 1497. Why should Cornwall, argued Joseph, be obliged to pay the king to send an army to squash the Scots? But Joseph was no rabble-rouser; people followed him because of his brave and clear opposition to injustice. The rebellion swiftly dissolved at the Battle of Blackheath, where Flamank and Joseph were taken prisoner. Their execution at Tyburn ten days later was an unpleasant exercise in Tudor butchery. Their frightened followers were sent home (no point executing all those taxpayers) and the county subjected to a humiliating and costly fine. A plaque on the churchyard wall honours Joseph in both Cornish and English.

Roskilly's Farm

Tregellast Barton Farm, TR12 6NX ✆ 01326 280479 ⌖ roskillys.co.uk ⊙ all year; Sat & Sun only in winter

The Roskillys – a talented and likeable family of farmers and artists – have been farming at Tregellast Barton just outside St Keverne for generations, and added artisanal ice cream-making to their activities in the 1980s. You can watch the beautiful herd of Jerseys being milked and drive yourself mad trying to choose from the long list of flavours available in the shop and farmyard café, **The Croust**. Gooseberry and elderflower sorbet topped my personal, and, I am proud to say, extensively researched, list of favourites. Toby Roskilly's furniture is on show in the gallery-shop and his sister, Bryanna Roskilly, is the stained-glass artist whose work decorates the café.

¶ FOOD & DRINK

Fat Apples The Old Vineyard, Porthallow TR12 6QH ☏ 01326 281559 ⌂ fatapplescafe. uk ⊙ closed Mon (except bank hols) & Tue; reduced winter opening; check website for full calendar and evening events. So many people have raved to me about this café – the wonderful soups, the amazing salads and sandwiches, the friendly family-run ambience – and I'm happy to say that they are right to do so. It's perfect, and less than a mile from little Porthallow Beach and the coast path. A simple camping field is also available.

18 GOONHILLY DOWNS

Head inland from the coastal villages and coves and you're soon confronted with an empty expanse of level moorland, dotted with grazing ponies as part of a heathland management scheme. Of course, it's far from empty, particularly from a naturalist's point of view – much of the heather is a type found only on the Lizard (and parts of Ireland) and there is a rich population of other heathland plants: tormentil and

RAF DRY TREE

A scattering of brick and concrete ruins, slowly disappearing beneath brambles and grass on Goonhilly Downs, is all that remains of a **World War II radar station**, staffed by women from the WAAF whose job it was to give early warning to the RAF bases at Predannack and Portreath of approaching enemy aircraft. Tracks fan out from the car park and a looping circular walk takes an hour or so to complete. There's a stillness and silence here, made all the more poignant by the looming presence of the giant satellite dish, Antenna One ('Arthur'; page 327), which soars above the northern perimeter fence. The base was named Dry Tree, rather grimly, after the gallows tree that stood at the junction of five parishes. The Dry Tree standing stone, which was set upright again in 1928 (after losing its head to careless road-makers), has a singular presence, which I will admit to finding rather unsettling.

ROGER DRISCOLL/S

CHILDREN'S SAILING TRUST

devil's-bit scabious, black bog-rush and purple moor-grass, as well as orchids and the extremely rare hairy buttercup.

Merlins and barn owls hunt here, and on still summer evenings the eerie cry of the nightjar can be heard. And there are butterflies in abundance – skippers, graylings, meadow browns and silver-studded blues. Tracks wander through the nature reserve, past the remnants of a World War II lookout station. Car parking is available close to the satellite station, on the B3292 – the road sign says National Nature Reserve) and a couple of hours can easily be lost, rambling around, with a pair of binoculars at the ready.

What makes walking here really interesting is that Goonhilly's history, both ancient and relatively modern, is never far from the surface – from the redundant satellite dishes of the Goonhilly Earth Station to the Bronze Age burial mounds and medieval turf stacks that litter the heath. Without some kind of guide, however, it's easy to be mistaken; the little hillocks dotted across the downs at regular intervals are neither Neolithic nor medieval in origin, but simply the remains of a grid of obstructions erected during World War II to prevent German gliders landing on the level, treeless plateau.

Merlin & Arthur: the Goonhilly Earth Station

The Goonhilly Earth Station must have been one of the most exciting places to work in Britain when it was at the cutting edge of communications technology in the early 1960s. The first aerial, nicknamed **Arthur**, tracked the Telstar satellite and its 79-foot-diameter dish is now a listed monument. It was followed by Uther and Guinivere, Lancelot, Tristan and Isolde to track the increasing number of satellites being launched into space. **Merlin**, the biggest dish at 98 feet in diameter, was constructed in 1985; in total there were 25 operational aerials of all shapes and sizes, transmitting international phone calls and TV programmes, as well as connecting shipping communications around the globe.

But in 2008, British Telecom announced it was transferring its satellite operations to Madley in Herefordshire, keeping Goonhilly open as a museum only. When the museum closed in 2010, there were fears that the whole station would go into decline, but the Earth Station has been

◀ **1** Bonython Garden. **2** Entrance to the prehistoric Halliggye Fogou, Trelowarren.
3 Learning to sail at Trevassack Lake with the Children's Sailing Trust.

given a new lease of life in recent years. Goonhilly is connected to a global radio-astronomy network, and the big dishes have been upgraded to provide a communications link with deep-space missions. Meanwhile, it serves to communicate with the Newquay Spaceport launches (page 94). There are no immediate plans to reopen the visitor centre, but you can still get up close to Arthur as he looms high over the security fence at the former Segway centre next door.

19 BONYTHON GARDEN

Cury Cross Lanes TR12 7BA ✆ 01326 240550 ⌨ bonythonmanor.co.uk ☉ mid-Apr–mid-Sep Mon–Fri

Cornish gardens, famed for their spring colour, are thick on the ground in the sheltered valleys of the Helford and Fal, but you really don't expect to find a great garden just a mile or two short of Goonhilly in the middle of the peninsula. What's more, Bonython has a style of its own, and is one of a handful of gardens which are redefining the Cornish garden scene that has been dominated for so long by the Victorian enthusiasm for spring-flowering showstoppers such as camellias, magnolias and rhododendrons.

Sue and Richard Nathan arrived at Bonython from South Africa in 1999, bringing with them a love of South African plants, buckets of horticultural curiosity and a sense of adventure. The walled gardens that you enter on arrival pay colourful though respectful homage to English mixed border planting, but once in the valley beyond, where a series of orchards, lakes and ornamental parkland merges with the tree-fringed landscape, the adventure starts. The lakeside slopes, planted with bold grasses and plants native to the Cape, have been established for almost two decades and offer an inspiring insight into how to break the Cornish mould.

A garden hut offers do-it-yourself teas and coffees, and Sue, who is a great plantswoman, is usually in the garden; she's a mine of friendly and helpful information.

20 TRELOWARREN & HALLIGGYE FOGOU

🏠 **Trelowarren** (page 420)

A long drive sweeps up and downhill through the wooded estate of **Trelowarren**, home to the Vyvyan family for over 600 years. The 13th baronet, Sir Ferrers Vyvyan, now runs the estate with impeccable green intelligence and the carbon-neutral holiday cottages, craft centre and restaurant are among the best of their kind in Cornwall.

But way before the drive straightens out in the final approach to the manor, there's a strange adventure to be enjoyed. A notice by a lay-by points the way to the **Halliggye Fogou**, a hundred yards or so up the hill that was once an Iron Age hillfort. During daylight hours between April and September, the iron gates are open at the entrance to this prehistoric underground chamber, which is thought to have been constructed at the same time as the fort. It's dark once you're down the steps, the roof is low and the passage twists away from the entrance, so a torch is essential. No-one knows the purpose of these fogous, about a dozen of which have been found in the far west of Cornwall, and this one is the longest and best preserved of them all. There is unlikely to be anyone else around; there is something surreal about returning to the world after a few minutes in the confines of this ancient, atmospheric place.

¶¶ FOOD & DRINK

Gear Farm Shop Just outside Trelowarren estate, on the road to St Martin TR12 6DE ✆ 01326 221150 ■. A wonderful place to pick up a pasty or a picnic. There's a quiet camping field too on this child-friendly farm.

New Yard Restaurant and Pantry Trelowarren TR12 6AF ✆ 01326 221595 ⌂ newyardrestaurant.co.uk. In a lovingly restored old farm building, with craft shops across the yard. Under new management since 2023, the restaurant continues to reflect the Vyvyan ethos of enjoying and making the best imaginative use of the estate, its own kitchen garden and other local farms' abundant seasonal resources.

21 TREVASSACK LAKE

Garras, TR12 6LH ✆ 01326 70326 ⌂ cstexperiences.co.uk

Between Trelowarren and Bonython, a beautifully landscaped lake formed from an old quarry is the wonderful home of the **Children's Sailing Trust**, a charity which offers year-round water-based activities for children with inclusivity as its guiding principle. Adults are also welcome to immerse themselves – literally – in the lake, with open-water swimming sessions and every other kind of watersport. There's a lovely café too, run by **Cornish Food Hub** (⌂ cornishfoodhub.com), and you can take it all in from the sunny terrace overlooking the water. On the bright but chilly February day when I last visited, the coffee was perfect and the lake serene, interrupted only by duck activity.

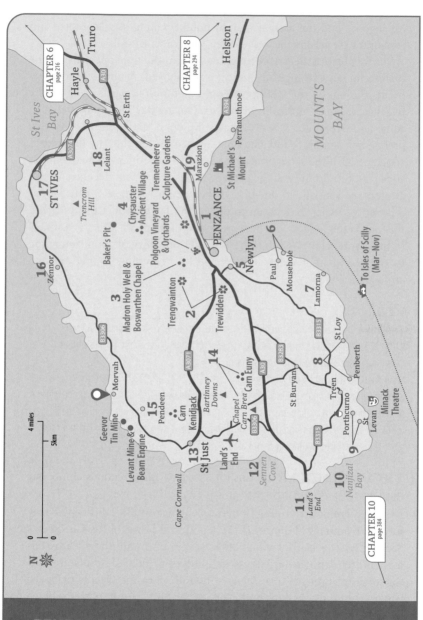

N

0 ___ 4 miles
0 ___ 5km

CHAPTER 6
page 216

St Ives
Bay

Truro

Hayle

A30

St Erth

CHAPTER 8
page 294

Helston

A394

Perranuthnoe

MOUNT'S
BAY

17 ST IVES

A3074

18 Lelant

Trencrom
Hill

Chysauster
Ancient Village
4

Tremenheere
Sculpture Gardens

Polgoon Vineyard
& Orchards

19 Marazion

St Michael's
Mount

1 PENZANCE

16 Zennor

Baker's Pit

Madron Holy Well &
Boswarthen Chapel
3

Trengwainton

2 Trewidden

5 Newlyn

Paul

6

Mousehole

To Isles of Scilly
(Mar–Nov)

B3306

14 Carn Euny

A3071

Bartinney
Downs

Chapel
Carn Brea

A30

B3283

B3315

7 Lamorna

St Loy

8

Penberth

Geevor
Tin Mine

Levant Mine &
Beam Engine

Morvah

15 Pendeen

Carn
Kenidjack

St Buryan

Treen

Cape Cornwall

13 St Just

Land's End

12 Sennen
Cove

B3306

B3315

Porthcurno

9 St
Levan

Minack
Theatre

11 Land's End

10

Nanjizal
Bay

Sennen
Bay

CHAPTER 10
page 384

PENZANCE, ST IVES & THE PENWITH PENINSULA

9
PENZANCE, ST IVES & THE PENWITH PENINSULA

A peninsula at the end of a peninsula: small wonder that Penwith feels remote from the rest of Cornwall, let alone the rest of the country. Driving down the long A30 can be a grim affair, but that first, almost unreal glimpse of St Michael's Mount and the wide blue sweep of Mount's Bay never fails to lift the spirits, creating the feeling that some kind of threshold is about to be crossed to a wilder, older, more mysterious part of Cornwall. **Penzance**, which dominates the bay and makes a kind of gateway to the peninsula, has a special character entirely in keeping with its position. It's no surprise that so many artists, writers, archaeologists and historians – as well as a healthy smattering of good old-fashioned eccentrics – have found their way down here over the years. As my Cornish neighbour likes to say, with enigmatic knowingness: 'shake the stocking and all the nuts will gather in the toe'.

From the summit of **Chapel Carn Brea** you get a feel for a good chunk of Penwith and its history, as well as its siren appeal to artists. Approached from the narrow, twisting road between Crows-an-Wra and the Land's End airport, this hill is a far from strenuous climb, but the visual reward suggests you've scaled something much bigger. Having ascended the heathery track from the car park, you can perch at the summit on a ruined Bronze Age burial chamber and think you're on an island, for on a clear day, sea and sky dominate for as far as you can swivel your head. The Isles of Scilly are a smudge on a horizon punctuated by ponderous tankers; smaller fishing vessels plough briskly through the white-capped swell; and waves which have travelled the Atlantic dash against the Longships lighthouse, enveloping it in dramatic clouds of foaming spray. Away to the east, **St Michael's Mount** is palely visible through a gap in the hills, and northwest beyond the offshore twin peaks of the Brisons, there's a glimpse of **Cape Cornwall**, believed for centuries to be the real Land's End.

At your feet, to the south and west, lies a green patchwork of fields and farms, bounded by hedges of wind-sculpted gorse and hawthorn; there are very few trees. Villages linked by ancient roads and tracks and the landmark church towers of St Buryan and Sennen are just discernible in the folded landscape where Davies Gilbert's rhymes, composed of nothing more than names of hamlets and farms, still echo down the lanes:

Vellandrucha, Cracka, Cudna,
Truzemenhall, Chun, Crowzenwra;
Bans, Burnnhal, Brane, Bosfranken,
Treeve, Trewidden, Try, Trembah.

Turn northwards, however, and **Penwith Moor** looms on the horizon, littered with prehistoric sites and abandoned tin mines, its craggy hilltop carns rising abruptly above the jagged north coast. There's a wild beauty here in the rough, windswept moors and cliffs, which is easy enough to appreciate when the sun is shining, but when the drenching clouds roll in, it can all feel rather raw and bleak. It's a welcome incongruity to find that **St Ives**, with its cosy and picturesque streets and alleyways, cosmopolitan galleries and lively, art-filled culture, is part of the north coast scenery too.

The eating is good in Penwith. Fish and crab from Newlyn and St Ives rarely come fresher to the fishmonger's slab; local dairies produce fabulous ice creams and farmers' markets start the season with astonishingly early potatoes and Cornish asparagus. Craft cider and even cider brandy is making a strong showing in Penwith, and many real-ale enthusiasts claim that (with no disrespect to Helston's Spingo) their favourite pint *ever* is to be found at the Star in Crowlas, where it is brewed on the premises.

GETTING AROUND

Penwith is well served by public transport, although you'd never guess, given the choked roads and bulging car parks at peak moments during the summer months. **Double-decker buses** (some open-topped in summer) trundle around the spectacular coast road, from Penzance to Land's End and on, with a change, to St Just, Zennor and St Ives, but I've rarely seen them more than half full. And St Ives, where it is particularly difficult to find a parking space outside the big field car parks on the outskirts, is reached by one of the prettiest rural **branch-line train** rides in England.

Yet you'll see lots of **cyclists** – and need to watch out for them – pedalling hard down the A30, particularly as you get close to Land's End – the end of the road, quite literally, for thousands of charity cyclists and walkers.

TRAINS

It's not quite the Orient Express, but the **Night Riviera** ($\oslash$ gwr.com) – the sleeper service which has rocked passengers to sleep between Paddington and Penzance since 1877 – is hard to beat for sheer civilisation and romance. I can't imagine anything sweeter than leaving Paddington shortly before midnight and waking up to find the Cornish coast outside your window. It's not often that arrival by train presents a visitor with the best introduction to a town, but **Penzance** offers a glorious exception to this dismal rule. As you roll into the terminus, decorated with huge panels of the Penwith landscape by local artist Kurt Jackson (page 362), it's hard not to be thrilled by the wide blue sweep of Mount's Bay, crowned at one end with the battlements of St Michael's Mount and at the other with the crowded slate rooftops of Newlyn. One stop before Penzance is **St Erth,** where the branch line to **St Ives** connects with the mainline service. Spared from Beeching's axe in the 1960s because of its popularity, the line skims the Lelant Saltings, a marshy sanctuary for migrating and native waders and seabirds. Climbing steadily, it turns to meet the surf and sandy beaches of St Ives Bay, where it runs along the rise above Porth Kidney Sands, Carbis Bay and, 15 minutes after leaving St Erth, enters St Ives. Train rides rarely come more appealing than this.

BUSES

The Land's End Coaster links **Penzance** to nearly every village on the 36-mile journey round **Land's End** to **St Ives**. This is an invaluable resource for Slow explorers and walkers doing the coast path in sections, wanting to get back to base or to visit the Minack Theatre (page 358). The Tin Coaster is another valuable service, running from Penzance across **Penwith moor** to St Just, Botallack and Geevor mines.

Other services cross the moor, and there are frequent buses from Penzance to St Ives. It's a pretty impressive, low-cost service, with all details to be found at ⊘ firstbus.co.uk/cornwall.

CYCLING

The wind blows hard in Penwith, and the hills are not for the faint-hearted. However, the visual rewards are staggering and for me the 18-mile, roller-coaster clifftop road from St Just to St Ives (with a pit stop in Zennor) provides some of the best (and sweatiest) hours to be had on a bike in Cornwall. **The First and Last Trail** is part of the Sustrans NCN Route 3 (the **Cornish Way**), linking Land's End to Bude, and this section takes you as far as Hayle, via a quiet and mainly inland route, with some decent stopping places for refreshment en route. Look out, too, for the **Beryl Bikes** (⊘ beryl.cc) stand by the station and elsewhere in Penzance, a new initiative from Cornwall council. The distinctively green e-bikes can be hired using an app for one-off trips or by the minute, hour or day.

 CYCLE HIRE & TOURS

Cornish Cycle Tours The Wesleyan, Rosenannon, St Wenn, Bodmin PL30 5PJ ⊘ 01637 889156 ⊘ cornishcycletours.co.uk. This company organises a number of tours (with routes and lengths designed to suit all levels of cycling fitness) of the Penwith peninsula and beyond. Accommodation and bike hire is included, though you have the option to bring your own bike.

Land's End Cycle Hire Geevor Mine, Pendeen TR19 7BA ⊘ 07885 452997 ⊘ landsendcyclehire.co.uk. Given a day's notice, they will deliver and collect your bike to a drop-off point around the coast and, if you're interested, suggest the least hilly routes.

Penzance Bike Hire Alexandra Rd, Penzance TR18 4LZ ⊘ 07764 225535 ⊘ penzancebikehire.co.uk. Offering tandems and electric bikes as well as the usual, with guided tours available on request.

WALKING

Penwith has some of the most dramatic of all Cornish **coastal walking**. The entire stretch is worth savouring, but particularly around Zennor Head, Gurnard's Head, Morvah and Cape Cornwall, and the superb walk from Land's End past Nanjizal and Treryn Dinas to Treen. Tim Locke, the author of *Slow Travel Sussex*, has a happy memory of taking the bus from Penzance to Land's End and following his favourite stretch of the coast path to Treen, before catching the same bus back to Penzance.

ℹ TOURIST INFORMATION

St Ives The Library, Gabriel St, TR26 2LS ✆ 01736 796297 ⊘ stives-cornwall.co.uk
St Just The Library, Market St, TR19 7HX ✆ 01736 788165

Inland, northern Penwith has the edge over the area further south: the moors, prehistoric sites and ruins of mine buildings punctuate the landscape perfectly with points of interest to head for, and an exceptionally fine route taking in all these aspects is described on page 368.

Further inland, the mini-summits of Chapel Carn Brea and Trencrom Hill give sweeping views quite out of scale with the minimal effort involved in getting to the top.

1 PENZANCE

🏠 **Chapel House** (page 421), 🏨 **The Abbey** (page 421)

Like many other coastal settlements in Cornwall, Penzance grew up in two parts – a cluster of houses around a natural safe haven and, on higher ground, the church and marketplace. There's been a long history of accusation that high-ground Penzance has always turned its back – socially, aesthetically and financially   on its seafront and harbour, but the whole town is united from top to bottom for the lively, week-long festivals of **Golowan** and **Montol**, which have revived the old Celtic summer and winter solstice celebrations respectively. Fancy dress and flaming torchlit processions are very much the thing.

EXPLORING THE TOWN

The quirky heart of Penzance lies on the slope between the harbour and the domed former **Corn Exchange** (Lloyds Bank). **Chapel Street**, uniting the port with its town, is a happy mix of Georgian and Recency town houses, as well as older buildings, many of which have been turned without loss of character into art galleries and antique shops, bars, restaurants and the odd specialist boutique. Sir John Betjeman may have grumbled that Penzance was 'turning into Slough', but you'd have to look beyond Chapel Street and be feeling fairly dyspeptic to agree. To the west, a labyrinth of squares and terraces of Regency houses, secret gardens and lamp-lit alleyways leading off **Morrab Road** reveals two of Penzance's finest treasures: **Penlee House**, set among exotic public gardens, contains the largest collection of work by the **Newlyn School**, and the **Morrab Library**, planted within the subtropical **Morrab Gardens**, is one of the last and most beautifully positioned independent libraries in the country.

If you arrive by train, you step straight out on to what used to be the northern dock of the **harbour**, partially filled in 1968 to create a large car park. The granite walls are still visible though, if you peer behind the cars. Nevertheless, the view across the bay is so entrancingly dominated by St Michael's Mount and the hope of seeing dolphins that you are distracted from some of the uglier planning decisions of the 20th century along the front. This is the leisure end of the harbour – and where on Monday and Thursday evenings you'll see the dinghy club setting out to race around Mount's Bay and pilot gig crews in training (page 403). The older, working harbour and dry dock is now much

SIR HUMPHRY DAVY

His statue, a favourite perch for seagulls, stands at the head of Market Jew Street, a stone's throw from the house where he was born. Davy, who was something of a Renaissance Man, admired by the likes of Napoleon and Samuel Coleridge, is best known for his invention of the miners' safety lamp in 1815 and his name must have been blessed a thousand times in coal miners' cottages up and down the country – ironically the lamp was unsuited to Cornish tin mines. Remarkably, Davy refused payment or patent – he knew he could help prevent the appalling methane explosions in the mines, caused by the naked flames of candles attached to the miners' helmets, and so he did. The principle was simple; by enclosing the oil-burning wick in a fine-gauge wire mesh cage, oxygen could enter and keep the flame alive, but the flame could not escape and ignite the methane.

There's an example of a Davy lamp, made around 1817, in the **Penlee House Gallery and Museum** (page 340).

It's rather unfortunate that Davy is also remembered for his discovery of nitrous oxide (laughing gas) which he considered an excellent cure for hangovers. It became a bit of an embarrassing obsession; his first lecture in 1801 at the Royal Institution in London on this very subject was a roaring success, and launched his career as a popular scientist.

An accident forced him to take on an assistant and his experiments with young Michael Faraday went far down the road in the development of electrical energy. (Davy reportedly said that Faraday was his greatest discovery.) Somehow, the brilliant polymath also found time to write *Salmonia*, a book on fly fishing published in 1828, a year before his death.

diminished as a commercial port and plans to redevelop it as a marina and bigger ferry terminal for the Isles of Scilly come and go with the tide. But this is where Penzance's story began: when merchant shipping travelling between the west of England or Ireland and the continent, fearful of the confused and treacherous seas beyond Land's End, would land and haul their cargo across the moors to and from boats moored at St Ives. A 6th-century chapel dedicated to St Anthony was built on the spur of granite that provided the earliest safe haven, and the harbour was called Pen Sans, the Holy Headland.

The chapel went centuries ago, but the granite spur remains visible. Known as the **Battery Rocks** (a small defensive position was built there during the Napoleonic Wars), it projects a little way into the sea beyond the high white walls of the splendid **Art Deco lido** (⊘ **jubileepool. co.uk**) that has won battle after battle against cuts in funding and wild storm damage to stay open during the summer months. (Be warned: there are days when dogs are invited to join their owners for a dip!) **St Mary's Church**, built in 1834, put an end to the long trudge up to the old parish church at Madron. You'll often hear choir and orchestra rehearsals as you pass and concerts in the church are frequent.

There are spring and autumn days when at high tide the waves dash against the Promenade, sending cliffs of spray over pedestrians, cars and guesthouses – and summer days when, beyond the flapping, colourful banners that line the seafront, tall ships lie peacefully at anchor in the quiet waters known as Gwavas Lake between the Battery Rocks and Newlyn. Occasionally, you'll see the square brown sails of a Cornish lugger, but best of all is when a pod of dolphins is sighted, arcing through the bay or riding the bow wave of a motor launch.

Up on the hill, in town, the main shopping streets, **Causeway Head** and **Market Jew Street** (jow being the old Cornish word for Thursday), hang on to a largely local identity; and though shops, galleries and restaurants come and go with alarming rapidity, Penzance retains a gritty vibrancy that has not submitted either to tourism or cloning.

The Morrab Library & Morrab Gardens

Morrab Pl, TR18 4DA ☏ 01738 364474 ⊘ morrablibrary.org.uk ⊙ Tue–Sat; free guided tours Fri 14.00

> If you have a library and a garden, you have everything you need.
> Cicero

Samuel Pidwell, brewer, mountain climber, mayor of Penzance and secretary of the Royal Geological Society, built this handsome, four-square house in 1841 with money made importing wine from Lisbon. The **library**, formed during the early years of the 19th century, has been in occupation since 1889, when the building was acquired by the town council.

Of just 39 independent libraries in the UK, this is the only one in Cornwall; the nicest thing about the Morrab ('by the sea' in Cornish) is the unstuffy atmosphere in the elegant, book-lined rooms and the colourful characters who work there and use it.

'You never know who's going to come through the door,' said Annabelle Read, the former chief librarian who was here for over 30 years. Her predecessor was a fan of the detective novel and besides Cornish history and periodicals, Celtic studies, art, biographies and travel, the largely open-access shelves are filled with crime fiction. Her successor since 2018, Lisa di Tommaso (it made my day to discover she had been given a copy of the second edition of this guide as a welcome present) is sure that the tradition won't change: 'Annabelle always said that lots of people come here to meet other people or borrow the latest Donna Leon, and I'm *"The Morrab has it all: winter lectures, coffee and good conversation – and enough rooms for peaceful browsing too."* sure that won't change.' The Morrab has it all: winter lectures, coffee and good conversation – and enough rooms for peaceful browsing too. Non-members can buy a very reasonably priced visitor's ticket for a single day.

It stands in over three acres of **subtropical gardens**, laid out in 1888 and much loved by the local community. Joe Palmese, the gardener, has acquired a reputation as a top propagator and locals will often bring back seeds from far-flung holidays for him to raise. When a letter appeared in the local newspaper criticising the gardens for their lack of colourful bedding and apparently unkempt appearance, there was an outcry as dozens of locals wrote back protesting the beauty of the gardens and the great work done by Joe and the volunteers.

◀ PENZANCE: **1** The Egyptian House. **2** Views towards the old Corn Exchange, now Lloyds Bank. **3** Exhibitions at Penlee House Gallery. **4** The Art Deco lido: Jubilee Pool. **5** Golowan Festival. **6** The subtropical Morrab Gardens.

Penlee House Gallery & Museum

Morrab Rd, TR18 4HE ✆ 01736 363625 ⌨ penleehouse.org.uk ⊙ Mon–Sat

This Victorian mansion in the lovely Penlee Memorial Gardens houses the country's largest collection of work by the Newlyn school, which included Stanhope and Elizabeth Forbes, Walter Langley and Norman Garstin – and their later successors, Alfred Munnings, Laura Knight and 'Lamorna' Birch. It's a friendly, busy gallery and the café that spills out into the gardens makes it a popular spot, especially on warm days. There are two floors of exhibition space where you can gaze happily at vanished Cornwall, its fishermen and their wives and children – one of my many favourites is a summery view of the Abbey Slip and inner

THE NEWLYN SCHOOL

Alison Bevan, former Director, Penlee House Gallery and Museum

In the 1880s, numerous British painters began to arrive in Newlyn, many of whom had trained in Paris or Antwerp. Most had also spent time painting in Brittany; in Newlyn they found a similar source of inspiration, but closer to home and with a direct rail link to London.

Like Brittany, Newlyn offered scenes and lives scarcely touched by the Industrial Revolution, with plentiful, willing models and cheap accommodation. Soon, a host of artists settled, forming the colony known as the 'Newlyn school'.

The first resident artist was Walter Langley, who moved to Newlyn in 1882. In 1884, Stanhope Forbes arrived, writing to his mother that 'Newlyn is a sort of English Concarneau and is the haunt of many artists.' By September 1884, there were at least 27 resident artists, including Frank Wright Bourdillon, Frank Bramley, Percy Craft, Elizabeth Forbes, Norman Garstin, Thomas Cooper Gotch, Frederick Hall, Edwin Harris, Harold Harvey, Albert Chevallier Tayler, Ralph Todd and Henry Scott Tuke. Many more artists visited the village during this period, for both long and short periods, while others who were recognised as part of the 'Newlyn school' based themselves in St Ives, Lelant or Falmouth.

Initially, the artists were united by a desire to paint '*en plein air*', depicting the lives of the villagers in a rural naturalist style. As the colony declined and the common ethos evaporated, Stanhope and Elizabeth Forbes founded their school of painting, bringing a new generation of artists to Newlyn, including Dod and Ernest Procter and Frank Gascoigne Heath.

This re-energising of the colony attracted further artists, including Samuel John 'Lamorna' Birch, Alfred Munnings, 'Seal' Weatherby, and Harold and Laura Knight, many of whom later settled in Lamorna, forming the Lamorna group, often referred to as the later Newlyn school.

harbour by Stanhope Forbes. What makes this painting particularly special is the plaque beside it which tells of the passion aroused locally by the threat of its sale and the successful campaign to keep it here at the Penlee.

There's no permanent collection on display, but there are frequently changing exhibitions, so check before coming if you've set your heart on seeing a particular painting (if it's not on display, and you give them a bit of notice, the director may open the storeroom for you).

Upstairs, a couple of rooms are dedicated to local history – there are some wonderful examples of Roman gold necklaces and wristlets found on a Penwith farm as well as costumes, mining equipment and examples of Newlyn copperware.

Chapel Street

A wander up Chapel Street from the harbour offers some rich pickings for Slow explorers. A plaque on number 25, the **Brontë House**, reveals that Maria Branwell, mother of the Brontë sisters, lived here. And so she did, until a visit to an uncle in Yorkshire in 1812 at the age of 29 changed her life forever. She died when her children, Charlotte, Anne, Emily and Branwell, were very young, and it became the turn of her sister Elizabeth to leave the Penzance family home for the parsonage at Haworth where she raised the infant writers, doubtless feeding them on Penwith legends and ghost stories, every bit as wild as stories bred on the Yorkshire moors. At least, that's how Daphne du Maurier liked to imagine things, *"The Egyptian House is an architectural curiosity – an eye-popping mixture of Georgian town house and painted sarcophagus."* endowing Elizabeth with the gift of having awakened in the authors of *Wuthering Heights* and *Jane Eyre*: 'that narrative power, that sense of the dramatic which is such a part of the Cornish character, moulding them, unconsciously, to the shape of their maternal forebears ... rugged as the granite on the moors of West Penwith.'

Further up the hill on the same side of the street, the **Egyptian House** is an architectural curiosity – an eye-popping mixture of Georgian town house and painted sarcophagus with a virtuoso display of geometry in the multi-paned windows. It's strange that the architect is something of a mystery, although the likeliest candidate is P F Robinson who had built the similarly styled Egyptian Hall in Piccadilly, London, in 1815, when the vogue for all things Egyptian was at a peak. The coade-stone façade (which was simply grafted on to a pair of much older shops) was created around 1835, for John Lavin, and created a suitably impressive entrance to a collection of minerals he displayed on the ground floor. The Landmark Trust acquired the building in 1968 and restored the façade to its former glory. Three apartments for holiday letting were also created, one on each floor above the shop which now occupies the ground floor.

On the other side of the road, the **Union Hotel** is worth a peep, although its finest treasure, an unrestored Georgian theatre, languishes out at the back, where it is used as a garage. An attempt to rescue the derelict building failed to gather enough support, but if you phone ahead to make an appointment when it's quiet behind the bar, you might be lucky enough to see the old theatre playbills, Georgian dining room and the Assembly Rooms on the first floor (where news of Trafalgar and the death of Nelson was first announced on English soil, which explains all the Nelsonabilia in the bar below). In the bar there are blackened stones on the wall by the entrance – apparently dating from when Penzance was torched by a Spanish marauding party in 1595. (The Turk's Head, also on Chapel Street, is one of the few buildings to have survived.) A step away, the telephone exchange building has been transformed into an important exhibition space for contemporary art. **The Exchange** (Princes St, TR18 2NL ✐ 01736 363715 ⟲ newlynartgallery.co.uk ☉ Tue–Sat; summer daily) is particularly striking after dark when its colourful glass exterior (designed by Penwith artist Peter Freeman) is lit up by green and blue ripples of LED lighting that responds to the weather or the movements of people on the pavement outside.

¶ FOOD & DRINK

Penzance **farmers' market** is held in and outside St John's Hall every Friday morning and you'll find several good places to pick up picnic ingredients in the surrounding streets – **Lavenders** in Alverton Street (⟲ lavendersdelibakery.co.uk), **The Granary** in Causeway Head (🅕), and **Archie Browns** in Bread Street (⟲ archiebrownscornwall.co.uk), which has a lunchtime restaurant upstairs, reminiscent of that icon of vegetarian cuisine, Cranks.

Artist Residence 20 Chapel St, TR18 4AW ✐ 01736 365664 ⟲ artistresidence.co.uk. Delicious, wholesome breakfasts, lunches and dinners featuring local, independent suppliers in a stunning townhouse.

The Bakehouse Old Bakehouse Lane, Chapel St, TR18 4AE⌀ 01736 331331
⌀ bakehouserestaurant.co.uk ⊙ check website in advance. Tucked away down an alley off Chapel Street, this is a long-established favourite with locals for brunch (Fri and Sat only) or dinner (Tues–Sat) and the occasional Monday night tapas. Food is fresh, local and beautifully presented by friendly staff.

Crown Victoria Sq, TR18 2EP ⌀ 01736 351070 ⌀ thecrownpenzance.co.uk. Always a good buzz in this small, friendly pub on the corner of a small square behind Market Jew Street. Real ales include Otter, Landlord and Heligan Honey, and there's a simple menu of homemade pizza at very reasonable prices (Fri & Sat eves only). Landlord Josh has his own very successful microbrewery, so look out for Cornish Crown on the pumps.

The Front Room 83 Market Jew St, TR18 3LG ⌀ 01736 448681 ⌀ thefrontroompz.co.uk. An established and popular addition to the eating and drinking scene in Penzance from breakfast through to tea. Pretty garden, cosy outdoor seating and a strong commitment to using fresh, seasonal, local produce.

Willy Wallers Ice Cream Parlour Unit 14B, The Wharf, TR18 2GB ⌀ willywallers.co.uk. Behind the vividly coloured shopfront, the homemade ice creams are as good as ice cream gets, which is saying a lot in these parts.

SHOPPING

The bright, contemporary **Lighthouse Gallery** (⌀ lighthouse-gallery.com) is in Causeway Head, a pedestrian street with a cinema and a good collection of independent shops that includes a specialist soap-maker, ironmonger, organic grocer, florist and clothing shops. In Chapel Street (page 341), galleries and vintage, antique and upmarket-design shops set the scene.

The Edge of the World Bookshop Market Jew St, TR18 2HR ⌀ edgeoftheworldbookshop.co.uk. A very appealing independent bookshop which has gone from strength to strength and garnered a heap of awards, thanks to the dedication and enthusiasm of owners James and Rachael Howorth. The pair have been huge supporters of this guide, and stalwarts of the now well-established **Penzance Literary Festival** (⌀ pzlitfest.co.uk), held in July.

PENZANCE'S HINTERLAND

As Penzance grew wealthy in the 17th and 18th centuries on the back of tin and copper, fish and farming, the grandees at the top of the economic pile built substantial houses for themselves on the hillside north of the town. They were not the first to appreciate the grand views over the bay: the Chysauster settlement of Iron Age roundhouses on the heights above Penzance commands a spectacular view of Mount's Bay and the surrounding moors. Down the deep lanes and ancient bridleways between Penzance and St Ives lie some of Cornwall's most secret and special places: Boswarthen Chapel, the Bodrifty roundhouse and Baker's Pit.

2 TREWIDDEN, TREREIFE & TRENGWAINTON GARDENS

Slow travel does not usually involve much excitement on the ring road, but the A30, as it bypasses Penzance to the north, is an exception.

Trewidden (TR20 8TT ✐ 01736 364275 🖱 trewiddengarden.co.uk) was built in the 1830s for the Bolitho family, who still live there. (Bolitho is a name synonymous in Penwith with tin mining and banking.) The house is not open, but there are 15 extravagantly leafy acres of gardens, planted in the 1880s on the site of an ancient tin mine – granite ingot moulds and smelting basins lie dotted about. Successive generations have added to the planting and the tree-fern pit, giant rhododendrons, a fabulous collection of camellias fringing secret pools and twisting paths create the impression of a lush, jungly maze. Head gardener Richard Morton is a mine of friendly information, well worth seeking out if you can catch him at a quiet moment. The tea room is a welcome new addition, sister to the popular Duke Street Café in Newlyn.

"Head gardener Richard Morton is a mine of friendly information, well worth seeking out if you can catch him."

Almost next door to Trewidden is the delightful **Trereife**, pronounced Treeve: a Queen Anne house and pretty gardens run by the endearingly eccentric Le Grice family. Changes are afoot, but it is very much to be hoped that the gardens at least will remain open to visits.

In contrast to Trewidden, **Trengwainton Gardens** (TR20 8RZ ✐ 01736 363148 ☉ closed Nov & Jan; special open days in Dec; National Trust), created around a long drive and lawn-with-a-view, seem open and airy, but are no less densely packed with sublime examples of magnolia, rhododendron, camellia, eucryphia, podocarpus and hundreds of other species of trees and shrubs. Vast walled gardens, originally constructed by sugar-cane magnate Sir Rose Price in the 19th century, are still used for growing vegetables, including some surprisingly exotic crops such as kumquats and avocados. On the main lawn, at the furthest reach of the garden, an eight-sided toposcope, carved in slate by a much-admired local artist, Joe Hemming, depicts all the real and symbolic ingredients of Penwith life, legend and industry: tinned sardines, a scythe, a tinner's shovel, a fishing boat, a mermaid, a woodcock, a lizard and the Bolitho emblem of lamb and flag. The gardens are owned by the National Trust, but the grand house at the end of the drive is still owned and lived in by a branch of the Bolitho family.

POLGOON VINEYARD & ORCHARDS

Rosehill, Penzance TR20 8TE 🕾 01736 333946 ⌘ polgoon.com ⊙ shop & guided tours all year

You see the elegant pink or green labels of Polgoon's wines, ciders and juices in all the best Cornish delis and restaurants these days, and further afield too, as the good news spreads. The leafy crown of Penzance and Mount's Bay makes a spectacular backdrop to the young vineyards and orchards, planted on the south-facing slopes of an old flower farm, although fine views often come with a weathery sting. Kim and John Coulson planted the first vines in 2003 and their success was instant: with the fruits of their first harvest in 2006, they won the Waitrose Trophy for the best still rosé in 2009. But thanks to the weather, the harvests in 2007 and 2008 were awful, so the enterprising Coulsons decided to plant apples, which are more weather-resistant than vines, and add sparkling cider, made the French way, to their stable of delicious drinks.

3 MADRON HOLY WELL & BOSWARTHEN CHAPEL

🏠 **Boscrowan Farm** Heamoor (page 421)

Leaving Madron on the narrow lane to Morvah, you'll see a sign on your right indicating the well and chapel. A woodland track takes you from the parking area for several hundred yards until the trees open out and a **pool** appears, overhung by a goat willow to which coloured strips of cloth and little personal items have been attached; 'clootie trees' are often seen by sacred Celtic wells and the hopeful-minded leave these fragments with their wishes or prayers in the tree. A little way beyond, in a walled enclosure are the remains of a simple **chapel** dating from the 6th century or possibly earlier; water from the same spring that feeds the well is channelled into a stone basin, which is why it's often described as a baptistry. There's no denying the atmosphere of peaceful sanctity here,

SS

while wilted flowers and candle stubs on the granite slab altar leave you in no doubt that this place still sees active worship.

4 CHYSAUSTER ANCIENT VILLAGE

Badger's Cross TR20 8XA ✆ 07831 757934 ⊙ Apr–Oct; English Heritage

A couple of miles northeast of Penzance, the Iron Age village of Chysauster is a hugely evocative archaeological site, set high on a south-facing slope looking over Mount's Bay. The remains of nine granite-walled Iron Age dwellings and a larger community building lead off what is thought to be the earliest identified village street in England and, although roofless, the mossy walls give a distinct impression of what family and community living would have been like before and during the Roman occupation. Each dwelling is composed of small, semi-circular chambers leading off a central, circular atrium that would have been open to the sky, a design peculiar to this part of Cornwall. It's a great place for children too: there are acres of cropped turf to run around (and a nice selection of wooden swords and bows at the entrance kiosk).

For more of the same, on a smaller scale, that you can wander into at any time of year, head for the remains of the Iron Age village at Bodrifty (♀ SW445354), which lie in a remote and rugged valley below Mulfra Quoit just three miles north of Penzance. A roundhouse has been constructed with the utmost authenticity at **Bodrifty Farm**, which can be visited by arrangement with the owners – and you can even stay in it (♂ canopyandstars.co.uk). **Carn Euny** (page 365) is equally remote, evocative and accessible all through the year.

Baker's Pit

♀ SW481359

With time on my hands after visiting Chysauster, I went looking for Baker's Pit, a wildlife reserve and wood-fringed lake buried in an unfrequented, though truly idyllic, Penwith valley.

Having returned to the road and turned left, the footpath I was looking for appeared after three or four hundred yards on my left. The path ran uphill, eventually passing the Castle an Dinas quarry on top, continuing on to Nancledra in the valley ahead. A purple sign on

◄ **1** Baker's Pit nature reserve. **2** The clootie tree at Madron Holy Well. **3** Chysauster Ancient Village. **4** Trengwainton Gardens.

my left indicated Baker's Pit, which ran down a flower-filled hillside, emerging eventually at a tree-fringed lake of quite staggering beauty. The path skirted the lake, arriving eventually at a preserved clay pit works and a concrete landing stage beside the water. The lake is the flooded clay pit, the water clear and very inviting on a hot August afternoon; two swimmers were quietly enjoying the cool green solitude far out in the middle of the water. I felt I was in the middle of nowhere, but just a short walk further down the same footpath by which I had arrived, took me to a tarmac road, a hamlet called Georgia and a tangle of footpaths offering alternative routes back to the Chysauster car park.

Cornwall Wildlife Trust (∂ cornwallwildlifetrust.org.uk) manages the nature reserve; there's a downloadable PDF of their leaflet on their website, including a map of a self-guided walking tour that starts from Georgia, where there is parking space for two or three cars.

THE SOUTH COAST

To the west of Penzance, the south coast, with its cosy, wooded valleys running down to the sea and picturesque fishing villages tucked into narrow coves, contrasts vividly with the bleakly craggy north coast and its ruined remnants of the mining industry. Mousehole, Lamorna and Porthcurno may have delivered themselves up gratefully to tourism, but a short walk inland and you are among old farming communities. The village scenes in the 1970s cult film *Straw Dogs* were filmed in St Buryan, where on a Friday evening the tractors parked outside the pub may outnumber the cars. Older communities lie hidden beneath the fields of 'broccly' (cauliflower to outsiders), daffodils and potatoes, emerging in desolate pastures as standing stones and circles and by roadsides as stumpy, weatherworn Celtic crosses.

5 NEWLYN

I have a soft spot for Newlyn: it's got the integrity of a hard-working community that is not overly concerned with how it looks to tourists and wears its cultural history without any great fuss. You hear French as well as Cornish trawlermen's voices in the mobile post office queue and around the harbour the air is thick with the screams of seagulls, the smell of diesel and fish. Net-makers and rope-makers, fish-packers and engineers all work from the sheds and warehouses around the

NEWLYN SCHOOL OF ART

newlynartschool.co.uk

Halfway up Newlyn's Chywoone Hill, a former primary school was given a new lease of life in 2011 as a high-quality art school, thanks to the vision and sheer determination of artist Henry Garfit. Henry had almost given up looking for studio space to rent (a startling shortage given the density of the artistic population in Penwith) when this building, with its huge and light-filled schoolroom windows, emerged as a candidate. Furthermore, it was only a step away from where Stanhope Forbes, 'the father of the Newlyn School', ran his own school of painting between 1899 and 1941. Offering local artists not only studio space but also the opportunity to teach, it's been a wild success: the calibre of the teachers – numbering 30 of Cornwall's most respected artists – many of whom have international reputations, and the joined-up co-operation with the Penlee, Exchange, Newlyn and Tate St Ives galleries, which are all on the doorstep, give students of all ages extraordinary advantages. Courses lasting from a few hours to four days cover subjects from drawing, painting and printmaking to sculpture, all very highly rated as well as being a lot of fun. The painting holidays on Tresco sound fantastic, and have gone from strength to strength. Henry deserves a medal.

harbour, and sitting on a bench with your ice cream or fish and chips you can take in all the activity of a working port, the largest and busiest in the southwest. Until 2018, the hugely popular **Fish Festival** was held here each year on the August bank holiday. The building of a new fish market, the pandemic and Brexit uncertainties all led to the festival being suspended, but at the time of writing there is unanimous support for it to return, spread over a number of days in the autumn, with a wider focus on the incredibly diverse range of industry and enterprise, including the arts, that makes Newlyn the unique fishing community it is.

Newlyn has always been famous for its coppersmiths (and in previous centuries, coppersmithing proved one way to keep unemployed local lads out of mischief). On top of the roof of the former **Seaman's Mission** perches a galleon-shaped weathervane, made by coppersmith Tom Batten in 1911. On the road out of Newlyn to Penzance there are more wonderful examples of the work of Arts and Crafts coppersmith John Mackenzie on the wall of the the **Newlyn Art Gallery** (✆ 01736 363715 newlynartgallery.co.uk Tue–Sat), sister gallery to the Exchange Gallery in Penzance, which puts on regularly changing exhibitions of contemporary and 20th-century art and has a café with a great view of the harbour. The large square panels on the façade, representing earth, air, fire and water, are all green and sadly corroded from exposure to the elements, but worth a respectful look. Today, Mike Johnson and his small team keep the Newlyn tradition of coppersmithing alive; it's possible to commission his work (⌂ thecopperworksnewlyn.com).

The very classy independent **cinema Newlyn Filmhouse** (The Combe, TR18 5HS ☎ 01736 332222 ⌂ newlynfilmhouse.com) opened its doors in 2016. Inside, there are two screens, state-of-the-art seating and a lovely bar-restaurant. Ex-Londoners Alastair and Suzie, who run the cinema, told me, 'We loved everything about Penwith, but we missed the kind of films we were able to see in London.' Newlyn is definitely on Penwith's cultural map these days.

One of the best times to visit Newlyn (and dinky, touristy Mousehole, just around the headland) is at Christmas, when both harbours are filled with an incredible display of lights, representing lobsters and mermaids as well as more traditional robins and sleighs, and many of the fishing boats are lit up too. Christmas light-watching is so popular that the narrow road from Newlyn into Mousehole gets choked with cars as dusk falls; it's essential to arrive early or prepare for a long walk.

¶¶ FOOD & DRINK

The independent butcher, baker, greengrocer, artisan cheese shop and three excellent (all slightly different) fishmongers make shopping for local food easy and enjoyable in Newlyn.

The pubs along the harbour are about as far removed from gastro-chic as you like, but brilliant for a pint of Betty Stogs or Doom Bar and fishy gossip, the best of which is completely unrepeatable. The more respectable stuff – including who's landed what – can be found on the harbour's entertaining blog (⌂ blog.through-the-gaps.co.uk).

Argoe The Strand, TR18 5HW ☎ 01736 362455 ⌂ argoenewlyn.co.uk ☉ Tue–Sat. This new harbourside restaurant has garnered heaps of praise for its menu of Cornish fish, seafood and tapas, that takes its inspiration from traditional European cooking. On warm days you can sit outside on the deck and watch the harbour activity while you eat.

---

1 Learning to paint with Newlyn School of Art. **2** The harbour at Mousehole. **3** The hugely popular Newlyn Fish Festival, set to make a comeback. **4** Cornish stargazy pie is made and served in pubs throughout Mousehole and Newlyn in the days before Christmas. ▶

Jelberts Ices Newlyn Rd, TR18 5HJ. Ice cream, made to a secret family recipe, handed down through generations, is sold in old-fashioned cornets or tubs and comes in one flavour only: vanilla. Mysteriously, the ice cream cannot be stored in a freezer.

Mackerel Sky Seafood Bar TR18 5HJ ⌂ mackerelskycafe.co.uk ☺ Mar–Oct; no bookings. A tiny restaurant with a big reputation locally for both lunches and dinners. Local fish and shellfish feature on an inventive menu that might include salt-and-pepper squid with wasabi aioli, grilled pollock with samphire butter or crab nachos.

The Tolcarne Inn Tolcarne Pl, TR18 5PR ✆ 01736 363074 ⌂ tolcarneinn.co.uk ☺ Tue–Sat. Highly acclaimed chef Ben Tunnicliffe is at the helm and has done much to put Newlyn on the culinary map; many make the pilgrimage from further afield to eat here. Fish, of course, comes straight to the kitchen from where it is landed – on the other side of the harbour.

6 MOUSEHOLE & PAUL

⌂ **The Old Coastguard** (page 421)

Dylan Thomas spent his honeymoon in **Mousehole** (pronounced 'Mouwzal') in 1937 and found it 'the loveliest village in England'. Clearly, the just-married man's thoughts were romantically inclined, but perhaps he would still approve, for despite the inevitable conflict between narrow, twisting streets and motor vehicles, second homes and tourist trade, the cosy, cottagey good looks and picturesque harbour with its tiny, sandy beach have remained intact. But the village only starts to reveal its character when you start pottering about the maze of tiny alleys behind the harbour. Here, you might find a retired fisherman's cottage, decorated all over with bits of painted boat and shell – or the plaque beside the oldest house in the village, its porch jutting over a courtyard on granite pillars, which records that 'Squire Jenkyn Keigwin was killed here 23rd July 1595 defending this house against the Spaniards.' (The offending cannonball sits on the windowsill of the house, now privately owned.) The rest of Mousehole's inhabitants, it appears, were paralysed by an attack of fatalism. The Spanish raid was the subject of a prophecy, inscribed in Cornish on the Merlin rock on the south side of the harbour. It read: 'They shall land on the Rock of Merlin, Those who shall burn Paul, Penzance and Newlyn.'

"You might find a retired fisherman's cottage, decorated all over with bits of painted boat and shell."

The tiny harbour is home to the finely restored Cornish lugger, *Barnabas*, whose square brown sail is a familiar sight on summer weekends and any other day that skipper Toby Floyer can rustle up a crew for a day's

THE PENLEE LIFEBOAT DISASTER

If you are making a special journey to see the Mousehole Christmas lights, you need to know why they are turned off for an hour each year on 19 December.

On 19 December 1981, the *Union Star*, a coaster with eight on board, suffered engine failure and was blown towards the coast by hurricane-force winds. As the urgency of the situation became clear to the Falmouth coastguard, the Penlee lifeboat, stationed in Mousehole, was requested to launch. Before the *Solomon Browne* slid down her ramp into towering waves, Coxswain Trevelyan Richards refused to allow the son of one crew member to board, saying 'No more than one from any family on a night like this.'

In an astonishing feat of bravery and seamanship, Richards managed to bring the lifeboat alongside the stricken ship and the message was received that four on board had been transferred to the lifeboat. However, when an attempt was made to go back for the remaining crew, radio contact with Falmouth abruptly ceased. In the terrible hours that followed, the truth dawned over Mousehole that all eight lifeboatmen had been lost to the storm, as well as all eight from the *Union Star*.

Today, the lifeboat operates out of Newlyn. The Penlee lifeboat station is closed and shuttered, and rarely opens to the public gaze; no lifeboat has since been launched from her ramp. The eight volunteer lifeboatmen of the *Solomon Browne* were posthumously honoured with RNLI medals and outside the lifeboat station a memorial plaque headed SERVICE NOT SELF lists their names.

Following the anguishing possibility that the boathouse might be demolished, in April 2023 the building was granted Grade II listed status and much to the relief and pride of local families, its future is now assured.

sailing around the coast or longer voyages to the Isles of Scilly or Brittany. Anyone with a taste for congenial sailing and the desire to pitch in (it takes at least four pairs of strong arms to 'walk' the sail and its heavy gaff around the front of the mast when changing tack) is welcome to join the merry crew. A donation is politely requested, and if the bug bites, the thing to do is join the Cornish Maritime Trust (⊘ cornishmaritimetrust. org) and become a regular, helping out with winter maintenance. The Trust has also restored a smaller lugger, *Softwing*, so there's rarely a shortage of available places. Every other (even-numbered) year, over a long weekend in July, Mousehole is host to the **Sea Salts and Sail festival** (⊘ seasalts.co.uk), which celebrates the village's maritime history. There are lots of boats – it's an informal warm-up for a much bigger, but similar festival later in the month at Douarnenez in Brittany – races, cook-ups on the beach, singing and fun to be had.

On the hill going out of Mousehole towards Raginnis, the **Wild Bird Hospital and Sanctuary** (✆ 01736 731386) was until recently open all year, receiving injured, orphaned and – occasionally – oiled birds. Founded in 1928 by sisters Dorothy and Phyllis Iglesias, the hospital hit the headlines in 1967 when the *Torrey Canyon*, carrying 120,000 tons of crude oil, foundered on the Seven Stones reef between Land's End and the Isles of Scilly. People everywhere, shocked by images of horribly oiled birds, were relieved by the news that in many cases they could be cleaned and saved. Over 8,000 oiled birds passed successfully through the hospital after the disaster. Avian flu has forced the centre to close to both birds and visitors, but fundraising to refurbish the hospital with improved biosecurity is underway. Find the Just Giving page on the hospital website ⊘ mouseholebirdhospital.org.uk.

Many Cornish villages by the sea are in two parts: the harbour and, on higher ground, where a church spire or tower might guide ships to the harbour entrance, the 'Churchtown'. **Paul**, on top of the hill behind Mousehole, is the village's 'Churchtown'. During the Spanish raid, the church was badly burned; it was rebuilt in 1600 and again as storms took their toll on the building. The churchyard wall contains a memorial to Dolly Pentreath, who died in 1777 at the age of 102, the last person in Cornwall to speak only Cornish.

¶¶ FOOD & DRINK

A few days before Christmas the traditional Cornish **stargazy pie** is made and served in pubs throughout Mousehole and Newlyn. It's a pie with no fixed ingredient, apart from whole, small fish, such as sardines, their heads poking through the pastry lid (to be fair, it's not everyone's cup of tea). Here the pie is made to celebrate Tom Bowcock's marvellous, life-saving haul, supposedly sometime during the 16th century, when terrible December weather had grounded the fishing fleet and the village faced starvation.

The Old Coastguard Hotel The Parade, TR19 6PR ✆ 01736 731222 ⊘ oldcoastguardhotel. co.uk. This place was given a breath of life by the Inkin brothers (who run the much-loved Gurnard's Head on the north coast). Beneath the hotel, the bar has splendid views and a garden looking out over the sea (as well as a basket of blankets to wrap up in on chilly evenings), a roaring fire in winter and a nice selection of books and paintings, country furniture and a relaxed atmosphere. Excellent local food, well-kept Cornish ales and superb wines at sensible prices, to ensure the local community do not feel this is for well-heeled visitors only.

7 LAMORNA

🏠 **Castallack Farm** (page 421) 🚶 **Into the Woods** (page 421)

Lamorna and Lamorna Cove are like chalk and cheese; the village is a ribbon of pretty houses in the deep and wooded Lamorna Valley, a mossy, ferny place, with orchards on the sunny slopes and an artist lurking behind nearly every window. The cove it opens on to is an oddly oppressive place. The eastern slopes, where granite used to build the Bishop Rock lighthouse was once quarried, appear threatened by an arrested granite rockslide and around the expensive harbour car park are notices beginning with a daunting list of Nos and Don'ts. If you can stomach these, then the coast path to Mousehole, returning by an inland route, is a very enjoyable three-mile circular walk.

If you find yourself in Lamorna during the summer months, look out for signs announcing that the garden at **Chygurno** is open. The garden clings to the side of a south-facing cliff overlooking the cove and is a tour de force of creative, subtropical gardening in a seemingly impossible location.

🍴 FOOD & DRINK

Lamorna Pottery Lamorna TR19 6NY ✆ 01736 810330 ⌂ lamornapottery.co.uk ⏲ Feb–Oct Wed–Sun. By the bus stop, in a wooded dell a mile short of Lamorna village. There's been a pottery here since the 1920s and a café since the seventies. Now owned by Jeremy and Munir, the café continues to offer homemade cakes and scones, and a good lunch menu – with a Bangladeshi twist – all served in a lovely garden when it's fine. Indoors, pottery classes are becoming popular. The location is also superb for short walks in the bluebell woods across the road.

8 ST LOY & PENBERTH

🏠 **The Summerhouse** St Loy (page 421)

The bus from Penzance to Land's End passes through St Buryan and Treen, making a superb four-mile **walk**, taking in the woodland cove of St Loy and the miniature fishing haven of Penberth, quite achievable in a morning or afternoon. A footpath from the pub in St Buryan runs in an almost straight line down to the coast at St Loy, crossing level farmland and ancient parish boundary stones. The downhill section through woods to St Loy cove is carpeted in bluebells in May. A rugged mile of coast path drops into Penberth, where you can pick up the footpath to Treen. You may, however, wish to wander up the lanes to

Sending a telegram from London to Cape Town was five times faster with Regen.

PORTHCURNO
(HOME)

Treen instead: the cottages and gardens are a treat and many have cut or potted flowers at the gate beside an honesty box. The short stretch of the B3283 encountered between Penberth and the turning to Treen has several salad and veg items on the roadside stalls. A good, traditional pub in Treen is well placed to while away the wait for the bus.

9 PORTHCURNO & ST LEVAN

The steep-sided valley ends in a **perfect beach** of soft white sand – and a second, smaller beach at low tide, when Pedn Vounder Beach (much loved by naturists) is accessible too. Here are a large car park, beach café and pub, but heaps of publicity in recent years have brought more visitors in the summer than the beaches and car park can absorb; on top of that 200,000 visitors a year venture down the narrow lane on their way to the **Minack Theatre** (page 358), perched high on the cliff overlooking the beach. A vertigo-inducing steep flight of steps leads from the beach to the theatre;

"The steep-sided valley ends in a perfect beach of soft white sand – and a second, smaller beach at low tide."

the road up is similarly tortuous, but the Penzance to Land's End service just about manages it (page 333). Come in February or March, by bus, and avoid the crowds that flock to the beaches and theatre in the summer months.

The lane continues past the entrance to the Minack as far as **St Levan**, an easy stroll away. The church has delightful bench-ends showing a jester, pilgrim, shepherd, fisherman (possibly St Levan himself) and some curious portraits. Outside in the churchyard is a smooth mound of granite, neatly split in two. Records of the rock go back to pre-Christian times when it was associated with fertility rites. The large granite cross was strategically interposed to prevent such goings-on. The coast path route back to the Minack takes you past the old holy well and the steep steps down to **Porth Chapel Beach** pass the barely identifiable cliffside ruins of St Levan's Chapel, thought to date from the 6th century. The beach has a dreamt-of beauty; I remember it on a sunny March morning at low tide. Two surfers and their little dog were making the first prints across the damp sand while a seal rolled around in the surf.

◀ **1** Minack Theatre, Porthcurno. **2** Nanjizal Bay. **3** Penberth Cove. **4** Porthcurno Telegraph Museum. **5** The church of St Levan contains some remarkable carved bench ends.

⅋ FOOD & DRINK

Just a short walk along the coast path from Porth Chapel Beach brings you to the tiny cluster of cottages at **Porthgwarra**. One of the smallest buildings turns out to be a shop, selling tea, coffee, ice creams, cakes and pasties (✆ 01736 871998 ⌂ staubynestatescottages. co.uk/porthgwarra-cove-cafe ⊙ reduced opening times in winter months), which is perfectly placed for coast-path walkers.

PK Porthcurno: Porthcurno Telegraph Museum

Eastern Hse, TR19 6JX ✆ 01736 810966 ⌂ pkporthcurno.com ⊙ Mar–Nov daily; Dec–Feb Sun & Mon

A £2.5-million refit in 2014 brought important changes to this historic hub of global communications. The museum always drew in those fascinated by old communications technology – from needle telegraph to ticker-tape telegrams – but there were still too many 'WWWICs' (Women Who Wait in Cars') for its liking. Accordingly, much thought and effort went in to presenting the exhibits in a more user-friendly way and a café was added. But nothing much changed in the Tunnels: a series of deeply evocative, bomb-proof chambers that were built into the cliff behind the telegraph station during World War II. The atmosphere is still authentically 1940s, and there are still some retired station employees among the wonderful volunteer staff, delighted to demonstrate how the old machines work.

The cable station (the whole village, in fact) dates from 1870, when the first cable to Bombay was laid, disappearing under the sea from Porthcurno Beach. It's quite a thought that by the turn of the century, the tiny valley, where young men from all over the world (for which, read 'Empire') came to be trained, was a multi-cultural community and hot spot of cutting-edge technology. The smart white houses and cottages all date from the centre's Edwardian heyday, though there are still plenty of people about who can remember when you needed to show your ID before you could enter Porthcurno.

Minack Theatre

TR19 6JU ✆ 01736 810181 ⌂ minack.com

Rowena Cade moved to Porthcurno from Derbyshire with her mother in the 1920s and soon after conceived a plan to construct an outdoor stage on a craggy bit of rock in the garden for a production of *The Tempest* by the local am-dram society. That was just the start; the production proved so successful – with the backdrop of the sea and sky, the acoustics of the cliffside gully so perfect – that she roped in her gardener and his apprentice to help her build a proper amphitheatre, with tiered banks, an access road and steps down to the beach,

The magic of the place is unfailing, even when the weather is unkind. Friends of mine saw *Under Milk Wood* at the Minack; a group of dolphins came out to play in the sea below, completely upstaging the actors for a moment or two, until with genius improvisation their antics were drawn into the play.

The visitor centre, café and extraordinary exotic garden are open all through the year. The programme of performances starts in May and finishes in September.

10 NANJIZAL BAY

During my time in Penwith, I considered myself indescribably fortunate to live within easy striking distance of this supremely beautiful beach, which has appeared more than once in the *Poldark* television series. There's no easy access by road (at Polgigga take the Porthgwarra turning and park by the side of the road after 400 yards), just a muddy farm track to Higher Bosistow Farm and then fields and heathery clifftops to the coast path. The beach – pale sand and a scattering of boulders – is finally reached by wooden steps. Despite the *Poldark* effect, you're more likely to see seals than other people, especially out of season. Look left for the Song of the Sea, a slender natural arch in the rock through which the sea glints, or rushes at high tide. Low tide is a good moment to find the beach, when caves and rock pools are revealed.

Nanjizal faces west, so is not much good for sun in the mornings, but wonderful for late summer evenings, when the water is almost warm enough for swimming in comfort. There's a pleasant, looping walk back, following the stream that gushes down on to the beach, through Bosistow Farm or you can branch left and follow the footpath to Trevilley Farm at Trevescan, for the bus stop and refreshments at the Apple Tree Café.

♦♦ FOOD & DRINK

Apple Tree Café Trevescan, Sennen TR19 7AQ ✆ 01736 872753 ⟲ appletreecafe.co.uk
◷ Feb–Dec Wed–Sun. This friendly pit stop is a welcome alternative to the tourist-orientated eateries at Land's End. Lunches, teas and very good 'fish and dips'.

11 LAND'S END

🏠 **Land's End Hostel** (page 421)

Coachloads of people arrive every day in the summer to wander up to the Land's End signpost, which points variously to the likes of the Falkland Isles (6,658 miles) and Moscow (1,586 miles), and then wander back through the sticky trap of shops, cafés and 'experiences' to the coach, no doubt relieved to have ticked that particular box. The relief must be enormous for those completing an 'End-to-Ender', having walked, jogged, cycled or wheelchaired from John o'Groats, 874 miles to the north, to glimpse the huddle of white buildings at mainland Britain's most southwesterly point. But consider the sadness of one charity fund-raiser, setting out for John o'Groats from Land's End, who tripped over the sign announcing his departure, broke his ankle, and got no further.

The best way to approach the headland is on foot, following the coast path from Sennen, just over a mile to the north. There's more of a sense of occasion as you approach over the cliffs, with the spray dashing over the Longships lighthouse and sea churning below, than arriving at a massive car park. This way too, you get to see the impressive remains of Maen Castle, a huge Iron Age hillfort, kept clear of undergrowth by the National Trust. Approaching from the south, the nearest parking to the coast path is in the village of Porthgwarra or as described for Nanjizal Bay (page 359).

12 SENNEN COVE

The beach is busy with families and surfers all through the summer – it's a beautiful sweep of sand, washed by some of the best surf in Cornwall, patrolled by lifeguards and fringed with rock pools. It's easily accessible, and parents of children taking part in the daily surf schools can sit on the raised terrace of the smart café-bar-restaurant **Surf Beach Bar** (𝒥 01736 871191 ⊘ surfbeachbar.co.uk) right by the beach and watch it all going on below. There's a small handful of beach-related shops at the harbour end of the cove and the **Roundhouse and Capstan** art and craft gallery (𝒥 01736 871859 ⊘ round-house.co.uk) in a black-timbered, circular building that houses the old capstan, formerly used for winching boats out of the water. More experienced surfers and those wanting to escape the crowds head further north to the next (un-lifeguarded) beach at

---

1 Sennen Cove. **2** Land's End, approached from the south. ▶

Gwynver, which is emptier and wilder as it involves a much longer walk. There is limited roadside parking on the road high above the beach.

THE NORTH COAST & PENWITH MOORS

The landscape takes on an entirely different character beyond Sennen. Remote, windswept and treeless, the granite mining villages that line the coast road have been repopulated in recent years by artists and writers, responding to the wild energy of the area's dramatic coast and wuthering moors.

13 ST JUST

🏠 **Bosavern Guesthouse** (page 421)

For a brief period during the mining boom in the 18th century, the population of St Just and Pendeen was greater than that of Liverpool and Manchester. Migrant families lived in disease-ridden, makeshift camps and shanty towns, which vanished as quickly as they sprang up, though the legacy of the industry is to be seen everywhere in the skeletal engine houses and chimneys on moorland and clifftops – and the rows of terraced granite cottages that housed the mining families once the population had shaken down to a sustainable level.

St Just, England's most westerly village, is a busy, likeable place, with a strong element of hand-knitted, community-minded folk, a surprising amount of things to see and do. There are numerous art galleries in and around the village, representing the work of local artists, and a fine collection of excellent places to eat or pick up picnic supplies, too.

"There are numerous art galleries in and around the village, representing the work of local artists."

It would be easy to spend a day pottering round St Just's studios: one which should not be missed is the new **Jackson Foundation Gallery** (✆ 01736 787638 ⊘ jacksonfoundationgallery. com ⊙ Tue–Sat). For over three decades Kurt Jackson and his wife Caroline have made Penwith their home, and the large – yet strikingly intimate – landscapes of this prolific artist are well known to collectors from all over the world. A large industrial building right in the middle of Penwith is now a superb exhibition space where you will find works by Jackson and other artists on display throughout the year.

The week-long community arts festival, **Lafrowda** ($\lozenge$ lafrowda. co.uk), is held in July, with outdoor events centring on the medieval Plain-an-Gwarry, a splendidly preserved, grassy medieval playing place. The highlight is Lafrowda Day, when the streets are decorated and there's live music, folk dancing and lots of people parading through the village in strange costumes.

¶ FOOD & DRINK

Tucked away on Chapel Road, **Vivian Olds**, the tiny butchers ($\mathscr{P}$ 01736 788520), has almost a cult following in Penwith. Pub menus and restaurants name him as their supplier with pride. **Bollowal Farm** (on the lane out to Cape Cornwall) has a stall of home-grown veg, always well stocked. The farm is now producing its own range of rum – not on sale at the farm gate, obviously ($\lozenge$ capecornwallrum.com).

Dog and Rabbit North Row, TR19 7LB $\mathscr{P}$ 01736 449811 $\odot$ Thu–Sun. This relaxed and cosy café, welcoming dogs and children, is clearly a favourite locals' hangout. Fine range of teas, cakes, breakfasts and lunches.

Kings Arms Market Sq, TR19 7HF $\mathscr{P}$ 01736 788545. A welcoming, beamy sort of pub with a log fire that positively beckons you in on chilly days and a deservedly good reputation for food and St Austell ales.

McFadden's Market Sq, TR19 7HD $\mathscr{P}$ 01736 788136. The steak pasties come in three sizes, but even a small one will set you up for a day's walking. Also good for local meats and cheeses.

The Square Market Sq, TR19 7HD ⬛ . A take-away café, located next to McFadden's, that is very popular with locals. Lots of vegan-friendly options, salads and exceptional pizzas.

The Star Inn 1 Fore St, TR19 7LL $\mathscr{P}$ 01736 788767. A St Austell Brewery pub which has retained its character as a popular locals' haunt. Monday evening is folk music night, when ten or more local musicians will gather round the table in the front window and play whatever takes their fancy.

Cape Cornwall

A cape is where two seas meet and for centuries the rocky promontory was thought to be the real Land's End. It's a good five miles north of the true southwestern tip of mainland Britain, but what it lacks in commercial razzamatazz, it gains in lonely grandeur. There is a National Trust car park and a rough footpath out to the topmost crag, where a chimney-like tower bears a plaque recording the gift of the promontory to the National Trust by Heinz in 1987. Almost invisible, perched on a

ROGER DRISCOLL/S

KIRSTY FERGUSSON

IAN WOOLCOCK/S

GEEVOR TIN MINE

CHRISDORNEY/S

ledge beneath the tower, is the volunteer coastguards hut: you can pop in and ask if there have been any sightings of dolphins or basking sharks – and beyond that, nothing but sea until the coast of Labrador.

By the side of the Carn Gloose road just southwest of Cape Cornwall, near a trig point and marked by an information sign, is **Ballowall Barrow**, an extraordinarily elaborate Bronze Age burial chamber. It was completely unknown until 1878 when Cornish antiquarian W C Borlase discovered it under mining rubble. The barrow includes an entrance grave, a cairn, several individual burial cists and a number of ritual pits. What you see is very striking, if not entirely authentic: a central oval structure, 35 feet across with

"Non-members are welcome at the café of the Cape Cornwall Golf Club, England's most westerly and most wind-blown course."

walls up to 10 feet high and all around this a passage with outside walls forming a 'collar' of the same height, built by Borlase to protect the interior. Close by, non-members are welcome at the café of the **Cape Cornwall Golf Club** (𝒽 capecornwallclub.com), England's most westerly and most wind-blown course. The egg and bacon baps are highly recommended.

14 CHAPEL CARN BREA & CARN EUNY

The dome-shaped hill between Crows-an-Wra and the little Land's End airport is known as **Chapel Carn Brea** (not to be confused with Carn Brea, which overlooks Camborne and Redruth). An easy walk from the small car park (♥ SW389284) to the summit reveals stunning views over the peninsula, described in the introduction to this chapter. An equally rewarding mile of footpath leads from the same car park, across the lane and northeast over Tredinney Common, in the shadow of Bartinney Down, past a very natural, gurgling holy well that marks the site of St Euny's Chapel, to the ancient hut settlement at **Carn Euny**. The site is managed by English Heritage, but there's no kiosk or fee for entering, and the sense of private discovery is overwhelming. The low stone walls of the roundhouses are clearly visible, beneath a soft blanket of turf and wildflowers, and the entrance to a mysterious fogou is also apparent.

◄ **1** The ancient hut settlement of Carn Euny. **2** Lafrowda Day, St Just. **3** Skeletal engine houses near St Just. **4** Panning for gems at the Geevor Tin Mine. **5** Levant Mine.

PREHISTORIC PENWITH

There is a greater concentration of prehistoric sites in Penwith than in any other part of England; the moors are littered with standing stones, circles and quoits (a capstone supported by three or more uprights), 3,000-year-old village settlements and mysterious fogous – subterranean passages of uncertain usage – which hide their secrets beneath the turf, gorse and bracken.

Some are easily seen from the road, such as **Lanyon Quoit**, beside the road from Madron to Morvah, or the **Merry Maidens**, a stone circle in a field adjoining the B3315 Lamorna–Land's End road. Iron Age cliff-forts at Treen (**Treryn Dinas**) on the south coast (confusingly there's another Treryn Dinas at Treen near Pendeen on the north coast) and Land's End (**Maen Castle**) can all be seen from the coast path. Others need to be tracked down on foot, with a map. The perfectly preserved **Boscawen-Un stone circle** is, local farmers tell me, occasionally still used for pagan celebrations and rites. This is no surprise – the local post office in St Buryan has a card in the window advertising the benign services of the village's resident witch. However, Boscawen-Un is so well hidden that it's more than likely (in daylight hours) you'll have the spot to yourself. There's limited space for parking beside the A30, a mile west of Drift, where a small sign indicates Boscawenoon Farm and the footpath to the circle.

Many, but not all, of Penwith's ancient sites come under the care and protection of CASPN (Cornwall Ancient Sites Protection Network) formed in 2000 after a number of sites were vandalised. The network involves organisations as diverse as English Heritage, the Cornwall Wildlife Trust and the Pagan Federation.

This remote and beautiful acre lies on a south-facing slope, overlooking the south coast; it's a place to linger, maybe with a picnic rug and a jug of local cider on a sunny afternoon.

15 PENDEEN

The village is typical of this part of the north coast – a huddle of granite miners' cottages, a village shop and pub, Methodist chapel and Anglican church – but Pendeen is a gateway to a section of the coast path that takes in an astonishing collection of **World Heritage mining sites**, from the desolate and much-photographed cliff-side ruins of **Botallack**, past a working beam engine at **Levant Mine** and **Geevor Tin Mine**, kept alive as a museum by the heroic efforts of former miners. The path continues past the windy headland and the lonely Pendeen lighthouse, before dropping down to the pristine, empty sands of Portheras Beach. Turn inland from Pendeen and you're straight on to the moors, dominated here by the craggy top of Carn Kenidjack overshadowing the **Tregeseal stone circle** to the south.

Levant Mine & Beam Engine

Trewellard TR19 7SX 🕿 01736 786156 ⊙ prebooked tours only, Sun–Thu; National Trust

Inside, the oldest working mine-serving steam engine in the country (1840) can be seen in the engine house of Levant Mine, which was close enough to be incorporated into the Geevor Tin Mine in the 1960s. Both mines had shafts running half a mile out to sea, and steam engines worked both the pumps and the winding mechanisms. Both mines are now flooded to sea level. Outside, the gritty post-industrial landscape is matched by remorseless cliffs and a turbulent sea; as you wander in the direction of Geevor, an information board shows photos of anguished women waiting for news of the 31 miners who lost their lives in 1919, when the crude mineshaft lift, known as a 'man-engine', collapsed. There are still a few old folk around Pendeen today who grew up never knowing their grandfathers.

Geevor Tin Mine

Trewellard TR19 7EW 🕿 01736 788662 🖰 geevor.com ⊙ Sun–Thu

Throughout the 1980s, Cornish tin mines that had survived the general decline of the previous century were forced, like their coal-producing counterparts elsewhere in the UK, to cease operations. The miners at Geevor, however, firmly believed that their profitable, productive mine would stay open. It was not to be. Nevertheless, after closure many from the community threw their indomitable spirit into keeping the pit alive as a museum. Alive is the right word: you can walk, stooping, down the narrow, damp passages once trodden by the tinners and meet former miners who will talk with pride and good humour about the lives they led before 1990. 'First day down there, it was the noise that got me. Three great drills going flat out and no escape from the noise. I got home that evening and told father it wasn't for me. I won't repeat his reply.' Above ground, everything has been preserved just as it was on the day the mine stopped working and a superb museum tells the whole story, including film footage of that last working day.

It's an exceptional and profoundly moving experience that fully justifies the slightly above-average admission fee. Do wear sensible shoes.

A circular walk from Morvah

✳ OS Explorer map 102 or OS Landranger map 203; start: Morvah Schoolhouse
📍 SW402355; seven miles; moderate–challenging, with some rough ground.

- -

This walk encompasses 4,000 years of history as well as offering grand views over moorland and sea and a wild stretch of coast path. Most – but not all – paths on the route are well signposted. There's limited roadside parking at Morvah; or use the lay-by at Bosullow Common at point 3. Morvah is on the A3 bus route from St Ives and has a coffee shop and gallery in the Schoolhouse Arts and Community Centre (☏ 01736 787808 🖰 morvah.com).

1 Leave Morvah on the B3306 St Ives road and at the first bend follow the marked footpath southeast over granite stiles and pasture towards Carn Farm. Film buffs will recognise the house where *Straw Dogs* was filmed in 1973, silhouetted on the skyline. Skirt the farm to the right and follow the signs uphill to Chun Quoit.

2 Chun Quoit, with its convex capstone, resembles a giant granite mushroom and you can just make out the remains of the cairn of boulders that once encircled it. This Neolithic burial chamber, along with Lanyon Quoit, just over the hill to the southeast, is one of the best preserved in Penwith. Turn left (due east, uphill) to **Chun Castle**.

Chun is a contraction of Chy-Woon, meaning 'House on the Hill'. First raised as a defensive stronghold in the 2nd or 3rd century BC, the circular remains of granite roundhouses can just about be discerned beneath the bracken and brambles. Leave the hillfort by the entrance and turn left, following a well-beaten track down the hill to the buildings of **Tregyllys Farm**. Here you find yourself at the start of the mile-long lane which joins the Madron–Morvah road almost opposite the lay-by.

3 Reach the road at **Bosullow Common** (note that the telephone box marked on the OS map at 📍 SW418344 has been removed), opposite a large lay-by. Cross over to the lay-by and follow the signed footpath.

4 After half a mile you reach a point where you can turn right into a field to see the Bronze Age monument **Men-an-Tol**, a striking stone alignment consisting of two pillars that stand either side of an upright stone ring, known as a crick stone. This arrangement of stones is unique and theories and superstitions have surrounded them for centuries. Return to the main track and continue up the hill. Soon on the left, in a field, there is a huge standing stone, **Men Scryfa** (said to be inscribed in Latin in the 5th century commemorating one Riolobran, son of Cunoval). (On a sunny day, you may want to walk up to the ruins of **Ding Dong Mine** from Men-an-Tol for the impressive views, before descending the hill and rejoining the walk at the Nine Maidens stone circle, but you'd miss Men Scryfa.)

5 At a grassy crossroads, 200 yards from Men Scryfa (♥ SW430354), branch off to the right and make your way up to the **Nine Maidens stone circle**. The name is misleading: there are 11 stones and it's thought there were at least another seven. With Ding Dong Mine now looming on the horizon, this is a rather brooding place, distinctly sinister in fog. Return to the grassy crossroads and go straight ahead. The path heads northwest over the hill and then drops with breathtaking loveliness towards the sea. Carn Galver looms craggily to the right.

6 Turn right on to the road at Rosemergy. Cross the cattle grid and turn left after 100 yards on to the signed footpath to the coast.

7 Turn left on the coast path; be prepared for some unavoidable and deeply boggy patches, particularly as you get close to Morvah. It's unwise to stray off the path to keep your feet dry, as there are several unmarked mineshafts in this area. But the views of the sea and fearsomely jagged Wolf Rocks are ample compensation for damp socks.

8 Turn left for the footpath inland to Morvah, emerging by the church.

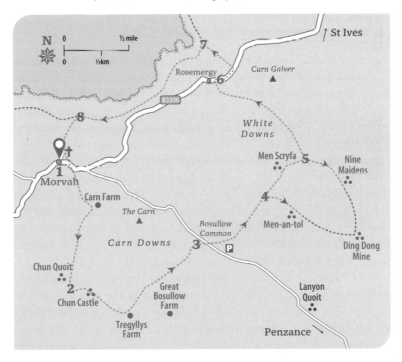

🍴 FOOD & DRINK

Lunches, including homemade soups and pasties in the **Counthouse Café** (✆ 01736 788662 ⌂ counthousecafe.com ⊙ Sun–Thu) at Geevor, are excellent, and locals book early in the week for the superb roast dinners cooked for Sunday lunchtimes only. There's a good crowd of pubs around Pendeen, too: the **Queen's Arms** at Botallack (⌂ queensarmscornwall.co.uk) and **Trewellard Arms** at Trewellard (⌂ goodpubfoodlandsend.com) are both good for local ales and traditional pub grub; in Pendeen itself, the **North Inn** (⌂ thenorthinnpendeen.co.uk) is a picturesque pub with a decent garden and camping field, and the **Radjel Inn** is a St Austell Brewery pub; both do good food and are family-friendly.

16 ZENNOR

🏠 **Gurnard's Head** (page 421)

> At Zennor one sees infinite Atlantic, all peacock-mingled colours, and the gorse is sunshine itself. Zennor is a most beautiful place: a tiny granite village nestling under high shaggy moor-hills and a big sweep of lovely sea beyond, such a lovely sea, lovelier even than the Mediterranean … It is the best place I have been in, I think.
>
> D H Lawrence, from a letter to Katherine Mansfield and John Murry (1916)

Lawrence was not alone; lots of people fall for Zennor's charm and the list of the village's notable residents, if only temporary, is quite astounding. In no particular order it includes the artist Patrick Heron, Emperor Haile Selassie (who sat out the war years here), Virginia Woolf, William Arnold-Forster, instrumental in setting up the League of Nations, and Vera Atkins (who directed an all-female British spy ring) – and one local resident told me they had encountered the Dalai Lama, roaming the hills above Zennor Quoit. Sadly for Lawrence, however, the couple he hoped would help him and his German wife, Frieda, found a writers' colony in Zennor refused to be seduced. Katherine Mansfield and her husband John Murry fled to Mylor (page 273) quite unable to appreciate Lawrence's passion for living 'like foxes under the hill' at their isolated farmhouse among the wild gorse and bleak granite.

Most visitors to Zennor make a beeline for the **church** and **Tinners Arms,** handily side by side. (The first version of the pub in fact, was built in 1271, to house the masons building the church.) The church's great treasure is a 600-year-old seat with a carving on its side panel of a mermaid, holding a comb and mirror. Zennor has a particular fascination with mermaids, stemming from the local legend of Matthew

Trewhella. Trewhella, the curate's son, had a fine singing voice, which proved irresistible to the mermaid Morveran, who flipped and flopped her way into the church to hear him sing. The moment he laid eyes on her, he was enchanted and following her back to the beach, disappeared under the waves of Pendour Cove, forever.

¶¶ FOOD & DRINK

Gurnard's Head Near Zennor, St Ives TR26 3DE ✎ 01736 796928 ✆ gurnardshead.co.uk. Standing alone on the coast road, this pub is a beacon for locals, walkers and get-away-from-it-all bon viveurs who travel great distances for the legendary food and hospitality. Log fires, flagstone floors and very decent pints of local ales and ciders.

Moomaid in the Village Café Bridge House, TR26 3DA ✆ moomaidofzennor.com. Moomaid ice creams and sorbets are made on the farm just above the village and there are several Moomaid cafés dotted around Penwith. It's a splendid pit stop for coast-path walkers and sweaty cyclists, set beside a granite stream and pretty garden.

Tinners Arms TR26 3BY ✎ 01736 796927. With flagstone floors, open fires, local ales and tasty food – as well as folk music on Thursday nights – the Tinners is under new management, with a jolly atmosphere on both sides of the bar.

17 ST IVES

🏠 **Primrose Valley Hotel** (page 421)

Crowning the north coast of the Penwith peninsula, where wide white beaches meet the gorgeously blue waters west of the Hayle estuary, St Ives has a luminous beauty quite unlike anywhere else in Cornwall. The town rises behind its working harbour and five sandy beaches – a maze of narrow streets and whitewashed fishing cottages (known as 'Downalong') giving way to Victorian terraces and villas tucked away behind leafy gardens ('Upalong'), sheltered from westerlies by the high Penwith Moors.

Drawn by the light and abundance of cheap studio space in old net lofts and pilchard cellars, artists have flocked here for well over a century. I have a particular fondness though, for Breon O'Casey, who had a slightly different take on St Ives's appeal. The artist moved to St Ives in the late 1950s, at a time when the town was attracting kindred rebel spirits from all over the international art world. 'They talked about the artists being attracted to St Ives because of the light,' O'Casey later wrote. 'That's all balls: it was the sense of camaraderie against an, at best, indifferent, and at worst, hostile, world that drew them.' Whatever the reason, as

Patrick Heron observed, St Ives is unique in being the only small town in Britain to have acquired an international reputation in the art world. That spontaneous assembling of artists such as Ben Nicholson, Barbara Hepworth, Naum Gabo, Peter Lanyon, Roger Hilton, Patrick Heron, Terry Frost and Bryan Wynter produced a dynamism and energy that lasted well into the 1970s; the town is still an important centre for art, but the original mood cannot be manufactured. There are times when St Ives reeks as much of nostalgia for its lost bohemia as of harbourside chips and pasties.

Today, the town is still rich in artist's studios and galleries, among which **Tate St Ives** (✆ 01736 796226 ⌂ tate.org.uk/stives) is pre-eminent. Built in 1993 on the site of an old gasworks, the gleaming white façade overlooks Porthmeor Beach and the curved entrance porch, where there are stands for surfboards, produces a subtle echo of the waves breaking on the shore below. Inside, the bright, white galleries host a broad programme of exhibitions of international modern and contemporary art as well as special commissions and works from the Tate collection. The new extension, completed in 2018, means that a larger selection of work by the St Ives school can now be displayed, although plenty of other works from the Tate's collection find their way into the new space, too. The views over sea and sky, framed by windows in the top floor café, are as riveting as any of the displays; for a moment, as you approach, you are beguiled into thinking you are looking at a blue abstract by Mark Rothko, who also visited St Ives and almost set up studio in Lelant. During the summer holidays the gallery organises beach workshops, popular with families; at all other times indoor 'art safaris' offer children a route round the gallery, providing buckets of crayons and paper.

The Tate also manages the **Barbara Hepworth Museum and Sculpture Garden** (✆ 01736 796226 ⌂ tate.org.uk/stives) a short, but steep, step away on the corner of Barnoon Hill and Ayr Lane. This is a delightful spot – far removed in spirit from the commercial tourist crush in the streets closer to the harbour and beaches. The museum occupies both floors of her studio: downstairs an informative introduction to

---

1 Lanyon Quoit. **2** The church at Zennor, home to a 600-year-old carving of a mermaid. **3** Leach Pottery offers courses for all ages and abilities in St Ives. **4** Barbara Hepworth's studio, St Ives. ▶

Hepworth's life and creative journey into abstract sculpture – and what binds it to human experience and the landscape – is a vital prelude to understanding the work on display in the room above and the leafily chambered garden with its summer house, untouched since her death in 1975. On my last visit, in 2023, I was impressed to see the garden looking extremely well cared for; a keen eye and unflinching hand on the pruning saw had done the place a power of good.

A wander up the hill known as The Stennack (the B3306) takes you to the hugely famous and influential **Leach Pottery** (✆ 01736 799703 ⌖ leachpottery.com), founded in 1920 by Bernard Leach and Japanese potter Shoji Hamada. Scores of potters were trained here, some from abroad, others from just down the road; while the museum celebrates the life, work and influence of its founders, the studios continue to produce 'Leachware' and provide training, apprenticeships and internships for international and local pottery students. There are family-friendly 'clay days' during the school holidays, perfect for budding potters. A superb collection of Leach/Hamada-inspired pottery can also be found down by the harbour, in Fish Street, in the spacious **St Ives Ceramics gallery** (✆ 01736 794930 ⌖ st-ives-ceramics.co.uk), set up by John Bedding, a former assistant to Leach.

It helps, but it's not essential, to be a fan of modern art in St Ives. The beaches are what bring the crowds flocking in. **Porthminster Beach**, just below the branch-line station, is a long, safe, clean sweep of sand with

THE KNILL LEGACY

It's hard to miss the odd, **pyramidal monument** on top of Worvas Hill, just south of St Ives. It was built in 1782 on the instructions of the mayor and customs inspector of St Ives, John Knill, who intended it to be his mausoleum. Even by Cornish standards, Knill was eccentric. In his will, he stipulated that he was to be remembered with a ceremony performed once every five years at the monument on the feast day of St James in July. In detail he described how the procession was to include ten little girls (daughters of sailors, fishermen or miners only, please) dressed in white, as well as two widows (in black) and a fiddler (colour of costume optional). They were to dance around the monument three times, then sing the Old 100th psalm, accompanied by the incumbent mayor, customs officer and vicar. Bizarrely, Knill insisted on attending the first of these ceremonies in 1811, a few months before his death. The tradition continues to this day; the next Knill ceremony is due to take place on 25 July 2026.

beach huts and a fine café-restaurant. **Porthmeor Beach**, in front of the Tate, is great for surfing, and the **Harbour Beach** is in the town centre, fronted by shops and cafés and backed by the solid granite harbour wall. Out of season, on a sunny morning, you may find you have it all to yourself; during the summer holidays it's chock-a-block with families and everyone with a take-away gravitates here for munching with a view.

At the end of the harbour, the **St Ives Museum** (Wheal Dream ⟨phone⟩ 01736 796005 ⊙ Apr–Oct Mon–Sat) makes a pleasant alternative to the crowded shops and streets just a short step away. The large building occupies the spot where stone was taken for filling in the granite walls of the harbour pier, designed by John Smeaton of Eddystone lighthouse fame in 1767, and has had a remarkable history – first constructed in the 18th century as a pilchard-curing cellar, it was then extended to become a chapel; in the 20th century it saw use as a laundry, cinema and hostel for shipwrecked sailors awaiting repatriation, with a dairy and pottery on the ground floor. The museum, which started in a small way when the Sailors' Mission closed in 1969, now fills both floors of the large building with an eclectic assortment of shipping, fishing, mining and farming memorabilia. Downstairs there are short films about local characters and life in St Ives; upstairs the volunteers are a cheerful bunch of gents who are happy to chat knowledgeably about the exhibits.

> "It helps, but it's not essential, to be a fan of modern art in St Ives. The beaches are what bring the crowds flocking in."

⟨icon⟩ FOOD & DRINK

Blas Burger Works The Warren, TR26 2EA ⟨phone⟩ 01736 797272 ⟨web⟩ blasburgerworks.co.uk ⊙ Wed–Sat eves only. With a reputation for fantastic food, including ethically sourced local meat and fish and veg from nearby allotments. (Locals are invited to contact them if they have a glut of 'yummy food'.) Small and cosy inside, but when full, takeaways are available – the beach is a short step away.

Porthminster Beach Café TR26 2EB ⟨phone⟩ 01736 795352 ⟨web⟩ porthminstercafe.co.uk. Much praise has been heaped upon this beachside café that grows its own salad greens on the slopes above the footpath from the branch-line station. Fresh, local and friendly – plus great views of sea, sky and beach.

Source Kitchen 6 The Digey, TR26 1HR ⟨phone⟩ 01736 799487 ⟨web⟩ sourcekitchen.co.uk. Rick Stein was impressed and so was I. Brunch, lunch, dinner and Sunday roasts with lovely vegetarian options have made the café a popular destination.

CROSSING THE PENINSULA: FROM ST IVES TO MARAZION

St Ives on the north coast and Marazion on the south coast are just six miles apart as the chough flies. The **St Michael's Way** – a fine cross-country walking route which traces an old pilgrim route to St Michael's Mount – manages to double the distance, starting in Lelant and following the glorious beaches on the western shores of the Hayle estuary northwards to St Ives, before turning south towards Trencrom Hill, from the summit of which the craggy form of St Michael's Mount can be seen, raising its glorious profile against the sparkling sea.

18 LELANT

Overlooking the salt marshes and mudflats of the Hayle estuary, Lelant is a favourite spot for birdwatchers, especially in the winter months when migrant wildfowl home in on the wide and tidal shoreline. There's no footpath between the railway and the water south of the village, so most serious twitchers head for the large car park at the Lelant Saltings station or go down to the hide at Ryan's Field, close to the A30. Walkers will find the start of the St Michael's Way at St Uny's Church and within five minutes the soft sandy path gives way to the fast-flowing River Hayle and the wide open expanse of Porthkidney Sands. The novelist Rosamunde Pilcher was born in the village, which makes it a place of pilgrimage for her enormous German following. Most of her novels, set in Penwith, have been televised in Germany where, by all accounts, they are prime Sunday evening viewing, which explains the obsession.

19 MARAZION

🏠 **Ednovean Farm** (page 421)

The pretty fishing village gets choked with visitors during the summer months, and the grassy seafront on the approach from Penzance is littered with expensive car parks. The bus is a better option, or if the tide's not too far in, it's a pleasant walk along the sandy beach from the car park at Long Rock (on the beach side of the railway line) a mile away. If you can coincide your visit to within an hour or so of low tide,

◀ **1** Porthkidney Sands. **2** *Skyspace*, Tremenheere Sculpture Gardens. **3** The Square, Marazion. **4** St Uny's Church, Lelant.

MARAZION MARSH

A very attractive section of the St Michael's Way passes through this RSPB reserve which occupies Cornwall's largest reedbed, noisy in spring with the songs of several different species of warbler. In autumn, two unusual migrants – the spotted crake and aquatic warbler – are regular visitors to the reedy marshes and bitterns have become regular winter visitors, although patience is required to see them.

the causeway to the Mount is exposed, but there are plenty of cafés, gift shops and galleries in Marazion to while away the wait.

A particularly interesting collection at the **Summerhouse Gallery** (✆ 01736 711400 ⌂ summerhousegallery.co.uk ⊙ closed Mon) exhibits the work of local artists. There is always something on display by Michael Praed, who paints not only the surrounding seascape, but the mines of the north Penwith coast. An extraordinary book he hand-wrote and illustrated as a young man in the 1960s was donated to the Penlee House museum (page 340) in Penzance: it documents his journey through the mining landscape, with pencil annotations by the miners he met on his fascinating journey.

St Michael's Mount

Marazion TR17 0EF ✆ 01736 710507 ⌂ stmichaelsmount.co.uk ⊙ castle Apr–Oct; gardens summer only

The entire essence of Cornwall appears to have been distilled into this immoderately picturesque icon of Cornish myth and history, a quarter of a mile from the mainland. Saints and tinners, soldiers and fishermen, Royalists and Parliamentarians, artists, gardeners and architects have all left their mark on the island, but it's far from pickled in its past. A community of about 30 islanders live in the houses and cottages clustered around the harbour and the castle is home to James and Mary St Aubyn, who have been in full-time residence since James's uncle, the late Lord St Levan, retired to the mainland in 2003. When the cobbled granite causeway is exposed at low tide, it's just a five-minute walk to the island from Marazion and a chalked notice informs you of the time by which you must leave in order to avoid being cut off by the tide. A boat service runs when the causeway is under water.

The Mount is distinctly busy in the high season. Nevertheless, there are grassy slopes for picnicking and the views from the castle battlements over the terraced gardens – cleverly planted to look good from an aerial perspective – and the wide blue expanse of Mount's Bay are astonishing, and there's much to see inside the castle too. Parts of the Benedictine monastery that was built here in the 12th century have been incorporated into the castle; the monks' refectory, now known as the Chevy Chase room, has a remarkable 15th-century ceiling and plaster frieze depicting hunting scenes and the Lady Chapel was converted into a drawing room during the 18th century. Much of the Victorian building work was designed by J P St Aubyn, the architect responsible for so much heavy-handed church restoration, though at home he seems to have had a lighter touch. And there's a model made of the Mount and castle, sculpted from hundreds of champagne corks by a butler who clearly had far too much time on his hands in his retirement.

It's hard not to find yourself wondering what it would be like to live here as part of the community in one of the cottages. I saw children's bikes and wellies and the amphibious boat trundling down the shore on 'the mum's run' to the local mainland primary school. What an idyllic existence, perhaps. 'It's not for everyone,' said the boatman on the way back. 'When the black flag is run up the flagpole, that means the weather's too bad for the boats and we're cut off then. Not everyone can endure that for very long.' I also heard how the island continues to release its hidden secrets every now and then. In July 2009, for example, Darren Little, an amateur archaeologist – and current head gardener – who lives on the island, was cutting back some long grass when he put his hand under a hedge and pulled out a smallish lump of metal. Another person might have tossed it aside, but Darren's curiosity was aroused. It turned out to be just the first piece in a hoard of 47 items – ranging from buckles to axe heads – thought to be a smith's 'scrap heap', dating from the late Bronze Age (1500–800BC). Having been authenticated by the British Museum, the find is now on display in the castle.

"The entire essence of Cornwall appears to have been distilled into this immoderately picturesque icon."

The Greek geographer Pytheas toured the south coast of Britain early in the 4th century BC and described an island called Ictis, accessible from the mainland at low tide. Wagonloads of tin, he wrote, were brought to the island, where lively commerce with Mediterranean traders had resulted in a 'civilised manner of life'. It's a pity that Pytheas (or Diodorus who more or less copied Pytheas's lost account 300 years later) doesn't mention the great forest that is thought to lie submerged beneath Mount's Bay and would have provided fuel for the smelting houses on the coast from the Bronze Age until the Dark Ages, when the seabed must have sunk dramatically for the story to be believed. But the old name for the island in Cornish is Carrek Luz en Cuz, 'the rock in the wood' and I'm sure I'm not the only person who has peered into the water from the side of a dinghy, hoping for a glimpse of a tree stump, far below.

James and Mary St Aubyn showed me the gardens, begun in the 18th century and added to over the centuries by previous generations of St Aubyns including four sisters who created three terraces of narrow walled gardens under the south face of the rock, whose pink brick walls give shelter to a colourful and tenderly exotic range of plants, a respite from the brutal granite and spiky succulents that bake on the exposed rock outside. 'The rock acts as a kind of giant night-storage heater,' explains Alan Cook, former head gardener. 'People ask how we can get away with planting such tender things in such an exposed place, but the rock creates its own microclimate.'

Some years ago, a vast chunk of rock, perched above the terraced gardens on the south side of the island, split away from the mother rock and fell at the feet of a couple of astonished German visitors. Months were spent assessing how to prevent further damage; the solution has been a series of long steel pins, bolted and cemented into the rock at its most vulnerable points like wall-ties – you can see them if you look up from the eastern terraces, but it's more likely that your gaze will be seized by the jewel-like succulents at your feet, that look like a coral reef when seen from the battlements.

The St Michael's Way

I think most people make up their own version of the route, using the OS Explorer map 102, as the published guide appears to be out of print and there are all sorts of route-shortening options. My own version is to start at the train station in **Carbis Bay**, and aim for **Trencrom Hill** via any one of the footpaths on the far side of the A3074, which soon link up with a scallop-shell waymarker, indicating you are on the

1 St Michael's Mount. 2 Marazion Marsh. ▶

St Michael's Way. Just west of Ludgvan, Tremenheere, an impressive sculpture garden with a terrific café (see below), lies right next to the footpath.

In **Ludgvan**, the White Hart is just the kind of village pub that a thirsty or hungry walker likes to see, and – if new tenants for this delightful old pub can be found – a good place to decide which route to take next. The options are to head southeast across the RSPB reserve at Marazion Marsh to **St Michael's Mount** (there are buses back to Carbis Bay from Marazion) or to head southwest, across farmland to Penzance (where either train or bus will take you back). Penzance to Marazion is a three-mile walk along the wide and sandy beach.

Tremenheere Sculpture Gardens
TR20 8YL ✆ 01736 448089 ⊘ tremenheere.co.uk

Since Tremenheere first opened its gates to the public in 2012, the compelling reasons to visit have multiplied: plantaholics will swoon over the maturing collection of rare, subtropical plants spread over south-facing slopes or the stream-fed valley woodland, threaded with wooden walkways and bridges, beside which a staggering collection of rhododendrons, azaleas and other plants native to Himalayan and Chinese slopes may be viewed at close quarters. Neil Armstrong, a Penzance GP, is the owner and creator of this remarkable place and is a passionate collector of contemporary sculpture, too; the number of sensitively placed pieces by internationally renowned artists continues to grow. A *Skyspace* at the summit of the garden, the work of Slow artist James Turrell, has a temple-like quality and is quietly awe-inspiring. Camera obscuras above and below ground also encourage visitors to slow down and take in the garden and landscape from unexpected angles.

"Plantaholics will swoon over the maturing collection of rare, subtropical plants spread over south-facing slopes."

More recent additions to the garden's wonders are a Restless Temple, a classical temple that shivers and floats in the breeze, and a stunning timber-built art gallery. Each time I visit, Armstrong has been busy, extending the garden, adding more rare trees and exotica, creating a new vantage point from which to observe the extraordinary landscape or adding a new piece of sculpture. The café at the entrance is a destination in itself, and a very popular lunch spot for locals (see opposite).

¶¶ FOOD & DRINK

Godolphin Arms West End, Marazion TR17 0EN ✆ 01736 888510 ⌂ godolphinarms. co.uk. Soak up the views of the Mount from the terrace or the blonde-wood Scandi-style restaurant, which boasts an impressive list of local suppliers.

Peppercorn Kitchen Lynfield Yard, Perranuthnoe TR20 9NE ✆ 01736 719584 ⌂ thepeppercorncafe.co.uk ⊙ closed Mon & Tues. A couple of miles east of Marazion, on the lane down to the beach beside the Cowhouse Gallery, this popular café offers a nice range of hot and cold snacks and lunches.

Tremenheere Kitchen Tremenheere Sculpture Gardens, TR20 8YL ⌂ tremenheerekitchen. com. A fabulous addition to the local lunchtime scene and deservedly popular. Everything on the menu is fresh, local and delicious. Wood-fired pizza and occasional fine-dining and film evenings are a huge success, too.

Victoria Inn Perranuthnoe TR20 9NP ✆ 01736 710309 ⌂ victoriainn-penzance.co.uk. Eye-catchingly pink and reputedly one of Cornwall's oldest pubs, the Victoria is one of the top eating places in west Cornwall, and has acquired shedloads of accolades and awards in the past few years. It's more of a restaurant with a bar than a pub, but the local ales are well kept and include Sharp's Doom Bar and Skinner's Heligan Honey.

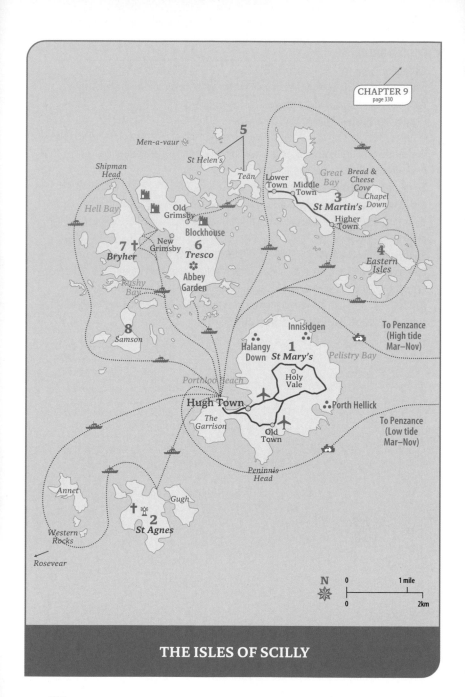

CHAPTER 9
page 330

Men-a-vaur

Shipman
Head

St Helen's

5

Teän

Lower
Town

Middle
Town

Great Bay

Bread &
Cheese
Cove

Hell Bay

Old
Grimsby

Blockhouse

New
Grimsby

6
Tresco

Abbey
Garden

3
St Martin's

Higher
Town

Chapel
Down

7 ✝
Bryher

*Rushy
Bay*

4
*Eastern
Isles*

8
Samson

Innisidgen

1
St Mary's

Halangy
Down

Holy
Vale

Pelistry Bay

To Penzance
(High tide
Mar–Nov)

Porthloo Beach

Hugh Town

The
Garrison

Old
Town

Porth Hellick

To Penzance
(Low tide
Mar–Nov)

*Peninnis
Head*

Annet

Gugh

✝ ☀
2
St Agnes

Western
Rocks

Rosevear

N
✳

0   1 mile
0   2km

THE ISLES OF SCILLY

10
THE ISLES
OF SCILLY

In many ways, life on the Isles of Scilly is an unselfconscious example of what the Slow concept is all about. Local culture and tradition, landscape, seascape, history and natural history are given affectionate respect here; people take time to enjoy what makes their islands so special. Traffic jams, chain stores and fast-food outlets belong to another world; everyone seems to have time to pause for a chat, leaning on the garden gate or over the shop counter. Children are able to roam and explore freely and safely, while wrinklier visitors remark that 'this is what Cornwall used to be like, 60 years ago'. And everywhere you go, you sense an enviably easy and relaxed sense of community among the 2,000 residents and a willingness to share their good-natured, ratracelessness with visitors, too.

Nevertheless, on a recent visit, I felt Scilly was going through a transitional phase, perhaps brought about by declining numbers of both residents and visitors of the Harold and Mary Wilson generation and a more 21st-century approach to what the islands have to offer: watersports – including the ultimate ÖTILLÖ challenge in inter-island sea swimming and running; coasteering; snorkelling with seals; paddleboarding – and yoga on pristine white beaches. ('Why go all the way to Sri Lanka, when it's all here?' I heard one woman say.) There's also been a perceptible upgrade in accommodation at all levels, combined with a new generation of cafés and restaurants that make simple and imaginative use of the highest-quality local ingredients. The entrancing landscape, however, has not changed. Five inhabited islands, 51 uninhabited islands and dozens of jagged rocks and deadly reefs make up the Scilly archipelago, 28 miles southwest of Land's End. But what you see are merely the hilltops of a submerged landmass, lost to an encroaching sea around a thousand years ago. Ancient field boundaries and Bronze Age settlements lie beneath the translucent waters that separate Bryher, Samson, Tresco, St Martin's and St Mary's (a deep channel has always set St Agnes apart) and, for a brief period during the extreme low tides of the spring equinox, it's possible to paddle between Bryher and Tresco. The islands are startlingly beautiful, with beaches that have an almost tropical quality – a turquoise sea, crystal clear and cool as jade, washes into shallow bays of sparkling white sand; spiky, succulent, showy subtropical plants flourish casually in gardens and waysides. And yet, on shores where the Atlantic crashes into the archipelago, the rock-strewn seascape is more Hebridean than Caribbean. Evidence of human occupation is not overwhelming – there are no big hotels or holiday villages – houses and cottages appear randomly among the lush vegetation or cluster around the curve of a harbour. Above the shoreline, chains of drystone walls coated in hairy lichen form a jigsaw of tiny fields, scattered across the sheltered, leeward slopes. Many, since the near-collapse of flower and potato farming, are abandoned to drifts of wild flowers, though some are still lined with sweet-scented narcissi or vegetables; elsewhere you might chance upon a couple of cows or a goat. On higher, exposed ground, it's all granite and gorse and cushions of heather and ling. Permissive footpaths thread across and around the islands – and while it's not difficult to get momentarily disorientated, it's impossible to get seriously lost. Walking on Scilly is quite unlike walking on the mainland: maps aren't really needed and in any case (with Tresco being a notable exception), waymarked routes and signs bearing place names don't exist. The fun lies in exploring, rather than notching up miles of path, in discovering the distinctive character of each island and in enjoying the pauses for the heart-stopping views across the misty recesses of the archipelago. That said, there are some fascinating guided walks to be done with local experts, details to be found chalked up on the TIC and Town Hall noticeboards.

"A turquoise sea, crystal clear and cool as jade, washes into shallow bays of sparkling white sand."

St Mary's, the largest of the inhabited islands, is the hub for all these adventures: flights from the mainland arrive here and the ferry from Penzance ties up at Town Quay, next to the busy inter-island boats. It's the only island with anything resembling a town, and most of the residential and holiday accommodation is to be found here. There's also a variety of holiday accommodation to be found on the

Off Islands – as the four other inhabited islands are known – each containing a loosely linked hamlet or two, where populations dwindle to a weather-beaten core in the winter. The uninhabited islands, many little more than a fist or spike of granite rising above the water, others with beaches and relics of past human occupation, are home to countless breeding populations of seabirds and seals. Each of the five inhabited islands has its own very distinct character, and it's funny how so many visitors end up with a partisan feeling for one island in particular. 'It was always St Martin's for me,' says the island's baker; 'the people, the beaches, the

"Each of the five inhabited islands has its own very distinct character, and many visitors end up with a partisan feeling for one."

starry night skies.' An elderly passenger on the ferry sighed, 'Bryher. For the solitude and the birds. I have to go every year, even if just for a day.' His wife chips in, 'St Mary's isn't appreciated enough outside Hugh Town: I love walking Up Country through the nature reserves to Pelistry Bay.' A giggling six-year-old says, 'I love camping at Troytown Farm [on St Agnes] because it's next to the beach and there are cows and ice cream.' And, 'We're third generation Tresco,' I overheard one woman say with pride – she was a holiday visitor, not a resident.

GETTING THERE

It's a bit of an adventure getting to Scilly, whatever the means of travel. By ferry there's always the chance of seeing dolphins and the slow revelation of the Cornish coast from Penzance to Land's End and arrival in the sheltering embrace of St Mary's harbour are unforgettable. From the air, the islands appear as scattered fragments of a stained-glass window: sapphire blue and pale jade sea surrounding cut-out pieces of land that are green and gold with daffodils and Bermuda buttercups in spring or russet red with dying bracken in autumn.

The **Isles of Scilly Steamship Company** (Isles of Scilly Travel Centre, Quay St, Penzance ✆ 01736 334220 ⌀ islesofscilly-travel. co.uk), which has run the vital ferry service from Penzance to St Mary's since 1926, also operates flights from Land's End and Newquay airports (and Exeter too, between March and October). The *Scillonian III* passenger ferry is your cheapest option and best for those travelling with dogs, children or camping gear (luggage space is very limited on the small aircraft). The crossing lasts just under three hours and departures are timed to give you a good four hours on St Mary's in the afternoon if you're only planning a day trip. Combined sea and air tickets are also an option.

During the winter months, when the passenger ferry is out of service for maintenance, the company's freight vessel, *Gry Maritha* (dubbed locally *The Grim Reaper* on account of her flat-bottomed and therefore stomach-churningly slow and rolling performance), takes the occasional and, it must be said, somewhat desperate passenger, but all but the hardiest take to the sky routes in winter. The fleet of small aircraft (an Islander plane is so small that if you lean forward your chin is on the pilot's shoulder) scoot above the waves at just 1,000 feet for the 20-minute flight, and there's a log burner for chilly days in the waiting room at Land's End airport. A superb helicopter service, taking less than 20 minutes, also flies between the new Penzance heliport (on Eastern Green, very close to the old one that closed in 2012) and either St Mary's or Tresco. For further details consult ⊘ penzancehelicopters.co.uk. Note that there are no flights or ferry services on a Sunday.

GETTING AROUND

For visitors, there is no option but to leave the car behind on the mainland: island taxis, golf buggies or tractors are there to transport new arrivals and/or their baggage to campsites or hotels if needed, but thereafter getting around the islands on foot, or perhaps bike – and between them by boat – is what it's all about.

INTER-ISLAND BOATS
⊘ scillyboating.co.uk & ⊘ visitislesofscilly.com/travel
Weather and tides permitting, there are boat trips from St Mary's to the Off Islands every day. The Off Islands run their own **daily ferry services** too, and there's also a fast water-taxi, taking up to 12 passengers.

TOURIST INFORMATION

Hugh Town (St Mary's) Porthcressa Beach, TR21 0LW ⊘ 01720 620600 ⊘ visitislesofscilly. com. Award-winning visitor centre, staffed by lovely volunteers.

WALK SCILLY

Scilly businessman Euan Rodger came up with the idea of organising a walking festival (⊘ visitislesofscilly.com/walkscilly) to kick start the pre-Easter holiday season. A relatively small affair when it started in 2006, the festival, held in April, offers a range of guided walks across the five inhabited islands as well as Samson, Teän and other uninhabited islands. Local guides are joined by specialists from the mainland and evening events add to the fun. The walks – graded easy, moderate and hard – are designed to celebrate the islands' cultural heritage and wildlife and include coastline foraging and rockpooling, star-gazing, farm visits and beachcombing.

Those who like to plan these trips ahead can do so at the ticket kiosk on the quay or the tourist information centre in Hugh Town. If you prefer a more serendipitous approach, the answer is to wander down to the quay, consult the chalked-up departure list, hop aboard and pay en route. If one boat is full, another is laid on, so there's never any stress about getting tickets in advance.

Often the boatmen will add an optional seal- and bird-spotting trip around a group of uninhabited islands to one of the regular routes.

CYCLING

Bikes are a great way to get around on **Tresco**, and useful if you are staying 'Up Country' on St Mary's and see yourself wanting to cycle in and out of Hugh Town each day. But with only nine miles of tarmac road on the islands, and all the interesting, sandy paths technically reserved for those on foot, you might regret the cost of taking your own bike on the *Scillonian III* ferry, and choose to hire a bike for a morning or day instead.

 CYCLE HIRE

St Mary's Bike Hire The Strand (opposite Holgates Green), Hugh Town, St Mary's TR21 0PS ⊘ 07552 994709 ⊘ stmarysbikehire.co.uk. Cross-country and hybrid bikes, tandems and tag-alongs available for a half or whole day, three days or a week. Electric bikes are available, too.
Tresco Bike Hire New Grimsby (next to Tresco Stores), Tresco TR24 0QQ ⊘ 01720 422849 ⊘ tresco.co.uk/arriving/pre-arrival/bicycle-hire. Adult and children's bikes, as well as e-bikes, all-terrain pushchairs and wheelchairs available for hire by the day or for longer periods.

Chilli Jam
made from
Scilly grown
Chillies
£2.50
Per Jar

SCILLONIAN III

SEA KAYAKING & WATERSPORTS

The first thing that hits you is the silence; getting around the islands by motor launch is practical and fun, but nothing beats the quiet enjoyment of moving silently through the water, and this is the way to get up close to nesting seabirds and sunbathing seals. Very calm seas and some previous paddling experience are necessary before you can venture out to the uninhabited rocks and islands, but even novices can enjoy pottering in shallow waters off the inward-facing beaches of the archipelago on stable, sit-on-top kayaks offered by the hire companies listed below.

 SEA KAYAK HIRE

Hut 62 Green Bay, Bryher TR23 0PR ✎ 07979 393206 ⚲ hut62.co.uk. Kayaks and other small water craft and sailing boats are available to hire by the day or half day. Paddling is restricted to the safe waters between Bryher, Tresco and St Martin's. Deliveries and pick-ups can also be organised from St Martin's (they have a base by the campsite) or Tresco. Novices are given friendly help and a safety boat patrols the waters.

Sailing Centre, Isles of Scilly Porthmellon Beach, St Mary's TR21 0NE & Raven's Porth Sailing Base, Old Grimsby, Tresco TR24 0PU ✎ 01720 422060 ⚲ sailingscilly.com. Kayak hire and tours, and lots of other watersport options, too.

St Agnes Watersports St Agnes, next to Troytown Farm (page 422), St Agnes TR22 0PL ✎ 01720 423207 ⚲ agneswatersports.co.uk. Kayaks and paddleboards, masks and snorkels for hire in the lovely sheltered and shallow waters off the western shore of St Agnes.

A TASTE OF THE ISLES OF SCILLY

You have superb opportunities on all the islands to eat fish and shellfish caught in Scilly's clear and unpolluted waters, with potatoes, asparagus or salads pulled from the sandy, seaweed-enriched soil just minutes before they arrive at the table. On all the islands you find garden or farm gate stalls, accompanied by an honesty box, selling eggs, honey, vegetables and fruit as the seasons dictate. There's plenty of wild food, too, if you know what you're looking for: you might see chefs foraging

◀ **1** The Isles of Scilly, offering ample opportunity for watersports. **2** Locally grown and made produce is in abundance on the islands. **3** The *Scillonian III* passenger ferry transporting people between the mainland and the islands.

for salty samphire, leafy Alexanders, or wild garlic and three-cornered leeks to go with a freshly caught crab or lobster. And that's not all: Veronica Farm fudge from Bryher and ice cream from the Troytown dairy herd on St Agnes are second to none – and the bakery on St Martin's continues to offer a fine range of artisan breads, thanks to its devoted baker, Barney McLachlan.

The near-collapse of flower growing on Scilly at the end of the 20th century led to a lot of abandoned small fields, but thankfully, a number of small **organic growers**, such as Jonathan Smith on St Martin's and Paul Whittaker on St Mary's have taken up the challenge to supply the islands with fresh greens (including some of the most delicious asparagus you will ever taste). There's a farmers' market in Hugh Town on the first Thursday of every month as well as a weekly local produce market on the green opposite the town hall every Wednesday morning, and a tempting Cornish deli in Hugh Street ($\mathscr{D}$ 01720 422734 $\mathring{\partial}$ hughstreetcafe.co.uk) in the town centre. Tresco's small supermarket (waggishly known as Trescos) is well stocked with Cornish produce and decent home-baked bread. Hugh Town has a Co-op supermarket (watch the milk and bread fly off the shelves when bad weather is forecast!) and the smaller islands make do with a post office-cum-shop that sells an increasingly upmarket range of products (Pukka teas and highest-quality local gin, distilled at Westward Farm on St Agnes) as well as those indispensable stalwarts of any camping expedition: tinned mushroom soup and Kit Kats.

Almost everything you need to know can be found in the latest (free) edition of *The Ultimate Food Guide,* available from the tourist office and lots of local outlets. Updates and details of the ten-day-long **Taste of Scilly Festival**, held in September with events on all the inhabited islands, are to be found at $\mathring{\partial}$ visitislesofscilly.com/tasteofscilly.

1 ST MARY'S

♠ **The Atlantic** (page 422), **Longstone Lodge** (page 422)
Å **The Garrison Campsite** (page 422), 🏠 **95 Watermill** (page 422)

Each morning there's what passes for a rush hour in **Hugh Town** as newspapers that have come in on the early flights are delivered to the shops, children hare off to school on bikes, dogs are walked and everyone stops whatever it is they're doing to discuss the weather. An hour or so later, there's a second rush hour as visitors emerge from the hotels and guesthouses and descend on the harbour to consult the boards and decide which of the Off Islands to explore that day. Later, towards the end of the afternoon, the ferries return, disgorge their passengers and the streets fill up with people making plans for the evening. In the summer this might mean a moonlit boat ride to another island for dinner, fish and chips on the beach, folk music in one of the pubs or taking in one of the frequent evening talks, given by local experts on Scillonian history or wildlife.

Tempting though it is to hop on an inter-island boat, there's lots to be said for spending a Slow day on St Mary's, pottering, chatting, walking or just soaking up the views. You might start by wandering through the **Garrison gate** (turn left in front of the chemist's in Hugh Town) and climb the steep hill to enjoy the views from the **Star Castle** – now a rather splendid hotel – built in 1595 within moated fortifications constructed in the shape of an eight-pointed star. From this wonderful vantage point you can look north across the wide blue waters to the twin peaks of barren Samson,

"Tempting though it is to hop on an inter-island boat, there's lots to be said for spending a Slow day on St Mary's."

the tree-fringed shores of Tresco and the white beaches of St Martin's. On Wednesday and Friday evenings in summer, you'll see the island gig crews at the oars, cheered on from a flotilla of small boats. Turn southwest and there's St Agnes, rising quietly to one side of the main archipelago and further still, beyond the seabird sanctuary of Annet and the Western Rocks, the lonely column of the Bishop Rock lighthouse.

A mile of level footpath runs around the coastline of the Garrison promontory, passing historic fortifications and cannon positions representing centuries of hostilities with the French, Dutch and Spanish. Circumnavigating the Garrison is an easy stroll, and on warm summer evenings it's almost a ritual pre-dinner promenade. On a winter's afternoon, in sharp slanting light, and with only seabirds for company, there's a different feeling altogether.

The **Isles of Scilly Museum** was forced to close in 2019, due to structural problems, and the collections have been farmed out to various pop-up exhibition spaces on all the inhabited islands. The more prestigious items, such as the Bronze Age Bryher Sword and Nornour brooches, can be found in the Town Hall on St Mary's, along with the museum shop and its helpful volunteer staff.

There are a number of art and craft galleries in Hugh Town, but it would be easy to miss the **Phoenix Craft workshops**, just beyond St Mary's Church, on the Porthmellon Industrial Estate. Here you'll see the work of artist Oriel Hicks (✎ 01720 422900 ⊘ phoenixstainedglass. co.uk), who has produced new stained-glass windows for all the islands' churches. They are immediately recognisable, letting in more light than their Victorian or Edwardian counterparts, and filled with the colours, birds and plants of the Scillonian landscape – and some well-known Scillonian faces, too (page 399).

Less than a mile away, on the far side of the hill dominated by the solid grey cylinder of **Buzza Tower** (originally built as a windmill, but now used as a landmark by boatmen entering the harbour from Tresco), is the former 'capital' of St Mary's, **Old Town**. The deep, snug bay still has the ragged remains of its granite harbour wall, a cluster of houses and, standing alone on the western shore of the bay, a little granite church, surrounded by a steeply tiered churchyard and elm trees. There was once a Norman castle on the slopes overlooking the harbour, but the whole town simply shifted its emphasis to the Hugh Town side of the hill, when the principal defences against the threat of invasion by the Spanish and French – the Star Castle and the Garrison ramparts – were built on the westernmost promontory of the island in the 16th century.

UP COUNTRY

Walk away from Hugh Town or Old Town, and within a few minutes you're in another world (referred to locally as 'Up Country'), where rural life goes on unperturbed by the busy comings and goings of the harbour or the grassy airport and helipad on the hill above Old Town. In fact, there are moments in the centre of the island where you lose sight and sound of the sea altogether. **Holy Vale**, a hamlet buried deep in a stream-fed valley, is picturesquely unspoilt, but it's the avenues and woods of mature elm (Dutch elm disease bypassed the islands) and the sight of thrushes, hopping tamely about the undergrowth, or an old red tractor in a sea of white-flowered three-cornered leeks that really make you feel the clock has been turned back 60 years. In the small but fragrant daffodil fields, the flowers are picked and bunched by farmers and their

◀ **1** St Mary's harbour. **2** Hugh Town, St Mary's. **3** Halangy Down. **4** Exotic puyas and palms at Carreg Dhu gardens.

THE WAR WITH THE NETHERLANDS

From 1649 to 1651 the Royalist Governor of Scilly, John Grenville, directed a fleet of privateers in a series of plundering attacks on Dutch (and English) merchant ships in order to raise money for Charles II and his exiled court in Scotland. Not surprisingly, the Dutch were a little annoyed. With 13 ships to back him up, the Dutch Admiral Maarten Harpertszoon Tromp landed on the islands demanding the release of all Dutch ships, crews and cargoes. Grenville, who was only 23 at the time, handed over the prisoners, but admitted (with what was perceived as youthful arrogance) that the ships and their cargoes had already been sold. An infuriated Tromp declared war on Scilly, but diplomatically left the fighting to the Roundhead army, which was already assembled on ships close to the islands. After fighting on Tresco and retreat to the Garrison on St Mary's, where he was besieged, Grenville and his men were forced to surrender (the terms were extraordinarily generous), but nobody remembered to sign a peace treaty with the Netherlands.

Until 1986 that is – when the chairman of the Isles of Scilly Council, Roy Duncan, decided enough was enough and wrote to the Dutch Embassy, asking for the continuing state of war to be brought to an end. Ambassador Huydecoper, recognising the gravity of the situation, leaped into action and on 17 April 1986 presented the islanders with a scroll, declaring an end to the hostilities. 'It must have been awful to know we could have attacked you at any moment,' he told the assembled Scillonians.

families, who pause to chat and straighten their backs. A vineyard and winery (see opposite) sit happily among the more traditional crops and a secret footpath leads you through woodland to the friendly café at Longstone Lodge. This café is just a short step from **Carreg Dhu**: an acre or two of exotic-looking shrubs and trees, semi-tender succulents and perennials, a thicket of towering camellias, broad grassy paths and a scattering of benches. It's open all year, and by the box for donations there's a list of jobs that need doing and a canvas bag of hand tools, for anyone to use who feels like a spot of weeding or dead-heading.

HISTORIC & PREHISTORIC SITES

You could also spend a day exploring the relics of Bronze Age settlements and burial chambers that lie dotted about the island. Information and maps are in the TIC, the museum space in the Town Hall, and the local newsagent and bookshop, but this being Scilly, it's just as easy to wander along the coastal paths (most Bronze Age sites are close to the sea) and stumble across the old stones at **Halangy Down** and **Innisidgen** along the way. One of the most impressive chambered barrows is close to **Porth Hellick** (there are signposts from the hamlet called Normandy), the wild and rock-strewn bay where **Sir Cloudesley Shovell**, Admiral of the Fleet, was washed ashore, either dead or dying in 1707; four ships in his fleet were wrecked on rocks off St Agnes and nearly 2,000 sailors also perished as a result of a miscalculation in navigation. A rough stone marks the spot where his body was found. Locals seem to enjoy the story that an arrogant Shovell disregarded the warning of a Scillonian sailor and hanged the man for his troubles. Perhaps local ill-feeling towards Shovell persists, making the storytellers happy to recount the equally unsubstantiated tale of the old lady who confessed on her deathbed that she had found the admiral still alive on the beach, stolen his ring and bopped him on the head. It spoils the story, perhaps, to remember that Shovell was as brave and talented a sailor as Nelson, and worked his way up from humble cabin boy to Admiral of the Fleet on merit alone.

🍴 FOOD & DRINK

Ales of Scilly Opposite Porthmellon Beach, St Mary's TR21 0JY ✆ 01720 423233 ⬧ alesofscilly.co.uk. Local beers are brewed here. Jennie Trevithick produces various strengths of ale, including the appropriately named Scuppered at 4.8%, which you'll see is the pint of choice for locals. Other brews are named after local shipwrecks. Jennie offers tastings, tours and tapas evenings for groups of two to ten.

Holy Vale Winery Holy Vale TR21 0NT ✆ 01720 422333 ☉ Mar–Oct Mon–Fri, by appt only Sat & Sun. In 2009, Robert Francis, owner of the Star Castle Hotel, planted 7,000 vines on the sunny slopes of this sheltered valley. The vagaries of the climate mean that supplies will always be limited but, as well as making his own wine, Robert keeps a fabulous international cellar and offers tastings in the winery. Lobster lunches (Robert's other passion is catching lobsters) are also held here. Booking is essential for both wine tastings and lunches.

Juliet's Garden Seaways Flower Farm, TR21 0NF ✆ 01720 422228 ⬧ julietsgardenrestaurant.co.uk. Everybody I've spoken to recommends this lovely spot, overlooking Porthloo Beach, about 20 minutes' walk from Hugh Town. You can go just for a coffee or cream tea or eat fish caught in the morning. If the restaurant is closed at lunchtime, it's because fishing is still in progress. Opening times vary; ring ahead to confirm.

Longstone Café TR21 0NW ✆ 01720 422410 ⬧ longstonecafe.co.uk ☉ Apr–Oct; closed Sun Apr–mid-May. Bang in the middle of the island, this café (and a very superior adjoining hostel; page 422) run by Amy Hiron and her family has been a runaway success. It's a great pit stop for coffee and homemade cake, and lunches often include crab, lobster or mackerel caught by Amy's husband.

On The Quay Hugh Town harbour, TR21 0HU ✆ 01720 423525 ◈ onthequay.com ☉ Apr–
Nov; closed Sun. Older Scillonians can remember going to tea dances in this fine old building,
located on the harbour quay. Phil and Sheryl Moon have brought the old place back to life
with great panache and given St Mary's a very fine restaurant, with a modishly open kitchen,
friendly bar and wonderful sheltered balcony for al fresco dining. The imaginative menu
makes the best of Scillonian produce and is beautifully presented. Downstairs, the **On the
Quay Café**, also run by Phil and Sheryl, is well placed for a last-minute coffee, ice cream or
grab-and-go picnic before hopping on an inter-island boat.

Tanglewood Kitchen Company The Post Office, Hugh St, TR21 0LR ✆ 01720 422454
◈ tanglewoodkitchen.co.uk ⬛. This is something different: housed in the old parcel office
at the back of the island's post office (there are interesting relics of the building's past on the
walls and under the glass-topped central table), you will find shelves crammed with lovely
deli items for sale. Euan and Lindsay Rodger also cook up a tempting range of ready meals
and dishes to take away, ranging from lobster salad to lamb tagine and some very naughty
puddings. They offer outside catering, too.

THE OFF ISLANDS

Each of the four inhabited Off Islands lie within a 20-minute boat
journey from St Mary's and ferry times are arranged so that you can
spend the best part of the day on an island; in summer, later boats allow
for an evening meal. Four or five hours is long enough to get a feel for the
character of each island, stretch your legs and find a deserted beach for a
picnic, a swim – or enjoy a pub lunch. It's only when you've visited them
all that you can be absolutely sure which one has claimed your heart.

2 ST AGNES

🏠 **Troytown Farm** (page 422)

Lying to the southwest of St Mary's, from which it is separated by deep
water, St Agnes feels cut off and remote from the other inhabited islands
which appear to face each other in a friendly kind of circle. But those who
love St Agnes and live there value it for this very isolation, the continuity
of its native families who fish and farm and the rare sculptural beauty
of its granite-stacked shores and moorland. 'It's how Scilly used to be,'
you'll hear. 'Not much changes on St Agnes.'

Arriving in the little harbour below the Turks Head, the island's only
pub, you can see the sandbar which connects the island at low tide to the
Gugh, a gorse-smothered crest of rock where Bronze Age burial mounds

are still discernible and a lonely standing stone, set aslant like the gnomon of a sundial, points towards the west. The only two houses on Gugh face the sandbar, their oddly curving roofs designed to withstand the winter gales. The rest of St Agnes's houses lie clustered close to or around the lighthouse (disused since the light was lit on Bishop's Rock) and much-loved church, less than half a mile from the harbour. Oriel Hicks, whose workshops on St Mary's can be visited (page 395), made the poignantly eloquent windows in this church, which depict two pilot gigs hastening towards a foundered ship. The faces of the rowers are portraits of much-loved Scillonians, not all of whom are alive today. The odd golf buggy or tractor shuttles up and down the tiny lane ferrying bags and camping gear; pursue the lane to the end and you arrive at the western end of the island, where Troytown Farm (page 422) has a miniature campsite just a drystone wall away from the beach.

Turn left, following the coast south from Troytown. Here, the pretty white beaches, piled with smooth round rocks and pebbles of the western shores, give way to spectacular coves and jutting cliffs of stacked granite. **St Warna** (the patron saint of shipwrecks) gives her name to the most dramatic of these and to a holy well close by. A sevenfold labyrinth laid out in stones on the turf by a lighthouse-keeper has been here since 1729, though it's possible he was retracing the lines of a much older pattern. The southern side of the island is all wild moor and the happily named **Wingletang Down** appears to resemble nothing so much as a giant's primitive sculpture garden; the level, heathery landscape is dotted with huge, sculptural crags and piles of granite that take little imagination to be transformed into faces, beasts or abstractions of the natural world.

The moor runs down to the arc of Beady Pool, a glittering white beach where shiny ochre, black and white beads can still be found, washed ashore from the wreck of a 17th-century merchant ship. Following the coast from Beady Pool to the Turks Head (page 400), it was little **Cove Vean** that really stole my heart, one bright May morning, when a cuckoo sang from the woods that enclosed the sandy beach and the water lapped gently over my toes as I made my way towards the pub above the ferry landing stage. Where could everyone have gone? The ferry from St Mary's had been crowded, but minutes after arrival, I felt I had this magical island almost to myself. It's funny how everyone says that.

❚❘ FOOD & DRINK

You won't find anything resembling a supermarket on St Agnes, but the **Post Office shop** (1 Coastguard Cottages, TR22 0PL) is good for basic groceries as well as being an outlet for local, organic produce.

Coastguards Café TR22 0PL ✆ 01720 423747. Tristan Hicks rustles up fresh produce for cream teas, lunches and packed picnics in a wooden building at the back of the coastguard cottages.

Troytown Farm Shop TR22 0PL ✆ 01720 422360 🖥 troytown.co.uk. This shop sells fresh milk, cream, butter and wonderful ice creams from its own small dairy herd. Sausages and bacon from home-reared pigs and seasonal veg from the polytunnels are also available here.

Turks Head TR22 0PL ✆ 01720 422434 🖥 turksheadscilly.co.uk. Britain's most southwesterly pub is cosy and welcoming inside and the garden in front has views over the harbour and the Gugh; on a sunny day it's the place to sit and wait for the passenger ferry to come in. Food is decent pub fare; pasties, fish and chips and ploughman's lunches, for example, and ales are from Sharp's.

Round the rugged rocks:
Annet, Rosevear & the Western Rocks

West of St Agnes the green-topped island is **Annet**, home to colonies of puffins and shearwaters, among thousands of other seabirds. Boats from St Agnes and St Mary's offer birdwatching trips around the islands, though landing is prohibited as Annet is a bird sanctuary. Sadly, the puffins find no sanctuary from black-backed gulls, who predate viciously on the vulnerable chicks at breeding time.

The boatmen will take you in as close as possible to the jagged rocks on the westernmost fringes of the archipelago, the **Western Rocks**, which have wrecked scores of ships over the centuries, in order to see seals who bask on the leeward shores. Among the screaming birds on barren, lonely **Rosevear,** you'll see a sobering sight: the ruins of stone huts, built as shelters for the men constructing the **Bishop Rock lighthouse**.

The original construction was designed by James Walker, the chief engineer to the British lighthouse authority, Trinity House, in 1847. His plan was to raise the tower on cast-iron legs, so that the sea could pass through. But it was swept away in 1850, before the paraffin lantern could

1 St Agnes. **2** Annet is home to colonies of puffins. **3** World Pilot Gig Championships. **4** A heathery footpath to Great Bay on St Martin's. ▶

JAMES LEPAGE/S

SS

SAMIB123/S

GLENMORE/S

be lit, revealing the extreme challenge of building a tower that could survive the full force of the Atlantic. Undeterred, Walker started again, raising a granite tower 120 feet high, built to a similar specification as the Eddystone lighthouse off Rame Head (page 160), which was finally lit in 1858. But the waves dashed over it in stormy weather – lifting the 550-pound fog bell from the top during one memorable storm – and the granite blocks started to crack, so Walker's successor, James Douglass, raised the tower by a further 55 feet and sheathed it all in a protective layer of concrete. It's the tallest of all pillar lighthouses around the British coast, and in gales the light at the top sways – by as much as six feet. It's a comfort to think that since 1992 it has been operated remotely from Trinity House headquarters in Harwich.

3 ST MARTIN'S

🏠 **Karma Hotel** (page 422), 🏡 **Little Arthur Crofter's Cabin** (page 422)

From St Mary's, the long gleam of white beach across the glittering sea to the north identifies St Martin's as surely as the red-and-white, bullet-shaped daymark identifies the island to shipping arriving from the east. The ferry deposits and collects passengers, depending on the tide, at either Higher or Lower Town quays, a 30-minute stroll apart, along a narrow concrete lane that winds between the straggle of houses that dot the south-facing slopes of the island. Flower farms, market gardens and even a vineyard flourish on these slopes, hidden behind high hedges of salt-tolerant *euonymus* and *pittosporum*. When people tell you why St Martin's is their favourite island, they usually mention two things: the empty, white beaches and the concentration of wonderful, simple food produced here from the land and the sea. A Slow day on St Martin's might start with a stroll to the **Island Bakery** (page 404) to scoop up a few picnic ingredients and a walk along **Par Beach** or along the gorse-covered inland ridge to **Chapel Down**, the easternmost rump of the island, less than a mile from Higher Town. The red-and-white nose of the daymark is a constant presence on the northern headland and the coastal path eventually runs past it. Looking west beyond the daymark you suddenly realise why there's so much talk of St Martin's perfect beaches: at your feet lies the horseshoe-shaped **Bread and Cheese Cove**, and around the headland the long, sparkling white sweep of **Great Bay**. (The sand is partly composed of tiny particles of quartz, which is why it appears to sparkle.) The sea is that particular shade of turquoise blue and jade green peculiar to Scilly. On a clear blue March day, I walked the length of both beaches without seeing a soul, and residents tell me that's it's rare to find more than a handful of families on

GIG RACING

✎ wpgc.uk

There's always been excitement and competition when gigs are launched, and never more so than during the first May bank holiday weekend, when the **World Pilot Gig Championships** see Scilly host 160 pilot gigs and their crews – some from as far afield as the Netherlands; even a team from the USA may put in an appearance. 'Once experienced, never forgotten!' says everybody fortunate enough to be participating or just visiting and cheering. It's a sporting event like no other – elite and yet open to all, pervaded throughout by the Scillonian spirit of fun and generosity. But take note: every available bed and camping pitch on Scilly is booked up months in advance of this weekend, so plan your trip carefully if you want to be lucky.

In the past, crews raced to be first to put a pilot on board ships entering Scilly's treacherous navigational passages; not for fun, but for the fee that was a vital source of income. There was no cash for coming second. Islanders would spring to the oars too, when a ship went down, racing to save lives and salvage cargo. Motorised pilot boats eventually replaced the gigs, but during the 1960s a few surviving elm-built gigs were revived for racing. The *Shah*, built in 1873, is still the pride of the St Agnes gig racers, and in April 2011 she carried the coffin of Osbert 'Obbie' Hicks from St Mary's to the

little island churchyard on St Agnes, where he had lived all his life. As a youngster, back in the 1930s, Obbie accompanied his father Jack on pilotage jobs – in fact, Jack was the last recorded pilot to be shipped by gig when he was put on board the SS *Foremost* in December 1938 by the gig *Gipsy*. Sadly, *Gipsy* was left to rot, but when gig racing started up, *Shah* was fit for action and so was Obbie; Jack stepped back into the old boat he knew so well as coxswain. If you find yourself on Scilly at the time of the championships, or during the summer evening practice events (○ women Wed, Men Fri), look out for Jack Hicks's great-grandchildren, still at the oars of the *Shah* today.

Keep an eye out too, for Tresco and Bryher's flagship gig, *Czar*, a gig with a history behind her. Peter Martin completed her restoration in 2008 at his workshop on St Mary's, but she had originally been built in 1879 by the best-known gig builder of his day, William Peters of St Mawes. Peters had already built a fast pilot gig for Bryher and designed the slightly longer *Czar* with a place for a seventh oar, reckoning that was the only way she could outrun her rival. *Czar* was delivered just ahead of a wild and stormy night during which two ships were wrecked. Immediately launched as a rescue and salvage vessel, she paid for herself on that first night in service.

either beach as most visitors opt for the instantly accessible splendour of the south coast sands of **Lawrence's Bay** and Par Beach. If the tide is out, **White Island** can be reached across a stony bar at the furthest tip of Great Bay. There are old kelp-burning pits ahead as you cross on to the island and the empty Atlantic to the north.

Following the coast path round the western headlands to **Lower Town** takes an easy half-hour; it doesn't take more than a couple of hours to circumnavigate the whole island. Allow much, much longer if you're easily distracted by beachcombing and rockpooling or unable to refrain from pausing to gape at the undiluted beauty of the land and sea and sky.

¶¶ FOOD & DRINK

The sheltered south coast is where Jonathan Smith grows an astonishing crop of organic vegetables at **Scilly Organics** (⌂ scillyorganics.com); there's a terrific display on sale at the farm gate from May to October and a helpfully signed route around the small fields for those keen to explore his six acres that run down to Lawrence's Bay. Further west, in the cluster of houses known as **Middle Town**, Churchtown Farm sells gorgeous bunches of scented narcissi and pinks (according to the season) and beef from their pedigree herd of ruby reds (⌂ scillyflowers.co.uk). In addition, **St Martin's Vineyard and winery** (✆ 07936 710262 ⌂ stmartinsvineyard.co.uk), at the easternmost end of Higher Town Bay, is open to visitors.

Adam's Fish and Chips Higher Town TR25 0QN ✆ 01720 423082 ⌂ adamsfishandchips. co.uk ⊙ eves only, generally April Tue & Thu, May–Sep Tue, Thu & Sat, but call to check. Adam Morton goes fishing for pollock in the morning, digs his spuds in the afternoon and produces superb fish and chips in the evening. That's how he started, and not much has changed, except that Adam has been able to build a wooden hut with seating for 50, overlooking Par Beach, beneath Little Arthur Farm, where he grew up. It's proved so successful that he has enlisted the help of another Scilly fisherman and his brother, James, is growing the potatoes. Booking essential if you want a table, but it's just as nice sitting on the beach.

Island Bakery Moo Green, Higher Town TR25 0QL ✆ 01720 422111 ⌂ theislandbakery-stmartins.com. Barney McLachlan makes artisan breads, traditional pasties and pizzas – perfect for an easy and delicious picnic. Coffee is also served here, and there are a couple of tables and benches outside.

Karma Hotel Lower Town TR25 0QW ✆ 01720 422368 ⌂ karmagroup.com. Built in 1989 to resemble a row of granite cottages and conveniently sited beside Lower Town Quay, the hotel is the island's smartest place to stay and eat. Posh picnics are available to eat on the pretty beach, just a step or two away. Special evening boats from Bryher, Tresco and St Mary's are laid on for diners here in the summer. Children and dogs are welcome.

Little Arthur Café & Bistro Higher Town TR25 0QL ℘ 01720 422779 ⊘ littlearthur. co.uk ⊙ closed Sun. The Morton family's organic smallholding has a small café perched on the hillside above Higher Town Quay, where you can munch sandwiches filled with crab or lobster, homemade mackerel pâté or salads. Eggs come from the hens in the garden.
Seven Stones Inn Lower Town TR25 0QW ℘ 01720 423777 ⊘ sevenstonesinn.com. A big, roomy pub with a friendly atmosphere, local ales and flowers on the bar. There's also lots of outdoor seating (which can get very busy at lunchtimes), with views over the harbour to Tresco and St Mary's. Real pride is taken in using as much island produce as possible on the menu (which might feature pan-fried mullet or a seafood linguine), at very reasonable prices.

4 THE EASTERN ISLES

Frequent boat trips tour around the craggy islands, but no landings are made as they are sanctuaries for breeding colonies of seals and seabirds. Even the boatman was surprised by the quantity of seals we discovered on a sheltered beach of Great Ganilly, when I visited. Upwards of 100 lay flopped on the beach or appeared close to the boat, heads bobbing with dog-like curiosity. Kayaking is a wonderful way to get even

WILDLIFE ON SCILLY

In 1985, the newly created Isles of Scilly Wildlife Trust (⊘ ios-wildlifetrust.org.uk) took on the mighty responsibility of leasing from the Duchy all the untenanted land in Scilly in order to safeguard the extraordinary biodiversity on the islands, which includes some home-grown specialities, such as the snouty little Scilly shrew and the chestnut-coloured Scilly bee. Many visitors to Scilly come specifically for the wildlife (including a few who come to volunteer their services to the Trust) and hordes of birdwatchers will descend on the islands whenever a rare migrant, such as a hoopoe or golden oriole which has been blown off-course, is spotted. I was impressed by the casual appearance of a ring ouzel during my first amble round St

Mary's one April, and even more impressed by the boatman who gently drew his boat in close to the rocky shore of Great Arthur in the Eastern Isles, where he had spotted a pair of diminutive purple sandpipers. But even non-birdwatchers will be astonished at the local blackbirds, which have distinctively reddish-orange – as opposed to yellow – beaks and at the tameness (let alone the quantity) of the sparrows and thrushes on the islands. I can't think when I last saw a thrush on mainland Cornwall.

The local bird expert (and fellow Bradt author) is Will Wagstaff; his guided walks, boat trips and hugely entertaining evening talks are advertised on the quay in St Mary's and in the tourist office.

closer to the wildlife (page 391), but you can get closer still with a snorkel and flippers. **Seal Snorkelling Adventures** (✆ 07340 055748 ⬧ sealsnorkellingadventures.com) equips you, gives instruction and leads swimmers (minimum age eight) into the seal-filled waters.

5 TEÄN & ST HELEN'S

Lying off the west coast of St Martin's, these two islands and their third, smaller neighbour, **Round Island,** are uninhabited, but often visited by private boats and specialist tour groups in the summer. On **St Helen's**, the remains of a Celtic oratory, overlaid with those of a medieval church maintained by the monks of Tavistock until the 15th century, a priest's house and small field system are still visible, and on the south shore of the island are the ruins of an 18th-century Pest House, intended – but scarcely used – for quarantining plague victims on ships headed for west coast English ports.

"Once a year, early in August, a pilgrimage to the island to honour St Elidius is led by the vicar of Scilly."

Once a year, early in August, a pilgrimage to the island to honour St Elidius is led by the vicar of Scilly, who holds a service in the chapel ruins, followed by a picnic on the beach (⬧.ioschurches.co.uk).

From St Martin's Hotel on the western tip of St Martin's, it looks as though you could swim to **Teän,** but the water's deep and the current in the narrow sound strong. Private boat trips are available or you can join a guided tour of the tiny island, which has a rich archaeological history. Worked flints are still found on the beach, and there are Bronze Age burial mounds and medieval graves beside the ruins of St Theona's Chapel. The most visible traces of human existence on the island are the remains of the house where the Nance family lived in the 17th and 18th centuries; the Nances introduced Scillonians to the foul-smelling burning dried-out kelp seaweed to make soda ash, which was sent to Bristol, where it was used in the manufacture of glass. The Scilly kelp-burners lost a vital part of their income when a similar product from Spain, called barilla, became cheaply available after the Napoleonic Wars ended in 1815.

◀ **1** Ariel view over Teän. **2** Snorkelling with seals. **3 & 4** Rare migrants such as golden oriole and hoopoe may occasionally find themselves blown off course.

THE ISLANDS, THE DUCHY & THE SMITHS

It's surprising how many people think that Scilly is a part of Cornwall, but it's not. It's a unitary authority (the smallest in the UK) in its own right. True, the islanders are represented in Parliament by the MP for St Ives and some areas of local government, such as Health and Local Enterprise Partnerships, are shared with Cornwall Council. But for many on the islands, the complex relationship with the mainland revolves mainly around the Duchy of Cornwall, from whom all buildings and land are leased. This goes back to 1337, when Edward III creatively rearranged an old earldom, incorporating choice bits of southwest England to form the Duchy of Cornwall, in order to provide an income for his eldest son, the Prince of Wales. It's fair to add that while the Isles of Scilly may look like a jewel in the Duchy crown, it's hardly a financial asset: overall, I was told, the Duchy spends more on the islands than it receives.

The entire island of Tresco is leased from the Duchy by the Dorrien-Smith family, which explains why it has such a strong and separate identity. This began in 1834, when Augustus Smith, a Hertfordshire banker, was granted the lease – and governorship – of not just Tresco, but all the islands. He seems to have been a benevolent kind of dictator, making sure that retired or disabled islanders were spared from poverty, building schools and creatively encouraging attendance by charging the children a penny a day if they went and a twopenny fine if they didn't. But his attempts to reform the economic and moral dereliction he perceived (which included waging war on smuggling and sending the unemployed and unemployable back to the mainland), did not endear him to everyone. Tresco alone now remains in the hands of his great-great-great nephew, Robert Dorrien-Smith, who continues the tradition of benevolent stewardship and personal investment in the island community. All 160 permanent residents on the smartly maintained island are employed and housed (a perk which continues after retirement) by the 'Boss'.

6 TRESCO

Tresco is as different from the other inhabited islands as Padstow is from Newlyn. The other islands give the impression of having grown haphazardly, with buildings casually strewn along the sandy sheltered shores and miniature fields sprouting long-abandoned varieties of narcissus. On Tresco, things look more organised, less dictated to by weather and tide and unfavourable economies. It is quite clear that someone with a spot of cash has stepped in and smartened things up in a tasteful way. Signposts give timings for the walks to the New Inn or to Pentle Bay, recycling bins are thoughtfully provided, polite notices explain which areas are private, and tarmac lanes are filled with smiling families on bicycles and Prince Harry lookalikes in sailing gear. There's no campsite and only a very limited number of bed and breakfast rooms, but timeshare flats are promoted, in a conscious effort to create a sort of extended 'Tresco family' – people who will come back year after year and regard it as a (second) home, rather than treat it as a holiday commodity for a week.

At the midpoint of the island, **New Grimsby** is a loose cluster of estate cottages and offices; the Tresco Stores and Flying Boat Club huddle at one end of the shallow bay, while at the harbour end stand an art and craft gallery and the New Inn. It's just a step from here to **St Nicholas's Church**, built in 1878 to the design of Thomas Dorrien-Smith (the nephew of Augustus), and over the hill lie the spectacular white beaches of **Old Grimsby** and **Pentle Bay**. A circular walk, taking in both the Grimsbys, an Elizabethan defensive fort known as the **Blockhouse**, and the east-coast beaches, with wonderful views over the Eastern Rocks, as well as the lakeside approach to the **Abbey**, takes a gentle hour.

It's only when you reach the rugged, northernmost acres of the island, covered in bracken and gorse, that the essential character of Scilly reasserts itself. Here is the sense of remoteness and silence, broken only by the cry of seabirds and the dash of sea on rocks. The remains of two defensive **fortresses** look across the western shore to Bryher. The higher of the two, which is just a ruin, is known as King Charles's Castle, though it was built long before his day by Henry VIII, in case of attack by the French. Some poor military architect's head must have rolled, for the

THE PRIVATE UTOPIA OF AUGUSTUS SMITH

What kind of man would want to leave his life as a successful merchant banker with a comfortable estate in Hertfordshire, and take on the lease and responsibility for five islands existing on the brink of extreme poverty? The complex, wealthy and socially imaginative Augustus Smith saw his opportunity to create a model society, founded on what he recognised as sound economic and moral principles. As an MP, Smith had already fought against the enclosure of Berkhamsted Common and improved access to education for the poor, but clearly this was just the start of a utopian vision that rapidly took shape when he bought the lease from the Duchy in 1834. In between restructuring the economy and population of the islands, Smith found time to start planting a magnificent garden, realising that he could grow just about anything the world had to offer. It's tempting to see it as a private Eden, but one in which Smith played the role of God, not Adam.

building was placed too high. There's a fine view over any ship attempting to enter the narrow sound below, but as soon as you point a cannon towards the channel below, gravity takes command of the cannonball before it can be fired. Oops.

In consequence, Henry ensured the second fort was built lower down, just above the high-tide mark (renamed Cromwell's Castle after the Civil War) and added a third fort for good measure (the Blockhouse) on the seaward-facing shore on the south point of Old Grimsby Bay. But neither saw any real action until 1651, when Parliamentarian troops under Admiral Blake fought the Royalist governor of Scilly, John Grenville, back to St Mary's. Cromwell's Castle was rebuilt as a solid tower and gun platform and a garrison of Roundheads was installed within. Some of the grafitti scratched on the stone walls is thought to have been left by soldiers manning the garrison.

Abbey Garden
TR24 0QQ ⌀ 01720 424105 ⌀ tresco.co.uk/enjoying/abbey-garden ☉ Mar–Nov

At the south end of the island, given shelter by a thick fringe of trees and a natural rise in the land to the north, these world-class gardens play a major part in drawing visitors to Tresco. What makes the gardens so special is the enormous range of plants from around the globe that flourish here, without glass or any kind of protection except the band of Monterey pines and cypresses and monumental hedges of evergreen oak that encircle the south-facing terraces. There are all the established favourites – exotics you see growing all over Scilly – such as giant blue echiums (known as Cornish foxgloves on the mainland), glossy purple-black aeoniums, fat, spiky aloes and a profusion of Watsonias. But there's so much more: enough to make seasoned curators of botanic gardens go weak at the knees and render the most senior garden writers speechless with wonder. The local microclimates within the 17 acres allow not only subtropical plants to be grown, but also New Zealand Pohutukawa trees with massive spreading branches, often smothered in crimson flowers, Australian banksias and South African proteas, Madeiran clethras and dozens of sweet, yellow-flowered mimosas.

◀ 1 Abbey Garden, Tresco. 2 Cromwell's Castle faces Bryher. 3 In a corner of Abbey Garden, the Valhalla Museum exhibits a collection of ships' figureheads. 4 Grey seal on the rocks.

Mike Nelhams, who recently retired after several decades as the garden's curator, was careful to stress, however, that it's not a botanic garden. 'Every plant here has to be garden worthy, fantastic to look at and play its part in the local and overall display. Andrew Lawson [the head gardener] and I are not into collecting rare plants just because we can grow them and make a collection.' Andrew Lawson has worked here for nearly three decades now, replanting, restoring and doing it all again after ravaging storms and freakishly cold winters. The impression as you enter – even in midwinter – is of lush scents, textures and flowers, but it's the sense of volume that draws you in. Like a classical Italian garden, there is height and structure, long vistas contained within high hedges; steps crowned with sculptures and the ruins of an ancient place of worship. It's a bit wild, too, just like a Tuscan garden, and plants are encouraged to self-seed and give each other support and shelter. Gardeners grow here too. Mike always encouraged his team, taking them to visit the best subtropical and Mediterranean gardens around Europe, organising international exchanges of plants and students, and arranging for Tresco to be twinned with the famous Hanbury gardens at La Mortola in Italy.

"The impression as you enter – even in midwinter – is of lush scents, textures and flowers, but it's the sense of volume that draws you in."

In a quiet corner of the gardens, the **Valhalla Museum** exhibits a collection of ships' figureheads, salvaged from wrecks around the treacherous coastline of the islands.

¶¶ FOOD & DRINK

Tresco's upmarket aspirations are reflected in the food and drink on the island and prices reflect the quality of what's on offer here. Budget-conscious visitors might want to bring a picnic.

Abbey Garden Café TR24 0QQ ✐ 01720 424108 ⊙ Mar–Nov. Occupying a part of the Abbey Garden visitor centre (page 411), with plenty of outdoor and indoor seating. It's the place to come at this end of the island for good coffee, cakes, sandwiches and the interesting specials board at lunchtime.

New Inn New Grimsby TR24 0QQ ✐ 01720 423006. Indoors, the bar is made from reclaimed driftwood; outdoors, in a sheltered courtyard and garden, are tables and chairs overlooking the harbour. The menu is designed to please foodies; Scillonian and Cornish ales are on tap.

Tresco Stores and Deli Smith Sq, New Grimsby TR24 0QQ ♪ 01720 422806. Not unlike Waitrose, this is more of a giant deli than a supermarket, with the emphasis firmly on Cornish produce. St Agnes's Troytown dairy ice cream and milk (page 400) can be found here, along with freshly baked bread and Tresco's delicious grass-fed beef.

7 BRYHER

⌂ **Hell Bay Hotel** (page 422)

The smallest of the inhabited islands has a simple, barefoot beauty that many feared would be lost when the Tresco estate took over the Hell Bay Hotel (page 422) and gave it an upmarket eco-makeover in 1999. Those fears turned out to be unfounded, more than 20 years on, for Bryher remains far from gentrified, and that feeling of wild remoteness remains unchanged, its beauty reflected in the extraordinary stained-glass windows in the little **church**, close to the quay. The windows, designed and made by Oriel Hicks (page 395), depict the flora and fauna of the island in jewel-like colours and loving detail. The north and south faces of the island couldn't be more different: **Rushy Bay** at the south end is pristine white sand and translucent jade and turquoise water. **Shipman Head Down**, to the north, has a wild, Hebridean look to it, and yet they are separated by just a mile of sandy tracks and paths. Similarly, the east coast turns a neighbourly face across a narrow stretch of water to Tresco while the west coast faces the onslaught of the Atlantic (**Hell Bay** did not acquire its name by chance) and sunsets that reduce everyone to silence. Bryher was my first introduction to the Isles of Scilly and the diversity of its beauty took my breath away. Like so many people arriving on Scilly for the first time, I found it hard to believe

"Like so many people arriving on Scilly for the first time, I found it hard to believe I was still in England."

I was still in England, just a few minutes' flight from the mainland. Katharine Sawyer, Scilly's resident archaeologist, who regularly leads guided walks around the islands (advertised on noticeboards and in the TIC on St Mary's; page 388) made the visit even more enjoyable. I could have scrunched my way quite happily alone up the granite-strewn slope to enjoy the views from Shipman Head Down, while little white-rumped birds sprang from the heather all round, but with Katharine guiding, our four-strong group discovered that some of the underfoot scrunch was flint, deposited on the northern points of the

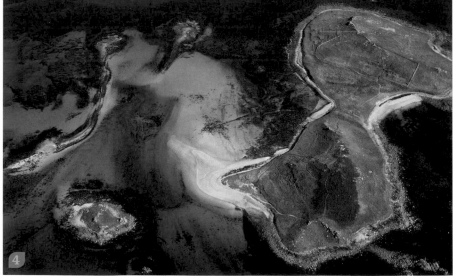

islands 20,000 years ago by south-bound glaciers crashing to a halt. Some of the granite boulders transpired to be remnants of **Bronze Age ramparts**, or a primitive customs barrier. The birds turned out to be wheatears, breaking the long journey from tropical Africa to more northerly parts of Europe. And the cushiony quilt of ling and bell heather, more properly known as 'maritime waved heathland,' sculpted by wind and salt spray, is grazed by ponies and cattle, as part of a land conservation scheme on Bryher. I was glad also, to be quietly informed on my first day, that islanders don't like it when people say 'Scilly Isles': it's always 'The Isles of Scilly' or just 'Scilly'. Information, especially when delivered by a friendly native with a dry sense of humour, is bliss.

FOOD & DRINK

Homegrown produce including eggs, jam, flowers and fudge and honesty boxes at garden gates are not uncommon sights on the island. The Pender family sell fresh fish, crab and lobster at **Island Fish** (✆ 01720 423880 ⌂ islandfish.co.uk ◷ Apr–Oct Mon–Sat, Jun–Aug Sun also). Phone ahead to see what's available.

The Crab Shack Hell Bay Hotel, TR23 0PR ✆ 01720 422947 ⌂ hellbay.co.uk ◷ May–Sep Mon–Wed & Fri, eves only. Part of the Hell Bay Hotel (page 422), the Crab Shack offers a gloriously messy evening to seafood lovers. Everyone is issued with an apron and seated at trestle tables armed with the tools for a shellfish feast. Very good shared fun even if you go on your own.

Fraggle Rock Bar and Café Norrard, TR23 0PR ✆ 01720 422222 ⌂ bryher.co ◷ closed Sun eve & Mon. A café-cum-pub at the north end of the Island. Convivial fish-and-chip nights are held on Fridays, and decent pub grub and Cornish ales on tap are available at other times.

Hell Bay Hotel TR23 0PR ✆ 01720 422947 ⌂ hellbay.co.uk. Hell Bay itself is a little further to the north; the hotel overlooks Great Porth beach – a superb spot for a morning coffee or afternoon tea. The upmarket bar menu is available at lunchtime, but you'll need to make a reservation for evening meals if you're not staying at the hotel. Many people I've spoken to reckon this is Scillonian cuisine at its best.

Island Fish Café TR23 0PR ✆ 01720 423880 ⌂ islandfish.co.uk ◷ Apr–Oct Mon–Sat, Jun–Sep Sun also. Brother and sister Mark and Amanda Pender added a small but very popular seafood café to this shop, which also does amazing pop-up paella events, including

◀ **1** Shipman Head Down, Byher. **2** Stained-glass window detail by Oriel Hicks (page 395) in the church on Bryher. **3** Kayaking between Bryher and Tresco. **4** Aerial view of Samson.

one held on the sand bar between Bryher and Tresco when the equinoctial low tides make it possible to walk between the two islands.

Olivia's Kitchen TR23 0PR ✆ 01720 423168 **[f]**. Close to the post office and shop, this delightful café offers a menu of light lunches, evening meals and Sunday roasts.

8 SAMSON

The twin, bosomy hills of Samson make it one of the more easily recognisable landmarks of the Scilly archipelago. Boats stop here en route to Bryher and drop adventurous passengers in the shallow water on the beach and pick them up again a few hours later. There are no loos, no shelter from sun or rain, nor are there any cafés on the island – just empty beaches, birds perching on the sad **ruins of cottages** last inhabited during the 1850s and the crumbling walls of the park, where deer were briefly kept by Augustus Smith, until they escaped on a low spring tide. There is much evidence of older populations that lived here when Samson was part of a single land mass: groups of open-mouthed, **Bronze Age burial cists** and **graves** are dotted about the island and low tides may reveal remnants of stone-edged **medieval field boundaries**.

On a recent visit I brought Philip Marsden's book, *Rising Ground*, with me and looked across the shallow waters at the prehistoric ritual landmarks he describes. Later, waiting for the boat to return to the beach, with my back to a sand dune, I put away the book and looked out at the islands, the sea, the birds and the sky. Like Marsden and so many others who come to Scilly, I find it impossible not to ask myself what it would be like to live on one of these islands. They are so remote and yet so connected in a deeper way – to the people, both past and present, and the places, both the dry and the submerged, that surround you. Questions of freedom and isolation, separation and belonging seem to take visible form here. Such musings are perhaps one of the most authentic Slow experiences to be enjoyed on Scilly. 'One day,' you might find yourself thinking. 'One day, I too might live here.'

ACCOMMODATION

The places to stay listed below are a personal selection of bed and breakfasts, campsites, self-catering cottages and one or two very special hotels – places that struck me for their location, friendliness or character, or a mixture of all three. For further reviews and additional listings, go to ⊘ bradtguides.com/cornwallsleeps. The hotels, bed and breakfasts and hostels are indicated by the symbol 🛏 under the heading for the nearest town or village in which they are located; self-catering options by 🏠. Camping options, which cover everything from full-on glamping to no-frills pitches, are indicated with a ⛺ symbol.

1 LAUNCESTON & THE NORTHEAST

Hotels
The Beach at Bude Bude EX23 8HJ ⊘ 01288 389800 ⊘ thebeachatbude. co.uk. Luxury boutique hotel with views over Summerleaze Beach.
The Beach House Widemouth Bay EX23 0AW ⊘ 01288 361256 ⊘ beachhousewidemouth. co.uk. With direct access to the beach, this hotel has ten rooms, all of which have been recently refurbished to a high standard. There's a lively bar-restaurant, too (page 50).
Mill House Inn Trebarwith PL34 0HD ⊘ 01840 770200 ⊘ themillhouseinn.co.uk. This comfortable hotel in a deep wooded valley setting is 15 minutes' walk from one of the north coast's best beaches.

B&Bs
The Old Rectory St Juliot, Boscastle PL35 0BT ⊘ 01840 250225 ⊘ stjuliot.com. Traditional comfort and exceptional breakfasts.

Self-catering
Coombe ⊘ 01628 825925 ⊘ landmarktrust. org.uk. A cluster of gorgeous cottages in an idyllic valley, sleeping three to six.
Pencuke Farm St Gennys (near Crackington Haven) EX23 0BH ⊘ 01840 230360 ⊘ pencukefarm.co.uk. A working farm that's especially good for families. The dog friendly cottages sleep between three and eight, and there are two shepherd's huts.

2 MID-CORNWALL NORTH: THE CAMEL ESTUARY TO HOLYWELL BAY

There are some very swanky places to stay in this area, which do not really fall within the Slow remit. However, special mention should be given to Mawgan Porth's **Bedruthan Hotel** (⊘ bedruthan.com), much loved by exhausted parents for its terrific programme of daytime and evening activities for children from babies to teens, and its very grown-up sister hotel next door, **The Scarlet** (⊘ scarlethotel.co.uk) – positively the last word in green luxury and eco-architecture.

Hotels

Lewinnick Lodge Pentire Headland, Newquay TR7 1QD ✎ 01637 878117 ⊘ lewinnicklodge. co.uk. Luxury boutique hotel in a spectacular clifftop location.

B&Bs

Roskear Tregunna, Wadebridge PL27 7HU ✎ 07748 432013 ⊘ roskear.com. Peaceful 18th-century farmhouse with two rooms and a shared bathroom.

Self-catering

Moyles Farm St Minver, Wadebridge PL27 6QT ✎ 01208 862331 ⊘ moylesfarm.co.uk. Upmarket cottages and barn conversions within easy reach of Rock and Polzeath's surfing beaches.

Camping

Cornish Tipi Holidays Tregeare, Pendoggett, St Kew PL30 3LW ✎ 01208 880781 ⊘ cornishtipiholidays.co.uk. Three sizes of tipi are available, sleeping up to seven in a lakeside woodland setting.

3 BODMIN MOOR

There are some spectacular camping opportunities around the Moor, ranging from luxury yurts to no-frills wild camping spots. Two of the best are included below.

Hotels

Bodmin Jail Hotel Scarlett's Well Rd, Bodmin PL31 2PL ✎ 01208 822844 ⊘ bodminjailhotel. com. This sensitive, multi-million-pound conversion of a historic building brings boutique luxury accommodation and dining to Bodmin.

B&Bs

The London Inn School Hill, St Neot PL14 6NG ✎ 01579 326728 ⊘ londoninnstneot.com. Three luxurious and beautifully decorated rooms are on offer in this superb village pub. Closed in winter.

The Old Deer House (formerly Cabilla Manor) Mount, near Warleggan PL30 4DW ✎ 01208 821224 ⊘ theolddeerhouse. co.uk. Old-fashioned hospitality and comfort in a contemporary building in a delightful rural location.

Self-catering

East Rose Farm St Breward, near Blisland, Bodmin PL30 4NL ✎ 01208 850674 ⊘ eastrose. co.uk. Seven cottages with a fishing lake and easy access to the Camel Trail.

Camping

South Penquite Farm Blisland, Bodmin PL30 4LH ✎ 01208 850491 ⊘ southpenquite.co.uk. An idyllic moorland farm, perfect for families.
Yurtworks Greyhayes, Row Hill, St Breward, near Blisland, Bodmin PL30 4LP ✎ 01208 850670 ⊘ yurtworks.co.uk. Three luxury yurts, set well apart for privacy, in glorious oak-fringed meadows.

4 SOUTHEAST CORNWALL

B&Bs

Coombeshead Farm Lewannick PL15 7QQ ✎ 01566 782009 ⊘ coombesheadfarm. co.uk. A beautifully restored Georgian farm and outbuildings provide very upmarket comfort amid 66 acres of rolling meadows and woodland. The acclaimed restaurant (page 142) is a destination in itself.

Talland Bay Hotel Porthallow Hse, Bridals Ln, Killigarth, Looe PL13 2JB ✎ 01503 272667 ⊘ tallandbayhotel.co.uk. Luxury accommodation with quirky character and pretty gardens. Located close to the beach.

Self-catering

Botelet Herodsfoot, Liskeard PL14 4RD
🖉 01503 220225 🖱 botelet.com. An idyllic
farm offering self-catering cottages and a yurt.
The Old Luggage Van and **The Travelling
Post Office** Railholiday Ltd, Haparanda Station,
Nut Tree Hill, St Germans PL12 5LU 🖉 01503
230783 🖱 railholiday.co.uk. Cosy, quirky
converted railway carriages only a short step
away from Port Eliot.
Spring Park Rezare PL15 9LX 🖉 07805 990302
🖱 quirky-holidays-cornwall.co.uk. A range
of delightful shepherd's huts, gypsy caravans
and cabins to choose from, each with its own
outdoor space.
Treworgey Farm Duloe, Liskeard PL14 4PP
🖉 01503 262730 🖱 hideawayhuts.co.uk &
🖱 treworgeycottages.com. The two luxury
shepherd's huts with bathroom, on a working
farm, are suitable for couples, while the holiday
cottages are perfect for families.
Windsworth The Old Coach Hse,
St Martin, Looe PL13 1NZ 🖉 01503 262671
🖱 windsworth.org. Off-grid but without
compromising comfort, and situated within a
gloriously preserved nature reserve, just a field
away from the coast path and 300m above its
own private beach. Sleeping six in two rooms.

Camping

Bush Farm Wild Camping Saltash PL12 6QY
🖉 07875 557160 🖱 bushfarmcampsite.co.uk.
Pitch anywhere you like on this idyllic, dog-
friendly farm.
Hawkins Battery The Earl's Dr,
Maker PL10 1JB 🖉 01752 823234
🖱 hawkinsbatteryholidaypark.co.uk.
Unchanging, secluded and well off the beaten
track, this is no-frills camping.
Highertown Farm Campsite Lansallos, Looe
PL13 2PX 🖉 01208 265211 🖱 nationaltrust.org.
uk. Between church and beach, a small National
Trust site popular with families.

5 THE FOWEY VALLEY & THE CORNISH ALPS

Hotels

Fowey Hall Hotel Hanson Dr, Fowey PL23 1ET
🖉 01726 833866 🖱 foweyhallhotel.co.uk.
Country-house style, very welcoming to children
and close to Readymoney Cove.

B&Bs

The Dwelling House at Fowey 6 Fore St,
Fowey PL23 1AQ 🖉 01726 833662. Just one
lovely bedroom if you can nab it, right in the
centre of Fowey.
Foye Old Exchange 12 Lostwithiel St, Fowey
PL23 1BD 🖉 01726 833252 🖱 foye-old-
exchange-bed-breakfast-fowey.hotelmix.co.uk.
Quirky but comfortable accommodation in the
centre of Fowey.

Self-catering

Bodrugan Barton Mevagissey PL26
6PT 🖉 01726 842094 🖱 bodrugan.co.uk.
Choose from glamping pods, cottages or a large
barn conversion on this working farm, within
walking distance of the beach.
Caerhays Estate Caerhays PL26 6IY 🖉 01872
500026 🖱 caerhaysholidays.co.uk. Twelve
cottages and houses set in glorious parkland,
close to the beach.

Camping

Court Farm Camping St Stephen PL26 7LE
🖉 01726 823684 🖱 courtfarmcornwall.co.uk.
Simple camping on quiet farmland; activities for
star-gazers.
Lombard Farm Mixtow PL23 1NA 🖉 07941
963124 🖱 lombardfarm.co.uk. Glamp above
the River Fowey in either a cabin, shepherd's
hut or yurt.

6 THE MINING HEARTLAND

Self-catering
Driftwood Beach Chalet Gwithian Towans, Hayle ☎ 01326 567838 ⌂ forevercornwall. co.uk. At the foot of the dunes, stylish and comfortable – and just a 20-minute walk to Gwithian beach. Sleeps six.
Godolphin House TR13 9RE ☎ 0344 800 2070 ⌂ nationaltrustcottages.co.uk. Atmospheric six-bedroom splendour in historic house with private garden space.

Camping
Beacon Cottage Camping Beacon Dr, St Agnes TR5 0NU ☎ 01872 552347 ⌂ beaconcottagefarmholidays.co.uk. Orchards and paddocks provide ample space for family-friendly camping on a working farm.
Mount Pleasant Eco Park Porthtowan TR4 8HL ☎ 01209 891500 ⌂ mpecopark.co.uk. Green credentials, yoga workshops and a vegan café close to beaches.

7 TRURO & THE FAL ESTUARY

Upmarket hotels and self-catering cottages are plentiful in this area. Various B&Bs and campsites are listed on ⌂ falriver.co.uk.

B&Bs
Hay Barton Tregony, Truro TR2 5TF ☎ 01872 530288 ⌂ haybarton.com. Elegant, grown-up accommodation on a working farm surrounded by bucolic scenery on the Roseland peninsula.

Self-catering
Come-to-Good Farm Feock TR3 6QS ☎ 01872 863828 ⌂ cometogoodfarm.com. With a barn, shepherd's hut and small campsite, the farm keeps chickens and sheep in a lovely rural location that's suitable for families.

St Anthony Head Cottages TR2 5HA ☎ 0844 800 2070 ⌂ nationaltrustcottages.co.uk. Four small holiday cottages, converted from former officers' quarters, look over the sea to Falmouth.

Camping
Treloan Coastal Holidays Gerrans, Portscatho TR2 5EF ☎ 01872 580989 ⌂ treloancoastalholidays.co.uk. Year-round mobile home options and clifftop pitches close to long sandy beaches on the Roseland peninsula.

8 SOUTHWEST CORNWALL: THE LIZARD PENINSULA

Hotels
Housel Bay Hotel Lizard TR12 7PG ☎ 01326 567500 ⌂ houselbay.com. Under new ownership, this grand old hotel on the cliffs is being slowly transformed into a haven of contemporary comfort, perfect for walkers, nature-lovers and gourmets.

B&Bs
The Old Temperance House St Keverne TR12 6NA ☎ 01326 280986 ⌂ oldtemperancehouse. co.uk. Four characterful rooms in a historic house between the pub and church in a popular village.

Self-catering
Kestle Barton Manaccan TR12 6HU ⌂ forevercornwall.co.uk. Three beautifully converted ancient barns, a lovely old farmhouse and Kestle Cottage, sleeping from two to eight. All have access to the art gallery's gardens, orchards and flower meadow.
Kynance Cottage Next to Kynance Cove Café, TR12 7PJ ☎ 01326 290436 ⌂ kynancecovecafe.co.uk. Sleeps two plus two small children right next to one of Cornwall's loveliest beaches.
Trelowarren Mawgan TR12 6AF ☎ 01326 221224 ⌂ trelowarren.com. Upmarket holiday

rentals on a historic estate with impeccable green credentials.

Camping

Henry's Campsite The Lizard TR12 7NX ✏ 01326 290596 ⌂ henryscampsite.co.uk. A legend among barefoot campers – perfect for old hippies and young travellers.
Penmarth Farm Coverack TR12 6SB ✏ 01326 281339 ⌂ coverackcamping.co.uk . Eco-friendly, no-frills camping on a small, friendly farm; some camping fields overlook the sea.

9 PENZANCE, ST IVES & THE PENWITH PENINSULA

The useful website ⌂ cornwallfarwest.co.uk, not affiliated to the tourist office, is used by owners of all types of accommodation in Penwith to advertise their stuff. The site has an excellent interactive map, particularly good for finding out-of-the-way campsites and B&Bs.

Hotels

Chapel House Chapel St, Penzance TR18 4AQ ✏ 07810 020617 ⌂ chapelhousepz.co.uk. A Georgian house transformed into an elegant boutique hotel with a relaxed atmosphere; they also run a supper club.
Gurnard's Head Near Zennor, St Ives TR26 3DE ✏ 01736 796928 ⌂ gurnardshead. co.uk. A fine pub (sister to The Old Coastguard in Mousehole) with very comfortable rooms, perched between granite moorland and wild coastal scenery.
The Old Coastguard Mousehole TR19 6PR ✏ 01726 731222 ⌂ theoldcoastguard.co.uk. Fourteen comfortable, stylish bedrooms, nearly all with views over the sea below, and a restaurant serving seriously good food.
Primrose Valley Hotel Porthminster Beach, St Ives TR26 2ED ✏ 01736 794939 ⌂ primroseonline.co.uk. An eleven-bedroom

family favourite, close to the beaches and town centre. A mezzanine apartment offers a self-catering option.

B&Bs

Bosavern Guesthouse St Just, Penzance TR19 7RD ✏ 01736 788301 ⌂ bosavern.com. Country-house comfort on the edge of the lovely Cot Valley, close to Land's End.
Ednovean Farm Perranuthnoe TR20 9LZ ✏ 01736 711883 ⌂ ednoveanfarm.co.uk. Beautiful gardens, stunning sea views and vintage-style luxury.

Self-catering

The Abbey Abbey St, Penzance TR18 4AR ✏ 01244 356666 ⌂ sykescottages.co.uk or hotelsincornwall.net; search for 'Abbey Villa'. A luxurious country house-style Georgian townhouse with open fires and seven en-suite bedrooms.
Boscrowan Farm Heamoor, near Penzance TR20 8UJ ✏ 01736 332396 ⌂ boscrowan.co.uk. Two cottages on a pretty smallholding, sleeping two and four.
Castallack Farm Mousehole TR19 6NL ✏ 01736 731969 ⌂ castallackfarm.co.uk. Dog-friendly cottages in a lovely rural spot, close to Mousehole and Lamorna.
The Summerhouse Cove Cottage St Loy, St Buryan TR19 6DH ✏ 01736 810010 ⌂ covecottagestloy.co.uk. A romantic hideaway in beautiful gardens above a sheltered cove.

Hostels

Land's End Hostel Trevescan, Land's End TR19 7AQ ✏ 07585 625774 ⌂ landsendholidays. co.uk. Good-value, spotless rooms, and within easy reach of the coast path and Land's End.

Camping

Into the Woods Chy An Goverrow, Lamorna TR19 6XW ⌂ woodlandchampions.co.uk. A bell tent offers authentic, off-grid escape from the outside world.

10 THE ISLES OF SCILLY

A comprehensive list of accommodation, from campsites to upmarket hotels, can be found at Ⓖ visitislesofscilly.com. By far the greatest number of B&Bs and self-catering cottages are to be found on St Mary's (though many of the B&Bs are being transformed into self-catering apartments these days); accommodation of all types is very limited on St Agnes, Bryher and St Martin's. The tourist information centre has a finger on the pulse of all availabilities, late deals and out-of-season offers. If looking for a cottage rental on Tresco, you can contact the island office directly on ✆ 01720 422849.

There are only four campsites spread across the islands – one each on St Mary's (The Garrison Campsite; see right), St Agnes (Troytown Farm; see right), Bryher (✆ 01720 422068 Ⓖ bryhercampsite.co.uk) and St Martin's (✆ 01720 422888 Ⓖ stmartinscampsite.co.uk). Reserving a pitch is essential, especially during the school holidays. Note that during the pilot gig championships in April/May, every bed and tent pitch is reserved months in advance.

Hotels

The Atlantic Hugh St, Hugh Town, St Mary's TR21 0PL ✆ 01720 422417 Ⓖ atlanticinnscilly. co.uk ☉ Feb–Nov. A small, friendly hotel with a lively bar overlooking the harbour.

Hell Bay Hotel Bryher TR23 0PR ✆ 01720 422947 Ⓖ hellbay.co.uk. A multi-award-winning treat for lovers of remote beauty who wish to retain all the sybaritic comforts of a small, modern hotel.

Karma Hotel Lower Town, St Martin's TR25 0QW ✆ 01720 422368 Ⓖ karmagroup.com. Luxurious rooms, spa and fine dining as close to the beach as you can get.

Self-catering

Little Arthur Crofter's Cabin St Martin's TR25 0QL ✆ 01720 422457 Ⓖ littlearthur.co.uk. A tiny, no-frills hideaway sleeping four, plus a summerhouse with bunks in the garden.

Troytown Farm St Agnes TR22 0PL ✆ 01720 422360 Ⓖ troytown.co.uk. Two cottages suitable for families and a studio on the island's ice-cream farm, close to the beach. No-frills campsite, too.

95 Watermill St Mary's TR21 0NS ✆ 07760 661627 Ⓖ canopyandstars.co.uk. A romantic shepherd's hut, offering the last word in luxury, set in an idyllic garden at the north end of the island.

Hostels

Longstone Lodge Holy Vale, St Mary's TR21 0NW ✆ 01720 422410 Ⓖ longstonecafe.co.uk/hostel. A stylish hostel in the rural centre of St Mary's with a variety of en-suite rooms.

Camping

The Garrison Campsite St Mary's TR21 0LS ✆ 01720 422670 Ⓖ garrisonholidaysscilly. co.uk. Campsite with far-ranging views and good amenities.

INDEX

Bold refers to main entries; *italics* to walking maps

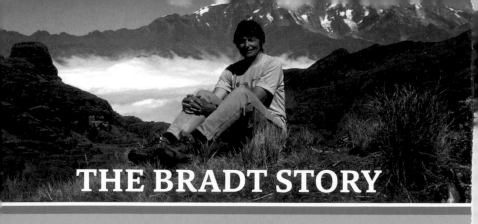

THE BRADT STORY

In the beginning

It all began in 1974 on an Amazon river barge. During an 18-month trip through South America, two adventurous young backpackers – Hilary Bradt and her then husband, George – decided to write about the hiking trails they had discovered through the Andes. *Backpacking Along Ancient Ways in Peru and Bolivia* included the very first descriptions of the Inca Trail. It was the start of a colourful journey to becoming one of the best-loved travel publishers in the world; you can read the full story on our website (**bradtguides. com/ourstory**).

Getting there first

Hilary quickly gained a reputation for being a true travel pioneer, and in the 1980s she started to focus on guides to places overlooked by other publishers. The Bradt Guides list became a roll call of guidebook 'firsts'. We published the first guide to Madagascar, followed by Mauritius, Czechoslovakia and Vietnam. The 1990s saw the beginning of our extensive coverage of Africa: Tanzania, Uganda, South Africa, and Eritrea. Later, post-conflict guides became a feature: Rwanda, Mozambique, Angola, and Sierra Leone, as well as the first standalone guides to the Baltic States following the fall of the Iron Curtain, and the first post-war guides to Bosnia, Kosovo and Albania.

Comprehensive – and with a conscience

Today, we are the world's largest independently owned travel publisher, with more than 200 titles. However, our ethos remains unchanged. Hilary is still keenly involved, and **we still get there first**: two-thirds of Bradt guides have no direct competition.

But we don't just get there first. Our guides are also known for being **more comprehensive** than any other series. We avoid templates and tick-lists. Each guide is a one-of-a-kind expression of an expert author's interests, knowledge and enthusiasm for telling it how it really is.

And a commitment to wildlife, conservation and respect for local communities has always been at the heart of our books. Bradt Guides was **championing sustainable travel** before any other guidebook publisher. We even have a series dedicated to Slow Travel in the UK, award-winning books that explore the country with a passion and depth you'll find nowhere else.

Thank you!

We can only do what we do because of the support of readers like you – people who value less-obvious experiences, less-visited places and a more thoughtful approach to travel. Those who, like us, take travel seriously.

Bradt GUIDES

TRAVEL TAKEN SERIOUSLY